FRE
Verbs

Second Edition

Christopher Kendris

B.S., M.S., Columbia University
M.A., Ph.D., Northwestern University

Former Chairman
Department of Foreign Languages
Farmingdale High School
Farmingdale, New York

BARRON'S

BARRON'S EDUCATIONAL SERIES, INC.

To my wife, Yolanda,
to my two sons, Alex and Ted,
to my daughters-in-law, Tina Marie and Francesca,
to my four grandsons,
Alexander Bryan, Daniel Patrick Christopher,
Matthew David, and Andrew Dimitri

with love

© Copyright 2001 by Barron's Educational Series, Inc.
Prior edition © Copyright 1990 by Barron's Educational
Series, Inc.
Adapted from *301 French Verbs,* © Copyright 1981
by Barron's Educational Series, Inc.

All inquiries should be addressed to:
Barron's Educational Series, Inc.
250 Wireless Boulevard
Hauppauge, New York 11788

http://www.barronseduc.com

Library of Congress Catalog Card No. 89-39626

International Standard Book No. 0-7641-1356-9

Library of Congress Cataloging-in-Publication Data

Kendris, Christopher.
    Spanish verbs / by Christopher Kendris.—2nd ed.
        p.   cm.
    Adapted from: 301 French verbs fully conjugated
in all the tenses. c1981.
Includes indexes.
    ISBN 0-8120-4294-8
    1. French language—Verb—Tables. I. Kendris,
Christopher. 301 French verbs fully conjugated in
all the tenses. II. Title.
PC2271 .K43 2001
448.2'421—dc20   89-39626
                                        CIP

PRINTED IN HONG KONG
9 8 7 6

Contents

About the Author

Christopher Kendris has taught French and Spanish at Northwestern University, at the College of the University of Chicago, at Rutgers University, at the State University of New York at Albany, and at Schenectady County Community College. For several years he also taught French and Spanish at Farmingdale High School, Farmingdale, New York, where he was chairman of the Department of Foreign Languages.

Dr. Kendris received his B.S. and M.S. degrees at Columbia University in the City of New York and his M.A. and Ph.D. degrees at Northwestern University in Evanston, Illinois. He also earned two certificates with *Mention très Honorable* at the Ecole Supérieure de Préparation et de Perfectionnement des Professeurs de Français à l'Etranger, Faculté des Lettres, Université de Paris.

Dr. Kendris is the author of many modern language books and workbooks, all of which have been published by Barron's Educational Series, Inc. All his French and Spanish books are listed **on-line** on the Internet, for example, on ***webmaster@barronseduc.com,*** on ***amazon.com,*** and on other popular web sites.

Abbreviations

adj.	adjectif (adjective)	*n.*	nom (noun)
adv.	adverbe (adverb)	*obj.*	objet (object)
ant.	antérieur (anterior)	*p.*	page
art.	article	*pp.*	pages
cond.	conditionnel (conditional)	*part.*	participe (participle)
def.	défini (definite)	*pl.*	pluriel (plural)
dir.	direct	*plpf.*	plus-que-parfait (pluperfect)
e.g.	for example	*pr.* or *prés.*	présent (present)
f. or *fem.*	féminin (feminine)	*prep.*	préposition (preposition)
fam.	familiar	*pron.*	pronom (pronoun)
fut.	futur (future)	*qqch*	quelque chose (something)
i.e.	that is, that is to say	*qqn*	quelqu'un (someone, somebody)
imp.	imparfait (imperfect)	*refl.*	reflexive
ind.	indicatif (indicative)	*s.* or *sing.*	singulier (singular)
inf.	infinitif (infinitive)	*subj.*	subjonctif (subjunctive)
m. or *masc.*	masculin (masculine)	*v.*	verbe (verb)

Introduction

The new edition of *French Verbs* includes improvements to the existing text and additional new material, and offers an important new feature—color as an aid to learning. In the front section of this book, rules regarding the use of verbs are made clearer by color highlights. In the body of the book, color takes the mystery out of conjugation. In all, the reader will find that color makes the entire book easier to use. Whatever facilitates learning enhances the ability to use what is learned. This pocket reference of over 300 commonly used French verbs for students, businesspeople, and travelers provides fingertip access to correct verb forms.

Verb conjugations are usually found scattered in French grammar books and they are difficult to find quickly when needed. Verbs have always been a major problem for students no matter what system or approach the teacher uses. You will master French verb forms if you study this book a few minutes every day, especially the pages before and after the alphabetical listing of the 301 verbs.

I compiled this book in order to help make your work easier and at the same time to teach you French verb forms systematically. It is a useful book because it provides a quick and easy way to find the full conjugation of many French verbs.

The verbs included here are arranged alphabetically by infinitive at the top of each page. The book contains many common verbs of high frequency, both reflexive and non-reflexive, that you need to know. It also contains many other frequently used verbs that are irregular in some way. On page 312 I give you an additional 1,000 French verbs that are conjugated in the same way as model verbs among the 301. If the verb you have in mind is not given, consult the list that begins on page 312. My other book, *501 French verbs fully conjugated in all the tenses,* fourth edition, contains two hundred additional verbs and new features.

The subject pronouns have been omitted from the conjugations in order to emphasize the verb forms. I give you the subject pronouns on page xxxii. Turn to that page now and become acquainted with them.

The first thing to do when you use this book is to become familiar with it from cover to cover—in particular, the front and back pages, where you will find valuable and useful information to make your work easier and more enjoyable. Take a minute right now and turn to the table of contents at the beginning of this book as I guide you in the following way:

(a)   On page vii I explain which verbs are conjugated with *avoir* or *être* to form a compound tense. Study those pages and refer to them frequently until you master those verbs.

(b)   On page viii I show you how to form a present participle regularly in French and I give you examples. I also give you the common irregular present participles on page ix.

(c)   On page ix I do the same for past participles. I give you the present and past participles of each verb at the top of the page where verb forms are given for a particular verb.

(d)   On page x you will find the principal parts of some important verbs which, in French, are called *Les temps primitifs*. This is useful because if you know these you can easily form all the tenses and moods from them.

(e)   On pages x and xi there are two tables showing the derivation of tenses of a typical verb conjugated with *avoir* and another conjugated with *être*. These are presented as in a picture so that you can see what tenses are derived from the principal parts.

(f)   On pages xii and xiii I give you a sample English verb conjugation so that you can get an idea of the way a verb is expressed in the English tenses. Many people do not know one tense from another because they have never learned the use of verb tenses in a systematic and organized way—not even in English! How can you know, for instance, that you need the conditional form of a verb in French when you want to say *"I would go* to the movies if . . ."* or the pluperfect tense in French if you want to say *"I had gone . . . ?"* The sample English verb conjugation with the names of the tenses and their numerical ranking will help you distinguish one tense from another so that you will know what tense you need to express a verb in French.

(g)   On page xiv I begin a summary of meanings and uses of French verb tenses and moods as related to English verb tenses and moods. That section is very important and useful because I separate the seven simple tenses from the seven compound tenses. I give you the name of each tense in French and English starting with the present indicative, which I call tense number 1, because it is the tense most frequently used. I assign a number to each tense name so that you can fix each one in your mind and associate the name and number in their logical order. I explain briefly what each tense is, when you use it, and I give examples using verbs in sentences in French and English.

(h)   On page xxvi I give you a summary of all the fourteen tenses in French with English equivalents, which I have divided into the seven simple tenses and the seven compound tenses. After referring to that summary frequently, you will soon know that tense number 1 is the present indicative, tense number 2 is the imperfect indicative, and so on.

(i)   On page xxix I show you how to form the seven simple tenses for regular verbs and here, again, I have assigned the same number to each tense name. I also explain how each compound tense is based on each simple tense in the table on pages xxxi–xxxii. Try to see these two divisions as two frames, two pictures, with the seven simple tenses in one frame and the seven compound tenses in another frame. Place them side by side in your mind, and you will see how tense number 8 is related to tense number 1, tense number 9 to tense number 2, and so on. If you study the numerical arrangement of each of the seven simple tenses and associate the tense number with the tense name, you will find it very easy to learn the names of the seven compound tenses, how they rank numerically according to use, how they are formed, and when they are used. Spend at least ten minutes every day studying these preliminary pages to help you understand better the fourteen tenses in French.

Finally, in the back pages of this book there are useful indexes and an additional 1,000 French verbs that are conjugated like model verbs among the 301.

I sincerely hope that this book will be of some help to you in learning and using French verbs.

CHRISTOPHER KENDRIS
B.S., M.S., M.A., Ph.D.

Verbs Conjugated with *avoir* or *être* to Form a Compound Tense

(a)   Generally speaking, a French verb is conjugated with *avoir* to form a compound tense.

(b)   All reflexive verbs, for example, *se laver,* are conjugated with *être*.

(c)   The following is a list of common non-reflexive verbs that are conjugated with *être*. The five verbs marked with asterisks (*) are conjugated with *avoir* when used with a direct object.

1. **aller** to go
   Elle est allée au cinéma.

2. **arriver** to arrive
   Elle est arrivée à une heure.

3. ***descendre** to go down, come down
   Elle est descendue vite.
   She came down quickly.
   BUT:
     *Elle a descendu la valise.
     She brought down the suitcase.

4. **devenir** to become
   Elle est devenue docteur.

5. **entrer** to enter, go in, come in
   Elle est entrée dans l'école.

6. ***monter** to go up, come up
   Elle est montée vite.
   She went up quickly.
   BUT:
     *Elle a monté l'escalier.
     She went up the stairs.

7. **mourir** to die
   Elle est morte hier.

8. **naître** to be born
   Elle est née hier.

9. **partir** to leave
   Elle est partie vite.

10. ***passer** to go by, to pass by
    Elle est passée chez moi.
    She came by my house.
    BUT:
      *Elle m'a passé le sel.
      She passed me the salt.
    AND:
      *Elle a passé un examen.
      She took an exam.

11. ***rentrer** to go in again, to return (home)
    Elle est rentrée tôt.
    She returned home early.
    BUT:
      *Elle a rentré le chat dans la maison.
      She brought (took) the cat into the house.

12. **rester** to remain, to stay
    Elle est restée chez elle.

13. **retourner** to return, to go back
    Elle est retournée à sa place.

14. **revenir** to come back
    Elle est revenue hier.

15. ***sortir** to go out
    Elle est sortie hier soir.
    She went out last night.
    BUT:
      *Elle a sorti son mouchoir.
      She took out her handkerchief.

16. **tomber** to fall
    Elle est tombée.

17. **venir** to come
    Elle est venue ce matin.

Formation of the Present and Past Participles in French

Formation of the present participle in French

The present participle is regularly formed in the following way. Take the **"nous"** form of the present indicative of the verb you have in mind, drop the ending **-ons** and add **-ant**. That ending is the equivalent to *-ing* in English. Examples:

chantons, chantant   vendons, vendant   allons, allant
finissons, finissant   mangeons, mangeant   travaillons,
travaillant

Common irregular present participles

The three common irregular present participles are: **ayant** from **avoir**;
étant from **être**; **sachant** from **savoir**.

Formation of the past participle in French

The past participle is regularly formed from the infinitive:

-er ending verbs, drop the **-er** and add **é**:   **donner, donné**
-ir ending verbs, drop the **-ir** and add **i**:   **finir, fini**
-re ending verbs, drop the **-re** and add **u**:   **vendre, vendu**

Common irregular past participles

INFINITIVE	PAST PARTICIPLE	INFINITIVE	PAST PARTICIPLE
apprendre	**appris**	naître	**né**
asseoir	**assis**	offrir	**offert**
avoir	**eu**	ouvrir	**ouvert**
boire	**bu**	paraître	**paru**
comprendre	**compris**	permettre	**permis**
conduire	**conduit**	plaire	**plu**
connaître	**connu**	pleuvoir	**plu**
construire	**construit**	pouvoir	**pu**
courir	**couru**	prendre	**pris**
couvrir	**couvert**	promettre	**promis**
craindre	**craint**	recevoir	**reçu**
croire	**cru**	revenir	**revenu**
devenir	**devenu**	rire	**ri**
devoir	**dû, due**	savoir	**su**
dire	**dit**	suivre	**suivi**
écrire	**écrit**	taire	**tu**
être	**été**	tenir	**tenu**
faire	**fait**	valoir	**valu**
falloir	**fallu**	venir	**venu**
lire	**lu**	vivre	**vécu**
mettre	**mis**	voir	**vu**
mourir	**mort**	vouloir	**voulu**

Principal Parts of Some Important Verbs
(Les temps primitifs de quelques verbes importants)

The principal parts of a verb are very important to know because from them you can easily form all the tenses. See the following pages where two tables are given, one showing the derivation of tenses of a verb conjugated with **avoir** and the other with **être.** Note that the headings at the top of each column are the same as the following headings.

INFINITIF	PARTICIPE PRÉSENT	PARTICIPE PASSÉ	PRÉSENT DE L'INDICATIF	PASSÉ SIMPLE
aller	allant	allé	je vais	j'allai
avoir	ayant	eu	j'ai	j'eus
battre	battant	battu	je bats	je battis
boire	buvant	bu	je bois	je bus
craindre	craignant	craint	je crains	je craignis
croire	croyant	cru	je crois	je crus
devoir	devant	dû, due	je dois	je dus
dire	disant	dit	je dis	je dis
écrire	écrivant	écrit	j'écris	j'écrivis
être	étant	été	je suis	je fus
faire	faisant	fait	je fais	je fis
lire	lisant	lu	je lis	je lus
mettre	mettant	mis	je mets	je mis
mourir	mourant	mort	je meurs	je mourus
naître	naissant	né	je nais	je naquis
ouvrir	ouvrant	ouvert	j'ouvre	j'ouvris
porter	portant	porté	je porte	je portai
pouvoir	pouvant	pu	je peux *or* je puis	je pus
prendre	prenant	pris	je prends	je pris
recevoir	recevant	reçu	je reçois	je reçus
savoir	sachant	su	je sais	je sus
venir	venant	venu	je viens	je vins
vivre	vivant	vécu	je vis	je vécus
voir	voyant	vu	je vois	je vis
voler	volant	volé	je vole	je volai

Tables Showing Derivation of Tenses of Verbs Conjugated with *avoir* and *être*

Derivation of Tenses of Verbs Conjugated with *avoir*

INFINITIF	PARTICIPE PRÉSENT	PARTICIPE PASSÉ	PRÉSENT DE L'INDICATIF	PASSÉ SIMPLE
donner	donnant	donné	je donne	je donnai

FUTUR	IMPARFAIT DE L'INDICATIF	PASSÉ COMPOSÉ	PRÉSENT DE L'INDICATIF	PASSÉ SIMPLE
donnerai	donnais	ai donné	donne	donnai
donneras	donnais	as donné	donnes	donnas
donnera	donnait	a donné	donne	donna
donnerons	donnions	avons donné	donnons	donnâmes
donnerez	donniez	avez donné	donnez	donnâtes
donneront	donnaient	ont donné	donnent	donnèrent

CONDITIONNEL	PLUS-QUE-PARFAIT DE L'INDICATIF	IMPÉRATIF	IMPARFAIT DU SUBJONCTIF
donnerais	avais donné	donne	donnasse
donnerais	avais donné	donnons	donnasses
donnerait	avait donné	donnez	donnât
donnerions	avions donné		donnassions
donneriez	aviez donné		donnassiez
donneraient	avaient donné		donnassent

	PASSÉ ANTÉRIEUR	PRÉSENT DU SUBJONCTIF
	eus donné	donne
	eus donné	donnes
	eut donné	donne
	eûmes donné	donnions
	eûtes donné	donniez
	eurent donné	donnent

FUTUR ANTÉRIEUR	CONDITIONNEL PASSÉ	PASSÉ DU SUBJONCTIF	PLUS-QUE-PARFAIT DU SUBJONCTIF
aurai donné	aurais donné	aie donné	eusse donné
auras donné	aurais donné	aies donné	eusses donné
aura donné	aurait donné	ait donné	eût donné
aurons donné	aurions donné	ayons donné	eussions donné
aurez donné	auriez donné	ayez donné	eussiez donné
auront donné	auraient donné	aient donné	eussent donné

Derivation of Tenses of Verbs Conjugated with *être*

INFINITIF	PARTICIPE PRÉSENT	PARTICIPE PASSÉ	PRÉSENT DE L'INDICATIF	PASSÉ SIMPLE
arriver	**arrivant**	**arrivé**	**j'arrive**	**j'arrivai**

FUTUR	IMPARFAIT DE L'INDICATIF	PASSÉ COMPOSÉ	PRÉSENT DE L'INDICATIF	PASSÉ SIMPLE
arriver**ai**	arriv**ais**	**suis** arrivé(e)	arrive	arriv**ai**
arriver**as**	arriv**ais**	**es** arrivé(e)	arrives	arriv**as**
arriver**a**	arriv**ait**	**est** arrivé(e)	arrives	arriv**a**
arriver**ons**	arriv**ions**	**sommes** arrivé(e)s	arriv**ons**	arriv**âmes**
arriver**ez**	arriv**iez**	**êtes** arrivé(e)(s)	arriv**ez**	arriv**âtes**
arriver**ont**	arriv**aient**	**sont** arrivé(e)s	arriv**ent**	arriv**èrent**

CONDITIONNEL		PLUS-QUE-PARFAIT DE L'INDICATIF	IMPÉRATIF	IMPARFAIT DU SUBJONCTIF
arriver**ais**		**étais** arrivé(e)	arrive	arriv**asse**
arriver**ais**		**étais** arrivé(e)	arriv**ons**	arriv**asses**
arriver**ait**		**était** arrivé(e)	arriv**ez**	arriv**ât**
arriver**ions**		**étions** arrivé(e)s		arriv**assions**
arriver**iez**		**étiez** arrivé(e)(s)		arriv**assiez**
arriver**aient**		**étaient** arrivé(e)s		arriv**assent**

		PASSÉ ANTÉRIEUR	PRÉSENT DU SUBJONCTIF	
		fus arrivé(e)	arrive	
		fus arrivé(e)	arrives	
		fut arrivé(e)	arrive	
		fûmes arrivé(e)s	arriv**ions**	
		fûtes arrivé(e)(s)	arriv**iez**	
		furent arrivé(e)s	arriv**ent**	

FUTUR ANTÉRIEUR	CONDITIONNEL PASSÉ	PASSÉ DU SUBJONCTIF	PLUS-QUE-PARFAIT DU SUBJONCTIF
serai arrivé(e)	**serais** arrivé(e)	**sois** arrivé(e)	**fusse** arrivé(e)
seras arrivé(e)	**serais** arrivé(e)	**sois** arrivé(e)	**fusses** arrivé(e)
sera arrivé(e)	**serait** arrivé(e)	**soit** arrivé(e)	**fût** arrivé(e)
serons arrivé(e)s	**serions** arrivé(e)s	**soyons** arrivé(e)s	**fussions** arrivé(e)s
serez arrivé(e)(s)	**seriez** arrivé(e)(s)	**soyez** arrivé(e)(s)	**fussiez** arrivé(e)(s)
seront arrivé(e)s	**seraient** arrivé(e)s	**soient** arrivé(e)s	**fussent** arrivé(e)s

Sample English Verb Conjugation

INFINITIVE **to go–aller**
PRESENT PARTICIPLE going   *PAST PARTICIPLE* gone

Tense no.	The seven simple tenses
1 *Present Indicative*	I go, you go, he (she, it) goes; we go, you go, they go
	or: I do go, you do go, he (she, it) does go; we do go, you do go, they do go
	or: I am going, you are going, he (she, it) is going; we are going, you are going, they are going
2 *Imperfect Indicative*	I was going, you were going, he (she, it) was going; we were going, you were going, they were going
	or: I went, you went, he (she, it) went; we went, you went, they went
	or: I used to go, you used to go, he (she, it) used to go; we used to go, you used to go, they used to go
3 *Passé Simple*	I went, you went, he (she, it) went; we went, you went, they went
	or: I did go, you did go, he (she, it) did go; we did go, you did go, they did go
4 *Future*	I shall go, you will go, he (she, it) will go; we shall go, you will go, they will go
5 *Conditional*	I would go, you would go, he (she, it) would go; we would go, you would go, they would go
6 *Present Subjunctive*	that I may go, that you may go, that he (she, it) may go; that we may go, that you may go, that they may go
7 *Imperfect Subjunctive*	that I might go, that you might go, that he (she, it) might go; that we might go, that you might go, that they might go

INFINITIVE **to go–aller**
PRESENT PARTICIPLE going   *PAST PARTICIPLE* gone

Tense no.	The seven compound tenses
8 *Passé Composé*	I have gone, you have gone, he (she, it) has gone; we have gone, you have gone, they have gone
or:	I went, you went, he (she, it) went; we went, you went, they went
or:	I did go, you did go, he (she, it) did go; we did go, you did go, they did go
9 *Pluperfect or Past Perfect Indicative*	I had gone, you had gone, he (she, it) had gone; we had gone, you had gone, they had gone
10 *Past Anterior*	I had gone, you had gone, he (she, it) had gone; we had gone, you had gone, they had gone
11 *Future Perfect or Future Anterior*	I shall have gone, you will have gone, he (she, it) will have gone; we shall have gone, you will have gone, they will have gone
12 *Conditional Perfect*	I would have gone, you would have gone, he (she, it) would have gone; we would have gone, you would have gone, they would have gone
13 *Past Subjunctive*	that I may have gone, that you may have gone, that he (she, it) may have gone; that we may have gone, that you may have gone, that they may have gone
14 *Pluperfect or Past Perfect Subjunctive*	that I might have gone, that you might have gone, that he (she, it) might have gone; that we might have gone, that you might have gone, that they might have gone

A Summary of Meanings and Uses of French Verb Tenses and Moods as Related to English Verb Tenses and Moods

A verb is where the action is! A verb is a word that expresses an action (like *go, eat, write*) or a state of being (like *think, believe, be*). Tense means time. French and English verb tenses are divided into three main groups of time: past, present, and future. A verb tense shows if an action or state of being took place, is taking place, or will take place.

French and English verbs are also used in four moods (or modes). Mood has to do with the *way* a person regards an action or a state. For example, a person may merely make a statement or ask a question— this is the Indicative Mood, which we use most of the time in French and English. A person may say that he *would do* something if something else were possible or that he *would have done* something if something else had been possible—this is the Conditional Mood. A person may use a verb *in such a way* to indicate a wish, a fear, a regret, a supposition, or something of this sort—this is the Subjunctive Mood. The Subjunctive Mood is used in French much more than in English. A person may command that something be done—this is the Imperative Mood.

There are six tenses in English: Present, Past, Future, Present Perfect, Past Perfect, and Future Perfect. The first three are simple tenses. The other three are compound tenses and are based on the simple tenses. In French, however, there are fourteen tenses, seven of which are simple and seven of which are compound.

In the pages that follow, the tenses and moods are given in French and the equivalent name or names in English are given in parentheses. I have numbered each tense name for easy reference and recognition. Although some of the names given in English are not considered to be tenses (for there are only six), they are given for the purpose of identification as they are related to the French names. The comparison includes only the essential points you need to know about the meanings and uses of French verb tenses and moods as related to English usage.

I shall use examples to illustrate their meanings and uses. See p. xxix for the formation of the seven simple tenses for regular verbs.

THE SEVEN SIMPLE TENSES

Tense No. 1   Le Présent de l'Indicatif
             (Present Indicative)

This tense is used most of the time in French and English. It indicates:

(a) An action or a state of being at the present time.
   EXAMPLES:
   1. Je **vais** à l'école maintenant. I *am going* to school now.
   2. Je **pense;** donc, je **suis.** I *think;* therefore, I *am.*

(b) Habitual action.
   EXAMPLE:
   Je **vais** à la bibliothèque tous les jours.
   I *go* to the library every day. OR: I *do go* to the library every day.

(c) A general truth, something that is permanently true.
   EXAMPLES:
   1. Deux et deux **font** quatre. Two and two *are* four.
   2. Voir c'**est** croire. Seeing *is* believing.

(d) Vividness when talking or writing about past events. This is called
   the *historical present.*
   EXAMPLE:
   Marie-Antoinette **est** condamnée à mort. Elle **monte** dans la charrette
   et **est** en route pour la guillotine.
   Marie-Antoinette *is* condemned to die. She *goes* into the cart and
   is on her way to the guillotine.

(e) A near future.
   EXAMPLE:
   Il **arrive** demain. He *arrives* tomorrow.

(f) An action or state of being that occurred in the past and
   continues up to the present. In English, this tense is the Present
   Perfect, which is formed with the present tense of *to have (have*
   or *has)* plus the past participle of the verb you are using.
   EXAMPLES:
   1. Je **suis** ici depuis dix minutes.
      I *have been* here for ten minutes. (I am still here at present)
   2. Elle **est** malade depuis trois jours.
      She *has been* sick for three days. (She is still sick at present)
   3. J'**attends** l'autobus depuis dix minutes.
      I *have been waiting* for the bus for ten minutes.

NOTE: In this last example the formation of the English verb tense is slightly different from the other two examples in English. The present participle *(waiting)* is used instead of the past participle *(waited)*.

NOTE ALSO: For the formation of this tense for regular verbs see p. xxix.

Tense No. 2 L'Imparfait de l'Indicatif
(Imperfect Indicative)

This is a past tense. It is used to indicate:

(a) An action that was going on in the past at the same time as another action.
EXAMPLE:
Il **lisait** pendant que j'**écrivais.** He *was reading* while I *was writing.*

(b) An action that was going on in the past when another action occurred.
EXAMPLE:
Il **lisait** quand je suis entré. He *was reading* when I came in.

(c) An action that a person did habitually in the past.
EXAMPLE:
Nous **allions** à la plage tous les jours. We *used to go* to the beach every day.
OR:
We *would go* to the beach every day.

(d) A description of a mental or physical condition in the past.
EXAMPLES:

(mental condition)	Il **était** triste quand je l'ai vu.
	He *was* sad when I saw him.
(physical condition)	Quand ma mère **était** jeune, elle **était** belle.
	When my mother *was* young, she *was* beautiful.

(e) An action or state of being that occurred in the past and *lasted for a certain length of time* prior to another past action. In English, it is usually translated as a pluperfect tense and is formed with *had been* plus the present participle of the verb you are using. It is like the special use of the **Présent de l'Indicatif** described in the above section (Tense No. 1) in paragraph (f), except that the action or state of being no longer exists at present.

EXAMPLE:

J'attendais l'autobus depuis dix minutes quand il est arrivé.

I *had been waiting* for the bus for ten minutes when it arrived.

NOTE: For the formation of this tense for regular verbs see p. xxix.

Tense No. 3   Le Passé Simple
(Past Definite or Simple Past)

This past tense is not ordinarily used in conversational French or in informal writing. It is a literary sense. It is used in formal writing, such as history and literature. You should be able merely to recognize this tense when you see it in your French readings. It should be noted that French writers use the **Passé Simple** less and less these days. The **Passé Composé** is taking its place in literature, except for **avoir** and **être,** which you must know in this tense.

EXAMPLES:

(a) Il **alla** en Afrique. He *went* to Africa.

(b) Il **voyagea** en Amérique. He *traveled* to America.

(c) Elle **fut** heureuse. She *was* happy.

(d) Elle **eut** un grand bonheur. She *had* great happiness.

NOTE: For the formation of this tense for regular verbs see p. xxx.

Tense No. 4   Le Futur
(Future)

In French and English this tense is used to express an action or a state of being that will take place at some time in the future.

EXAMPLES:

(a) J'**irai** en France l'été prochain.
I *shall go* to France next summer.

OR:

I *will go* to France next summer.

(b) J'y **penserai.**
I *shall think* about it.
OR:
I *will think* about it.

(c) Je **partirai** dès qu'il arrivera.
I *shall leave* as soon as he arrives.

(d) Je te **dirai** tout quand tu seras ici.
I *shall tell* you all when you are here.

If the action of the verb you are using is not past or present and if future time is implied, the future tense is used when the clause begins with any of the following conjunctions: **aussitôt que** (as soon as), **dès que** (as soon as), **quand** (when), **lorsque** (when), and **tant que** (as long as).

NOTE: For the formation of this tense for regular verbs see p. xxx.

Tense No. 5   Le Conditionnel Présent
           (Conditional)

The Conditional is used in French and English to express:

(a) An action that you would do if something else were possible.
   EXAMPLE:
   Je **ferais** le travail si j'avais le temps.
   I *would do* the work if I had the time.

(b) A conditional desire. This is the Conditional of courtesy in French.
   EXAMPLES:
   J'**aimerais** du thé. I *would like* some tea.
   Je **voudrais** du café. I *would like* some coffee.

(c)   An obligation or duty.
   EXAMPLE:
   Je **devrais** étudier pour l'examen. I *should* study for the examination.
   OR: I *ought* to study for the examination.

   NOTE (1): The French verb **devoir** plus the infinitive is used to express the idea of *should* when you mean *ought*.

   NOTE (2): When the Conditional of the verb **pouvoir** is used in French, it is translated into English as *could* or *would be able*.

   EXAMPLE:
   Je **pourrais** venir après le dîner. I *could come* after dinner.
   OR: I *would be able* to come after dinner.

   NOTE: For the formation of this tense for regular verbs see p. xxx.

Tense No. 6   Le Présent du Subjonctif
                (Present Subjunctive)

The Subjunctive is used in French much more than in English. It is disappearing in English, except for the following major uses:

  (a) The Subjunctive is used in French and English to express a command.
      EXAMPLE:
      Soyez à l'heure! *Be* on time!
      NOTE: In English, the form in the Subjunctive applies mainly to the
      verb *to be*. Also, note that all the verbs in French are not in the
      Subjunctive when expressing a command. See **L'Impératif** on
      p. xxviii.

  (b) The Subjunctive is commonly used in English to express a condition
      contrary to fact.
      EXAMPLE:
      If I *were* you, I would not do it.
      NOTE: In French the Subjunctive is not used in this instance. Instead,
      the *Imparfait de l'Indicatif* is used if what precedes is *si (if)*. Same
      example in French: Si j'**étais** vous, je ne le ferais pas.

  (c) The Present Subjunctive is used in French and English after a verb
      that expresses some kind of insistence, preference, or suggestion.
      EXAMPLES:
      1. Je préfère qu'il **fasse** le travail maintenant.
         I prefer that *he do* the work now.
      2. J'exige qu'il **soit** puni.
         I demand that *he be* punished.

  (d) The Subjunctive is used in French after a verb that expresses doubt,
      fear, joy, sorrow, or some other emotion. Notice in the following
      examples that the Subjunctive is not used in English but it is in
      French.
EXAMPLES:
      1. Je doute qu'il **vienne.**
         I doubt that he *is coming.*   OR: I doubt that he *will come.*
      2. J'ai peur qu'il ne **soit** malade.
         I'm afraid that he *is* sick.
      3. Je suis heureux qu'il **vienne.**
         I'm happy that he *is coming.*
      4. Je regrette qu'il **soit** malade.
         I'm sorry that he *is* sick.

(e) The Present Subjunctive is used in French after certain conjunctions. Notice, however, that the Subjunctive is not always used in English.

EXAMPLES:

1. Je partirai **à moins qu'il ne vienne.**
   I shall leave unless he *comes.*
2. Je resterai **jusqu'à ce qu'il vienne.**
   I shall stay until he *comes.*
3. **Quoiqu'elle soit** belle, il ne l'aime pas.
   Although she *is* beautiful, he does not love her.
4. Je l'explique **pour qu'elle comprenne.**
   I'm explaining it *so that she may understand.*

(f) The Present Subjunctive is used in French after certain impersonal expressions that show a need, doubt, possibility or impossibility. Notice, however, that the Subjunctive is not always used in English in the following examples:

1. Il est urgent qu'il **vienne.**
   It is urgent that he *come.*
2. Il vaut mieux qu'il **vienne.**
   It is better that he *come.*
3. Il est possible qu'il **vienne.**
   It is possible that he *will come.*
4. Il est douteux qu'il **vienne.**
   It is doubtful that he *will come.*
5. Il est nécessaire qu'il **vienne.**
   It is necessary that he *come.* OR: He must come.
6. Il faut qu'il **vienne.**
   It is necessary that he *come.* OR: He must come.
7. Il est important que vous **fassiez** le travail.
   It is important that you *do* the work.
8. Il est indispensable qu'elle **fasse** le travail.
   It is required that she *do* the work.

NOTE: For the formation of this tense for regular verbs see p. xxx.

Tense No. 7 L'Imparfait du Subjonctif
            (Imperfect Subjunctive)

L'Imparfait du Subjonctif is used for the same reasons as the **Présent du Subjonctif**—that is, after certain verbs, conjunctions, and impersonal expressions that were used in examples above under the section **le Présent du Subjonctif.** The main difference between these two is the time of the action. If present, use the **Présent du Subjonctif** (Tense No. 6). If the action is related to the past, the **Imparfait du Subjonctif** (this tense) is used, provided that the action was *not* completed. If the action was completed, the **Plus-que-parfait du Subjonctif** is used. See below under the section **Plus-que-parfait du Subjonctif** (Tense No. 14).

Since the Subjunctive Mood is troublesome in French and English, you may be pleased to know that this tense is rarely used in English. It is used in French, however, but only in formal writing and in literature. For that reason, you should merely be familiar with it so you can recognize it when you see it in your French readings. In conversational French and in informal writing, **l'Imparfait du Subjonctif** is avoided. Use, instead, the **Présent du Subjonctif.**

Notice that the **Imparfait du Subjonctif** is used in French in both of the following examples, but is used in English only in the second example, (b):

EXAMPLES:
(a) Je voulais qu'il vînt. I wanted him to come.
   (action not completed; he did not come while I wanted him to come)

   NOTE: The Subjunctive of **venir** is used because the verb that precedes is one that requires the Subjunctive *after* it—in this example it is **vouloir.** In conversational French and informal writing, the **Imparfait du Subjonctif** is avoided. Use, instead, the **Présent du Subjonctif:** Je voulais qu'il **vienne.**

(b) Je le lui expliquais **pour qu'elle le comprît.**
   I was explaining it to her *so that she might understand it.* (action not completed; the understanding was not completed at the time of the explaining)

   NOTE: The Subjunctive of **comprendre** is used because the conjunction that precedes is one that requires the Subjunctive *after* it—in this example it is **pour que.** In conversational French and informal writing, the **Imparfait du Subjonctif** is avoided. Use, instead, the **Présent du Subjunctif:** Je le lui expliquais pour qu'elle le **comprenne.**

   NOTE: For the formation of this tense for regular verbs see p. xxx.

THE SEVEN COMPOUND TENSES

Tense No. 8   Le Passé Composé
         (Past Indefinite or Compound Past)

This past tense is used in conversational French, correspondence, and other informal writing. The **Passé Composé** is used more and more in literature these days and is taking the place of the **Passé Simple** (Tense

No. 3). It is a compound tense because it is formed with the **Présent de l'Indicatif** (Tense No. 1) of *avoir* or *être* (depending on which of these two auxiliaries is required to form a compound tense) plus the past participle. See page vii for the distinction made between verbs conjugated with *avoir* or *être*.

EXAMPLES:

1. Il **est allé** à l'école. He *went* to school.
2. Il **est allé** à l'école. He *did go* to school.
3. Il **est allé** à l'école. He *has gone* to school.
4. J'**ai mangé** dans ce restaurant beaucoup de fois.
   I *have eaten* in this restaurant many times.

NOTE: In examples 3 and 4 in English the verb is formed with the Present tense of *to have (have* or *has)* plus the past participle of the verb you are using. In English, this form is called the Present Perfect.

5. J'**ai parlé** au garçon. I *spoke* to the boy. OR: I *have spoken* to the boy.
   OR: I *did speak* to the boy.

Tense No. 9   Le Plus-que-parfait de l'Indicatif
                (Pluperfect or Past Perfect Indicative)

In French and English this tense is used to express an action that happened in the past *before* another past action. Since it is used in relation to another past action, the other past action is expressed in either the **Passé Composé** (Tense No. 8) or the **Imparfait de l'Indicatif** (Tense No. 2) in French. This tense is used in formal writing and literature as well as in conversational French and informal writing. The correct use of this tense is strictly observed in French. In English, however, too often we neglect to use it correctly. It is a compound tense because it is formed with the **Imparfait de l'Indicatif** of *avoir* or *être* (depending on which of these two auxiliaries is required to form a compound tense) plus the past participle. See page vii for the distinction made between verbs conjugated with *avoir* or *être*. In English, this tense is formed with the Past Tense of *to have* *(had)* plus the past participle of the verb you are using.

EXAMPLES:

(a) Je me suis rappelé que j'**avais oublié** de le lui dire.
    I remembered that I *had forgotten* to tell him.

NOTE: It would be incorrect in English to say: I remembered that I *forgot* to tell him. The point here is that *first* I forgot; then, I remembered. Both actions are in the past. The action that occurred in the past *before* the other past action is in the Pluperfect. And in this example it is *I had forgotten* (**j'avais oublié**).

(b) J'**avais étudié** la leçon que le professeur a expliquée.
I *had studied* the lesson that the teacher explained.

> NOTE: *First* I studied the lesson; then, the teacher explained it. Both actions are in the past. The action that occurred in the past *before* the other past action is in the Pluperfect. And in this example it is *I had studied* (**j'avais étudié**). If you say **J'ai étudié la leçon que le professeur avait expliquée,** you are saying that you *studied* the lesson that the teacher *had explained.* In other words, the teacher explained the lesson first and then you studied it.

(c) J'étais fatigué ce matin parce que je n'**avais** pas **dormi.**
I was tired this morning because I *had* not *slept.*

Tense No. 10   Le Passé Antérieur
(Past Anterior)

This tense is similar to the **Plus-que-parfait de l'Indicatif** (Tense No. 9). The main difference is that in French it is a literary tense; that is, it is used in formal writing, such as history and literature. More and more French writers today use the **Plus-que-parfait de l'Indicatif** instead of this tense. Generally speaking, the **Passé Antérieur** is to the **Plus-que-parfait** what the **Passé Simple** is to the **Passé Composé.** The **Passé Antérieur** is a compound tense. In French, it is formed with the **Passé Simple** of *avoir* or *être* (depending on which of these two auxiliaries is required to form a compound tense) plus the past participle. In English, it is formed in the same way as the Pluperfect or Past Perfect. This tense is ordinarily introduced by conjunctions of time: **après que, aussitôt que, dès que, lorsque, quand.**

> EXAMPLE:
> Quand il **eut mangé** tout, il partit. When he *had eaten* everything, he left.

> NOTE: In conversational French and informal writing, the **Plus-que-parfait de l'Indicatif** is used instead: Quand il **avait mangé** tout, il est parti. The translation into English is the same.

Tense No. 11   Le Futur Antérieur
(Future Perfect or Future Anterior)

In French and English this tense is used to express an action that will happen in the future *before* another future action. Since it is used in relation to another future action, the other future action is expressed in the simple Future in French, but not always in the simple Future in English. In French, it is used in conversation and informal writing as well as in formal writing and in literature. It is a compound tense because it is formed with the **Futur** of *avoir* and *être* (depending on which of these two auxiliaries is required to form a compound tense) plus the past participle of the verb you are using. In English, it is formed by using *shall have* or *will have* plus the past participle of the verb you are using.

EXAMPLES:
(a) Elle arrivera demain et j'**aurai fini** le travail.
   She will arrive tomorrow and I *shall have finished* the work.

> NOTE: First, I shall finish the work; then, she will arrive. The action that will occur in the future *before* the other future action is in the **Futur Antérieur.**

(b) Quand elle arrivera demain, j'**aurai fini** le travail.
   When she arrives tomorrow, I *shall have finished* the work.

> NOTE: The idea of future time here is the same as in example (a) above. In English, the Present tense is used *(When she arrives . . .)* to express a near future. In French the **Futur** is used **(Quand elle arrivera . . .)** because **quand** precedes and the action will take place in the future. Study Tense No. 4 on page xviii.

Tense No. 12   Le Conditionnel Passé
                  (Conditional Perfect)

This is used in French and English to express an action that you *would have done* if something else had been possible; that is, you would have done something *on condition* that something else had been possible. It is a compound tense because it is formed with the **Conditionnel Présent** of *avoir* or *être* plus the past participle of the verb you are using. In English, it is formed by using *would have* plus the past participle. Observe the difference between the following examples and the one given for the use of the **Conditionnel Présent,** which was explained and illustrated in Tense No. 5 above.

EXAMPLES:
(a) J'**aurais fait** le travail si j'avais étudié.
   I *would have done* the work if I had studied.
(b) J'**aurais fait** le travail si j'avais eu le temps.
   I *would have done* the work if I had had the time.

> NOTE: Review the **Plus-que-parfait de l'Indicatif,** which was explained above in Tense No. 9, in order to understand the use of *if I had studied* **(si j'avais étudié)** and *if I had had the time* **(si j'avais eu le temps).**

NOTE FURTHER: The French verb **devoir** plus the infinitive is used to express the idea of *should* when you mean *ought to*. The past participle of **devoir** is **dû.** It is conjugated with **avoir.**

EXAMPLE:
J'**aurais dû** étudier.
I *should have* studied. OR: I *ought to have* studied.

Tense No. 13   Le Passé du Subjonctif
                  (Past or Perfect Subjunctive)

This tense is used to express an action that took place in the past in relation to the present time. It is like the **Passé Composé,** except that the auxiliary verb *(avoir* or *être)* is in the **Présent du Subjonctif.** The Subjunctive is used (as was noted in the previous sections of verb tenses in the Subjunctive) because what precedes is a certain verb, a certain conjunction, or a certain impersonal expression. The **Passé du Subjonctif** is also used in relation to a future time when another action will be completed. This tense is rarely used in English. In French, however, this tense is used in formal writing and in literature as well as in conversational French and informal writing. It is a compound tense because it is formed with the **Présent du Subjonctif** of *avoir* or *être* as the auxiliary plus the past participle of the verb you are using.

EXAMPLES:
(a) A past action in relation to the present

Il est possible qu'elle **soit partie.**
It is possible that she *may have left.* OR: It is possible that she *has left.*
Je doute qu'il **ait fait** cela.
I doubt that he *did* that.

(b) An action that will take place in the future

J'insiste que vous **soyez rentré** avant dix heures.
I insist that you *be back* before ten o'clock.

Tense No. 14   Le Plus-que-parfait du Subjonctif
                  (Pluperfect or Past Perfect Subjunctive)

This tense is used for the same reasons as the **Imparfait du Subjonctif** (Tense No. 7)—that is, after certain verbs, conjunctions and impersonal expressions that were used in examples previously under **le Présent du**

Subjonctif. The main difference between the **Imparfait du Subjonctif** and this tense is the time of the action in the past. If the action was *not* completed, the **Imparfait du Subjonctif** is used. If the action was completed, this tense is used. It is rarely used in English. In French, it is used only in formal writing and in literature. For that reason, you should merely be familiar with it so you can recognize it in your readings in French literature. In conversational French and in informal writing, this tense is avoided. Use, instead, the **Passé du Subjonctif** (Tense No. 13).

This is a compound tense. It is formed by using the **Imparfait du Subjonctif** of *avoir* or *être* plus the past participle. This tense is like the **Plus-que-parfait de l'Indicatif**, except that the auxiliary verb *(avoir or être)* is in the **Imparfait du Subjonctif.** Review the uses of the Subjunctive mood in Tense No. 6.

EXAMPLES:
(a) Il était possible qu'elle **fût partie.**
    It was possible that she *might have left.*

NOTE: Avoid this tense in conversational and informal French.
Use, instead, **le Passé du Subjonctif:**
Il était possible qu'elle **soit partie.**

(b) Je ne croyais pas qu'elle **eût dit** cela.
    I did not believe that she *had said* that.

NOTE: Avoid this tense in conversational and informal French.
Use, instead, **le Passé du Subjonctif:**
Je ne croyais pas qu'elle **ait dit** cela.

(c) Je n'ai pas cru qu'elle **eût dit** cela.
    I did not believe that she *had said* that.

NOTE FURTHER: The French verb **devoir** plus the infinitive is used to express the idea of *should* when you mean *ought.* The past participle of **devoir** is **dû.** It is conjugated with **avoir.**

(d) J'ai craint que vous ne **fussiez tombé.**
    I was afraid that you *had fallen.*

NOTE: Avoid this tense in conversational and informal French.
Use, instead, **le Passé du Subjonctif:**
J'ai craint que vous ne **soyez tombé.**

L'Impératif
(Imperative or Command)

The Imperative mood is used in French and English to express a command or a request. It is also used to express an indirect request made in the third person, as in (e) and (f) below. In both languages it is formed by dropping the subject pronoun and using the present tense. There are a few exceptions in both languages when the **Présent du Subjonctif** is used.

EXAMPLES:

(a) **Sortez!** Get out!

(b) **Entrez!** Come in!

(c) **Buvons!** Let's drink!

(d) **Soyez** à l'heure! *Be* on time! (Subjunctive is used)

(e) Dieu le **veuille!** May God *grant* it! (Subjunctive is used)

(f) Qu'ils **mangent du** gâteau! Let them *eat* cake! (Subjunctive is used)

(g) **Asseyez-vous!** Sit down!

(h) **Levez-vous!** Get up!

(i) **Ne vous asseyez pas!** Don't sit down!

(j) **Ne vous levez pas!** Don't get up!

NOTE: The Imperative is not a tense. It is a mood.

NOTE FURTHER: If you use a reflexive verb in the Imperative, drop the subject pronoun but keep the reflexive pronoun. Example: **Lavez-vous!** Wash yourself! See also examples (g) through (j).

Summary of verb tenses and moods in French with English equivalents

Les sept temps simples *The seven simple tenses*		Les sept temps composés *The seven compound tenses*	
Tense No.	Tense Name	Tense No.	Tense Name
1	**Présent de l'indicatif** *Present indicative*	8	**Passé Composé**
2	**Imparfait de l'indicatif** *Imperfect indicative*	9	**Plus-que-parfait de l'indicatif** *Pluperfect indicative*

3	**Passé simple**	10	**Passé antérieur**
	Past definite or Simple past		*Past anterior*
4	**Futur**	11	**Futur antérieur**
	Future		*Future perfect*
5	**Conditionnel**	12	**Conditionnel passé**
	Conditional		*Conditional perfect*
6	**Présent du subjonctif**	13	**Passé du subjonctif**
	Present subjunctive		*Past subjunctive*
7	**Imparfait du subjonctif**	14	**Plus-que-parfait du subjonctif**
	Imperfect subjunctive		*Pluperfect subjunctive*

The Imperative is not a tense; it is a mood.

Formation of the Tenses

In French there are seven simple tenses and seven compound tenses. A simple tense means that the verb form consists of one word. A compound tense is a verb form that consists of two words (the auxiliary verb and the past participle). The auxiliary verb is also called a helping verb and in French it is any of the seven simple tenses of **avoir** or **être.**

FORMATION OF THE SEVEN SIMPLE TENSES
FOR REGULAR VERBS

Tense No. 1   Présent de l'Indicatif
            (Present Indicative)

-er verbs: drop **-er** and add **e, es, e; ons, ez, ent**

-ir verbs: drop **-ir** and add **is, is, it; issons, issez, issent**

-re verbs: drop **-re** and add **s, s, -; ons, ez, ent**

Tense No. 2   Imparfait de l'Indicatif
            (Imperfect Indicative)

For **-er, -ir, -re** verbs, take the **"nous"** form in the present indicative of the verb you have in mind, drop the ending **-ons** and add **ais, ais, ait; ions, iez, aient**

Tense No. 3 Passé Simple
              (Past Definite or Simple Past)

For all **-er** verbs, drop **-er** and add **ai, as, a; âmes, âtes, èrent**

For **-ir** and **-re** verbs, drop the ending of the infinitive and add **is, is, it; îmes, îtes, irent**

Tense No. 4 Futur
              (Future)

Add the following endings to the whole infinitive, but for **-re** verbs drop **e** in **-re** before adding the future endings, which are: **ai, as, a; ons, ez, ont**Tense **No. 5 Conditionnel**
              (Conditional)

Add the following endings to the whole infinitive, but for **-re** verbs drop **e** in **-re** before adding the conditional endings, which are: **ais, ais, ait; ions, iez, aient.** Note that these endings are the same as those for the imperfect indicative (Tense No. 2).

Tense No. 6 Présent du Subjonctif
              (Present Subjunctive)

Drop **-ant** ending of the present participle of the verb you have in mind and add **e, es, e; ions, iez, ent**

Tense No. 7 Imparfait du Subjonctif
              (Imperfect Subjunctive)

There is a shortcut to finding the forms of this difficult tense. Go straight to the 3ʳᵈ person, singular, **passé simple** tense of the verb you have in mind. If the ending is **-a**, as in **parla (parler)**, drop **-a** and add **-asse, -asses, -ât; -assions, -assiez, -assent.** If the ending is **-it**, as in **finit (finir)** or **vendit (vendre)**, drop **-it** and add **-isse, isses, -ît; -issions, -issiez, -issent.** If you find the ending **-ut**, as in many irregular **-re** verbs (**lire/lut**), drop **-ut** and add **-usse, -usses, -ût; -ussions, -ussiez, -ussent.** Note the accent mark (ˆ) on **-ât, -ît, -ût.**

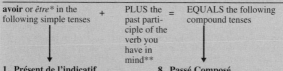

Each compound tense is based on each simple tense. The fourteen tenses given on page xxvi are arranged in a logical order which is numerical. Here is how you form each of the seven compound tenses:

Tense number 8 is based on Tense number 1; in other words, you form the **passé composé** by using the auxiliary **avoir** or **être** (whichever is appropriate) in the **présent de l'indicatif** plus the past participle of the verb you have in mind. Examples: **j'ai parlé; je suis allé(e).**

Tense number 9 is based on Tense number 2; in other words, you form the **plus-que-parfait de l'indicatif** by using the auxiliary **avoir** or *être* (whichever is appropriate) in the **imparfait de l'indicatif** plus the past participle of the verb you have in mind. Examples: **j'avais parlé; j'étais allé(e).**

Tense number 10 is based on Tense number 3; in other words, you form the **passé antérieur** by using the auxiliary **avoir** or **être** (whichever is appropriate) in the **passé simple** plus the past participle of the verb you have in mind. Examples: **j'eus parlé; je fus allé(e).**

Tense number 11 is based on Tense number 4; in other words, you form the **futur antérieur** by using the auxiliary **avoir** or **être** (whichever is appropriate) in the **futur** plus the past participle of the verb you have in mind. Examples: **j'aurai parlé; je serai allé(e).**

Tense number 12 is based on Tense number 5; in other words, you form the **conditionnel passé** by using the auxiliary **avoir** or **être** (whichever is appropriate) in the **conditionnel** plus the past participle of the verb you have in mind. Examples: **j'aurais parlé; je serais allé(e).**

Tense number 13 is based on Tense number 6; in other words, you form the **passé du subjonctif** by using the auxiliary **avoir** or **être** (whichever is appropriate) in the **présent du subjonctif** plus the past participle of the verb you have in mind. Examples: **que j'aie parlé; que je sois allé(e).** This tense is like the **passé composé** (tense number 8), except that the auxiliary verb **avoir** or **être** is in the present subjunctive.

Tense number 14 is based on Tense number 7; in other words, you form the **plus-que-parfait du subjonctif** by using the auxiliary **avoir** or **être** (whichever is appropriate) in the **imparfait du subjonctif** plus the past participle of the verb you have in mind. Examples: **que j'eusse parlé; que je fusse allé(e).**

If you ever expect to know or even recognize the meaning of any of the seven compound tenses, or to know how to form them, you certainly have to know **avoir** and **être** in the seven simple tenses. If you do not, you cannot form the seven compound tenses—and they are the easiest to form. This is one perfect example to illustrate that learning French verb forms is a cumulative experience because in order to know the seven compound tenses, you must first know the forms of **avoir** and **être** in the seven simple tenses. They are found on pages 31 and 119 in this book.

To know which verbs are conjugated with **avoir** or **être** to form the seven compound tenses, see page vii. To understand the uses of the seven simple tenses, see pages xvi–xxii. To understand the uses of the seven compound tenses, see pages xxii–xxvii. To know the translation of all fourteen tenses into English, see pages xiii–xiv.

Subject Pronouns

    (a) The subject pronouns for all verb forms on the following pages have been omitted in order to emphasize the verb forms, which is what this book is all about.

    (b) The subject pronouns that have been omitted are, as you know, as follows:

	singular		plural
	je *or* **j'**		**nous**
	tu		**vous**
	il, elle, on		**ils, elles**

(c) You realize, of course, that when you use a verb form in the Imperative (Command) you do not use the subject pronoun with it, as is also done in English. Example: **Parlez!** *Speak!* If you use a reflexive verb in the Imperative, drop the subject pronoun but keep the reflexive pronoun. Example: **Lavez-vous!** *Wash yourself!*

Subject Pronouns

singular		plural
je *or* **j'**		**nous**
tu		**vous**
il, elle, on		**ils, elles**

to accept

The Seven Simple Tenses		The Seven Compound Tenses	
Singular	Plural	Singular	Plural
1 présent de l'indicatif		8 passé composé	
accepte	acceptons	ai accepté	avons accepté
acceptes	acceptez	as accepté	avez accepté
accepte	acceptent	a accepté	ont accepté
2 imparfait de l'indicatif		9 plus-que-parfait de l'indicatif	
acceptais	acceptions	avais accepté	avions accepté
acceptais	acceptiez	avais accepté	aviez accepté
acceptait	acceptaient	avait accepté	avaient accepté
3 passé simple		10 passé antérieur	
acceptai	acceptâmes	eus accepté	eûmes accepté
acceptas	acceptâtes	eus accepté	eûtes accepté
accepta	acceptèrent	eut accepté	eurent accepté
4 futur		11 futur antérieur	
accepterai	accepterons	aurai accepté	aurons accepté
accepteras	accepterez	auras accepté	aurez accepté
acceptera	accepteront	aura accepté	auront accepté
5 conditionnel		12 conditionnel passé	
accepterais	accepterions	aurais accepté	aurions accepté
accepterais	accepteriez	aurais accepté	auriez accepté
accepterait	accepteraient	aurait accepté	auraient accepté
6 présent du subjonctif		13 passé du subjonctif	
accepte	acceptions	aie accepté	ayons accepté
acceptes	acceptiez	aies accepté	ayez accepté
accepte	acceptent	ait accepté	aient accepté
7 imparfait du subjonctif		14 plus-que-parfait du subjonctif	
acceptasse	acceptassions	eusse accepté	eussions accepté
acceptasses	acceptassiez	eusses accepté	eussiez accepté
acceptât	acceptassent	eût accepté	eussent accepté
		Impératif	
		accepte	
		acceptons	
		acceptez	

Ce matin Madame Pompidou a téléphoné à son amie, Madame Dulac, pour accepter une invitation à dîner chez elle. Voici leur conversation:

Madame Pompidou: **Je viens de recevoir votre aimable invitation. J'accepte avec plaisir. J'ai déjà accepté une invitation pour déjeuner chez une autre amie le même jour. Alors, après le déjeuner chez elle, j'irai en ville pour faire du shopping et je serai chez vous à huit heures pour le dîner.**

Madame Dulac: **Vous acceptez? C'est merveilleux. Alors, vous n'aurez pas besoin de faire la cuisine ce jour-là! Merci pour votre acceptation.**

1

accompagner   Part. pr. **accompagnant**   Part. passé **accompagné**

to accompany

The Seven Simple Tenses		The Seven Compound Tenses	
Singular	Plural	Singular	Plural
1 présent de l'indicatif		8 passé composé	
accompagne	accompagnons	ai accompagné	avons accompagné
accompagnes	accompagnez	as accompagné	avez accompagné
accompagne	accompagnent	a accompagné	ont accompagné
2 imparfait de l'indicatif		9 plus-que-parfait de l'indicatif	
accompagnais	accompagnions	avais accompagné	avions accompagné
accompagnais	accompagniez	avais accompagné	aviez accompagné
accompagnait	accompagnaient	avait accompagné	avaient accompagné
3 passé simple		10 passé antérieur	
accompagnai	accompagnâmes	eus accompagné	eûmes accompagné
accompagnas	accompagnâtes	eus accompagné	eûtes accompagné
accompagna	accompagnèrent	eut accompagné	eurent accompagné
4 futur		11 futur antérieur	
accompagnerai	accompagnerons	aurai accompagné	aurons accompagné
accompagneras	accompagnerez	auras accompagné	aurez accompagné
accompagnera	accompagneront	aura accompagné	auront accompagné
5 conditionnel		12 conditionnel passé	
accompagnerais	accompagnerions	aurais accompagné	aurions accompagné
accompagnerais	accompagneriez	aurais accompagné	auriez accompagné
accompagnerait	accompagneraient	aurait accompagné	auraient accompagné
6 présent du subjonctif		13 passé du subjonctif	
accompagne	accompagnions	aie accompagné	ayons accompagné
accompagnes	accompagniez	aies accompagné	ayez accompagné
accompagne	accompagnent	ait accompagné	aient accompagné
7 imparfait du subjonctif		14 plus-que-parfait du subjonctif	
accompagnasse	accompagnassions	eusse accompagné	eussions accompagné
accompagnasses	accompagnassiez	eusses accompagné	eussiez accompagné
accompagnât	accompagnassent	eût accompagné	eussent accompagné

	Impératif	
	accompagne	
	accompagnons	
	accompagnez	

Hier après-midi Monsieur Durand, professeur de français, a accompagné ses étudiants au Bois de Boulogne pour pique-niquer. Les étudiants étaient accompagnés aussi de leurs parents. Avez-vous jamais accompagné un groupe d'élèves? C'est de la bonne compagnie!

s'accompagner de   to be accompanied by
un accompagnement   accompanying, accompaniment (music)
un accompagnateur, une accompagnatrice   accompanist (music)
un compagnon, une compagne   companion

to greet, welcome

The Seven Simple Tenses		The Seven Compound Tenses	
Singular	Plural	Singular	Plural
1 présent de l'indicatif		8 passé composé	
accueille	accueillons	ai accueilli	avons accueilli
accueilles	accueillez	as accueilli	avez accueilli
accueille	accueillent	a accueilli	ont accueilli
2 imparfait de l'indicatif		9 plus-que-parfait de l'indicatif	
accueillais	accueillions	avais accueilli	avions accueilli
accueillais	accueilliez	avais accueilli	aviez accueilli
accueillait	accueillaient	avait accueilli	avaient accueilli
3 passé simple		10 passé antérieur	
accueillis	accueillîmes	eus accueilli	eûmes accueilli
accueillis	accueillîtes	eus accueilli	eûtes accueilli
accueillit	accueillirent	eut accueilli	eurent accueillli
4 futur		11 futur antérieur	
accueillerai	accueillerons	aurai accueilli	aurons accueilli
accueilleras	accueillerez	auras accueilli	aurez accueilli
accueillera	accueilleront	aura accueilli	auront accueilli
5 conditionnel		12 conditionnel passé	
accueillerais	accueillerions	aurais accueilli	aurions accueilli
accueillerais	accueilleriez	aurais accueilli	auriez accueilli
accueillerait	accueilleraient	aurait accueilli	auraient accueilli
6 présent du subjonctif		13 passé du subjonctif	
accueille	accueillions	aie accueilli	ayons accueilli
accueilles	accueilliez	aies accueilli	ayez accueilli
accueille	accueillent	ait accueilli	aient accueilli
7 imparfait du subjonctif		14 plus-que-parfait du subjonctif	
accueillisse	accueillisslons	eusse accueilli	eussions accueilli
accueillisses	accueillissiez	eusses accueilli	eussiez accueilli
accueillît	accueillissent	eût accueilli	eussent accueilli

Impératif
accueille
accueillons
accueillez

Avez-vous jamais été accueilli aimablement? C'est bon. Avez-vous jamais été accueilli froidement? Ce n'est pas bon! Chaque fois que je rends visite à mes grands-parents, ils m'accueillent chaleureusement. Ils me font toujours bon accueil.

un accueil   welcome, reception; **un accueil chaleureux**   warm welcome
accueillant, accueillante   hospitable

For other words and expressions related to this verb, see **cueillir.**

to buy, to purchase

The Seven Simple Tenses		The Seven Compound Tenses	
Singular	Plural	Singular	Plural
1 présent de l'indicatif		8 passé composé	
achète	achetons	ai acheté	avons acheté
achètes	achetez	as acheté	avez acheté
achète	achètent	a acheté	ont acheté
2 imparfait de l'indicatif		9 plus-que-parfait de l'indicatif	
achetais	achetions	avais acheté	avions acheté
achetais	achetiez	avais acheté	aviez acheté
achetait	achetaient	avait acheté	avaient acheté
3 passé simple		10 passé antérieur	
achetai	achetâmes	eus acheté	eûmes acheté
achetas	achetâtes	eus acheté	eûtes acheté
acheta	achetèrent	eut acheté	eurent acheté
4 futur		11 futur antérieur	
achèterai	achèterons	aurai acheté	aurons acheté
achèteras	achèterez	auras acheté	aurez acheté
achètera	achèteront	aura acheté	auront acheté
5 conditionnel		12 conditionnel passé	
achèterais	achèterions	aurais acheté	aurions acheté
achèterais	achèteriez	aurais acheté	auriez acheté
achèterait	achèteraient	aurait acheté	auraient acheté
6 présent du subjonctif		13 passé du subjonctif	
achète	achetions	aie acheté	ayons acheté
achètes	achetiez	aies acheté	ayez acheté
achète	achètent	ait acheté	aient acheté
7 imparfait du subjonctif		14 plus-que-parfait du subjonctif	
achetasse	achetassions	eusse acheté	eussions acheté
achetasses	achetassiez	eusses acheté	eussiez acheté
achetât	achetassent	eût acheté	eussent acheté

	Impératif	
achète	achetons	achetez

Samedi je vais en ville pour acheter quelques cadeaux. La semaine dernière mon père a acheté une nouvelle automobile et ma mère a acheté une jolie robe. Quand je leur ai dit que je voulais faire quelques achats, ils m'ont demandé:—Qu'est-ce que tu achèteras?

Je leur ai répondu:—Je ne suis pas acheteur d'un grand magasin! J'achèterai un petit cadeau pour toi et pour toi!

un achat   purchase; **acheter qqch à qqn**   to buy something from someone
un acheteur, une acheteuse   buyer, purchaser
achetable   purchasable; **racheter**   to ransom; to buy back
acheter comptant   to buy in cash; **acheter à crédit**   to buy on credit

to admit

The Seven Simple Tenses		The Seven Compound Tenses	
Singular	Plural	Singular	Plural
1 présent de l'indicatif		8 passé composé	
admets	admettons	ai admis	avons admis
admets	admettez	as admis	avez admis
admet	admettent	a admis	ont admis
2 imparfait de l'indicatif		9 plus-que-parfait de l'indicatif	
admettais	admettions	avais admis	avions admis
admettais	admettiez	avais admis	aviez admis
admettait	admettaient	avait admis	avaient admis
3 passé simple		10 passé antérieur	
admis	admîmes	eus admis	eûmes admis
admis	admîtes	eus admis	eûtes admis
admit	admirent	eut admis	eurent admis
4 futur		11 futur antérieur	
admettrai	admettrons	aurai admis	aurons admis
admettras	admettrez	auras admis	aurez admis
admettra	admettront	aura admis	auront admis
5 conditionnel		12 conditionnel passé	
admettrais	admettrions	aurais admis	aurions admis
admettrais	admettriez	aurais admis	auriez admis
admettrait	admettraient	aurait admis	auraient admis
6 présent du subjonctif		13 passé du subjonctif	
admette	admettions	aie admis	ayons admis
admettes	admettiez	aies admis	ayez admis
admette	admettent	ait admis	aient admis
7 imparfait du subjonctif		14 plus-que-parfait du subjonctif	
admisse	admissions	eusse admis	eussions admis
admisses	admissiez	eusses admis	eussiez admis
admît	admissent	eût admis	eussent admis

Impératif
admets   admettons   admettez

Je connais un élève qui n'admet pas toujours ses fautes. Un jour, dans la classe de français, Robert a lancé son crayon contre le mur. Le professeur lui a dit: Robert, ce que tu viens de faire n'est pas admissible dans cette classe.

Robert a répondu:—Mais, monsieur, ce n'est pas moi qui ai lancé ce crayon. C'est Georges.

—Ce n'est pas vrai! dit Georges. Admets la vérité, Robert. Après quelques minutes, Robert a admis que c'était lui.

admis, admise   admitted, accepted
une admission   admission, admittance
C'est chose admise que . . .   It's generally admitted that . . .

admirer   Part. pr. **admirant**   Part. passé **admiré**

to admire

The Seven Simple Tenses		The Seven Compound Tenses	
Singular	Plural	Singular	Plural
1 présent de l'indicatif		8 passé composé	
admire	admirons	ai admiré	avons admiré
admires	admirez	as admiré	avez admiré
admire	admirent	a admiré	ont admiré
2 imparfait de l'indicatif		9 plus-que-parfait de l'indicatif	
admirais	admirions	avais admiré	avions admiré
admirais	admiriez	avais admiré	aviez admiré
admirait	admiraient	avait admiré	avaient admiré
3 passé simple		10 passé antérieur	
admirai	admirâmes	eus admiré	eûmes admiré
admiras	admirâtes	eus admiré	eûtes admiré
admira	admirèrent	eut admiré	eurent admiré
4 futur		11 futur antérieur	
admirerai	admirerons	aurai admiré	aurons admiré
admireras	admirerez	auras admiré	aurez admiré
admirera	admireront	aura admiré	auront admiré
5 conditionnel		12 conditionnel passé	
admirerais	admirerions	aurais admiré	aurions admiré
admirerais	admireriez	aurais admiré	auriez admiré
admirerait	admireraient	aurait admiré	auraient admiré
6 présent du subjonctif		13 passé du subjonctif	
admire	admirions	aie admiré	ayons admiré
admires	admiriez	aies admiré	ayez admiré
admire	admirent	ait admiré	aient admiré
7 imparfait du subjonctif		14 plus-que-parfait du subjonctif	
admirasse	admirassions	eusse admiré	eussions admiré
admirasses	admirassiez	eusses admiré	eussiez admiré
admirât	admirassent	eût admiré	eussent admiré

	Impératif
	admire
	admirons
	admirez

Il y a des personnes admirables, n'est-ce pas? Quelle personne admirez-vous le plus? Est-ce que vous aimez une personne qui vous admire? Avez-vous des admirateurs, des admiratrices? Moi, j'admire l'art d'Auguste Rodin. Je suis toujours en admiration devant ses oeuvres sculptées.

une admiration admiration, wonder
admirativement admiringly
admiratif, admirative admiring
un admirateur, une admiratrice admirer

to worship, to adore

The Seven Simple Tenses		The Seven Compound Tenses	
Singular	Plural	Singular	Plural
1 présent de l'indicatif		8 passé composé	
adore	adorons	ai adoré	avons adoré
adores	adorez	as adoré	avez adoré
adore	adorent	a adoré	ont adoré
2 imparfait de l'indicatif		9 plus-que-parfait de l'indicatif	
adorais	adorions	avais adoré	avions adoré
adorais	adoriez	avais adoré	aviez adoré
adorait	adoraient	avait adoré	avaient adoré
3 passé simple		10 passé antérieur	
adorai	adorâmes	eus adoré	eûmes adoré
adoras	adorâtes	eus adoré	eûtes adoré
adora	adorèrent	eut adoré	eurent adoré
4 futur		11 futur antérieur	
adorerai	adorerons	aurai adoré	aurons adoré
adoreras	adorerez	auras adoré	aurez adoré
adorera	adoreront	aura adoré	auront adoré
5 conditionnel		12 conditionnel passé	
adorerais	adorerions	aurais adoré	aurions adoré
adorerais	adoreriez	aurais adoré	auriez adoré
adorerait	adoreraient	aurait adoré	auraient adoré
6 présent du subjonctif		13 passé du subjonctif	
adore	adorions	aie adoré	ayons adoré
adores	adoriez	aies adoré	ayez adoré
adore	adorent	ait adoré	aient adoré
7 imparfait du subjonctif		14 plus-que-parfait du subjonctif	
adorasse	adorassions	eusse adoré	eussions adoré
adorasses	adorassiez	eusses adoré	eussiez adoré
adorât	adorassent	eût adoré	eussent adoré
		Impératif	
		adore	
		adorons	
		adorez	

Claudette adore dancer avec les beaux garçons. Elle adore mettre tous ses bijoux avant d'aller au bal. Elle est adorable, gracieuse, et danse adorablement.

adorable adorable, charming, delightful
une adoration adoration, worship
adorablement adorably
un adorateur, une adoratrice adorer, worshipper
dorer to gild

s'agir　　　　　　　Part. pr. —　　　　　Part. passé **agi**

to be the matter, to be a question of

The Seven Simple Tenses	The Seven Compound Tenses
Singular	Singular
1 présent de l'indicatif **il s'agit**	8 passé composé **il s'est agi**
2 imparfait de l'indicatif **il s'agissait**	9 plus-que-parfait de l'indicatif **il s'était agi**
3 passé simple **il s'agit**	10 passé antérieur **il se fut agi**
4 futur **il s'agira**	11 futur antérieur **il se sera agi**
5 conditionnel **il s'agirait**	12 conditionnel passé **il se serait agi**
6 présent du subjonctif **qu'il s'agisse**	13 passé du subjonctif **qu'il se soit agi**
7 imparfait du subjonctif **qu'il s'agît**	14 plus-que-parfait du subjonctif **qu'il se fût agi**
	Impératif —

Hier, le petit Michel est entré dans la maison en pleurant.
—De quoi s'agit-il?! s'exclame sa mère.
—Il s'agit . . . il s'agit . . . de mon vélo. Quelqu'un a volé mon vélo!

s'agir de　to have to do with, to be a matter of
De quoi s'agit-il?　What's the matter? What's up?
Voici ce dont il s'agit.　This is what it's about.
Il s'agit de mon vélo.　It's about my bike.

Note that this verb is impersonal and is used primarily in the tenses given above.

to aid, to help, to assist

The Seven Simple Tenses		The Seven Compound Tenses	
Singular	Plural	Singular	Plural
1 présent de l'indicatif		8 passé composé	
aide	aidons	ai aidé	avons aidé
aides	aidez	as aidé	avez aidé
aide	aident	a aidé	ont aidé
2 imparfait de l'indicatif		9 plus-que-parfait de l'indicatif	
aidais	aidions	avais aidé	avions aidé
aidais	aidiez	avais aidé	aviez aidé
aidait	aidaient	avait aidé	avaient aidé
3 passé simple		10 passé antérieur	
aidai	aidâmes	eus aidé	eûmes aidé
aidas	aidâtes	eus aidé	eûtes aidé
aida	aidèrent	eut aidé	eurent aidé
4 futur		11 futur antérieur	
aiderai	aiderons	aurai aidé	aurons aidé
aideras	aiderez	auras aidé	aurez aidé
aidera	aideront	aura aidé	auront aidé
5 conditionnel		12 conditionnel passé	
aiderais	aiderions	aurais aidé	aurions aidé
aiderais	aideriez	aurais aidé	auriez aidé
aiderait	aideraient	aurait aidé	auraient aidé
6 présent du subjonctif		13 passé du subjonctif	
aide	aidions	aie aidé	ayons aidé
aides	aidiez	aies aidé	ayez aidé
aide	aident	ait aidé	aient aidé
7 imparfait du subjonctif		14 plus-que-parfait du subjonctif	
aidasse	aidassions	eusse aidé	eussions aidé
aidasses	aidassiez	eusses aidé	eussiez aidé
aidât	aidassent	eût aidé	eussent aidé
		Impératif	
		aide	
		aidons	
		aidez	

Tous les soirs Roger aide son petit frère à faire sa leçon de mathématiques. Ce soir, le petit frère lui demande:—Après cette leçon, veux-tu m'aider à écrire une composition?

—Aide-toi et le ciel t'aidera, lui répond son grand frère.

aider qqn à faire qqch to help someone do something
s'aider to help oneself; to help each other
une aide aid, assistance, help; **à l'aide de** with the help of
un aide-mémoire handbook, memory aid
Aide-toi et le ciel t'aidera. God helps those who help themselves.

aimer   Part. pr. **aimant**   Part. passé **aimé**

to love, to like

The Seven Simple Tenses		The Seven Compound Tenses	
Singular	Plural	Singular	Plural
1 présent de l'indicatif		8 passé composé	
aime	aimons	ai aimé	avons aimé
aimes	aimez	as aimé	avez aimé
aime	aiment	a aimé	ont aimé
2 imparfait de l'indicatif		9 plus-que-parfait de l'indicatif	
aimais	aimions	avais aimé	avions aimé
aimais	aimiez	avais aimé	aviez aimé
aimait	aimaient	avait aimé	avaient aimé
3 passé simple		10 passé antérieur	
aimai	aimâmes	eus aimé	eûmes aimé
aimas	aimâtes	eus aimé	eûtes aimé
aima	aimèrent	eut aimé	eurent aimé
4 futur		11 futur antérieur	
aimerai	aimerons	aurai aimé	aurons aimé
aimeras	aimerez	auras aimé	aurez aimé
aimera	aimeront	aura aimé	auront aimé
5 conditionnel		12 conditionnel passé	
aimerais	aimerions	aurais aimé	aurions aimé
aimerais	aimeriez	aurais aimé	auriez aimé
aimerait	aimeraient	aurait aimé	auraient aimé
6 présent du subjonctif		13 passé du subjonctif	
aime	aimions	aie aimé	ayons aimé
aimes	aimiez	aies aimé	ayez aimé
aime	aiment	ait aimé	aient aimé
7 imparfait du subjonctif		14 plus-que-parfait du subjonctif	
aimasse	aimassions	eusse aimé	eussions aimé
aimasses	aimassiez	eusses aimé	eussiez aimé
aimât	aimassent	eût aimé	eussent aimé

Impératif
aime   aimons   aimez

Qu'est-ce que vous aimez faire après le dîner? Etudier? Jouer? Regarder la télé? Est-ce que vous êtes aimable? Etes-vous aimable avec tout le monde? Est-ce que vous aimez mieux étudier ou jouer?

amour m.   love; **une chanson d'amour**   love song (song of love)
aimer bien qqn   to like somebody
aimer (à) faire qqch   to enjoy doing something
aimer mieux   to prefer, to like better
aimable   friendly, amiable, pleasant
un amant   lover; **une amante**   mistress; **amoureux, amoureuse de**   in love with;
    tomber amoureux, amoureuse   to fall in love

The Seven Simple Tenses		The Seven Compound Tenses	
Singular	Plural	Singular	Plural
1 présent de l'indicatif		8 passé composé	
ajoute	ajoutons	ai ajouté	avons ajouté
ajoutes	ajoutez	as ajouté	avez ajouté
ajoute	ajoutent	a ajouté	ont ajouté
2 imparfait de l'indicatif		9 plus-que-parfait de l'indicatif	
ajoutais	ajoutions	avais ajouté	avions ajouté
ajoutais	ajoutiez	avais ajouté	aviez ajouté
ajoutait	ajoutaient	avait ajouté	avaient ajouté
3 passé simple		10 passé antérieur	
ajoutai	ajoutâmes	eus ajouté	eûmes ajouté
ajoutas	ajoutâtes	eus ajouté	eûtes ajouté
ajouta	ajoutèrent	eut ajouté	eurent ajouté
4 futur		11 futur antérieur	
ajouterai	ajouterons	aurai ajouté	aurons ajouté
ajouteras	ajouterez	auras ajouté	aurez ajouté
ajoutera	ajouteront	aura ajouté	auront ajouté
5 conditionnel		12 conditionnel passé	
ajouterais	ajouterions	aurais ajouté	aurions ajouté
ajouterais	ajouteriez	aurais ajouté	auriez ajouté
ajouterait	ajouteraient	aurait ajouté	auraient ajouté
6 présent du subjonctif		13 passé du subjonctif	
ajoute	ajoutions	aie ajouté	ayons ajouté
ajoutes	ajoutiez	ales ajouté	ayez ajouté
ajoute	ajoutent	ait ajouté	aient ajouté
7 imparfait du subjonctif		14 plus-que-parfait du subjonctif	
ajoutasse	ajoutassions	eusse ajouté	eussions ajouté
ajoutasses	ajoutassiez	eusses ajouté	eussiez ajouté
ajoutât	ajoutassent	eût ajouté	eussent ajouté
		Impératif	
		ajoute	
		ajoutons	
		ajoutez	

Si vous aimez faire un ragoût délicieux, ajoutez-y quelques petits oignons, du sel, du poivre, et une gousse d'ail pour obtenir une saveur piquante. Il y a d'autres assaisonnements et condiments que vous pouvez y ajouter aussi. Un assaisonnement ajoute du piquant dans votre ragoût.

un ajout   addition, additive
ajouter foi à   to add credence to, to give credence to
jouter   to tilt, to joust; to dispute, to fight
une joute   contest, tournament

11

aller	Part. pr. **allant**	Part. passé **allé(e)(s)**

to go

The Seven Simple Tenses		The Seven Compound Tenses	
Singular	Plural	Singular	Plural
1 présent de l'indicatif		8 passé composé	
vais	**allons**	**suis allé(e)**	**sommes allé(e)s**
vas	**allez**	**es allé(e)**	**êtes allé(e)(s)**
va	**vont**	**est allé(e)**	**sont allé(e)s**
2 imparfait de l'indicatif		9 plus-que-parfait de l'indicatif	
allais	**allions**	**étais allé(e)**	**étions allé(e)s**
allais	**alliez**	**étais allé(e)**	**étiez allé(e)(s)**
allait	**allaient**	**était allé(e)**	**étaient allé(e)s**
3 passé simple		10 passé antérieur	
allai	**allâmes**	**fus allé(e)**	**fûmes allé(e)s**
allas	**allâtes**	**fus allé(e)**	**fûtes allé(e)(s)**
alla	**allèrent**	**fut allé(e)**	**furent allé(e)s**
4 futur		11 futur antérieur	
irai	**irons**	**serai allé(e)**	**serons allé(e)s**
iras	**irez**	**seras allé(e)**	**serez allé(e)(s)**
ira	**iront**	**sera allé(e)**	**seront allé(e)s**
5 conditionnel		12 conditionnel passé	
irais	**irions**	**serais allé(e)**	**serions allé(e)s**
irais	**iriez**	**serais allé(e)**	**seriez allé(e)(s)**
irait	**iraient**	**serait allé(e)**	**seraient allé(e)s**
6 présent du subjonctif		13 passé du subjonctif	
aille	**allions**	**sois allé(e)**	**soyons allé(e)s**
ailles	**alliez**	**sois allé(e)**	**soyez allé(e)(s)**
aille	**aillent**	**soit allé(e)**	**soient allé(e)s**
7 imparfait du subjonctif		14 plus-que-parfait du subjonctif	
allasse	**allassions**	**fusse allé(e)**	**fussions allé(e)s**
allasses	**allassiez**	**fusses allé(e)**	**fussiez allé(e)(s)**
allât	**allassent**	**fût allé(e)**	**fussent allé(e)s**

	Impératif	
va	allons	allez

Comment allez-vous? **Je vais bien, je vais mal, je vais mieux.**

aller à la pêche to go fishing
aller à la rencontre de quelqu'un to go to meet someone
aller à pied to walk, to go on foot
aller au fond des choses to get to the bottom of things
Ça va? Is everything O.K.? **Oui, ça va!**
Le ver vert va vers le verre vert. The green worm is going toward the green glass.

to go away

The Seven Simple Tenses		The Seven Compound Tenses	
Singular	Plural	Singular	Plural
1 présent de l'indicatif		8 passé composé	
m'en vais	nous en allons	m'en suis allé(e)	nous en sommes allé(e)s
t'en vas	vous en allez	t'en es allé(e)	vous en êtes allé(e)(s)
s'en va	s'en vont	s'en est allé(e)	s'en sont allé(e)s
2 imparfait de l'indicatif		9 plus-que-parfait de l'indicatif	
m'en allais	nous en allions	m'en étais allé(e)	nous en étions allé(e)s
t'en allais	vous en alliez	t'en étais allé(e)	vous en étiez allé(e)(s)
s'en allait	s'en allaient	s'en était allé(e)	s'en étaient allé(e)s
3 passé simple		10 passé antérieur	
m'en allai	nous en allâmes	m'en fus allé(e)	nous en fûmes allé(e)s
t'en allas	vous en allâtes	t'en fus allé(e)	vous en fûtes allé(e)(s)
s'en alla	s'en allèrent	s'en fut allé(e)	s'en furent allé(e)s
4 futur		11 futur antérieur	
m'en irai	nous en irons	m'en serai allé(e)	nous en serons allé(e)s
t'en iras	vous en irez	t'en seras allé(e)	vous en serez allé(e)(s)
s'en ira	s'en iront	s'en sera allé(e)	s'en seront allé(e)s
5 conditionnel		12 conditionnel passé	
m'en irais	nous en irions	m'en serais allé(e)	nous en serions allé(e)s
t'en irais	vous en iriez	t'en serais allé(e)	vous en seriez allé(e)(s)
s'en irait	s'en iraient	s'en serait allé(e)	s'en seraient allé(e)s
6 présent du subjonctif		13 passé du subjonctif	
m'en aille	nous en allions	m'en sois allé(e)	nous en soyons allé(e)s
t'en ailles	vous en alliez	t'en sois allé(e)	vous en soyez allé(e)(s)
s'en aille	s'en aillent	s'en soit allé(e)	s'en soient allé(e)s
7 imparfait du subjonctif		14 plus-que-parfait du subjonctif	
m'en allasse	nous en allassions	m'en fusse allé(e)	nous en fussions allé(e)s
t'en allasses	vous en allassiez	t'en fusses allé(e)	vous en fussiez allé(e)(s)
s'en allât	s'en allassent	s'en fût allé(e)	s'en fussent allé(e)s

Impératif
va-t'en; ne t'en va pas   allons-nous-en; ne nous en allons pas
allez-vous-en; ne vous en allez pas

This verb also has the following idiomatic meanings: to move away (from one residence to another), to die, to pass away, to steal away.

Monsieur et Madame Moreau n'habitent plus ici. Ils s'en sont allés. Je crois qu'ils sont maintenant à Bordeaux.

Madame Morel est gravement malade; elle s'en va.

Le cambrioleur s'en est allé furtivement avec l'argent et les bijoux.

amener   Part. pr. **amenant**   Part. passé **amené**

to bring, to lead

The Seven Simple Tenses		The Seven Compound Tenses	
Singular	Plural	Singular	Plural
1 présent de l'indicatif		8 passé composé	
amène	amenons	ai amené	avons amené
amènes	amenez	as amené	avez amené
amène	amènent	a amené	ont amené
2 imparfait de l'indicatif		9 plus-que-parfait de l'indicatif	
amenais	amenions	avais amené	avions amené
amenais	ameniez	avais amené	aviez amené
amenait	amenaient	avait amené	avaient amené
3 passé simple		10 passé antérieur	
amenai	amenâmes	eus amené	eûmes amené
amenas	amenâtes	eus amené	eûtes amené
amena	amenèrent	eut amené	eurent amené
4 futur		11 futur antérieur	
amènerai	amènerons	aurai amené	aurons amené
amèneras	amènerez	auras amené	aurez amené
amènera	amèneront	aura amené	auront amené
5 conditionnel		12 conditionnel passé	
amènerais	amènerions	aurais amené	aurions amené
amènerais	amèneriez	aurais amené	auriez amené
amènerait	amèneraient	aurait amené	auraient amené
6 présent du subjonctif		13 passé du subjonctif	
amène	amenions	aie amené	ayons amené
amènes	ameniez	aies amené	ayez amené
amène	amènent	ait amené	aient amené
7 imparfait du subjonctif		14 plus-que-parfait du subjonctif	
amenasse	amenassions	eusse amené	eussions amené
amenasses	amenassiez	eusses amené	eussiez amené
amenât	amenassent	eût amené	eussent amené
		Impératif	
		amène	
		amenons	
		amenez	

Aujourd'hui ma mère a amené ma petite soeur chez le dentiste. Quand elles sont entrées chez lui, le dentiste leur a demandé:—Quel bon vent vous amène ici??

amener une conversation to direct, lead a conversation
amène pleasant, agreeable
Qu'est-ce qui vous amène ici?   What brings you here?

to amuse, to entertain

The Seven Simple Tenses		The Seven Compound Tenses	
Singular	Plural	Singular	Plural
1 présent de l'indicatif		8 passé composé	
amuse	amusons	ai amusé	avons amusé
amuses	amusez	as amusé	avez amusé
amuse	amusent	a amusé	ont amusé
2 imparfait de l'indicatif		9 plus-que-parfait de l'indicatif	
amusais	amusions	avais amusé	avions amusé
amusais	amusiez	avais amusé	aviez amusé
amusait	amusaient	avait amusé	avaient amusé
3 passé simple		10 passé antérieur	
amusai	amusâmes	eus amusé	eûmes amusé
amusas	amusâtes	eus amusé	eûtes amusé
amusa	amusèrent	eut amusé	eurent amusé
4 futur		11 futur antérieur	
amuserai	amuserons	aurai amusé	aurons amusé
amuseras	amuserez	auras amusé	aurez amusé
amusera	amuseront	aura amusé	auront amusé
5 conditionnel		12 conditionnel passé	
amuserais	amuserions	aurais amusé	aurions amusé
amuserais	amuseriez	aurais amusé	auriez amusé
amuserait	amuseraient	aurait amusé	auraient amusé
6 présent du subjonctif		13 passé du subjonctif	
amuse	amusions	aie amusé	ayons amusé
amuses	amusiez	aies amusé	ayez amusé
amuse	amusent	ait amusé	aient amusé
7 imparfait du subjonctif		14 plus-que-parfait du subjonctif	
amusasse	amusassions	eusse amusé	eussions amusé
amusasses	amusassiez	eusses amusé	eussiez amusé
amusât	amusassent	eût amusé	eussent amusé

Impératif
amuse
amusons
amusez

Cet acteur sait bien jouer son rôle. Il amuse les spectateurs. C'est un comédien accompli. Il est amusant, n'est-ce pas?

amusant, amusante amusing
un amuseur amuser, entertainer
un amuse-gueule tidbit, titbit
une amusette diversion, pastime
un amusement amusement, entertainment

See also **s'amuser**.

to have a good time, to amuse oneself, to enjoy oneself

The Seven Simple Tenses		The Seven Compound Tenses	
Singular	Plural	Singular	Plural
1 présent de l'indicatif		8 passé composé	
m'amuse	nous amusons	me suis amusé(e)	nous sommes amusé(e)s
t'amuses	vous amusez	t'es amusé(e)	vous êtes amusé(e)(s)
s'amuse	s'amusent	s'est amusé(e)	se sont amusé(e)s
2 imparfait de l'indicatif		9 plus-que-parfait de l'indicatif	
m'amusais	nous amusions	m'étais amusé(e)	nous étions amusé(e)s
t'amusais	vous amusiez	t'étais amusé(e)	vous étiez amusé(e)(s)
s'amusait	s'amusaient	s'était amusé(e)	s'étaient amusé(e)s
3 passé simple		10 passé antérieur	
m'amusai	nous amusâmes	me fus amusé(e)	nous fûmes amusé(e)s
t'amusas	vous amusâtes	te fus amusé(e)	vous fûtes amusé(e)(s)
s'amusa	s'amusèrent	se fut amusé(e)	se furent amusé(e)s
4 futur		11 futur antérieur	
m'amuserai	nous amuserons	me serai amusé(e)	nous serons amusé(e)s
t'amuseras	vous amuserez	te seras amusé(e)	vous serez amusé(e)(s)
s'amusera	s'amuseront	se sera amusé(e)	se seront amusé(e)s
5 conditionnel		12 conditionnel passé	
m'amuserais	nous amuserions	me serais amusé(e)	nous serions amusé(e)s
t'amuserais	vous amuseriez	te serais amusé(e)	vous seriez amusé(e)(s)
s'amuserait	s'amuseraient	se serait amusé(e)	se seraient amusé(e)s
6 présent du subjonctif		13 passé du subjonctif	
m'amuse	nous amusions	me sois amusé(e)	nous soyons amusé(e)s
t'amuses	vous amusiez	te sois amusé(e)	vous soyez amusé(e)(s)
s'amuse	s'amusent	se soit amusé(e)	se soient amusé(e)s
7 imparfait du subjonctif		14 plus-que-parfait du subjonctif	
m'amusasse	nous amusassions	me fusse amusé(e)	nous fussions amusé(e)s
t'amusasses	vous amusassiez	te fusses amusé(e)	vous fussiez amusé(e)(s)
s'amusât	s'amusassent	se fût amusé(e)	se fussent amusé(e)s

Impératif
amuse-toi; ne t'amuse pas
amusons-nous; ne nous amusons pas
amusez-vous; ne vous amusez pas

Il y a des élèves qui s'amusent à mettre le professeur en colère. Est-ce que vous vous amusez dans la classe de français? Moi, je m'amuse beaucoup dans cette classe.

Hier soir je suis allé au cinéma et j'ai vu un film très amusant. Je me suis bien amusé. Mon amie, Françoise, s'est bien amusée aussi.

Que faites-vous pour vous amuser?

s'amuser à + inf.   to enjoy oneself + pres. part.
s'amuser de   to make fun of
s'amuser avec   to play with

    See also **amuser**.

to call, to name, to appeal

The Seven Simple Tenses		The Seven Compound Tenses	
Singular	Plural	Singular	Plural
1 présent de l'indicatif		8 passé composé	
appelle	**appelons**	**ai appelé**	**avons appelé**
appelles	**appelez**	**as appelé**	**avez appelé**
appelle	**appellent**	**a appelé**	**ont appelé**
2 imparfait de l'indicatif		9 plus-que-parfait de l'indicatif	
appelais	**appelions**	**avais appelé**	**avions appelé**
appelais	**appeliez**	**avais appelé**	**aviez appelé**
appelait	**appelaient**	**avait appelé**	**avaient appelé**
3 passé simple		10 passé antérieur	
appelai	**appelâmes**	**eus appelé**	**eûmes appelé**
appelas	**appelâtes**	**eus appelé**	**eûtes appelé**
appela	**appelèrent**	**eut appelé**	**eurent appelé**
4 futur		11 futur antérieur	
appellerai	**appellerons**	**aurai appelé**	**aurons appelé**
appelleras	**appellerez**	**auras appelé**	**aurez appelé**
appellera	**appelleront**	**aura appelé**	**auront appelé**
5 conditionnel		12 conditionnel passé	
appellerais	**appellerions**	**aurais appelé**	**aurions appelé**
appellerais	**appelleriez**	**aurais appelé**	**auriez appelé**
appellerait	**appelleraient**	**aurait appelé**	**auraient appelé**
6 présent du subjonctif		13 passé du subjonctif	
appelle	**appelions**	**aie appelé**	**ayons appelé**
appelles	**appeliez**	**aies appelé**	**ayez appelé**
appelle	**appellent**	**ait appelé**	**aient appelé**
7 imparfait du subjonctif		14 plus-que-parfait du subjonctif	
appelasse	**appelassions**	**eusse appelé**	**eussions appelé**
appelasses	**appelassiez**	**eusses appelé**	**eussiez appelé**
appelât	**appelassent**	**eût appelé**	**eussent appelé**
		Impératif	
		appelle	
		appelons	
		appelez	

Madame Dubois va appeler le médecin parce qu'elle ne va pas bien aujourd'hui.

—As-tu appelé le docteur, chérie? lui demande son mari.
—Non, mon chéri—répond sa femme. Je souffre. Veux-tu l'appeler, s'il te plaît?

une appellation appellation; **un appel** appeal, summons
en appeler à qqn to appeal to someone
rappeler to call back, to remind, to recall
un appel call; **appel téléphonique** telephone call; **faire l'appel** to call the roll

s'appeler Part. pr. **s'appelant** Part. passé **appelé(e)(s)**

to be named, to call oneself

The Seven Simple Tenses		The Seven Compound Tenses	
Singular	Plural	Singular	Plural
1 présent de l'indicatif		8 passé composé	
m'appelle	nous appelons	me suis appelé(e)	nous sommes appelé(e)s
t'appelles	vous appelez	t'es appelé(e)	vous êtes appelé(e)(s)
s'appelle	s'appellent	s'est appelé(e)	se sont appelé(e)s
2 imparfait de l'indicatif		9 plus-que-parfait de l'indicatif	
m'appelais	nous appelions	m'étais appelé(e)	nous étions appelé(e)s
t'appelais	vous appeliez	t'étais appelé(e)	vous étiez appelé(e)(s)
s'appelait	s'appelaient	s'était appelé(e)	s'étaient appelé(e)s
3 passé simple		10 passé antérieur	
m'appelai	nous appelâmes	me fus appelé(e)	nous fûmes appelé(e)s
t'appelas	vous appelâtes	te fus appelé(e)	vous fûtes appelé(e)(s)
s'appela	s'appelèrent	se fut appelé(e)	se furent appelé(e)s
4 futur		11 futur antérieur	
m'appellerai	nous appellerons	me serai appelé(e)	nous serons appelé(e)s
t'appelleras	vous appellerez	te seras appelé(e)	vous serez appelé(e)(s)
s'appellera	s'appelleront	se sera appelé(e)	se seront appelé(e)s
5 conditionnel		12 conditionnel passé	
m'appellerais	nous appellerions	me serais appelé(e)	nous serions appelé(e)s
t'appellerais	vous appelleriez	te serais appelé(e)	vous seriez appelé(e)(s)
s'appellerait	s'appelleraient	se serait appelé(e)	se seraient appelé(e)s
6 présent du subjonctif		13 passé du subjonctif	
m'appelle	nous appelions	me sois appelé(e)	nous soyons appelé(e)s
t'appelles	vous appeliez	te sois appelé(e)	vous soyez appelé(e)(s)
s'appelle	s'appellent	se soit appelé(e)	se soient appelé(e)s
7 imparfait du subjonctif		14 plus-que-parfait du subjonctif	
m'appelasse	nous appelassions	me fusse appelé(e)	nous fussions appelé(e)s
t'appelasses	vous appelassiez	te fusses appelé(e)	vous fussiez appelé(e)(s)
s'appelât	s'appelassent	se fût appelé(e)	se fussent appelé(e)s

Impératif
appelle-toi; ne t'appelle pas
appelons-nous; ne nous appelons pas
appelez-vous; ne vous appelez pas

—Bonjour, mon enfant. Comment t'appelles-tu?
—Je m'appelle Henri.
—As-tu des frères et des soeurs?
—Oui, j'ai deux frères et trois soeurs. Ils s'appellent Joseph, Bernard, Thérèse, Paulette, et Andrée.

For other words and expressions related to this verb, see **appeler, rappeler,** and **se rappeler.**

to bring, to bear

The Seven Simple Tenses		The Seven Compound Tenses	
Singular	Plural	Singular	Plural
1 présent de l'indicatif		8 passé composé	
apporte	apportons	ai apporté	avons apporté
apportes	apportez	as apporté	avez apporté
apporte	apportent	a apporté	ont apporté
2 imparfait de l'indicatif		9 plus-que-parfait de l'indicatif	
apportais	apportions	avais apporté	avions apporté
apportais	apportiez	avais apporté	aviez apporté
apportait	apportaient	avait apporté	avaient apporté
3 passé simple		10 passé antérieur	
apportai	apportâmes	eus apporté	eûmes apporté
apportas	apportâtes	eus apporté	eûtes apporté
apporta	apportèrent	eut apporté	eurent apporté
4 futur		11 futur antérieur	
apporterai	apporterons	aurai apporté	aurons apporté
apporteras	apporterez	auras apporté	aurez apporté
apportera	apporteront	aura apporté	auront apporté
5 conditionnel		12 conditionnel passé	
apporterais	apporterions	aurais apporté	aurions apporté
apporterais	apporteriez	aurais apporté	auriez apporté
apporterait	apporteraient	aurait apporté	auraient apporté
6 présent du subjonctif		13 passé du subjonctif	
apporte	apportions	aie apporté	ayons apporté
apportes	apportiez	aies apporté	ayez apporté
apporte	apportent	ait apporté	aient apporté
7 imparfait du subjonctif		14 plus-que-parfait du subjonctif	
apportasse	apportassions	eusse apporté	eussions apporté
apportasses	apportassiez	eusses apporté	eussiez apporté
apportât	apportassent	eût apporté	eussent apporté

Impératif
apporte
apportons
apportez

Hier soir, j'ai dîné dans un restaurant français. Quand le garçon m'a apporté mon repas, je lui ai dit:—Apportez-moi du pain, aussi, s'il vous plaît et n'oubliez pas de m'apporter un verre de vin rouge.

—Tout de suite, monsieur—il m'a répondu. Voulez-vous que je vous apporte l'addition maintenant ou après le dîner? Aimez-vous la salade que je vous ai apportée?

un apport   something brought; **un apport dotal**   wife's dowry
un apporteur   a person who brings something (usually news); **un apporteur de bonnes nouvelles**   bearer of good news

See also **porter**.

19

to learn

The Seven Simple Tenses		The Seven Compound Tenses	
Singular	Plural	Singular	Plural
1 présent de l'indicatif		8 passé composé	
apprends	**apprenons**	**ai appris**	**avons appris**
apprends	**apprenez**	**as appris**	**avez appris**
apprend	**apprennent**	**a appris**	**ont appris**
2 imparfait de l'indicatif		9 plus-que-parfait de l'indicatif	
apprenais	**apprenions**	**avais appris**	**avions appris**
apprenais	**appreniez**	**avais appris**	**aviez appris**
apprenait	**apprenaient**	**avait appris**	**avaient appris**
3 passé simple		10 passé antérieur	
appris	**apprîmes**	**eus appris**	**eûmes appris**
appris	**apprîtes**	**eus appris**	**eûtes appris**
apprit	**apprirent**	**eut appris**	**eurent appris**
4 futur		11 futur antérieur	
apprendrai	**apprendrons**	**aurai appris**	**aurons appris**
apprendras	**apprendrez**	**auras appris**	**aurez appris**
apprendra	**apprendront**	**aura appris**	**auront appris**
5 conditionnel		12 conditionnel passé	
apprendrais	**apprendrions**	**aurais appris**	**aurions appris**
apprendrais	**apprendriez**	**aurais appris**	**auriez appris**
apprendrait	**apprendraient**	**aurait appris**	**auraient appris**
6 présent du subjonctif		13 passé du subjonctif	
apprenne	**apprenions**	**aie appris**	**ayons appris**
apprennes	**appreniez**	**aies appris**	**ayez appris**
apprenne	**apprennent**	**ait appris**	**aient appris**
7 imparfait du subjonctif		14 plus-que-parfait du subjonctif	
apprisse	**apprissions**	**eusse appris**	**eussions appris**
apprisses	**apprissiez**	**eusses appris**	**eussiez appris**
apprît	**apprissent**	**eût appris**	**eussent appris**
		Impératif	
		apprends	
		apprenons	
		apprenez	

A l'école j'apprends à lire en français. J'apprends à écrire et à parler. Ce matin mon maître de français m'a dit:—Robert, apprends ce poème par coeur pour demain.

La semaine dernière j'ai appris un poème de Verlaine. Pour demain j'apprendrai la conjugaison du verbe *apprendre*.

apprendre par coeur   to memorize
apprendre à qqn à faire qqch   to teach somebody to do something
apprendre qqch à qqn   to inform someone of something; to teach someone something
apprendre à faire qqch   to learn to do something

The Seven Simple Tenses		The Seven Compound Tenses	
Singular	Plural	Singular	Plural
1 présent de l'indicatif		8 passé composé	
arrange	arrangeons	ai arrangé	avons arrangé
arranges	arrangez	as arrangé	avez arrangé
arrange	arrangent	a arrangé	ont arrangé
2 imparfait de l'indicatif		9 plus-que-parfait de l'indicatif	
arrangeais	arrangions	avais arrangé	avions arrangé
arrangeais	arrangiez	avais arrangé	aviez arrangé
arrangeait	arrangeaient	avait arrangé	avaient arrangé
3 passé simple		10 passé antérieur	
arrangeai	arrangeâmes	eus arrangé	eûmes arrangé
arrangeas	arrangeâtes	eus arrangé	eûtes arrangé
arrangea	arrangèrent	eut arrangé	eurent arrangé
4 futur		11 futur antérieur	
arrangerai	arrangerons	aurai arrangé	aurons arrangé
arrangeras	arrangerez	auras arrangé	aurez arrangé
arrangera	arrangeront	aura arrangé	auront arrangé
5 conditionnel		12 conditionnel passé	
arrangerais	arrangerions	aurais arrangé	aurions arrangé
arrangerais	arrangeriez	aurais arrangé	auriez arrangé
arrangerait	arrangeraient	aurait arrangé	auraient arrangé
6 présent du subjonctif		13 passé du subjonctif	
arrange	arrangions	aie arrangé	ayons arrangé
arranges	arrangiez	aies arrangé	ayez arrangé
arrange	arrangent	ait arrangé	aient arrangé
7 imparfait du subjonctif		14 plus-que-parfait du subjonctif	
arrangeasse	arrangeassions	eusse arrangé	eussions arrangé
arrangeasses	arrangeassiez	eusses arrangé	eussiez arrangé
arrangeât	arrangeassent	eût arrangé	eussent arrangé
		Impératif	
		arrange	
		arrangeons	
		arrangez	

J'aime beaucoup un joli arrangement de fleurs. Aimez-vous les fleurs que j'ai arrangées dans ce vase? Les Japonais savent bien arranger les fleurs. Quand mon père apporte des fleurs à ma mère, nous les arrangeons dans un joli vase.

arranger qqch   to arrange, contrive something
arranger l'affaire   to straighten out a matter
arranger qqn   to accommodate, suit someone; **Ça m'arrange bien.**   That suits me fine.   **Ça s'arrangera.**   It will turn out all right.

| arrêter | Part. pr. **arrêtant** | Part. passé **arrêté** |

to arrest, to stop (someone or something)

The Seven Simple Tenses		The Seven Compound Tenses	
Singular	Plural	Singular	Plural
1 présent de l'indicatif		8 passé composé	
arrête	**arrêtons**	**ai arrêté**	**avons arrêté**
arrêtes	**arrêtez**	**as arrêté**	**avez arrêté**
arrête	**arrêtent**	**a arrêté**	**ont arrêté**
2 imparfait de l'indicatif		9 plus-que-parfait de l'indicatif	
arrêtais	**arrêtions**	**avais arrêté**	**avions arrêté**
arrêtais	**arrêtiez**	**avais arrêté**	**aviez arrêté**
arrêtait	**arrêtaient**	**avait arrêté**	**avaient arrêté**
3 passé simple		10 passé antérieur	
arrêtai	**arrêtâmes**	**eus arrêté**	**eûmes arrêté**
arrêtas	**arrêtâtes**	**eus arrêté**	**eûtes arrêté**
arrêta	**arrêtèrent**	**eut arrêté**	**eurent arrêté**
4 futur		11 futur antérieur	
arrêterai	**arrêterons**	**aurai arrêté** ·	**aurons arrêté**
arrêteras	**arrêterez**	**auras arrêté**	**aurez arrêté**
arrêtera	**arrêteront**	**aura arrêté**	**auront arrêté**
5 conditionnel		12 conditionnel passé	
arrêterais	**arrêterions**	**aurais arrêté**	**aurions arrêté**
arrêterais	**arrêteriez**	**aurais arrêté**	**auriez arrêté**
arrêterait	**arrêteraient**	**aurait arrêté**	**auraient arrêté**
6 présent du subjonctif		13 passé du subjonctif	
arrête	**arrêtions**	**aie arrêté**	**ayons arrêté**
arrêtes	**arrêtiez**	**aies arrêté**	**ayez arrêté**
arrête	**arrêtent**	**ait arrêté**	**aient arrêté**
7 imparfait du subjonctif		14 plus-que-parfait du subjonctif	
arrêtasse	**arrêtassions**	**eusse arrêté**	**eussions arrêté**
arrêtasses	**arrêtassiez**	**eusses arrêté**	**eussiez arrêté**
arrêtât	**arrêtassent**	**eût arrêté**	**eussent arrêté**

Impératif
arrête
arrêtons
arrêtez

**L'agent de police a arrêté les voitures pour laisser les piétons traverser la rue.
Il a crié:—Arrêtez! Arrêtez!**

un arrêt   halt, stop, arrest
arrêt d'autobus   bus stop
un arrêté ministériel   decree
arrêter qqn de faire qqch   to stop someone from doing something
une arrestation   arrest, apprehension
arrêter un jour   to set a date; **arrêter un marché**   to make a deal

See also **s'arrêter.**

Part. pr. **s'arrêtant**   Part. passé **arrêté(e)(s)**   **s'arrêter**

to stop (oneself, itself), to pause

The Seven Simple Tenses		The Seven Compound Tenses	
Singular	Plural	Singular	Plural
1 présent de l'indicatif		8 passé composé	
m'arrête	nous arrêtons	me suis arrêté(e)	nous sommes arrêté(e)s
t'arrêtes	vous arrêtez	t'es arrêté(e)	vous êtes arrêté(e)(s)
s'arrête	s'arrêtent	s'est arrêté(e)	se sont arrêté(e)s
2 imparfait de l'indicatif		9 plus-que-parfait de l'indicatif	
m'arrêtais	nous arrêtions	m'étais arrêté(e)	nous étions arrêté(e)s
t'arrêtais	vous arrêtiez	t'étais arrêté(e)	vous étiez arrêté(e)(s)
s'arrêtait	s'arrêtaient	s'était arrêté(e)	s'étaient arrêté(e)s
3 passé simple		10 passé antérieur	
m'arrêtai	nous arrêtâmes	me fus arrêté(e)	nous fûmes arrêté(e)s
t'arrêtas	vous arrêtâtes	te fus arrêté(e)	vous fûtes arrêté(e)(s)
s'arrêta	s'arrêtèrent	se fut arrêté(e)	se furent arrêté(e)s
4 futur		11 futur antérieur	
m'arrêterai	nous arrêterons	me serai arrêté(e)	nous serons arrêté(e)s
t'arrêteras	vous arrêterez	te seras arrêté(e)	vous serez arrêté(e)(s)
s'arrêtera	s'arrêteront	se sera arrêté(e)	se seront arrêté(e)s
5 conditionnel		12 conditionnel passé	
m'arrêterais	nous arrêterions	me serais arrêté(e)	nous serions arrêté(e)s
t'arrêterais	vous arrêteriez	te serais arrêté(e)	vous seriez arrêté(e)(s)
s'arrêterait	s'arrêteraient	se serait arrêté(e)	se seraient arrêté(e)s
6 présent du subjonctif		13 passé du subjonctif	
m'arrête	nous arrêtions	me sois arrêté(e)	nous soyons arrêté(e)s
t'arrêtes	vous arrêtiez	te sois arrêté(e)	vous soyez arrêté(e)(s)
s'arrête	s'arrêtent	se soit arrêté(e)	se soient arrêté(e)s
7 imparfait du subjonctif		14 plus-que-parfait du subjonctif	
m'arrêtasse	nous arrêtassions	me fusse arrêté(e)	nous fussions arrêté(e)s
t'arrêtasse	vous arrêtassiez	te fusses arrêté(e)	vous fussiez arrêté(e)(s)
s'arrêtât	s'arrêtassent	se fût arrêté(e)	se fussent arrêté(e)s

Impératif
arrête-toi; ne t'arrête pas
arrêtons-nous; ne nous arrêtons pas
arrêtez-vous; ne vous arrêtez pas

Madame Dumont s'est arrêtée devant une pâtisserie pour acheter une belle tarte aux cerises. Deux autres dames se sont arrêtées derrière elle et les trois sont entrées dans le magasin.

s'arrêter de faire qqch   to desist from doing something

For other words and expressions related to this verb, see **arrêter.**

to arrive, to happen

The Seven Simple Tenses		The Seven Compound Tenses	
Singular	Plural	Singular	Plural
1 présent de l'indicatif		8 passé composé	
arrive	arrivons	suis arrivé(e)	sommes arrivé(e)s
arrives	arrivez	es arrivé(e)	êtes arrivé(e)(s)
arrive	arrivent	est arrivé(e)	sont arrivé(e)s
2 imparfait de l'indicatif		9 plus-que-parfait de l'indicatif	
arrivais	arrivions	étais arrivé(e)	étions arrivé(e)s
arrivais	arriviez	étais arrivé(e)	étiez arrivé(e)(s)
arrivait	arrivaient	était arrivé(e)	étaient arrivé(e)s
3 passé simple		10 passé antérieur	
arrivai	arrivâmes	fus arrivé(e)	fûmes arrivé(e)s
arrivas	arrivâtes	fus arrivé(e)	fûtes arrivé(e)(s)
arriva	arrivèrent	fut arrivé(e)	furent arrivé(e)s
4 futur		11 futur antérieur	
arriverai	arriverons	serai arrivé(e)	serons arrivé(e)s
arriveras	arriverez	seras arrivé(e)	serez arrivé(e)(s)
arrivera	arriveront	sera arrivé(e)	seront arrivé(e)s
5 conditionnel		12 conditionnel passé	
arriverais	arriverions	serais arrivé(e)	serions arrivé(e)s
arriverais	arriveriez	serais arrivé(e)	seriez arrivé(e)(s)
arriverait	arriveraient	serait arrivé(e)	seraient arrivé(e)s
6 présent du subjonctif		13 passé du subjonctif	
arrive	arrivions	sois arrivé(e)	soyons arrivé(e)s
arrives	arriviez	sois arrivé(e)	soyez arrivé(e)(s)
arrive	arrivent	soit arrivé(e)	soient arrivé(e)s
7 imparfait du subjonctif		14 plus-que-parfait du subjonctif	
arrivasse	arrivassions	fusse arrivé(e)	fussions arrivé(e)s
arrivasses	arrivassiez	fusses arrivé(e)	fussiez arrivé(e)(s)
arrivât	arrivassent	fût arrivé(e)	fussent arrivé(e)s

Impératif
arrive
arrivons
arrivez

Paulette est arrivée à la gare à deux heures. Le train pour Paris arrivera à trois heures. Elle passera une heure dans la salle d'attente. Après quelques minutes, elle voit beaucoup de personnes qui courent frénétiquement. Elle n'arrive pas à comprendre ce qui se passe.
—Qu'est-ce qui arrive? elle demande.
—Il y a eu un accident! on lui répond.

arriver à faire qqch to succeed in + pres. part.; to manage to do something
arriver à to happen to **Cela n'arrive qu'à moi!** It's just my luck! That would happen to me!

The Seven Simple Tenses		The Seven Compound Tenses	
Singular	Plural	Singular	Plural
1 présent de l'indicatif		8 passé composé	
m'assieds	**nous asseyons**	**me suis assis(e)**	**nous sommes assis(es)**
t'assieds	**vous asseyez**	**t'es assis(e)**	**vous êtes assis(e)(es)**
s'assied	**s'asseyent**	**s'est assis(e)**	**se sont assis(es)**
2 imparfait de l'indicatif		9 plus-que-parfait de l'indicatif	
m'asseyais	**nous asseyions**	**m'étais assis(e)**	**nous étions assis(es)**
t'asseyais	**vous asseyiez**	**t'étais assis(e)**	**vous étiez assis(e)(es)**
s'asseyait	**s'asseyaient**	**s'était assis(e)**	**s'étaient assis(es)**
3 passé simple		10 passé antérieur	
m'assis	**nous assîmes**	**me fus assis(e)**	**nous fûmes assis(es)**
t'assis	**vous assîtes**	**te fus assis(e)**	**vous fûtes assis(e)(es)**
s'assit	**s'assirent**	**se fut assis(e)**	**se furent assis(es)**
4 futur		11 futur antérieur	
m'assiérai	**nous assiérons**	**me serai assis(e)**	**nous serons assis(es)**
t'assiéras	**vous assiérez**	**te seras assis(e)**	**vous serez assis(e)(es)**
s'assiéra	**s'assiéront**	**se sera assis(e)**	**se seront assis(es)**
5 conditionnel		12 conditionnel passé	
m'assiérais	**nous assiérions**	**me serais assis(e)**	**nous serions assis(es)**
t'assiérais	**vous assiériez**	**te serais assis(e)**	**vous seriez assis(e)(es)**
s'assiérait	**s'assiéraient**	**se serait assis(e)**	**se seraient assis(es)**
6 présent du subjonctif		13 passé du subjonctif	
m'asseye	**nous asseyions**	**me sois assis(e)**	**nous soyons assis(es)**
t'asseyes	**vous asseyiez**	**te sois assis(e)**	**vous soyez assis(e)(es)**
s'asseye	**s'asseyent**	**se soit assis(e)**	**se soient assis(es)**
7 imparfait du subjonctif		14 plus-que-parfait du subjonctif	
m'assisse	**nous assissions**	**me fusse assis(e)**	**nous fussions assis(es)**
t'assisses	**vous assissiez**	**te fusses assis(e)**	**vous fussiez assis(e)(es)**
s'assît	**s'assissent**	**se fût assis(e)**	**se fussent assis(es)**

Impératif
assieds-toi; ne t'assieds pas
asseyons-nous; ne nous asseyons pas
asseyez-vous; ne vous asseyez pas

Quand je voyage en train, je m'assieds toujours près d'une fenêtre si c'est possible.

Une fois, pendant un voyage, une belle jeune fille s'est approchée de moi et m'a demandé:

—Puis-je m'asseoir ici? Est-ce que cette place est libre?

—Certainement, j'ai répondu—asseyez-vous, je vous en prie.

Elle s'est assise auprès de moi et nous nous sommes bien amusés à raconter des histoires drôles.

asseoir qqn   to seat someone: **se rasseoir**   to sit down again
resseoir   to seat again, to reseat

25

assister	Part. pr. **assistant**	Pàrt. passé **assisté**

to assist (at), to be present (at), to attend

The Seven Simple Tenses		The Seven Compound Tenses	
Singular	Plural	Singular	Plural
1 présent de l'indicatif		8 passé composé	
assiste	assistons	ai assisté	avons assisté
assistes	assistez	as assisté	avez assisté
assiste	assistent	a assisté	ont assisté
2 imparfait de l'indicatif		9 plus-que-parfait de l'indicatif	
assistais	assistions	avais assisté	avions assisté
assistais	assistiez	avais assisté	aviez assisté
assistait	assistaient	avait assisté	avaient assisté
3 passé simple		10 passé antérieur	
assistai	assistâmes	eus assisté	eûmes assisté
assistas	assistâtes	eus assisté	eûtes assisté
assista	assistèrent	eut assisté	eurent assisté
4 futur		11 futur antérieur	
assisterai	assisterons	aurai assisté	aurons assisté
assisteras	assisterez	auras assisté	aurez assisté
assistera	assisteront	aura assisté	auront assisté
5 conditionnel		12 conditionnel passé	
assisterais	assisterions	aurais assisté	aurions assisté
assisterais	assisteriez	aurais assisté	auriez assisté
assisterait	assisteraient	aurait assisté	auraient assisté
6 présent du subjonctif		13 passé du subjonctif	
assiste	assistions	aie assisté	ayons assisté
assistes	assistiez	aies assisté	ayez assisté
assiste	assistent	ait assisté	aient assisté
7 imparfait du subjonctif		14 plus-que-parfait du subjonctif	
assistasse	assistassions	eusse assisté	eussions assisté
assistasses	assistassiez	eusses assisté	eussiez assisté
assistât	assistassent	eût assisté	eussent assisté

Impératif
assiste
assistons
assistez

Lundi prochain j'assisterai à une conférence de musiciens. L'année dernière j'ai assisté à la même conférence et il y avait beaucoup de monde.

assistance *f.* assistance, help; attendance; audience
assister à to be present at, to attend
assister de to help with
les assistants those present; spectators

to make sure, to assure oneself, to insure oneself

The Seven Simple Tenses		The Seven Compound Tenses	
Singular	Plural	Singular	Plural
1 présent de l'indicatif		8 passé composé	
m'assure	nous assurons	me suis assuré(e)	nous sommes assuré(e)s
t'assures	vous assurez	t'es assuré(e)	vous êtes assuré(e)(s)
s'assure	s'assurent	s'est assuré(e)	se sont assuré(e)s
2 imparfait de l'indicatif		9 plus-que-parfait de l'indicatif	
m'assurais	nous assurions	m'étais assuré(e)	nous étions assuré(e)s
t'assurais	vous assuriez	t'étais assuré(e)	vous étiez assuré(e)(s)
s'assurait	s'assuraient	s'était assuré(e)	s'étaient assuré(e)s
3 passé simple		10 passé antérieur	
m'assurai	nous assurâmes	me fus assuré(e)	nous fûmes assuré(e)s
t'assuras	vous assurâtes	te fus assuré(e)	vous fûtes assuré(e)(s)
s'assura	s'assurèrent	se fut assuré(e)	se furent assuré(e)s
4 futur		11 futur antérieur	
m'assurerai	nous assurerons	me serai assuré(e)	nous serons assuré(e)s
t'assureras	vous assurerez	te seras assuré(e)	vous serez assuré(e)(s)
s'assurera	s'assureront	se sera assuré(e)	se seront assuré(e)s
5 conditionnel		12 conditionnel passé	
m'assurerais	nous assurerions	me serais assuré(e)	nous serions assuré(e)s
t'assurerais	vous assureriez	te serais assuré(e)	vous seriez assuré(e)(s)
s'assurerait	s'assureraient	se serait assuré(e)	se seraient assuré(e)s
6 présent du subjonctif		13 passé du subjonctif	
m'assure	nous assurions	me sois assuré(e)	nous soyons assuré(e)s
t'assures	vous assuriez	te sois assuré(e)	vous soyez assuré(e)(s)
s'assure	s'assurent	se soit assuré(e)	se soient assuré(e)s
7 imparfait du subjonctif		14 plus-que-parfait du subjonctif	
m'assurasse	nous assurassions	me fusse assuré(e)	nous fussions assuré(e)s
t'assurasses	vous assurassiez	te fusses assuré(e)	vous fussiez assuré(e)(s)
s'assurât	s'assurassent	se fût assuré(e)	se fussent assuré(e)s

Impératif
assure-toi; ne t'assure pas
assurons-nous; ne nous assurons pas
assurez-vous; ne vous assurez pas

Pour s'assurer que la porte était bien fermée, Madame Lafontaine l'a fermée à clef. Puis elle a fermé toutes les fenêtres pour avoir de l'assurance et un sentiment de sécurité.

Assurément, elle a raison. Il y a des cambrioleurs dans le voisinage.

assurément   assuredly
assurance *f.*   assurance, insurance
s'assurer de la protection de qqn   to secure someone's protection
assurance sur la vie   life insurance, life assurance

attendre   Part. pr. **attendant**   Part. passé **attendu**

to wait, to wait for, to expect

The Seven Simple Tenses		The Seven Compound Tenses	
Singular	Plural	Singular	Plural
1 présent de l'indicatif		8 passé composé	
attends	attendons	ai attendu	avons attendu
attends	attendez	as attendu	avez attendu
attend	attendent	a attendu	ont attendu
2 imparfait de l'indicatif		9 plus-que-parfait de l'indicatif	
attendais	attendions	avais attendu	avions attendu
attendais	attendiez	avais attendu	aviez attendu
attendait	attendaient	avait attendu	avaient attendu
3 passé simple		10 passé antérieur	
attendis	attendîmes	eus attendu	eûmes attendu
attendis	attendîtes	eus attendu	eûtes attendu
attendit	attendirent	eut attendu	eurent attendu
4 futur		11 futur antérieur	
attendrai	attendrons	aurai attendu	aurons attendu
attendras	attendrez	auras attendu	aurez attendu
attendra	attendront	aura attendu	auront attendu
5 conditionnel		12 conditionnel passé	
attendrais	attendrions	aurais attendu	aurions attendu
attendrais	attendriez	aurais attendu	auriez attendu
attendrait	attendraient	aurait attendu	auraient attendu
6 présent du subjonctif		13 passé du subjonctif	
attende	attendions	aie attendu	ayons attendu
attendes	attendiez	aies attendu	ayez attendu
attende	attendent	ait attendu	aient attendu
7 imparfait du subjonctif		14 plus-que-parfait du subjonctif	
attendisse	attendissions	eusse attendu	eussions attendu
attendisses	attendissiez	eusses attendu	eussiez attendu
attendît	attendissent	eût attendu	eussent attendu
		Impératif	
		attends	
		attendons	
		attendez	

J'attends l'autobus depuis vingt minutes. Hier j'ai attendu dix minutes. Quand il arrivera, je m'attendrai à trouver une place libre.

faire attendre qqch à qqn   to make someone wait for something; to keep someone waiting for something
en attendant   meanwhile, in the meantime
Cela peut attendre!   It can wait!
s'attendre à   to expect; **s'attendre que + subjunctive**
J'attends l'autobus depuis vingt minutes!   I have been waiting for the bus for 20 minutes!

28

The Seven Simple Tenses		The Seven Compound Tenses	
Singular	Plural	Singular	Plural
1 présent de l'indicatif		**8 passé composé**	
attrape	attrapons	ai attrapé	avons attrapé
attrapes	attrapez	as attrapé	avez attrapé
attrape	attrapent	a attrapé	ont attrapé
2 imparfait de l'indicatif		**9 plus-que-parfait de l'indicatif**	
attrapais	attrapions	avais attrapé	avions attrapé
attrapais	attrapiez	avais attrapé	aviez attrapé
attrapait	attrapaient	avait attrapé	avaient attrapé
3 passé simple		**10 passé antérieur**	
attrapai	attrapâmes	eus attrapé	eûmes attrapé
attrapas	attrapâtes	eus attrapé	eûtes attrapé
attrapa	attrapèrent	eut attrapé	eurent attrapé
4 futur		**11 futur antérieur**	
attraperai	attraperons	aurai attrapé	aurons attrapé
attraperas	attraperez	auras attrapé	aurez attrapé
attrapera	attraperont	aura attrapé	auront attrapé
5 conditionnel		**12 conditionnel passé**	
attraperais	attraperions	aurais attrapé	aurions attrapé
attraperais	attraperiez	aurais attrapé	auriez attrapé
attraperait	attraperaient	aurait attrapé	auraient attrapé
6 présent du subjonctif		**13 passé du subjonctif**	
attrape	attrapions	aie attrapé	ayons attrapé
attrapes	attrapiez	aies attrapé	ayez attrapé
attrape	attrapent	ait attrapé	aient attrapé
7 imparfait du subjonctif		**14 plus-que-parfait du subjonctif**	
attrapasse	attrapassions	eusse attrapé	eussions attrapé
attrapasses	attrapassiez	eusses attrapé	eussiez attrapé
attrapât	attrapassent	eût attrapé	eussent attrapé
		Impératif	
		attrape	
		attrapons	
		attrapez	

—Si tu ne veux pas attraper un rhume, mets ton manteau parce qu'il fait froid dehors.

—Je n'ai pas le temps maintenant, maman—je dois attraper l'autobus.

attraper un rhume to catch cold
attraper qqn à qqch to catch someone at something (to surprise)
s'attraper to be catching, infectious
une attrape snare
un attrape-mouches flypaper (sticky paper to catch flies)

to advance, to go forward

The Seven Simple Tenses		The Seven Compound Tenses	
Singular	Plural	Singular	Plural
1 présent de l'indicatif		8 passé composé	
avance	avançons	ai avancé	avons avancé
avances	avancez	as avancé	avez avancé
avance	avancent	a avancé	ont avancé
2 imparfait de l'indicatif		9 plus-que-parfait de l'indicatif	
avançais	avancions	avais avancé	avions avancé
avançais	avanciez	avais avancé	aviez avancé
avançait	avançaient	avait avancé	avaient avancé
3 passé simple		10 passé antérieur	
avançai	avançâmes	eus avancé	eûmes avancé
avanças	avançâtes	eus avancé	eûtes avancé
avança	avancèrent	eut avancé	eurent avancé
4 futur		11 futur antérieur	
avancerai	avancerons	aurai avancé	aurons avancé
avanceras	avancerez	auras avancé	aurez avancé
avancera	avanceront	aura avancé	auront avancé
5 conditionnel		12 conditionnel passé	
avancerais	avancerions	aurais avancé	aurions avancé
avancerais	avanceriez	aurais avancé	auriez avancé
avancerait	avanceraient	aurait avancé	auraient avancé
6 présent du subjonctif		13 passé du subjonctif	
avance	avancions	aie avancé	ayons avancé
avances	avanciez	aies avancé	ayez avancé
avance	avancent	ait avancé	aient avancé
7 imparfait du subjonctif		14 plus-que-parfait du subjonctif	
avançasse	avançassions	eusse avancé	eussions avancé
avançasses	avançassiez	eusses avancé	eussiez avancé
avançât	avançassent	eût avancé	eussent avancé

	Impératif	
avance	avançons	avancez

Le docteur a dit au petit garçon:—Ouvre la bouche et avance la langue.
Le garçon n'a pas ouvert la bouche et il n'a pas avancé la langue.
Le docteur a insisté:—Ouvrons la bouche et avançons la langue!

une avance advance, progress
à l'avance, d'avance in advance, beforehand
arriver en avance to arrive early
Ta montre avance. Your watch is fast.
avancer une théorie to promote a theory
Comment avance le travail? How is the work coming along?

to have

The Seven Simple Tenses		The Seven Compound Tenses	
Singular	Plural	Singular	Plural
1 présent de l'indicatif		8 passé composé	
ai	avons	al eu	avons eu
as	avez	as eu	avez eu
a	ont	a eu	ont eu
2 imparfait de l'indicatif		9 plus-que-parfait de l'indicatif	
avais	avions	avais eu	avions eu
avais	aviez	avais eu	aviez eu
avait	avaient	avait eu	avaient eu
3 passé simple		10 passé antérieur	
eus	eûmes	eus eu	eûmes eu
eus	eûtes	eus eu	eûtes eu
eut	eurent	eut eu	eurent eu
4 futur		11 futur antérieur	
aurai	aurons	aurai eu	aurons eu
auras	aurez	auras eu	aurez eu
aura	auront	aura eu	auront eu
5 conditionnel		12 conditionnel passé	
aurais	aurions	aurais eu	aurions eu
aurais	auriez	aurais eu	auriez eu
aurait	auraient	aurait eu	auraient eu
6 présent du subjonctif		13 passé du subjonctif	
aie	ayons	aie eu	ayons eu
ales	ayez	aies eu	ayez eu
ait	aient	ait eu	aient eu
7 imparfait du subjonctif		14 plus-que-parfait du subjonctif	
eusse	eussions	eusse eu	eussions eu
eusses	eussiez	eusses eu	eussiez eu
eût	eussent	eût eu	eussent eu
		Impératif	
		aie	
		ayons	
		ayez	

avoir ... ans   to be ... years old
avoir à + inf.   to have to, to be obliged to + inf.
avoir besoin de   to need, to have need of
avoir chaud   to be (feel) warm (persons)
avoir froid   to be (feel) cold (persons)
avoir sommeil   to be (feel) sleepy

avoir qqch à faire   to have something to do
avoir de la chance   to be lucky
avoir faim   to be hungry
avoir soif   to be thirsty
avoir mal à la gorge   to have a sore throat

balayer   Part. pr. **balayant**   Part. passé **balayé**

to sweep

The Seven Simple Tenses		The Seven Compound Tenses	
Singular	Plural	Singular	Plural
1 présent de l'indicatif		8 passé composé	
balaye	balayons	ai balayé	avons balayé
balayes	balayez	as balayé	avez balayé
balaye	balayent	a balayé	ont balayé
2 imparfait de l'indicatif		9 plus-que-parfait de l'indicatif	
balayais	balayions	avais balayé	avions balayé
balayais	balayiez	avais balayé	aviez balayé
balayait	balayaient	avait balayé	avaient balayé
3 passé simple		10 passé antérieur	
balayai	balayâmes	eus balayé	eûmes balayé
balayas	balayâtes	eus balayé	eûtes balayé
balaya	balayèrent	eut balayé	eurent balayé
4 futur		11 futur antérieur	
balayerai	balayerons	aurai balayé	aurons balayé
balayeras	balayerez	auras balayé	aurez balayé
balayera	balayeront	aura balayé	auront balayé
5 conditionnel		12 conditionnel passé	
balayerais	balayerions	aurais balayé	aurions balayé
balayerais	balayeriez	aurais balayé	auriez balayé
balayerait	balayeraient	aurait balayé	auraient balayé
6 présent du subjonctif		13 passé du subjonctif	
balaye	balayions	aie balayé	ayons balayé
balayes	balayiez	aies balayé	ayez balayé
balaye	balayent	ait balayé	aient balayé
7 imparfait du subjonctif		14 plus-que-parfait du subjonctif	
balayasse	balayassions	eusse balayé	eussions balayé
balayasses	balayassiez	eusses balayé	eussiez balayé
balayât	balayassent	eût balayé	eussent balayé
		Impératif	
		balaye	
		balayons	
		balayez	

—Marie, as-tu balayé les chambres?
—Non, madame.
—Et pourquoi pas?
—Parce que je n'ai pas de balai, je n'ai pas de balayette, et je ne suis pas balayeuse. Voilà pourquoi!

un balai broom; **une balayette** small broom; **un balayeur, une balayeuse**
  sweeper
Verbs ending in *-ayer* may change *y* to *i* before mute *e* or may keep *y*.

to build, to construct

The Seven Simple Tenses		The Seven Compound Tenses	
Singular	Plural	Singular	Plural
1 présent de l'indicatif		8 passé composé	
bâtis	bâtissons	ai bâti	avons bâti
bâtis	bâtissez	as bâti	avez bâti
bâtit	bâtissent	a bâti	ont bâti
2 imparfait de l'indicatif		9 plus-que-parfait de l'indicatif	
bâtissais	bâtissions	avais bâti	avions bâti
bâtissais	bâtissiez	avais bâti	aviez bâti
bâtissait	bâtissaient	avait bâti	avaient bâti
3 passé simple		10 passé antérieur	
bâtis	bâtîmes	eus bâti	eûmes bâti
bâtis	bâtîtes	eus bâti	eûtes bâti
bâtit	bâtirent	eut bâti	eurent bâti
4 futur		11 futur antérieur	
bâtirai	bâtirons	aurai bâti	aurons bâti
bâtiras	bâtirez	auras bâti	aurez bâti
bâtira	bâtiront	aura bâti	auront bâti
5 conditionnel		12 conditionnel passé	
bâtirais	bâtirions	aurais bâti	aurions bâti
bâtirais	bâtiriez	aurais bâti	auriez bâti
bâtirait	bâtiraient	aurait bâti	auraient bâti
6 présent du subjonctif		13 passé du subjonctif	
bâtisse	bâtissions	aie bâti	ayons bâti
bâtisses	bâtissiez	aies bâti	ayez bâti
bâtisse	bâtissent	ait bâti	aient bâti
7 imparfait du subjonctif		14 plus-que-parfait du subjonctif	
bâtisse	bâtissions	eusse bâti	eussions bâti
bâtisses	bâtissiez	eusses bâti	eussiez bâti
bâtît	bâtissent	eût bâti	eussent bâti
		Impératif	
		bâtis	
		bâtissons	
		bâtissez	

—Est-ce que tu aimes bâtir des maisons en papier mâché?
—Oui, beaucoup. J'aime surtout bâtir des petits avions en papier. Je les lance contre le mur dans la salle de classe.
—Et ton père? Aime-t-il bâtir?
—Non, il ne bâtit jamais. Il a fait bâtir cette maison. Nous bâtissons des châteaux en Espagne en employant notre imagination.
—Moi, j'aime les grands bâtiments.

un bâtiment   building, edifice; **un bâtisseur**   builder
bâtir   to baste; **du fil à bâtir**   basting thread

battre	Part. pr. **battant**	Part. passé **battu**

to beat, to hit, to strike

The Seven Simple Tenses		The Seven Compound Tenses	
Singular	Plural	Singular	Plural
1 présent de l'indicatif		8 passé composé	
bats	battons	ai battu	avons battu
bats	battez	as battu	avez battu
bat	battent	a battu	ont battu
2 imparfait de l'indicatif		9 plus-que-parfait de l'indicatif	
battais	battions	avais battu	avions battu
battais	battiez	avais battu	aviez battu
battait	battaient	avait battu	avaient battu
3 passé simple		10 passé antérieur	
battis	battîmes	eus battu	eûmes battu
battis	battîtes	eus battu	eûtes battu
battit	battirent	eut battu	eurent battu
4 futur		11 futur antérieur	
battrai	battrons	aurai battu	aurons battu
battras	battrez	auras battu	aurez battu
battra	battront	aura battu	auront battu
5 conditionnel		12 conditionnel passé	
battrais	battrions	aurais battu	aurions battu
battrais	battriez	aurais battu	auriez battu
battrait	battraient	aurait battu	auraient battu
6 présent du subjonctif		13 passé du subjonctif	
batte	battions	aie battu	ayons battu
battes	battiez	aies battu	ayez battu
batte	battent	ait battu	aient battu
7 imparfait du subjonctif		14 plus-que-parfait du subjonctif	
battisse	battissions	eusse battu	eussions battu
battisses	battissiez	eusses battu	eussiez battu
battît	battissent	eût battu	eussent battu

	Impératif	
bats	battons	battez

Notre femme de chambre est dans la cour. Elle est en train de battre les tapis. Elle les bat tous les samedis. Samedi dernier, pendant qu'elle battait les tapis, mon frère jouait au tennis et il a battu son adversaire.

battre des mains   to clap, to applaud
battre la campagne   to scour the countryside
le battant   leaf, flap (of a table)
une porte à deux battants   double door
une batte   bat, beater
le battement   banging (of a door); throbbing, flutter, beating

to fight

The Seven Simple Tenses		The Seven Compound Tenses	
Singular	Plural	Singular	Plural
1 présent de l'indicatif		8 passé composé	
me bats	nous battons	me suis battu(e)	nous sommes battu(e)s
te bats	vous battez	t'es battu(e)(s)	vous êtes battu(e)(s)
se bat	se battent	s'est battu(e)	se sont battu(e)s
2 imparfait de l'indicatif		9 plus-que-parfait de l'indicatif	
me battais	nous battions	m'étais battu(e)	nous étions battu(e)s
te battais	vous battiez	t'étais battu(e)	vous étiez battu(e)(s)
se battait	se battaient	s'était battu(e)	s'étaient battu(e)s
3 passé simple		10 passé antérieur	
me battls	nous battîmes	me fus battu(e)	nous fûmes battu(e)s
te battis	vous battîtes	te fus battu(e)	vous fûtes battu(e)(s)
se battit	se battirent	se fut battu(e)	se furent battu(e)s
4 futur		11 futur antérieur	
me battrai	nous battrons	me serai battu(e)	nous serons battu(e)s
te battras	vous battrez	te seras battu(e)	vous serez battu(e)(s)
se battra	se battront	se sera battu(e)	se seront battu(e)s
5 conditionnel		12 conditionnel passé	
me battrais	nous battrions	me serais battu(e)	nous serions battu(e)s
te battrais	vous battriez	te serais battu(e)	vous seriez battu(e)(s)
se battrait	se battraient	se serait battu(e)	se seraient battu(e)s
6 présent du subjonctif		13 passé du subjonctif	
me batte	nous battlons	me sois battu(e)	nous soyons battu(e)s
te battes	vous battiez	te sois battu(e)	vous soyez battu(e)(s)
se batte	se battent	se soit battu(e)	se soient battu(e)s
7 imparfait du subjonctif		14 plus-que-parfait du subjonctif	
me battisse	nous battissions	me fusse battu(e)	nous fussions battu(e)s
te battisses	vous battissiez	te fusses battu(e)	vous fussiez battu(e)(s)
se battît	se battissent	se fût battu(e)	se fussent battu(e)s

Impératif
bats-toi; ne te bats pas
battons-nous; ne nous battons pas
battez-vous; ne vous battez pas

Ecoutez! Nos voisins commencent à se battre. Ils se battent toujours. La dernière fois ils se sont battus à coups de poings. Il y a toujours un grand combat chez eux.

For other words and expressions related to this verb, see **battre**.

bavarder	Part.pr. **bavardant**	Part.passé **bavardé**

to chat, to chatter, to babble, to gossip

The Seven Simple Tenses		The Seven Compound Tenses	
Singular	Plural	Singular	Plural
1 présent de l'indicatif		8 passé composé	
bavarde	bavardons	ai bavardé	avons bavardé
bavardes	bavardez	as bavardé	avez bavardé
bavarde	bavardent	a bavardé	ont bavardé
2 imparfait de l'indicatif		9 plus-que-parfait de l'indicatif	
bavardais	bavardions	avais bavardé	avions bavardé
bavardais	bavardiez	avais bavardé	aviez bavardé
bavardait	bavardaient	avait bavardé	avaient bavardé
3 passé simple		10 passé antérieur	
bavardai	bavardâmes	eus bavardé	eûmes bavardé
bavardas	bavardâtes	eus bavardé	eûtes bavardé
bavarda	bavardèrent	eut bavardé	eurent bavardé
4 futur		11 futur antérieur	
bavarderai	bavarderons	aurai bavardé	aurons bavardé
bavarderas	bavarderez	auras bavardé	aurez bavardé
bavardera	bavarderont	aura bavardé	auront bavardé
5 conditionnel		12 conditionnel passé	
bavarderais	bavarderions	aurais bavardé	aurions bavardé
bavarderais	bavarderiez	aurais bavardé	auriez bavardé
bavarderait	bavarderaient	aurait bavardé	auraient bavardé
6 présent du subjonctif		13 passé du subjonctif	
bavarde	bavardions	aie bavardé	ayons bavardé
bavardes	bavardiez	aies bavardé	ayez bavardé
bavarde	bavardent	ait bavardé	aient bavardé
7 imparfait du subjonctif		14 plus-que-parfait du subjonctif	
bavardasse	bavardassions	eusse bavardé	eussions bavardé
bavardasses	bavardassiez	eusses bavardé	eussiez bavardé
bavardât	bavardassent	eût bavardé	eussent bavardé
		Impératif	
		bavarde	
		bavardons	
		bavardez	

Aimez-vous les personnes qui bavardent tout le temps? Je connais un homme qui est bavard. Sa femme est bavarde aussi. Elle aime à parler avec abondance. Moi, je n'aime pas le bavardage. Je ne bavarde pas parce que je n'aime pas perdre mon temps.

le bavardage chitchat, chattering, talkativeness
bavard, bavarde talkative, loquacious, garrulous
perdre son temps à bavarder to waste one's time babbling

to harm, to hurt, to injure, to wound, to offend

The Seven Simple Tenses		The Seven Compound Tenses	
Singular	Plural	Singular	Plural
1 présent de l'indicatif		8 passé composé	
blesse	blessons	ai blessé	avons blessé
blesses	blessez	as blessé	avez blessé
blesse	blessent	a blessé	ont blessé
2 imparfait de l'indicatif		9 plus-que-parfait de l'indicatif	
blessais	blessions	avais blessé	avions blessé
blessais	blessiez	avais blessé	aviez blessé
blessait	blessaient	avait blessé	avaient blessé
3 passé simple		10 passé antérieur	
blessal	blessâmes	eus blessé	eûmes blessé
blessas	blessâtes	eus blessé	eûtes blessé
blessa	blessèrent	eut blessé	eurent blessé
4 futur		11 futur antérieur	
blesserai	blesserons	aurai blessé	aurons blessé
blesseras	blesserez	auras blessé	aurez blessé
blessera	blesseront	aura blessé	auront blessé
5 conditionnel		12 conditionnel passé	
blesserais	blesserions	aurais blessé	aurions blessé
blesserais	blesseriez	aurais blessé	auriez blessé
blesserait	blesseraient	aurait blessé	auraient blessé
6 présent du subjonctif		13 passé du subjonctif	
blesse	blessions	aie blessé	ayons blessé
blesses	blessiez	aies blessé	ayez blessé
blesse	blessent	ait blessé	aient blessé
7 imparfait du subjonctif		14 plus-que-parfait du subjonctif	
blessasse	blessassions	eusse blessé	eussions blessé
blessasses	blessassiez	eusses blessé	eussiez blessé
blessât	blessassent	eût blessé	eussent blessé

Impératif
blesse
blessons
blessez

Ma soeur est tombée sur un rocher qui l'a blessée au visage. C'était une blessure grave.

blesser à mort   to wound mortally
une blessure   wound, injury
une parole blessante   a cutting word

See also **se blesser.** Do not confuse **blesser** with **bénir,** which means *to bless.*

se blesser   Part. pr. **se blessant**   Part. passé **blessé(e)(s)**

to hurt oneself, to injure oneself, to wound oneself

The Seven Simple Tenses		The Seven Compound Tenses	
Singular	Plural	Singular	Plural
1 présent de l'indicatif		8 passé composé	
me blesse	nous blessons	me suis blessé(e)	nous sommes blessé(e)s
te blesses	vous blessez	t'es blessé(e)	vous êtes blessé(e)(s)
se blesse	se blessent	s'est blessé(e)	se sont blessé(e)s
2 imparfait de l'indicatif		9 plus-que-parfait de l'indicatif	
me blessais	nous blessions	m'étais blessé(e)	nous étions blessé(e)s
te blessais	vous blessiez	t'étais blessé(e)	vous étiez blessé(e)(s)
se blessait	se blessaient	s'était blessé(e)	s'étaient blessé(e)s
3 passé simple		10 passé antérieur	
me blessai	nous blessâmes	me fus blessé(e)	nous fûmes blessé(e)s
te blessas	vous blessâtes	te fus blessé(e)	vous fûtes blessé(e)(s)
se blessa	se blessèrent	se fut blessé(e)	se furent blessé(e)s
4 futur		11 futur antérieur	
me blesserai	nous blesserons	me serai blessé(e)	nous serons blessé(e)s
te blesseras	vous blesserez	te seras blessé(e)	vous serez blessé(e)(s)
se blessera	se blesseront	se sera blessé(e)	se seront blessé(e)s
5 conditionnel		12 conditionnel passé	
me blesserais	nous blesserions	me serais blessé(e)	nous serions blessé(e)s
te blesserais	vous blesseriez	te serais blessé(e)	vous seriez blessé(e)(s)
se blesserait	se blesseraient	se serait blessé(e)	se seraient blessé(e)s
6 présent du subjonctif		13 passé du subjonctif	
me blesse	nous blessions	me sois blessé(e)	nous soyons blessé(e)s
te blesses	vous blessiez	te sois blessé(e)	vous soyez blessé(e)(s)
se blesse	se blessent	se soit blessé(e)	se soient blessé(e)s
7 imparfait du subjonctif		14 plus-que-parfait du subjonctif	
me blessasse	nous blessassions	me fusse blessé(e)	nous fussions blessé(e)s
te blessasses	vous blessassiez	te fusses blessé(e)	vous fussiez blessé(e)(s)
se blessât	se blessassent	se fût blessé(e)	se fussent blessé(e)s

Impératif
blesse-toi; ne te blesse pas
blessons-nous; ne nous blessons pas
blessez-vous; ne vous blessez pas

Madame Leblanc est tombée dans la rue et elle s'est blessée au genou. C'était une blessure légère, heureusement.

se blesser de   to take offense at

For other words and expressions related to this verb, see **blesser.** Do not confuse **blesser** and **se blesser** with **bénir,** which means *to bless.*

The Seven Simple Tenses		The Seven Compound Tenses	
Singular	Plural	Singular	Plural
1 présent de l'indicatif		8 passé composé	
bois	buvons	ai bu	avons bu
bois	buvez	as bu	avez bu
boit	boivent	a bu	ont bu
2 imparfait de l'indicatif		9 plus-que-parfait de l'indicatif	
buvais	buvions	avais bu	avions bu
buvais	buviez	avais bu	aviez bu
buvait	buvaient	avait bu	avaient bu
3 passé simple		10 passé antérieur	
bus	bûmes	eus bu	eûmes bu
bus	bûtes	eus bu	eûtes bu
but	burent	eut bu	eurent bu
4 futur		11 futur antérieur	
boirai	boirons	aurai bu	aurons bu
boiras	boirez	auras bu	aurez bu
boira	boiront	aura bu	auront bu
5 conditionnel		12 conditionnel passé	
boirais	boirions	aurais bu	aurions bu
boirais	boiriez	aurais bu	auriez bu
boirait	boiraient	aurait bu	auraient bu
6 présent du subjonctif		13 passé du subjonctif	
boive	buvions	aie bu	ayons bu
boives	buviez	aies bu	ayez bu
boive	boivent	ait bu	aient bu
7 imparfait du subjonctif		14 plus-que-parfait du subjonctif	
busse	bussions	eusse bu	eussions bu
busses	bussiez	eusses bu	eussiez bu
bût	bussent	eût bu	eussent bu
		Impératif	
	bois buvons buvez		

—Michel, as-tu bu ton lait?
—Non, maman, je ne l'ai pas bu.
—Bois-le tout de suite, je te dis.
—Tous les jours je bois du lait. N'y a-t-il pas d'autres boissons dans la maison?
—Si, il y a d'autres boissons dans la maison mais les bons garçons comme toi boivent du lait.

boire à la santé de qqn   to drink to someone's health
une boisson   drink; **boisson gazeuse**   carbonated drink
un buveur, une buveuse   drinker; **une buvette**   bar
un buvard   ink blotter; **boire un coup**   to have a drink

brosser   Part. pr. **brossant**   Part. passé **brossé**

to brush

The Seven Simple Tenses		The Seven Compound Tenses	
Singular	Plural	Singular	Plural
1 présent de l'indicatif		8 passé composé	
brosse	brossons	ai brossé	avons brossé
brosses	brossez	as brossé	avez brossé
brosse	brossent	a brossé	ont brossé
2 imparfait de l'indicatif		9 plus-que-parfait de l'indicatif	
brossais	brossions	avais brossé	avions brossé
brossais	brossiez	avais brossé	aviez brossé
brossait	brossaient	avait brossé	avaient brossé
3 passé simple		10 passé antérieur	
brossai	brossâmes	eus brossé	eûmes brossé
brossas	brossâtes	eus brossé	eûtes brossé
brossa	brossèrent	eut brossé	eurent brossé
4 futur		11 futur antérieur	
brosserai	brosserons	aurai brossé	aurons brossé
brosseras	brosserez	auras brossé	aurez brossé
brossera	brosseront	aura brossé	auront brossé
5 conditionnel		12 conditionnel passé	
brosserais	brosserions	aurais brossé	aurions brossé
brosserais	brosseriez	aurais brossé	auriez brossé
brosserait	brosseraient	aurait brossé	auraient brossé
6 présent du subjonctif		13 passé du subjonctif	
brosse	brossions	aie brossé	ayons brossé
brosses	brossiez	aies brossé	ayez brossé
brosse	brossent	ait brossé	aient brossé
7 imparfait du subjonctif		14 plus-que-parfait du subjonctif	
brossasse	brossassions	eusse brossé	eussions brossé
brossasses	brossassiez	eusses brossé	eussiez brossé
brossât	brossassent	eût brossé	eussent brossé

	Impératif	
brosse	brossons	brossez

—Henriette, as-tu brossé tes souliers?
—Non, maman, je ne les ai pas brossés.
—Et pourquoi pas, ma petite?
—Parce que je n'ai pas de brosse.

une brosse brush; **brosse à chaussures** shoebrush; **brosse à dents** toothbrush;
   brosse à ongles nailbrush
donner un coup de brosse to brush

See also **se brosser.**

to brush oneself

The Seven Simple Tenses		The Seven Compound Tenses	
Singular	Plural	Singular	Plural
1 présent de l'indicatif		8 passé composé	
me brosse	nous brossons	me suis brossé(e)	nous sommes brossé(e)s
te brosses	vous brossez	t'es brossé(e)	vous êtes brossé(e)s
se brosse	se brossent	s'est brossé(e)	se sont brossé(e)s
2 imparfait de l'indicatif		9 plus-que-parfait de l'indicatif	
me brossais	nous brossions	m'étais brossé(e)	nous étions brossé(e)s
te brossais	vous brossiez	t'étais brossé(e)	vous étiez brossé(e)(s)
se brossait	se brossaient	s'était brossé(e)	s'étaient brossé(e)s
3 passé simple		10 passé antérieur	
me brossai	nous brossâmes	me fus brossé(e)	nous fûmes brossé(e)s
te brossas	vous brossâtes	te fus brossé(e)	vous fûtes brossé(e)(s)
se brossa	se brossèrent	se fut brossé(e)	se furent brossé(e)s
4 futur		11 futur antérieur	
me brosserai	nous brosserons	me serai brossé(e)	nous serons brossé(e)s
te brosseras	vous brosserez	te seras brossé(e)	vous serez brossé(e)(s)
se brossera	se brosseront	se sera brossé(e)	se seront brossé(e)s
5 conditionnel		12 conditionnel passé	
me brosserais	nous brosserions	me serais brossé(e)	nous serions brossé(e)s
te brosserais	vous brosseriez	te serais brossé(e)	vous seriez brossé(e)(s)
se brosserait	se brosseraient	se serait brossé(e)	se seraient brossé(e)s
6 présent du subjonctif		13 passé du subjonctif	
me brosse	nous brossions	me sois brossé(e)	nous soyons brossé(e)s
te brosses	vous brossiez	te sois brossé(e)	vous soyez brossé(e)(s)
se brosse	se brossent	se soit brossé(e)	se soient brossé(e)s
7 imparfait du subjonctif		14 plus-que-parfait du subjonctif	
me brossasse	nous brossassions	me fusse brossé(e)	nous fussions brossé(e)s
te brossasses	vous brossassiez	te fusses brossé(e)	vous fussiez brossé(e)(s)
se brossât	se brossassent	se fût brossé(e)	se fussent brossé(e)s

Impératif
brosse-toi; ne te brosse pas
brossons-nous; ne nous brossons pas
brossez-vous; ne vous brossez pas

—Tina Marie, est-ce que tu t'es brossée?
—Non, maman, je ne me suis pas brossée.
—Et pourquoi pas? Brosse-toi vite!
—Parce que je n'ai pas de brosse à habits, je n'ai pas de brosse à cheveux, je n'ai pas de brosse à chaussures. Je n'ai aucune brosse. Je n'ai pas de brosse à dents, non plus.
—Quelle fille!

se brosser les dents, les cheveux, etc.   to brush one's teeth, hair, etc.

For other words and expressions related to this verb, see **brosser**.

brûler

Part. pr. **brûlant**   Part. passé **brûlé**

to burn

The Seven Simple Tenses		The Seven Compound Tenses	
Singular	Plural	Singular	Plural
1 présent de l'indicatif		8 passé composé	
brûle	**brûlons**	**ai brûlé**	**avons brûlé**
brûles	**brûlez**	**as brûlé**	**avez brûlé**
brûle	**brûlent**	**a brûlé**	**ont brûlé**
2 imparfait de l'indicatif		9 plus-que-parfait de l'indicatif	
brûlais	**brûlions**	**avais brûlé**	**avions brûlé**
brûlais	**brûliez**	**avais brûlé**	**aviez brûlé**
brûlait	**brûlaient**	**avait brûlé**	**avaient brûlé**
3 passé simple		10 passé antérieur	
brûlai	**brûlâmes**	**eus brûlé**	**eûmes brûlé**
brûlas	**brûlâtes**	**eus brûlé**	**eûtes brûlé**
brûla	**brûlèrent**	**eut brûlé**	**eurent brûlé**
4 futur		11 futur antérieur	
brûlerai	**brûlerons**	**aurai brûlé**	**aurons brûlé**
brûleras	**brûlerez**	**auras brûlé**	**aurez brûlé**
brûlera	**brûleront**	**aura brûlé**	**auront brûlé**
5 conditionnel		12 conditionnel passé	
brûlerais	**brûlerions**	**aurais brûlé**	**aurions brûlé**
brûlerais	**brûleriez**	**aurais brûlé**	**auriez brûlé**
brûlerait	**brûleraient**	**aurait brûlé**	**auraient brûlé**
6 présent du subjonctif		13 passé du subjonctif	
brûle	**brûlions**	**aie brûlé**	**ayons brûlé**
brûles	**brûliez**	**aies brûlé**	**ayez brûlé**
brûle	**brûlent**	**ait brûlé**	**aient brûlé**
7 imparfait du subjonctif		14 plus-que-parfait du subjonctif	
brûlasse	**brûlassions**	**eusse brûlé**	**eussions brûlé**
brûlasses	**brûlassiez**	**eusses brûlé**	**eussiez brûlé**
brûlât	**brûlassent**	**eût brûlé**	**eussent brûlé**
		Impératif	
		brûle	
		brûlons	
		brûlez	

—Joséphine, avez-vous brûlé les vieux papiers que je vous ai donnés?
—Oui, madame, et je me suis brûlée. J'ai une brûlure aux doigts.

une brûlure   burn
un brûleur   burner, roaster
brûler d'amour   to be madly in love
brûler de faire qqch   to be eager to do something
brûler un feu rouge   to pass through a red traffic light

The Seven Simple Tenses		The Seven Compound Tenses	
Singular	Plural	Singular	Plural
1 présent de l'indicatif		8 passé composé	
cache	cachons	ai caché	avons caché
caches	cachez	as caché	avez caché
cache	cachent	a caché	ont caché
2 imparfait de l'indicatif		9 plus-que-parfait de l'indicatif	
cachais	cachions	avais caché	avions caché
cachais	cachiez	avais caché	aviez caché
cachait	cachaient	avait caché	avaient caché
3 passé simple		10 passé antérieur	
cachai	cachâmes	eus caché	eûmes caché
cachas	cachâtes	eus caché	eûtes caché
cacha	cachèrent	eut caché	eurent caché
4 futur		11 futur antérieur	
cacherai	cacherons	aurai caché	aurons caché
cacheras	cacherez	auras caché	aurez caché
cachera	cacheront	aura caché	auront caché
5 conditionnel		12 conditionnel passé	
cacherais	cacherions	aurais caché	aurions caché
cacherais	cacheriez	aurais caché	auriez caché
cacherait	cacheraient	aurait caché	auraient caché
6 présent du subjonctif		13 passé du subjonctif	
cache	cachions	aie caché	ayons caché
caches	cachiez	aies caché	ayez caché
cache	cachent	ait caché	aient caché
7 imparfait du subjonctif		14 plus-que-parfait du subjonctif	
cachasse	cachassions	eusse caché	eussions caché
cachasses	cachassiez	eusses caché	eussiez caché
cachât	cachassent	eût caché	eussent caché

	Impératif	
cache	cachons	cachez

—Pierre, qu'est-ce que tu as caché derrière toi?
—Rien, papa.
—Ne me dis pas ça. Tu caches quelque chose.
—Voilà, papa, c'est un petit chat que j'ai trouvé dans le parc.

une cache, une cachette hiding place
un cachet seal, mark
un cachetage sealing
cacher qqch à qqn to hide something from someone

cacheter to seal up
cache-cache hide-and-seek
vin cacheté vintage wine
un cache-poussière dust coat (**des cache-poussière**)

See also **se cacher.**

se cacher   Part. pr. **se cachant**   Part. passé **caché(e)(s)**

to hide oneself

The Seven Simple Tenses		The Seven Compound Tenses	
Singular	Plural	Singular	Plural
1 présent de l'indicatif		8 passé composé	
me cache	nous cachons	me suis caché(e)	nous sommes caché(e)s
te caches	vous cachez	t'es caché(e)	vous êtes caché(e)(s)
se cache	se cachent	s'est caché(e)	se sont caché(e)s
2 imparfait de l'indicatif		9 plus-que-parfait de l'indicatif	
me cachais	nous cachions	m'étais caché(e)	nous étions caché(e)s
te cachais	vous cachiez	t'étais caché(e)	vous étiez caché(e)(s)
se cachait	se cachaient	s'était caché(e)	s'étaient caché(e)s
3 passé simple		10 passé antérieur	
me cachai	nous cachâmes	me fus caché(e)	nous fûmes caché(e)s
te cachas	vous cachâtes	te fus caché(e)	vous fûtes caché(e)(s)
se cacha	se cachèrent	se fut caché(e)	se furent caché(e)s
4 futur		11 futur antérieur	
me cacherai	nous cacherons	me serai caché(e)	nous serons caché(e)s
te cacheras	vous cacherez	te seras caché(e)	vous serez caché(e)(s)
se cachera	se cacheront	se sera caché(e)	se seront caché(e)s
5 conditionnel		12 conditionnel passé	
me cacherais	nous cacherions	me serais caché(e)	nous serions caché(e)s
te cacherais	vous cacheriez	te serais caché(e)	vous seriez caché(e)(s)
se cacherait	se cacheraient	se serait caché(e)	se seraient caché(e)s
6 présent du subjonctif		13 passé du subjonctif	
me cache	nous cachions	me sois caché(e)	nous soyons caché(e)s
te caches	vous cachiez	te sois caché(e)	vous soyez caché(e)(s)
se cache	se cachent	se soit caché(e)	se soient caché(e)s
7 imparfait du subjonctif		14 plus-que-parfait du subjonctif	
me cachasse	nous cachassions	me fusse caché(e)	nous fussions caché(e)s
te cachasses	vous cachassiez	te fusses caché(e)	vous fussiez caché(e)(s)
se cachât	se cachassent	se fût caché(e)	se fussent caché(e)s

Impératif
cache-toi; ne te cache pas
cachons-nous; ne nous cachons pas
cachez-vous; ne vous cachez pas

J'ai un petit chien que j'appelle Coco. Quelquefois je ne peux pas le trouver parce qu'il se cache sous mon lit ou derrière l'arbre dans le jardin. La semaine dernière il s'est caché sous le chapeau de mon père. Il aime jouer à cache-cache. Il est très intelligent.

une cache, une cachette hiding place	cacheter to seal up
un cachet seal, mark	cache-cache hide-and-seek
un cachetage sealing	vin cacheté vintage wine
se cacher de qqn to hide from someone	un cachot cell, prison

    See also **cacher.**

to break

The Seven Simple Tenses		The Seven Compound Tenses	
Singular	Plural	Singular	Plural
1 présent de l'indicatif		8 passé composé	
casse	cassons	ai cassé	avons cassé
casses	cassez	as cassé	avez cassé
casse	cassent	a cassé	ont cassé
2 imparfait de l'indicatif		9 plus-que-parfait de l'indicatif	
cassais	cassions	avais cassé	avions cassé
cassais	cassiez	avais cassé	aviez cassé
cassait	cassaient	avait cassé	avaient cassé
3 passé simple		10 passé antérieur	
cassai	cassâmes	eus cassé	eûmes cassé
cassas	cassâtes	eus cassé	eûtes cassé
cassa	cassèrent	eut cassé	eurent cassé
4 futur		11 futur antérieur	
casserai	casserons	aurai cassé	aurons cassé
casseras	casserez	auras cassé	aurez cassé
cassera	casseront	aura cassé	auront cassé
5 conditionnel		12 conditionnel passé	
casserais	casserions	aurais cassé	aurions cassé
casserais	casseriez	aurais cassé	auriez cassé
casserait	casseraient	aurait cassé	auraient cassé
6 présent du subjonctif		13 passé du subjonctif	
casse	cassions	aie cassé	ayons cassé
casses	cassiez	aies cassé	ayez cassé
casse	cassent	ait cassé	aient cassé
7 imparfait du subjonctif		14 plus-que-parfait du subjonctif	
cassasse	cassassions	eusse cassé	eussions cassé
cassasses	cassassiez	eusses cassé	eussiez cassé
cassât	cassassent	eût cassé	eussent cassé
		Impératif	
		casse	
		cassons	
		cassez	

—Jean, c'est toi qui as cassé mon joli vase?
—Non, maman, c'est Mathilde.
—Mathilde, c'est toi qui as cassé mon joli vase?
—Non, maman, c'est Jean.
—Quels enfants!

une casse breakage, damage
un casse-croûte snack
un casse-noisettes, un casse-noix
  nutcracker

casser la croûte to have a snack
un casse-pieds a bore, a pain in the neck
un cassement de tête puzzle, worry
concasser to crush (cereal, stones)

See also **se casser**.

to break (a part of one's body, *e.g.,* leg, arm, nose)

The Seven Simple Tenses		The Seven Compound Tenses	
Singular	Plural	Singular	Plural
1 présent de l'indicatif		8 passé composé	
me casse	nous cassons	me suis cassé(e)	nous sommes cassé(e)s
te casses	vous cassez	t'es cassé(e)	vous êtes cassé(e)(s)
se casse	se cassent	s'est cassé(e)	se sont cassé(e)s
2 imparfait de l'indicatif		9 plus-que-parfait de l'indicatif	
me cassais	nous cassions	m'étais cassé(e)	nous étions cassé(e)s
te cassais	vous cassiez	t'étais cassé(e)	vous étiez cassé(e)(s)
se cassait	se cassaient	s'était cassé(e)	s'étaient cassé(e)s
3 passé simple		10 passé antérieur	
me cassai	nous cassâmes	me fus cassé(e)	nous fûmes cassé(e)s
te cassas	vous cassâtes	te fus cassé(e)	vous fûtes cassé(e)(s)
se cassa	se cassèrent	se fut cassé(e)	se furent cassé(e)s
4 futur		11 futur antérieur	
me casserai	nous casserons	me serai cassé(e)	nous serons cassé(e)s
te casseras	vous casserez	te seras cassé(e)	vous serez cassé(e)(s)
se cassera	se casseront	se sera cassé(e)	se seront cassé(e)s
5 conditionnel		12 conditionnel passé	
me casserais	nous casserions	me serais cassé(e)	nous serions cassé(e)s
te casserais	vous casseriez	te serais cassé(e)	vous seriez cassé(e)(s)
se casserait	se casseraient	se serait cassé(e)	se seraient cassé(e)s
6 présent du subjonctif		13 passé du subjonctif	
me casse	nous cassions	me sois cassé(e)	nous soyons cassé(e)s
te casses	vous cassiez	te sois cassé(e)	vous soyez cassé(e)(s)
se casse	se cassent	se soit cassé(e)	se soient cassé(e)s
7 imparfait du subjonctif		14 plus-que-parfait du subjonctif	
me cassasse	nous cassassions	me fusse cassé(e)	nous fussions cassé(e)s
te cassasses	vous cassassiez	te fusses cassé(e)	vous fussiez cassé(e)(s)
se cassât	se cassassent	se fût cassé(e)	se fussent cassé(e)s

	Impératif
	casse-toi . . .; ne te casse pas . . .
	cassons-nous . . .; ne nous cassons pas . . .
	cassez-vous . . .; ne vous cassez pas . . .

Pendant les vacances d'hiver, nous sommes allés faire du ski dans les montagnes. Mon père s'est cassé le bras, ma mère s'est cassé la jambe, et moi, je me suis cassé le pied.

se casser la tête   to rack one's brains
se casser le nez   to find nobody answering the door
casser la tête à qqn   to annoy someone

See also **casser.**

to cause, to chat

The Seven Simple Tenses		The Seven Compound Tenses	
Singular	Plural	Singular	Plural
1 présent de l'indicatif		8 passé composé	
cause	**causons**	ai causé	avons causé
causes	causez	as causé	avez causé
cause	causent	a causé	ont causé
2 imparfait de l'indicatif		9 plus-que-parfait de l'indicatif	
causais	causions	avais causé	avions causé
causais	causiez	avais causé	aviez causé
causait	causaient	avait causé	avaient causé
3 passé simple		10 passé antérieur	
causai	causâmes	eus causé	eûmes causé
causas	causâtes	eus causé	eûtes causé
causa	causèrent	eut causé	eurent causé
4 futur		11 futur antérieur	
causerai	causerons	aurai causé	aurons causé
causeras	causerez	auras causé	aurez causé
causera	causeront	aura causé	auront causé
5 conditionnel		12 conditionnel passé	
causerais	causerions	aurais causé	aurions causé
causerais	causeriez	aurais causé	auriez causé
causerait	causeraient	aurait causé	auraient causé
6 présent du subjonctif		13 passé du subjonctif	
cause	causions	aie causé	ayons causé
causes	causiez	aies causé	ayez causé
cause	causent	ait causé	aient causé
7 imparfait du subjonctif		14 plus-que-parfait du subjonctif	
causasse	causassions	eusse causé	eussions causé
causasses	causassiez	eusses causé	eussiez causé
causât	causassent	eût causé	eussent causé
		Impératif	
		cause	
		causons	
		causez	

Quand je voyage, j'aime beaucoup causer avec les passagers. Est-ce que vous causez avec vos voisins dans la salle de classe? En français, bien sûr! Je connais un garçon qui n'est pas très causant.

causant, causante talkative
causatif, causative causative
une cause cause, reason
causer de la pluie et du beau temps
  to chat about the weather

une cause célèbre famous trial
une causerie chat, informal talk
causeur, causeuse talkative

47

céder	Part. pr. **cédant**	Part. passé **cédé**

to yield, to cede

The Seven Simple Tenses		The Seven Compound Tenses	
Singular	Plural	Singular	Plural
1 présent de l'indicatif		8 passé composé	
cède	cédons	ai cédé	avons cédé
cèdes	cédez	as cédé	avez cédé
cède	cèdent	a cédé	ont cédé
2 imparfait de l'indicatif		9 plus-que-parfait de l'indicatif	
cédais	cédions	avais cédé	avions cédé
cédais	cédiez	avais cédé	aviez cédé
cédait	cédaient	avait cédé	avaient cédé
3 passé simple		10 passé antérieur	
cédai	cédâmes	eus cédé	eûmes cédé
cédas	cédâtes	eus cédé	eûtes cédé
céda	cédèrent	eut cédé	eurent cédé
4 futur		11 futur antérieur	
céderai	céderons	aurai cédé	aurons cédé
céderas	céderez	auras cédé	aurez cédé
cédera	céderont	aura cédé	auront cédé
5 conditionnel		12 conditionnel passé	
céderais	céderions	aurais cédé	aurions cédé
céderais	céderiez	aurais cédé	auriez cédé
céderait	céderaient	aurait cédé	auraient cédé
6 présent du subjonctif		13 passé du subjonctif	
cède	cédions	aie cédé	ayons cédé
cèdes	cédiez	aies cédé	ayez cédé
cède	cèdent	ait cédé	aient cédé
7 imparfait du subjonctif		14 plus-que-parfait du subjonctif	
cédasse	cédassions	eusse cédé	eussions cédé
cédasses	cédassiez	eusses cédé	eussiez cédé
cédât	cédassent	eût cédé	eussent cédé
		Impératif	
		cède	
		cédons	
		cédez	

Hier soir j'ai pris l'autobus pour rentrer chez moi. J'ai pris la dernière place libre. Après quelques minutes, une vieille dame est entrée dans l'autobus et j'ai cédé ma place à cette aimable personne.

céder à to give up, give in, yield to	**céder par faiblesse** to give in out
accéder à to accede to, to comply with	of weakness
concéder à to concede to, to grant	**céder à la tentation** to give in to
céder le pas à qqn to give way to someone	temptation

to cease

The Seven Simple Tenses		The Seven Compound Tenses	
Singular	Plural	Singular	Plural
1 présent de l'indicatif		8 passé composé	
cesse	cessons	ai cessé	avons cessé
cesses	cessez	as cessé	avez cessé
cesse	cessent	a cessé	ont cessé
2 imparfait de l'indicatif		9 plus-que-parfait de l'indicatif	
cessais	cessions	avais cessé	avions cessé
cessais	cessiez	avais cessé	aviez cessé
cessait	cessaient	avait cessé	avaient cessé
3 passé simple		10 passé antérieur	
cessai	cessâmes	eus cessé	eûmes cessé
cessas	cessâtes	eus cessé	eûtes cessé
cessa	cessèrent	eut cessé	eurent cessé
4 futur		11 futur antérieur	
cesserai	cesserons	aurai cessé	aurons cessé
cesseras	cesserez	auras cessé	aurez cessé
cessera	cesseront	aura cessé	auront cessé
5 conditionnel		12 conditionnel passé	
cesserais	cesserions	aurais cessé	aurions cessé
cesserais	cesseriez	aurais cessé	auriez cessé
cesserait	cesseraient	aurait cessé	auraient cessé
6 présent du subjonctif		13 passé du subjonctif	
cesse	cessions	aie cessé	ayons cessé
cesses	cessiez	aies cessé	ayez cessé
cesse	cessent	ait cessé	aient cessé
7 imparfait du subjonctif		14 plus-que-parfait du subjonctif	
cessasse	cessassions	eusse cessé	eussions cessé
cessasses	cessassiez	eusses cessé	eussiez cessé
cessât	cessassent	eût cessé	eussent cessé
		Impératif	
		cesse	
		cessons	
		cessez	

—Robert, cesse de parler, s'il te plaît! Tu es trop bavard dans cette classe.
—Oui, monsieur. Je cesse de parler. Je me tais.

une cesse   cease, ceasing
cesser de se voir   to stop seeing each other
cesser le feu   to cease fire

cesser de faire qqch   to stop doing
something

For **je me tais,** see **se taire.** See also **bavarder.**

changer   Part. pr. **changeant**   Part. passé **changé**

to change

The Seven Simple Tenses		The Seven Compound Tenses	
Singular	Plural	Singular	Plural
1 présent de l'indicatif		8 passé composé	
change	changeons	ai changé	avons changé
changes	changez	as changé	avez changé
change	changent	a changé	ont changé
2 imparfait de l'indicatif		9 plus-que-parfait de l'indicatif	
changeais	changions	avais changé	avions changé
changeais	changiez	avais changé	aviez changé
changeait	changeaient	avait changé	avaient changé
3 passé simple		10 passé antérieur	
changeai	changeâmes	eus changé	eûmes changé
changeas	changeâtes	eus changé	eûtes changé
changea	changèrent	eut changé	eurent changé
4 futur		11 futur antérieur	
changerai	changerons	aurai changé	aurons changé
changeras	changerez	auras changé	aurez changé
changera	changeront	aura changé	auront changé
5 conditionnel		12 conditionnel passé	
changerais	changerions	aurais changé	aurions changé
changerais	changeriez	aurais changé	auriez changé
changerait	changeraient	aurait changé	auraient changé
6 présent du subjonctif		13 passé du subjonctif	
change	changions	aie changé	ayons changé
changes	changiez	aies changé	ayez changé
change	changent	ait changé	aient changé
7 imparfait du subjonctif		14 plus-que-parfait du subjonctif	
changeasse	changeassions	eusse changé	eussions changé
changeasses	changeassiez	eusses changé	eussiez changé
changeât	changeassent	eût changé	eussent changé
		Impératif	
		change	
		changeons	
		changez	

    Je vais changer de vêtements maintenant parce que je prends le train pour Paris et là je vais changer de train pour aller à Marseille.

changer d'avis to change one's mind	**échanger** to exchange
changer de route to take another road	**Plus ça change, plus c'est la même chose!**
un changement soudain a sudden change	The more it changes, the more it remains the same!

to sing

The Seven Simple Tenses		The Seven Compound Tenses	
Singular	Plural	Singular	Plural
1 présent de l'indicatif		8 passé composé	
chante	chantons	ai chanté	avons chanté
chantes	chantez	as chanté	avez chanté
chante	chantent	a chanté	ont chanté
2 imparfait de l'indicatif		9 plus-que-parfait de l'indicatif	
chantais	chantions	avais chanté	avions chanté
chantais	chantiez	avais chanté	aviez chanté
chantait	chantaient	avait chanté	avaient chanté
3 passé simple		10 passé antérieur	
chantai	chantâmes	eus chanté	eûmes chanté
chantas	chantâtes	eus chanté	eûtes chanté
chanta	chantèrent	eut chanté	eurent chanté
4 futur		11 futur antérieur	
chanterai	chanterons	aurai chanté	aurons chanté
chanteras	chanterez	auras chanté	aurez chanté
chantera	chanteront	aura chanté	auront chanté
5 conditionnel		12 conditionnel passé	
chanterais	chanterions	aurais chanté	aurions chanté
chanterais	chanteriez	aurais chanté	auriez chanté
chanterait	chanteraient	aurait chanté	auraient chanté
6 présent du subjonctif		13 passé du subjonctif	
chante	chantions	aie chanté	ayons chanté
chantes	chantiez	aies chanté	ayez chanté
chante	chantent	ait chanté	aient chanté
7 imparfait du subjonctif		14 plus-que-parfait du subjonctif	
chantasse	chantassions	eusse chanté	eussions chanté
chantasses	chantassiez	eusses chanté	eussiez chanté
chantât	chantassent	eût chanté	eussent chanté

Impératif
chante
chantons
chantez

Madame Chanteclaire aime bien chanter en jouant du piano. Tous les matins elle chante dans la salle de bains et quelquefois elle chante quand elle dort. Elle donne des leçons de chant.

une chanson song	**chanson de geste** epic poem
chansons! fiddlesticks! nonsense!	**un chant** carol, chant, singing
C'est une autre chanson! That's another story!	**le chantage** blackmail
chanson d'amour love song	**chanteur, chanteuse** singer
Si ça vous chante . . . If you are in the mood for it . . .	**enchanter** to enchant

51

to burden, to charge, to load

The Seven Simple Tenses		The Seven Compound Tenses	
Singular	Plural	Singular	Plural
1 présent de l'indicatif		8 passé composé	
charge	chargeons	ai chargé	avons chargé
charges	chargez	as chargé	avez chargé
charge	chargent	a chargé	ont chargé
2 imparfait de l'indicatif		9 plus-que-parfait de l'indicatif	
chargeais	chargions	avais chargé	avions chargé
chargeais	chargiez	avais chargé	aviez chargé
chargeait	chargeaient	avait chargé	avaient chargé
3 passé simple		10 passé antérieur	
chargeai	chargeâmes	eus chargé	eûmes chargé
chargeas	chargeâtes	eus chargé	eûtes chargé
chargea	chargèrent	eut chargé	eurent chargé
4 futur		11 futur antérieur	
chargerai	chargerons	aurai chargé	aurons chargé
chargeras	chargerez	auras chargé	aurez chargé
chargera	chargeront	aura chargé	auront chargé
5 conditionnel		12 conditionnel passé	
chargerais	chargerions	aurais chargé	aurions chargé
chargerais	chargeriez	aurais chargé	auriez chargé
chargerait	chargeraient	aurait chargé	auraient chargé
6 présent du subjonctif		13 passé du subjonctif	
charge	chargions	aie chargé	ayons chargé
charges	chargiez	aies chargé	ayez chargé
charge	chargent	ait chargé	aient chargé
7 imparfait du subjonctif		14 plus-que-parfait du subjonctif	
chargeasse	chargeassions	eusse chargé	eussions chargé
chargeasses	chargeassiez	eusses chargé	eussiez chargé
chargeât	chargeassent	eût chargé	eussent chargé
		Impératif	
		charge	
		chargeons	
		chargez	

Je connais une dame qui charge son mari de paquets chaque fois qu'ils vont faire des emplettes. Une fois quand je les ai vus en ville, il a chargé sa femme de malédictions.

une charge a load, burden
chargé d'impôts heavily taxed
un chargé d'affaires envoy
Je m'en charge. I'll take care of it.

charger de malédictions to curse
charger de louanges to overwhelm with praises

to hunt, to pursue, to chase, to drive out

The Seven Simple Tenses		The Seven Compound Tenses	
Singular	Plural	Singular	Plural
1 présent de l'indicatif		8 passé composé	
chasse	chassons	ai chassé	avons chassé
chasses	chassez	as chassé	avez chassé
chasse	chassent	a chassé	ont chassé
2 imparfait de l'indicatif		9 plus-que-parfait de l'indicatif	
chassais	chassions	avais chassé	avions chassé
chassais	chassiez	avais chassé	aviez chassé
chassait	chassaient	avait chassé	avaient chassé
3 passé simple		10 passé antérieur	
chassai	chassâmes	eus chassé	eûmes chassé
chassas	chassâtes	eus chassé	eûtes chassé
chassa	chassèrent	eut chassé	eurent chassé
4 futur		11 futur antérieur	
chasserai	chasserons	aurai chassé	aurons chassé
chasseras	chasserez	auras chassé	aurez chassé
chassera	chasseront	aura chassé	auront chassé
5 conditionnel		12 conditionnel passé	
chasserais	chasserions	aurais chassé	aurions chassé
chasserais	chasseriez	aurais chassé	auriez chassé
chasserait	chasseraient	aurait chassé	auraient chassé
6 présent du subjonctif		13 passé du subjonctif	
chasse	chassions	aie chassé	ayons chassé
chasses	chassiez	aies chassé	ayez chassé
chasse	chassent	ait chassé	aient chassé
7 imparfait du subjonctif		14 plus-que-parfait du subjonctif	
chassasse	chassassions	eusse chassé	eussions chassé
chassasses	chassassiez	eusses chassé	eussiez chassé
chassât	chassassent	eût chassé	eussent chassé
		Impératif	
		chasse	
		chassons	
		chassez	

Avez-vous jamais chassé des papillons? Tout le monde aime chasser de temps en temps. Les chasseurs aiment chasser. Les chats aiment chasser les souris. Et les garçons aiment chasser les jolies jeunes filles.

Pronounce out loud this tongue twister as fast as you can:
Le chasseur, sachant chasser sans son chien, chassera.
(The hunter, knowing how to hunt without his dog, will hunt.)

Sachant is the pres. part. of **savoir**.

chercher	Part. pr. **cherchant**	Part. passé **cherché**

to look for, to search, to seek

The Seven Simple Tenses		The Seven Compound Tenses	
Singular	Plural	Singular	Plural
1 présent de l'indicatif		8 passé composé	
cherche	cherchons	ai cherché	avons cherché
cherches	cherchez	as cherché	avez cherché
cherche	cherchent	a cherché	ont cherché
2 imparfait de l'indicatif		9 plus-que-parfait de l'indicatif	
cherchais	cherchions	avais cherché	avions cherché
cherchais	cherchiez	avais cherché	aviez cherché
cherchait	cherchaient	avait cherché	avaient cherché
3 passé simple		10 passé antérieur	
cherchai	cherchâmes	eus cherché	eûmes cherché
cherchas	cherchâtes	eus cherché	eûtes cherché
chercha	cherchèrent	eut cherché	eurent cherché
4 futur		11 futur antérieur	
chercherai	chercherons	aurai cherché	aurons cherché
chercheras	chercherez	auras cherché	aurez cherché
cherchera	chercheront	aura cherché	auront cherché
5 conditionnel		12 conditionnel passé	
chercherais	chercherions	aurais cherché	aurions cherché
chercherais	chercheriez	aurais cherché	auriez cherché
chercherait	chercheraient	aurait cherché	auraient cherché
6 présent du subjonctif		13 passé du subjonctif	
cherche	cherchions	aie cherché	ayons cherché
cherches	cherchiez	aies cherché	ayez cherché
cherche	cherchent	ait cherché	aient cherché
7 imparfait du subjonctif		14 plus-que-parfait du subjonctif	
cherchasse	cherchassions	eusse cherché	eussions cherché
cherchasses	cherchassiez	eusses cherché	eussiez cherché
cherchât	cherchassent	eût cherché	eussent cherché

	Impératif	
cherche	cherchons	cherchez

—Monsieur, monsieur, j'ai perdu mon livre de français. J'ai cherché partout et je n'arrive pas à le trouver.
—Continue à chercher parce que demain je donnerai un examen.

se chercher to look for one another
chercheur seeker, investigator
aller chercher to go and get
chercher à to attempt to, to try to
aller chercher qqn ou qqch to go get someone or something

rechercher to investigate, to seek, to look for again
faire des travaux de recherches to carry out research work
envoyer chercher to send for

to choose, to select, to pick

The Seven Simple Tenses		The Seven Compound Tenses	
Singular	Plural	Singular	Plural
1 présent de l'indicatif		8 passé composé	
choisis	choisissons	ai choisi	avons choisi
choisis	choisissez	as choisi	avez choisi
choisit	choisissent	a choisi	ont choisi
2 imparfait de l'indicatif		9 plus-que-parfait de l'indicatif	
choisissais	choisissions	avais choisi	avions choisi
choisissais	choisissiez	avais choisi	aviez choisi
choisissait	choisissaient	avait choisi	avaient choisi
3 passé simple		10 passé antérieur	
choisis	choisîmes	eus choisi	eûmes choisi
choisis	choisîtes	eus choisi	eûtes choisi
choisit	choisirent	eut choisi	eurent choisi
4 futur		11 futur antérieur	
choisirai	choisirons	aurai choisi	aurons choisi
choisiras	choisirez	auras choisi	aurez choisi
choisira	choisiront	aura choisi	auront choisi
5 conditionnel		12 conditionnel passé	
choisirais	choisirions	aurais choisi	aurions choisi
choisirais	choisiriez	aurais choisi	auriez choisi
choisirait	choisiraient	aurait choisi	auraient choisi
6 présent du subjonctif		13 passé du subjonctif	
choisisse	choisissions	aie choisi	ayons choisi
choisisses	choisissiez	aies choisi	ayez choisi
choisisse	choisissent	ait choisi	aient choisi
7 imparfait du subjonctif		14 plus-que-parfait du subjonctif	
choisisse	choisissions	eusse choisi	eussions choisi
choisisses	choisissiez	eusses choisi	eussiez choisi
choisît	choisissent	eût choisi	eussent choisi
		Impératif	
		choisis	
		choisissons	
		choisissez	

Hier soir j'ai dîné dans un restaurant français avec des amis. J'ai choisi du poisson. Raymond a choisi de la viande et Joseph a choisi une omelette.

un choix choice	**Il faut savoir choisir ses amis.** You must
faire choix de to make choice of	know how to choose your friends.
l'embarras du choix too much to	**Il n'y a pas grand choix.** There's not
choose from	much choice.

to command, to order

The Seven Simple Tenses		The Seven Compound Tenses	
Singular	Plural	Singular	Plural
1 présent de l'indicatif		8 passé composé	
commande	commandons	ai commandé	avons commandé
commandes	commandez	as commandé	avez commandé
commande	commandent	a commandé	ont commandé
2 imparfait de l'indicatif		9 plus-que-parfait de l'indicatif	
commandais	commandions	avais commandé	avions commandé
commandais	commandiez	avais commandé	aviez commandé
commandait	commandaient	avait commandé	avaient commandé
3 passé simple		10 passé antérieur	
commandai	commandâmes	eus commandé	eûmes commandé
commandas	commandâtes	eus commandé	eûtes commandé
commanda	commandèrent	eut commandé	eurent commandé
4 futur		11 futur antérieur	
commanderai	commanderons	aurai commandé	aurons commandé
commanderas	commanderez	auras commandé	aurez commandé
commandera	commanderont	aura commandé	auront commandé
5 conditionnel		12 conditionnel passé	
commanderais	commanderions	aurais commandé	aurions commandé
commanderais	commanderiez	aurais commandé	auriez commandé
commanderait	commanderaient	aurait commandé	auraient commandé
6 présent du subjonctif		13 passé du subjonctif	
commande	commandions	aie commandé	ayons commandé
commandes	commandiez	aies commandé	ayez commandé
commande	commandent	ait commandé	aient commandé
7 imparfait du subjonctif		14 plus-que-parfait du subjonctif	
commandasse	commandassions	eusse commandé	eussions commandé
commandasses	commandassiez	eusses commandé	eussiez commandé
commandât	commandassent	eût commandé	eussent commandé

Impératif
commande
commandons
commandez

Hier soir mes amis et moi avons dîné dans un restaurant chinois. Nous avons commandé beaucoup de choses intéressantes.

un commandant   commanding officer
une commande   an order
commander à qqn de faire qqch   to order someone to do something
recommander   to recommend; **recommander à qqn de faire qqch**   to advise
   someone to do something
décommander un rendez-vous   to cancel a date, an appointment

Part pr. **commençant** Part. passé **commencé** **commencer**

to begin, to start, to commence

The Seven Simple Tenses		The Seven Compound Tenses	
Singular	Plural	Singular	Plural
1 présent de l'indicatif		8 passé composé	
commence	commençons	ai commencé	avons commencé
commences	commencez	as commencé	avez commencé
commence	commencent	a commencé	ont commencé
2 imparfait de l'indicatif		9 plus-que-parfait de l'indicatif	
commençais	commencions	avais commencé	avions commencé
commençais	commenciez	avais commencé	aviez commencé
commençait	commençaient	avait commencé	avaient commencé
3 passé simple		10 passé antérieur	
commençai	commençâmes	eus commencé	eûmes commencé
commenças	commençâtes	eus commencé	eûtes commencé
commença	commencèrent	eut commencé	eurent commencé
4 futur		11 futur antérieur	
commencerai	commencerons	aurai commencé	aurons commencé
commenceras	commencerez	auras commencé	aurez commencé
commencera	commenceront	aura commencé	auront commencé
5 conditionnel		12 conditionnel passé	
commencerais	commencerions	aurais commencé	aurions commencé
commencerais	commenceriez	aurais commencé	auriez commencé
commencerait	commenceraient	aurait commencé	auraient commencé
6 présent du subjonctif		13 passé du subjonctif	
commence	commencions	aie commencé	ayons commencé
commences	commenciez	aies commencé	ayez commencé
commence	commencent	ait commencé	aient commencé
7 imparfait du subjonctif		14 plus-que-parfait du subjonctif	
commençasse	commençassions	eusse commencé	eussions commencé
commençasses	commençassiez	eusses commencé	eussiez commencé
commençât	commençassent	eût commencé	eussent commencé

Impératif
commence   commençons   commencez

—Alexandre, as-tu commencé tes devoirs pour la classe de français?
—Non, maman, pas encore. Je vais faire une promenade maintenant.
—Tu ne vas pas faire une promenade parce qu'il commence à pleuvoir.
—Commence à faire tes devoirs tout de suite!

commencer à + inf.   to begin + inf.   pour commencer   to begin with
le commencement   the beginning   commencer par   to begin by
au commencement   in the beginning   recommencer à   to begin again + inf.
du commencement à la fin   from
  beginning to end

57

comprendre   Part. pr. **comprenant**   Part. passé **compris**

to understand

The Seven Simple Tenses		The Seven Compound Tenses	
Singular	Plural	Singular	Plural
1 présent de l'indicatif		8 passé composé	
comprends	**comprenons**	**ai compris**	**avons compris**
comprends	**comprenez**	**as compris**	**avez compris**
comprend	**comprennent**	**a compris**	**ont compris**
2 imparfait de l'indicatif		9 plus-que-parfait de l'indicatif	
comprenais	**comprenions**	**avais compris**	**avions compris**
comprenais	**compreniez**	**avais compris**	**aviez compris**
comprenait	**comprenaient**	**avait compris**	**avaient compris**
3 passé simple		10 passé antérieur	
compris	**comprîmes**	**eus compris**	**eûmes compris**
compris	**comprîtes**	**eus compris**	**eûtes compris**
comprit	**comprirent**	**eut compris**	**eurent compris**
4 futur		11 futur antérieur	
comprendrai	**comprendrons**	**aurai compris**	**aurons compris**
comprendras	**comprendrez**	**auras compris**	**aurez compris**
comprendra	**comprendront**	**aura compris**	**auront compris**
5 conditionnel		12 conditionnel passé	
comprendrais	**comprendrions**	**aurais compris**	**aurions compris**
comprendrais	**comprendriez**	**aurais compris**	**auriez compris**
comprendrait	**comprendraient**	**aurait compris**	**auraient compris**
6 présent du subjonctif		13 passé du subjonctif	
comprenne	**comprenions**	**aie compris**	**ayons compris**
comprennes	**compreniez**	**aies compris**	**ayez compris**
comprenne	**comprennent**	**ait compris**	**aient compris**
7 imparfait du subjonctif		14 plus-que-parfait du subjonctif	
comprisse	**comprissions**	**eusse compris**	**eussions compris**
comprisses	**comprissiez**	**eusses compris**	**eussiez compris**
comprît	**comprissent**	**eût compris**	**eussent compris**
		Impératif	
		comprends	
		comprenons	
		comprenez	

Je ne comprends jamais la prof de biologie. Je n'ai pas compris la leçon d'hier, je ne comprends pas la leçon d'aujourd'hui, et je ne comprendrai jamais rien.

faire comprendre à qqn que . . . to make it clear to someone that . . .
la compréhension comprehension, understanding
Ça se comprend. Of course; That is understood.
y compris included, including

to count, to intend, to expect to

The Seven Simple Tenses		The Seven Compound Tenses	
Singular	Plural	Singular	Plural
1 présent de l'indicatif		8 passé composé	
compte	comptons	ai compté	avons compté
comptes	comptez	as compté	avez compté
compte	comptent	a compté	ont compté
2 imparfait de l'indicatif		9 plus-que-parfait de l'indicatif	
comptais	comptions	avais compté	avions compté
comptais	comptiez	avais compté	aviez compté
comptait	comptaient	avait compté	avaient compté
3 passé simple		10 passé antérieur	
comptai	comptâmes	eus compté	eûmes compté
comptas	comptâtes	eus compté	eûtes compté
compta	comptèrent	eut compté	eurent compté
4 futur		11 futur antérieur	
compterai	compterons	aurai compté	aurons compté
compteras	compterez	auras compté	aurez compté
comptera	compteront	aura compté	auront compté
5 conditionnel		12 conditionnel passé	
compterais	compterions	aurais compté	aurions compté
compterais	compteriez	aurais compté	auriez compté
compterait	compteraient	aurait compté	auraient compté
6 présent du subjonctif		13 passé du subjonctif	
compte	comptions	aie compté	ayons compté
comptes	comptiez	aies compté	ayez compté
compte	comptent	ait compté	aient compté
7 imparfait du subjonctif		14 plus-que-parfait du subjonctif	
comptasse	comptassions	eusse compté	eussions compté
comptasses	comptassiez	eusses compté	eussiez compté
comptât	comptassent	eût compté	eussent compté

Impératif
compte
comptons
comptez

**Je compte aller en France l'été prochain avec ma femme pour voir nos amis
français.**

la comptabilité bookkeeping	**compter sur** to count (rely) on; **Puis-je y**
comptable accountable	**compter?** Can I depend on it?
le comptage accounting	**escompter** to discount; **un escompte** discount
payer comptant to pay cash	**donner sans compter** to give generously
compter faire qqch to expect	**sans compter . . .** say nothing of
to do something	**le comptoir** counter (in a store)

to lead, to drive, to conduct, to manage

The Seven Simple Tenses		The Seven Compound Tenses	
Singular	Plural	Singular	Plural
1 présent de l'indicatif		8 passé composé	
conduis	conduisons	ai conduit	avons conduit
conduis	conduisez	as conduit	avez conduit
conduit	conduisent	a conduit	ont conduit
2 imparfait de l'indicatif		9 plus-que-parfait de l'indicatif	
conduisais	conduisions	avais conduit	avions conduit
conduisais	conduisiez	avais conduit	aviez conduit
conduisait	conduisaient	avait conduit	avaient conduit
3 passé simple		10 passé antérieur	
conduisis	conduisîmes	eus conduit	eûmes conduit
conduisis	conduisîtes	eus conduit	eûtes conduit
conduisit	conduisirent	eut conduit	eurent conduit
4 futur		11 futur antérieur	
conduirai	conduirons	aurai conduit	aurons conduit
conduiras	conduirez	auras conduit	aurez conduit
conduira	conduiront	aura conduit	auront conduit
5 conditionnel		12 conditionnel passé	
conduirais	conduirions	aurais conduit	aurions conduit
conduirais	conduiriez	aurais conduit	auriez conduit
conduirait	conduiraient	aurait conduit	auraient conduit
6 présent du subjonctif		13 passé du subjonctif	
conduise	conduisions	aie conduit	ayons conduit
conduises	conduisiez	aies conduit	ayez conduit
conduise	conduisent	ait conduit	aient conduit
7 imparfait du subjonctif		14 plus-que-parfait du subjonctif	
conduisisse	conduisissions	eusse conduit	eussions conduit
conduisisses	conduisissiez	eusses conduit	eussiez conduit
conduisît	conduisissent	eût conduit	eussent conduit

	Impératif	
conduis	conduisons	conduisez

—Savez-vous conduire?
—Oui, je sais conduire. Je conduis une voiture, je dirige un orchestre, et hier j'ai conduit quelqu'un à la gare. Attendez, je vais vous conduire à la porte.
—Merci. Vous êtes très aimable.

un conducteur, une conductrice driver   conduire une voiture to drive a car
la conduite conduct, behavior   se conduire to conduct (behave)
induire to induce   oneself
induire en to lead into

See also **introduire, produire,** and **traduire.**

to know, to be acquainted with, to make the acquaintance of

The Seven Simple Tenses		The Seven Compound Tenses	
Singular	Plural	Singular	Plural
1 présent de l'indicatif		8 passé composé	
connais	connaissons	ai connu	avons connu
connais	connaissez	as connu	avez connu
connaît	connaissent	a connu	ont connu
2 imparfait de l'indicatif		9 plus-que-parfait de l'indicatif	
connaissais	connaissions	avais connu	avions connu
connaissais	connaissiez	avais connu	aviez connu
connaissait	connaissaient	avait connu	avaient connu
3 passé simple		10 passé antérieur	
connus	connûmes	eus connu	eûmes connu
connus	connûtes	eus connu	eûtes connu
connut	connurent	eut connu	eurent connu
4 futur		11 futur antérieur	
connaîtrai	connaîtrons	aurai connu	aurons connu
connaîtras	connaîtrez	auras connu	aurez connu
connaîtra	connaîtront	aura connu	auront connu
5 conditionnel		12 conditionnel passé	
connaîtrais	connaîtrions	aurais connu	aurions connu
connaîtrais	connaîtriez	aurais connu	auriez connu
connaîtrait	connaîtraient	aurait connu	auraient connu
6 présent du subjonctif		13 passé du subjonctif	
connaisse	connaissions	aie connu	ayons connu
connaisses	connaissiez	aies connu	ayez connu
connaisse	connaissent	ait connu	aient connu
7 imparfait du subjonctif		14 plus-que-parfait du subjonctif	
connusse	connussions	eusse connu	eussions connu
connusses	connussiez	eusses connu	eussiez connu
connût	connussent	eût connu	eussent connu

Impératif
connais
connaissons
connaissez

—Connaissez-vous quelqu'un qui puisse m'aider? Je suis touriste et je ne connais pas cette ville.
—Non, je ne connais personne. Je suis touriste aussi.
—Voulez-vous aller prendre un café? Nous pouvons faire connaissance.

la **connaissance**   knowledge, understanding, acquaintance
connaisseur, connaisseuse   expert
se **connaître**   to know each other, to know oneself
faire connaissance   to get acquainted

61

construire	Part. pr. **construisant**	Part. passé **construit**

to construct, to build

The Seven Simple Tenses		The Seven Compound Tenses	
Singular	Plural	Singular	Plural
1 présent de l'indicatif		8 passé composé	
construis	construisons	ai construit	avons construit
construis	construisez	as construit	avez construit
construit	construisent	a construit	ont construit
2 imparfait de l'indicatif		9 plus-que-parfait de l'indicatif	
construisais	construisions	avais construit	avions construit
construisais	construisiez	avais construit	aviez construit
construisait	construisaient	avait construit	avaient construit
3 passé simple		10 passé antérieur	
construisis	construisîmes	eus construit	eûmes construit
construisis	construisîtes	eus construit	eûtes construit
construisit	construisirent	eut construit	eurent construit
4 futur		11 futur antérieur	
construirai	construirons	aurai construit	aurons construit
construiras	construirez	auras construit	aurez construit
construira	construiront	aura construit	auront construit
5 conditionnel		12 conditionnel passé	
construirais	construirions	aurais construit	aurions construit
construirais	construiriez	aurais construit	auriez construit
construirait	construiraient	aurait construit	auraient construit
6 présent du subjonctif		13 passé du subjonctif	
construise	construisions	aie construit	ayons construit
construises	construisiez	aies construit	ayez construit
construise	construisent	ait construit	aient construit
7 imparfait du subjonctif		14 plus-que-parfait du subjonctif	
construisisse	construisissions	eusse construit	eussions construit
construisisses	construisissiez	eusses construit	eussiez construit
construisît	construisissent	eût construit	eussent construit

Impératif
construis
construisons
construisez

—Je vois que vous êtes en train de construire quelque chose. Qu'est-ce que vous construisez?

—Je construis une tour comme la Tour Eiffel. Aimez-vous ce bateau que j'ai construit?

un constructeur a manufacturer, builder, constructor
une construction construction, building
reconstruire to reconstruct, to rebuild

to relate, to narrate

The Seven Simple Tenses		The Seven Compound Tenses	
Singular	Plural	Singular	Plural
1 présent de l'indicatif		8 passé composé	
conte	contons	ai conté	avons conté
contes	contez	as conté	avez conté
conte	content	a conté	ont conté
2 imparfait de l'indicatif		9 plus-que-parfait de l'indicatif	
contais	contions	avais conté	avions conté
contais	contiez	avais conté	aviez conté
contait	contaient	avait conté	avaient conté
3 passé simple		10 passé antérieur	
contai	contâmes	eus conté	eûmes conté
contas	contâtes	eus conté	eûtes conté
conta	contèrent	eut conté	eurent conté
4 futur		11 futur antérieur	
conterai	conterons	aurai conté	aurons conté
conteras	conterez	auras conté	aurez conté
contera	conteront	aura conté	auront conté
5 conditionnel		12 conditionnel passé	
conterais	conterions	aurais conté	aurions conté
conterais	conteriez	aurais conté	auriez conté
conterait	conteraient	aurait conté	auraient conté
6 présent du subjonctif		13 passé du subjonctif	
conte	contions	aie conté	ayons conté
contes	contiez	aies conté	ayez conté
conte	content	ait conté	aient conté
7 imparfait du subjonctif		14 plus-que-parfait du subjonctif	
contasse	contassions	eusse conté	eussions conté
contasses	contassiez	eusses conté	eussiez conté
contât	contassent	eût conté	eussent conté

	Impératif
	conte
	contons
	contez

**Notre professeur de français nous conte toujours des histoires intéressantes.
Son conte favori est *Un coeur simple* de Flaubert.**

un conte   a story, tale
un conte de fées   fairy tale
un conte à dormir debout   cock-and-bull story
un conteur, une conteuse   writer of short stories

See also **raconter.**

continuer   Part. pr. **continuant**   Part. passé **continué**

to continue

The Seven Simple Tenses		The Seven Compound Tenses	
Singular	Plural	Singular	Plural
1 présent de l'indicatif		8 passé composé	
continue	continuons	ai continué	avons continué
continues	continuez	as continué	avez continué
continue	continuent	a continué	ont continué
2 imparfait de l'indicatif		9 plus-que-parfait de l'indicatif	
continuais	continuions	avais continué	avions continué
continuais	continuiez	avais continué	aviez continué
continuait	continuaient	avait continué	avaient continué
3 passé simple		10 passé antérieur	
continuai	continuâmes	eus continué	eûmes continué
continuas	continuâtes	eus continué	eûtes continué
continua	continuèrent	eut continué	eurent continué
4 futur		11 futur antérieur	
continuerai	continuerons	aurai continué	aurons continué
continueras	continuerez	auras continué	aurez continué
continuera	continueront	aura continué	auront continué
5 conditionnel		12 conditionnel passé	
continuerais	continuerions	aurais continué	aurions continué
continuerais	continueriez	aurais continué	auriez continué
continuerait	continueraient	aurait continué	auraient continué
6 présent du subjonctif		13 passé du subjonctif	
continue	continuions	aie continué	ayons continué
continues	continuiez	aies continué	ayez continué
continue	continuent	ait continué	aient continué
7 imparfait du subjonctif		14 plus-que-parfait du subjonctif	
continuasse	continuassions	eusse continué	eussions continué
continuasses	continuassiez	eusses continué	eussiez continué
continuât	continuassent	eût continué	eussent continué
		Impératif	
		continue	
		continuons	
		continuez	

—Allez-vous continuer à étudier le français l'année prochaine?
—Certainement. Je compte étudier cette belle langue continuellement.

la continuation continuation	**continuer à + inf.** to continue + inf.
continuel, continuelle continual	**continuer de + inf.** to continue (persist) in
continuellement continually	**Cet ivrogne continue de boire.** This
	drunkard persists in drinking (habit).

to correct

The Seven Simple Tenses		The Seven Compound Tenses	
Singular	Plural	Singular	Plural
1 présent de l'indicatif		8 passé composé	
corrige	corrigeons	ai corrigé	avons corrigé
corriges	corrigez	as corrigé	avez corrigé
corrige	corrigent	a corrigé	ont corrigé
2 imparfait de l'indicatif		9 plus-que-parfait de l'indicatif	
corrigeais	corrigions	avais corrigé	avions corrigé
corrigeais	corrigiez	avais corrigé	aviez corrigé
corrigeait	corrigeaient	avait corrigé	avaient corrigé
3 passé simple		10 passé antérieur	
corrigeai	corrigeâmes	eus corrigé	eûmes corrigé
corrigeas	corrigeâtes	eus corrigé	eûtes corrigé
corrigea	corrigèrent	eut corrigé	eurent corrigé
4 futur		11 futur antérieur	
corrigerai	corrigerons	aurai corrigé	aurons corrigé
corrigeras	corrigerez	auras corrigé	aurez corrigé
corrigera	corrigeront	aura corrigé	auront corrigé
5 conditionnel		12 conditionnel passé	
corrigerais	corrigerions	aurais corrigé	aurions corrigé
corrigerais	corrigeriez	aurais corrigé	auriez corrigé
corrigerait	corrigeraient	aurait corrigé	auraient corrigé
6 présent du subjonctif		13 passé du subjonctif	
corrige	corrigions	aie corrigé	ayons corrigé
corriges	corrigiez	aies corrigé	ayez corrigé
corrige	corrigent	ait corrigé	aient corrigé
7 imparfait du subjonctif		14 plus-que-parfait du subjonctif	
corrigeasse	corrigeassions	eusse corrigé	eussions corrigé
corrigeasses	corrigeassiez	eusses corrigé	eussiez corrigé
corrigeât	corrigeassent	eût corrigé	eussent corrigé
		Impératif	
		corrige	
		corrigeons	
		corrigez	

Dans la classe de français nous corrigeons toujours nos devoirs en classe. La prof de français écrit les corrections au tableau.

une correction correction; **recorriger** to correct again
corriger qqn de to correct someone of
se corriger de to correct one's ways
corrigible corrigible; **incorrigible** incorrigible
incorrectement inaccurately, incorrectly

se coucher Part. pr. **se couchant** Part. passé **couché(e)(s)**

to go to bed, to lie down

The Seven Simple Tenses		The Seven Compound Tenses	
Singular	Plural	Singular	Plural
1 présent de l'indicatif		8 passé composé	
me couche	nous couchons	me suis couché(e)	nous sommes couché(e)s
te couches	vous couchez	t'es couché(e)	vous êtes couché(e)(s)
se couche	se couchent	s'est couché(e)	se sont couché(e)s
2 imparfait de l'indicatif		9 plus-que-parfait de l'indicatif	
me couchais	nous couchions	m'étais couché(e)	nous étions couché(e)s
te couchais	vous conchiez	t'étais couché(e)	vous étiez couché(e)(s)
se couchait	se couchaient	s'était couché(e)	s'étaient couché(e)s
3 passé simple		10 passé antérieur	
me couchai	nous couchâmes	me fus couché(e)	nous fûmes couché(e)s
te couchas	vous couchâtes	te fus couché(e)	vous fûtes couché(e)(s)
se coucha	se couchèrent	se fut couché(e)	se furent couché(e)s
4 futur		11 futur antérieur	
me coucherai	nous coucherons	me serai couché(e)	nous serons couché(e)s
te coucheras	vous coucherez	te seras couché(e)	vous serez couché(e)(s)
se couchera	se coucheront	se sera couché(e)	se seront couché(e)s
5 conditionnel		12 conditionnel passé	
me coucherais	nous coucherions	me serais couché(e)	nous serions couché(e)s
te coucherais	vous coucheriez	te serais couché(e)	vous seriez couché(e)(s)
se coucherait	se coucheraient	se serait couché(e)	se seraient couché(e)s
6 présent du subjonctif		13 passé du subjonctif	
me couche	nous couchions	me sois couché(e)	nous soyons couché(e)s
te couches	vous couchiez	te sois couché(e)	vous soyez couché(e)(s)
se couche	se couchent	se soit couché(e)	se soient couché(e)s
7 imparfait du subjonctif		14 plus-que-parfait du subjonctif	
me couchasse	nous couchassions	me fusse couché(e)	nous fussions couché(e)s
te couchasses	vous couchassiez	te fusses couché(e)	vous fussiez couché(e)(s)
se couchât	se couchassent	se fût couché(e)	se fussent couché(e)s

Impératif
couche-toi; ne te couche pas
couchons-nous; ne nous couchons pas
couchez-vous; ne vous couchez pas

—Couche-toi, Hélène! Il est minuit. Hier soir tu t'es couchée tard.
—Donne-moi ma poupée pour nous coucher ensemble.

le coucher du soleil sunset	**se recoucher** to go back to bed
une couche a layer	**se coucher tôt** to go to bed early
une couchette bunk, cot	**Comme on fait son lit on se couche!**
Le soleil se couche. The sun is setting.	You've made your bed; now lie in it!

to cut, to switch off

The Seven Simple Tenses		The Seven Compound Tenses	
Singular	Plural	Singular	Plural
1 présent de l'indicatif		8 passé composé	
coupe	coupons	ai coupé	avons coupé
coupes	coupez	as coupé	avez coupé
coupe	coupent	a coupé	ont coupé
2 imparfait de l'indicatif		9 plus-que-parfait de l'indicatif	
coupais	coupions	avais coupé	avions coupé
coupais	coupiez	avais coupé	aviez coupé
coupait	coupaient	avait coupé	avaient coupé
3 passé simple		10 passé antérieur	
coupai	coupâmes	eus coupé	eûmes coupé
coupas	coupâtes	eus coupé	eûtes coupé
coupa	coupèrent	eut coupé	eurent coupé
4 futur		11 futur antérieur	
couperai	couperons	aurai coupé	aurons coupé
couperas	couperez	auras coupé	aurez coupé
coupera	couperont	aura coupé	auront coupé
5 conditionnel		12 conditionnel passé	
couperais	couperions	aurais coupé	aurions coupé
couperais	couperiez	aurais coupé	auriez coupé
couperait	couperaient	aurait coupé	auraient coupé
6 présent du subjonctif		13 passé du subjonctif	
coupe	coupions	aie coupé	ayons coupé
coupes	coupiez	aies coupé	ayez coupé
coupe	coupent	ait coupé	aient coupé
7 imparfait du subjonctif		14 plus-que-parfait du subjonctif	
coupasse	coupassions	eusse coupé	eussions coupé
coupasses	coupassiez	eusses coupé	eussiez coupé
coupât	coupassent	eût coupé	eussent coupé

Impératif
coupe
coupons
coupez

Ce morceau de pain est trop grand. Je vais le couper en deux.

un coupon coupon	**découper** to cut out
une coupure cut, gash, crack	**entrecouper** to interrupt
couper les cheveux en quatre to split hairs	**couper la fièvre** to reduce a fever
se faire couper les cheveux to have one's hair cut	**une coupe de cheveux** haircut **une coupe au rasoir** razor cut
une coupe goblet	**une coupe croisée** crosscut
la coupe de France de football French football cup	

to run, to race

The Seven Simple Tenses		The Seven Compound Tenses	
Singular	Plural	Singular	Plural
1 présent de l'indicatif		8 passé composé	
cours	courons	ai couru	avons couru
cours	courez	as couru	avez couru
court	courent	a couru	ont couru
2 imparfait de l'indicatif		9 plus-que-parfait de l'indicatif	
courais	courions	avais couru	avions couru
courais	couriez	avais couru	aviez couru
courait	couraient	avait couru	avaient couru
3 passé simple		10 passé antérieur	
courus	courûmes	eus couru	eûmes couru
courus	courûtes	eus couru	eûtes couru
courut	coururent	eut couru	eurent couru
4 futur		11 futur antérieur	
courrai	courrons	aurai couru	aurons couru
courras	courrez	auras couru	aurez couru
courra	courront	aura couru	auront couru
5 conditionnel		12 conditionnel passé	
courrais	courrions	aurais couru	aurions couru
courrais	courriez	aurais couru	auriez couru
courrait	courraient	aurait couru	auraient couru
6 présent du subjonctif		13 passé du subjonctif	
coure	courions	aie couru	ayons couru
coures	couriez	aies couru	ayez couru
coure	courent	ait couru	aient couru
7 imparfait du subjonctif		14 plus-que-parfait du subjonctif	
courusse	courussions	eusse couru	eussions couru
courusses	courussiez	eusses couru	eussiez couru
courût	courussent	eût couru	eussent couru
		Impératif	
		cours	
		courons	
		courez	

Les enfants sont toujours prêts à courir. Quand on est jeune on court sans se fatiguer. Michel a couru de la maison jusqu'à l'école. Il a seize ans.

le courrier courier, messenger, mail	**accourir vers** to come running toward
un coureur runner	**courir les rues** to run about the streets
faire courir un bruit to spread a rumor	**par le temps qui court** these days,
courir une course to run a race	nowadays
courir le monde to roam all over the world	**parcourir** to go through, to travel through, to cover (distance)

68

to cost

The Seven Simple Tenses		The Seven Compound Tenses	
Singular	Plural	Singular	Plural
1 présent de l'indicatif		8 passé composé	
il coûte	**ils coûtent**	**il a coûté**	**ils ont coûté**
2 imparfait de l'indicatif		9 plus-que-parfait de l'indicatif	
il coûtait	**ils coûtaient**	**il avait coûté**	**ils avaient coûté**
3 passé simple		10 passé antérieur	
il coûta	**ils coûtèrent**	**il eut coûté**	**ils eurent coûté**
4 futur		11 futur antérieur	
il coûtera	**ils coûteront**	**il aura coûté**	**ils auront coûté**
5 conditionnel		12 conditionnel passé	
il coûterait	**ils coûteraient**	**il aurait coûté**	**ils auraient coûté**
6 présent du subjonctif		13 passé du subjonctif	
qu'il coûte	**qu'ils coûtent**	**qu'il ait coûté**	**qu'ils aient coûté**
7 imparfait du subjonctif		14 plus-que-parfait du subjonctif	
qu'il coûtât	**qu'ils coûtassent**	**qu'il eût coûté**	**qu'ils eussent coûté**

Impératif
—

—Combien coûte cette table?
—Elle coûte dix mille francs.
—Et combien coûte ce lit?
—Il coûte dix mille francs aussi.
—Ils coûtent joliment cher!

coûteusement   expensively, dearly
coûte que coûte   at any cost
coûteux, coûteuse   costly, expensive
Cela coûte joliment cher.   That costs a pretty penny.
coûter cher, coûter peu   to be expensive, inexpensive
coûter à qqn   to cost someone;
  Cela lui en a coûté la vie.   That cost him his life.

This verb is generally regarded as impersonal and is used primarily in the third person singular and plural.

couvrir   Part. pr. **couvrant**   Part. passé **couvert**

to cover

The Seven Simple Tenses		The Seven Compound Tenses	
Singular	Plural	Singular	Plural
1 présent de l'indicatif		8 passé composé	
couvre	couvrons	ai couvert	avons couvert
couvres	couvrez	as couvert	avez couvert
couvre	couvrent	a couvert	ont couvert
2 imparfait de l'indicatif		9 plus-que-parfait de l'indicatif	
couvrais	couvrions	avais couvert	avions couvert
couvrais	couvriez	avais couvert	aviez couvert
couvrait	couvraient	avait couvert	avaient couvert
3 passé simple		10 passé antérieur	
couvris	couvrîmes	eus couvert	eûmes couvert
couvris	couvrîtes	eus couvert	eûtes couvert
couvrit	couvrirent	eut couvert	eurent couvert
4 futur		11 futur antérieur	
couvrirai	couvrirons	aurai couvert	aurons couvert
couvriras	couvrirez	auras couvert	aurez couvert
couvrira	couvriront	aura couvert	auront couvert
5 conditionnel		12 conditionnel passé	
couvrirais	couvririons	aurais couvert	aurions couvert
couvrirais	couvririez	aurais couvert	auriez couvert
couvrirait	couvriraient	aurait couvert	auraient couvert
6 présent du subjonctif		13 passé du subjonctif	
couvre	couvrions	aie couvert	ayons couvert
couvres	couvriez	aies couvert	ayez couvert
couvre	couvrent	ait couvert	aient couvert
7 imparfait du subjonctif		14 plus-que-parfait du subjonctif	
couvrisse	couvrissions	eusse couvert	eussions couvert
couvrisses	couvrissiez	eusses couvert	eussiez couvert
couvrît	couvrissent	eût couvert	eussent couvert

Impératif
couvre
couvrons
couvrez

Avant de quitter la maison, Madame Champlain a couvert le lit d'un dessus-de-lit. Puis, elle a couvert son mari de caresses et de baisers.

un couvert place setting (spoon, knife, fork, *etc.*)
acheter des couverts to buy cutlery
mettre le couvert to lay the table
une couverture blanket
Le temps se couvre. The sky is overcast.

découvrir to discover, disclose, uncover
se couvrir to cover oneself, to put on one's hat
le couvre-feu curfew
un couvre-lit bedspread (**des couvre-lits**)
un dessus-de-lit bedspread (**des dessus-de-lits**)

70   See also **découvrir.**

to fear, to be afraid

The Seven Simple Tenses		The Seven Compound Tenses	
Singular	Plural	Singular	Plural
1 présent de l'indicatif		8 passé composé	
crains	craignons	ai craint	avons craint
crains	craignez	as craint	avez craint
craint	craignent	a craint	ont craint
2 imparfait de l'indicatif		9 plus-que-parfait de l'indicatif	
craignais	craignions	avais craint	avions craint
craignais	craigniez	avais craint	aviez craint
craignait	craignaient	avait craint	avaient craint
3 passé simple		10 passé antérieur	
craignis	craignîmes	eus craint	eûmes craint
craignis	craignîtes	eus craint	eûtes craint
craignit	craignirent	eut craint	eurent craint
4 futur		11 futur antérieur	
craindrai	craindrons	aurai craint	aurons craint
craindras	craindrez	auras craint	aurez craint
craindra	craindront	aura craint	auront craint
5 conditionnel		12 conditionnel passé	
craindrais	craindrions	aurais craint	aurions craint
craindrais	craindriez	aurais craint	auriez craint
craindrait	craindraient	aurait craint	auraient craint
6 présent du subjonctif		13 passé du subjonctif	
craigne	craignions	aie craint	ayons craint
craignes	craigniez	aies craint	ayez craint
craigne	craignent	ait craint	aient craint
7 imparfait du subjonctif		14 plus-que-parfait du subjonctif	
craignisse	craignissions	eusse craint	eussions craint
craignisses	craignissiez	eusses craint	eussiez craint
craignît	craignissent	eût craint	eussent craint
		Impératif	
		crains	
		craignons	
		craignez	

Le petit garçon craint de traverser le parc pendant la nuit. Il a raison parce que c'est dangereux. Il a des craintes.

une crainte fear, dread	craintif, craintive fearful
craindre pour sa vie to be in fear of one's life	craintivement fearfully
sans crainte fearless	

crier	Part. pr. **criant**	Part. passé **crié**

to shout, to cry out

The Seven Simple Tenses		The Seven Compound Tenses	
Singular	Plural	Singular	Plural
1 présent de l'indicatif		8 passé composé	
crie	crions	ai crié	avons crié
cries	criez	as crié	avez crié
crie	crient	a crié	ont crié
2 imparfait de l'indicatif		9 plus-que-parfait de l'indicatif	
criais	criions	avais crié	avions crié
criais	criiez	avais crié	aviez crié
criait	criaient	avait crié	avaient crié
3 passé simple		10 passé antérieur	
criai	criâmes	eus crié	eûmes crié
crias	criâtes	eus crié	eûtes crié
cria	crièrent	eut crié	eurent crié
4 futur		11 futur antérieur	
crierai	crierons	aurai crié	aurons crié
crieras	crierez	auras crié	aurez crié
criera	crieront	aura crié	auront crié
5 conditionnel		12 conditionnel passé	
crierais	crierions	aurais crié	aurions crié
crierais	crieriez	aurais crié	auriez crié
crierait	crieraient	aurait crié	auraient crié
6 présent du subjonctif		13 passé du subjonctif	
crie	criions	aie crié	ayons crié
cries	criiez	aies crié	ayez crié
crie	crient	ait crié	aient crié
7 imparfait du subjonctif		14 plus-que-parfait du subjonctif	
criasse	criassions	eusse crié	eussions crié
criasses	criassiez	eusses crié	eussiez crié
criât	criassent	eût crié	eussent crié
		Impératif	
		crie	
		crions	
		criez	

Cet enfant crie toujours. Hier il a crié à tue-tête quand il a vu un avion dans le ciel.

un cri a shout, a cry
pousser un cri to utter a cry
crier à tue-tête to shout one's head off
un crieur hawker
un crieur de journaux newsboy

un criailleur, une criailleuse nagger
un criard, une criarde someone who
constantly shouts, nags, scolds;
screecher

to believe

The Seven Simple Tenses		The Seven Compound Tenses	
Singular	Plural	Singular	Plural
1 présent de l'indicatif		8 passé composé	
crois	**croyons**	**ai cru**	**avons cru**
crois	**croyez**	**as cru**	**avez cru**
croit	**croient**	**a cru**	**ont cru**
2 imparfait de l'indicatif		9 plus-que-parfait de l'indicatif	
croyais	**croyions**	**avais cru**	**avions cru**
croyais	**croyiez**	**avais cru**	**aviez cru**
croyait	**croyaient**	**avait cru**	**avaient cru**
3 passé simple		10 passé antérieur	
crus	**crûmes**	**eus cru**	**eûmes cru**
crus	**crûtes**	**eus cru**	**eûtes cru**
crut	**crurent**	**eut cru**	**eurent cru**
4 futur		11 futur antérieur	
croirai	**croirons**	**aurai cru**	**aurons cru**
croiras	**croirez**	**auras cru**	**aurez cru**
croira	**croiront**	**aura cru**	**auront cru**
5 conditionnel		12 conditionnel passé	
croirais	**croirions**	**aurais cru**	**aurions cru**
croirais	**croiriez**	**aurais cru**	**auriez cru**
croirait	**croiraient**	**aurait cru**	**auraient cru**
6 présent du subjonctif		13 passé du subjonctif	
croie	**croyions**	**aie cru**	**ayons cru**
croies	**croyiez**	**aies cru**	**ayez cru**
croie	**croient**	**ait cru**	**aient cru**
7 imparfait du subjonctif		14 plus-que-parfait du subjonctif	
crusse	**crussions**	**eusse cru**	**eussions cru**
crusses	**crussiez**	**eusses cru**	**eussiez cru**
crût	**crussent**	**eût cru**	**eussent cru**
		Impératif	
		crois	
		croyons	
		croyez	

Est-ce que vous croyez tout ce que vous entendez? Avez-vous cru l'histoire que je vous ai racontée?

Croyez-m'en! Take my word for it!
se croire to think oneself; to consider oneself
Paul se croit beau. Paul thinks himself handsome.
croyable believable

incroyable unbelievable
croire à qqch to believe in something
croire en qqn to believe in someone

73

cueillir   Part. pr. **cueillant**   Part. passé **cueilli**

to gather, to pick

The Seven Simple Tenses		The Seven Compound Tenses	
Singular	Plural	Singular	Plural
1 présent de l'indicatif		8 passé composé	
cueille	cueillons	ai cueilli	avons cueilli
cueilles	cueillez	as cueilli	avez cueilli
cueille	cueillent	a cueilli	ont cueilli
2 imparfait de l'indicatif		9 plus-que-parfait de l'indicatif	
cueillais	cueillions	avais cueilli	avions cueilli
cueillais	cueilliez	avais cueilli	aviez cueilli
cueillait	cueillaient	avait cueilli	avaient cueilli
3 passé simple		10 passé antérieur	
cueillis	cueillîmes	eus cueilli	eûmes cueilli
cueillis	cueillîtes	eus cueilli	eûtes cueilli
cueillit	cueillirent	eut cueilli	eurent cueilli
4 futur		11 futur antérieur	
cueillerai	cueillerons	aurai cueilli	aurons cueilli
cueilleras	cueillerez	auras cueilli	aurez cueilli
cueillera	cueilleront	aura cueilli	auront ceuilli
5 conditionnel		12 conditionnel passé	
cueillerais	cueillerions	aurais cueilli	aurions cueilli
cueillerais	cueilleriez	aurais cueilli	auriez cueilli
cueillerait	cueilleraient	aurait cueilli	auraient cueilli
6 présent du subjonctif		13 passé du subjonctif	
cueille	cueillions	aie cueilli	ayons cueilli
cueilles	cueilliez	aies cueilli	ayez cueilli
cueille	cueillent	ait cueilli	aient cueilli
7 imparfait du subjonctif		14 plus-que-parfait du subjonctif	
cueillisse	cueillissions	eusse cueilli	eussions cueilli
cueillisses	cueillissiez	eusses cueilli	eussiez cueilli
cueillît	cueillissent	eût cueilli	eussent cueilli
		Impératif	
		cueille	
		cueillons	
		cueillez	

Je vois que tu cueilles des fleurs. As-tu cueilli toutes les fleurs qui sont dans ce vase?

un cueilleur, une cueilleuse   gatherer, picker
la cueillaison, la cueillette   gathering, picking
un cueilloir   basket for picking fruit; instrument for picking fruit on high branches
Cueillez, cueillez votre jeunesse (Ronsard)—Seize the day (Horace: *Carpe diem*).

For other words related to this verb, see **accueillir**.

The Seven Simple Tenses		The Seven Compound Tenses	
Singular	Plural	Singular	Plural
1 présent de l'indicatif		8 passé composé	
cuis	cuisons	ai cuit	avons cuit
cuis	cuisez	as cuit	avez cuit
cuit	cuisent	a cuit	ont cuit
2 imparfait de l'indicatif		9 plus-que-parfait de l'indicatif	
cuisais	cuisions	avais cuit	avions cuit
cuisais	cuisiez	avais cuit	aviez cuit
cuisait	cuisaient	avait cuit	avaient cuit
3 passé simple		10 passé antérieur	
cuisis	cuisîmes	eus cuit	eûmes cuit
cuisis	cuisîtes	eus cuit	eûtes cuit
cuisit	cuisirent	eut cuit	eurent cuit
4 futur		11 futur antérieur	
cuirai	cuirons	aurai cuit	aurons cuit
cuiras	cuirez	auras cuit	aurez cuit
cuira	cuiront	aura cuit	auront cuit
5 conditionnel		12 conditionnel passé	
cuirais	cuirions	aurais cuit	aurions cuit
cuirais	cuiriez	aurais cuit	auriez cuit
cuirait	cuiraient	aurait cuit	auraient cuit
6 présent du subjonctif		13 passé du subjonctif	
cuise	cuisions	aie cuit	ayons cuit
cuises	cuisiez	aies cuit	ayez cuit
cuise	cuisent	ait cuit	aient cuit
7 imparfait du subjonctif		14 plus-que-parfait du subjonctif	
cuisisse	cuisissions	eusse cuit	eussions cuit
cuisisses	cuisissiez	eusses cuit	eussiez cuit
cuisît	cuisissent	eût cuit	eussent cuit

Impératif
cuis
cuisons
cuisez

Qui a cuit ce morceau de viande? C'est dégoûtant! Il est trop cuit. Ne savez-vous pas faire cuire un bon morceau de viande? Vous n'êtes pas bon cuisinier.

la cuisine kitchen	**une cuisinière** kitchen range (stove)
cuisinier, cuisinière cook	**un cuiseur** pressure cooker
faire cuire à la poêle to pan fry	**trop cuit** overcooked, overdone
Il est cuit. He's done for; His goose is cooked.	**la cuisson** cooking (time)

danser   Part. pr. **dansant**   Part. passé **dansé**

to dance

The Seven Simple Tenses		The Seven Compound Tenses	
Singular	Plural	Singular	Plural
1 présent de l'indicatif		8 passé composé	
danse	dansons	ai dansé	avons dansé
danses	dansez	as dansé	avez dansé
danse	dansent	a dansé	ont dansé
2 imparfait de l'indicatif		9 plus-que-parfait de l'indicatif	
dansais	dansions	avais dansé	avions dansé
dansais	dansiez	avais dansé	aviez dansé
dansait	dansaient	avait dansé	avaient dansé
3 passé simple		10 passé antérieur	
dansai	dansâmes	eus dansé	eûmes dansé
dansas	dansâtes	eus dansé	eûtes dansé
dansa	dansèrent	eut dansé	eurent dansé
4 futur		11 futur antérieur	
danserai	danserons	aurai dansé	aurons dansé
danseras	danserez	auras dansé	aurez dansé
dansera	danseront	aura dansé	auront dansé
5 conditionnel		12 conditionnel passé	
danserais	danserions	aurais dansé	aurions dansé
danserais	danseriez	aurais dansé	auriez dansé
danserait	danseraient	aurait dansé	auraient dansé
6 présent du subjonctif		13 passé du subjonctif	
danse	dansions	aie dansé	ayons dansé
danses	dansiez	aies dansé	ayez dansé
danse	dansent	ait dansé	aient dansé
7 imparfait du subjonctif		14 plus-que-parfait du subjonctif	
dansasse	dansassions	eusse dansé	eussions dansé
dansasses	dansassiez	eusses dansé	eussiez dansé
dansât	dansassent	eût dansé	eussent dansé

	Impératif	
danse	dansons	dansez

René: **Veux-tu danser avec moi?**
Renée: **Je ne sais pas danser.**
René: **Je suis bon danseur. Je vais t'apprendre à danser. Viens! Dansons!**

danser de joie to dance for joy
une soirée dansante evening dancing
  party
un thé dansant tea dance
  (usually 5 o'clock)

un danseur, une danseuse dancer
une danse dance; **un bal** ball
  (dance)

to discover, to uncover

The Seven Simple Tenses		The Seven Compound Tenses	
Singular	Plural	Singular	Plural
1 présent de l'indicatif		8 passé composé	
découvre	découvrons	ai découvert	avons découvert
découvres	découvrez	as découvert	avez découvert
découvre	découvrent	a découvert	ont découvert
2 imparfait de l'indicatif		9 plus-que-parfait de l'indicatif	
découvrais	découvrions	avais découvert	avions découvert
découvrais	découvriez	avais découvert	aviez découvert
découvrait	découvraient	avait découvert	avaient découvert
3 passé simple		10 passé antérieur	
découvris	découvrîmes	eus découvert	eûmes découvert
découvris	découvrîtes	eus découvert	eûtes découvert
découvrit	découvrirent	eut découvert	eurent découvert
4 futur		11 futur antérieur	
découvrirai	découvrirons	aurai découvert	aurons découvert
découvriras	découvrirez	auras découvert	aurez découvert
découvrira	découvriront	aura découvert	auront découvert
5 conditionnel		12 conditionnel passé	
découvrirais	découvririons	aurais découvert	aurions découvert
découvrirais	découvririez	aurais découvert	auriez découvert
découvrirait	découvriraient	aurait découvert	auraient découvert
6 présent du subjonctif		13 passé du subjonctif	
découvre	découvrions	aie découvert	ayons découvert
découvres	découvriez	aies découvert	ayez découvert
découvre	découvrent	ait découvert	aient découvert
7 imparfait du subjonctif		14 plus-que-parfait du subjonctif	
découvrisse	découvrissions	eusse découvert	eussions découvert
découvrisses	découvrissiez	eusses découvert	eussiez découvert
découvrît	découvrissent	eût découvert	eussent découvert

Impératif
découvre   découvrons   découvrez

Ce matin j'ai couvert ce panier de fruits et maintenant il est découvert. Qui l'a découvert?

un découvreur   discoverer
une découverte   a discovery, invention
se découvrir   to take off one's clothes; to take off one's hat
aller à la découverte   to explore
Découvrir saint Pierre pour couvrir saint Paul.   To rob Peter to pay Paul.

See also **couvrir.**

to describe

The Seven Simple Tenses		The Seven Compound Tenses	
Singular	Plural	Singular	Plural
1 présent de l'indicatif		8 passé composé	
décris	décrivons	ai décrit	avons décrit
décris	décrivez	as décrit	avez décrit
décrit	décrivent	a décrit	ont décrit
2 imparfait de l'indicatif		9 plus-que-parfait de l'indicatif	
décrivais	décrivions	avais décrit	avions décrit
décrivais	décriviez	avais décrit	aviez décrit
décrivait	décrivaient	avait décrit	avaient décrit
3 passé simple		10 passé antérieur	
décrivis	décrivîmes	eus décrit	eûmes décrit
décrivis	décrivîtes	eus décrit	eûtes décrit
décrivit	décrivirent	eut décrit	eurent décrit
4 futur		11 futur antérieur	
décrirai	décrirons	aurai décrit	aurons décrit
décriras	décrirez	auras décrit	aurez décrit
décrira	décriront	aura décrit	auront décrit
5 conditionnel		12 conditionnel passé	
décrirais	décririons	aurais décrit	aurions décrit
décrirais	décririez	aurais décrit	auriez décrit
décrirait	décriraient	aurait décrit	auraient décrit
6 présent du subjonctif		13 passé du subjonctif	
décrive	décrivions	aie décrit	ayons décrit
décrives	décriviez	aies décrit	ayez décrit
décrive	décrivent	ait décrit	aient décrit
7 imparfait du subjonctif		14 plus-que-parfait du subjonctif	
décrivisse	décrivissions	eusse décrit	eussions décrit
décrivisses	décrivissiez	eusses décrit	eussiez décrit
décrivît	décrivissent	eût décrit	eussent décrit
		Impératif	
		décris	
		décrivons	
		décrivez	

Quel beau paysage! Je le décrirai dans une lettre à mon ami. Je ferai une description en détail.

une description	description	**proscrire**	to proscribe
écrire	to write	**prescrire**	to prescribe, stipulate
		une prescription	prescription (law)

See also **écrire**.

78

to defend, to forbid, to prohibit

The Seven Simple Tenses		The Seven Compound Tenses	
Singular	Plural	Singular	Plural
1 présent de l'indicatif		8 passé composé	
défends	**défendons**	**ai défendu**	**avons défendu**
défends	**défendez**	**as défendu**	**avez défendu**
défend	**défendent**	**a défendu**	**ont défendu**
2 imparfait de l'indicatif		9 plus-que-parfait de l'indicatif	
défendais	**défendions**	**avais défendu**	**avions défendu**
défendais	**défendiez**	**avais défendu**	**aviez défendu**
défendait	**défendaient**	**avait défendu**	**avaient défendu**
3 passé simple		10 passé antérieur	
défendis	**défendîmes**	**eus défendu**	**eûmes défendu**
défendis	**défendîtes**	**eus défendu**	**eûtes défendu**
défendit	**défendirent**	**eut défendu**	**eurent défendu**
4 futur		11 futur antérieur	
défendrai	**défendrons**	**aurai défendu**	**aurons défendu**
défendras	**défendrez**	**auras défendu**	**aurez défendu**
défendra	**défendront**	**aura défendu**	**auront défendu**
5 conditionnel		12 conditionnel passé	
défendrais	**défendrions**	**aurais défendu**	**aurions défendu**
défendrais	**défendriez**	**aurais défendu**	**auriez défendu**
défendrait	**défendraient**	**aurait défendu**	**auraient défendu**
6 présent du subjonctif		13 passé du subjonctif	
défende	**défendions**	**aie défendu**	**ayons défendu**
défendes	**défendiez**	**aies défendu**	**ayez défendu**
défende	**défendent**	**ait défendu**	**aient défendu**
7 imparfait du subjonctif		14 plus-que-parfait du subjonctif	
défendisse	**défendissions**	**eusse défendu**	**eussions défendu**
défendisses	**défendissiez**	**eusses défendu**	**eussiez défendu**
défendît	**défendissent**	**eût défendu**	**eussent défendu**

Impératif
défends
défendons
défendez

Le père: **Je te défends de fumer. C'est une mauvaise habitude.**
Le fils: **Alors, pourquoi fumes-tu, papa?**

une défense defense	**se défendre** to defend oneself
DÉFENSE DE FUMER SMOKING PROHIBITED	**défensif, défensive** defensive
défendable justifiable	**défensivement** defensively
défendre qqch à qqn to forbid someone something	**se défendre d'avoir fait qqch** to deny having done something

déjeuner Part. pr. **déjeunant** Part. passé **déjeuné**

to lunch, to have lunch, breakfast

The Seven Simple Tenses		The Seven Compound Tenses	
Singular	Plural	Singular	Plural
1 présent de l'indicatif		8 passé composé	
déjeune	déjeunons	ai déjeuné	avons déjeuné
déjeunes	déjeunez	as déjeuné	avez déjeuné
déjeune	déjeunent	a déjeuné	ont déjeuné
2 imparfait de l'indicatif		9 plus-que-parfait de l'indicatif	
déjeunais	déjeunions	avais déjeuné	avions déjeuné
déjeunais	déjeuniez	avais déjeuné	aviez déjeuné
déjeunait	déjeunaient	avait déjeuné	avaient déjeuné
3 passé simple		10 passé antérieur	
déjeunai	déjeunâmes	eus déjeuné	eûmes déjeuné
déjeunas	déjeunâtes	eus déjeuné	eûtes déjeuné
déjeuna	déjeunèrent	eut déjeuné	eurent déjeuné
4 futur		11 futur antérieur	
déjeunerai	déjeunerons	aurai déjeuné	aurons déjeuné
déjeuneras	déjeunerez	auras déjeuné	aurez déjeuné
déjeunera	déjeuneront	aura déjeuné	auront déjeuné
5 conditionnel		12 conditionnel passé	
déjeunerais	déjeunerions	aurais déjeuné	aurions déjeuné
déjeunerais	déjeuneriez	aurais déjeuné	auriez déjeuné
déjeunerait	déjeuneraient	aurait déjeuné	auraient déjeuné
6 présent du subjonctif		13 passé du subjonctif	
déjeune	déjeunions	aie déjeuné	ayons déjeuné
déjeunes	déjeuniez	aies déjeuné	ayez déjeuné
déjeune	déjeunent	ait déjeuné	aient déjeuné
7 imparfait du subjonctif		14 plus-que-parfait du subjonctif	
déjeunasse	déjeunassions	eusse déjeuné	eussions déjeuné
déjeunasses	déjeunassiez	eusses déjeuné	eussiez déjeuné
déjeunât	déjeunassent	eût déjeuné	eussent déjeuné

	Impératif
	déjeune
	déjeunons
	déjeunez

Tous les matins je me lève et je prends mon petit déjeuner à sept heures et demie. A midi je déjeune avec mes camarades à l'école. Avec qui déjeunez-vous?

le déjeuner lunch
le petit déjeuner breakfast
jeûner to fast
le jeûne fast, fasting

rompre le jeûne to break one's fast
un jour de jeûne a day of fasting
déjeuner sur l'herbe to have a picnic
 lunch (on the grass)

to ask (for), to request

The Seven Simple Tenses		The Seven Compound Tenses	
Singular	Plural	Singular	Plural
1 présent de l'indicatif		8 passé composé	
demande	demandons	ai demandé	avons demandé
demandes	demandez	as demandé	avez demandé
demande	demandent	a demandé	ont demandé
2 imparfait de l'indicatif		9 plus-que-parfait de l'indicatif	
demandais	demandions	avais demandé	avions demandé
demandais	demandiez	avais demandé	aviez demandé
demandait	demandaient	avait demandé	avaient demandé
3 passé simple		10 passé antérieur	
demandai	demandâmes	eus demandé	eûmes demandé
demandas	demandâtes	eus demandé	eûtes demandé
demanda	demandèrent	eut demandé	eurent demandé
4 futur		11 futur antérieur	
demanderai	demanderons	aurai demandé	aurons demandé
demanderas	demanderez	auras demandé	aurez demandé
demandera	demanderont	aura demandé	auront demandé
5 conditionnel		12 conditionnel passé	
demanderais	demanderions	aurais demandé	aurions demandé
demanderais	demanderiez	aurais demandé	auriez demandé
demanderait	demanderaient	aurait demandé	auraient demandé
6 présent du subjonctif		13 passé du subjonctif	
demande	demandions	aie demandé	ayons demandé
demandes	demandiez	aies demandé	ayez demandé
demande	demandent	ait demandé	aient demandé
7 imparfait du subjonctif		14 plus-que-parfait du subjonctif	
demandasse	demandassions	eusse demandé	eussions demandé
demandasses	demandassiez	eusses demandé	eussiez demandé
demandât	demandassent	eût demandé	eussent demandé

Impératif
demande
demandons
demandez

J'ai demandé à une dame où s'arrête l'autobus. Elle m'a répondu: —Je ne sais pas, monsieur. Demandez à l'agent de police.

une demande a request	**mander** to send word by letter
sur demande on request, on application	**un mandat** mandate; **un mandat-lettre**
faire une demande de to apply for	letter money order; **un mandat-poste**
se demander to wonder	postal money order

demeurer　　　Part. pr. **demeurant**　　　Part. passé **demeuré**

to reside, to live, to remain, to stay

The Seven Simple Tenses		The Seven Compound Tenses	
Singular	Plural	Singular	Plural
1　présent de l'indicatif		8　passé composé	
demeure	demeurons	ai demeuré	avons demeuré
demeures	demeurez	as demeuré	avez demeuré
demeure	demeurent	a demeuré	ont demeuré
2　imparfait de l'indicatif		9　plus-que-parfait de l'indicatif	
demeurais	demeurions	avais demeuré	avions demeuré
demeurais	demeuriez	avais demeuré	aviez demeuré
demeurait	demeuraient	avait demeuré	avaient demeuré
3　passé simple		10　passé antérieur	
demeurai	demeurâmes	eus demeuré	eûmes demeuré
demeuras	demeurâtes	eus demeuré	eûtes demeuré
demeura	demeurèrent	eut demeuré	eurent demeuré
4　futur		11　futur antérieur	
demeurerai	demeurerons	aurai demeuré	aurons demeuré
demeureras	demeurerez	auras demeuré	aurez demeuré
demeurera	demeureront	aura demeuré	auront demeuré
5　conditionnel		12　conditionnel passé	
demeurerais	demeurerions	aurais demeuré	aurions demeuré
demeurerais	demeureriez	aurais demeuré	auriez demeuré
demeurerait	demeureraient	aurait demeuré	auraient demeuré
6　présent du subjonctif		13　passé du subjonctif	
demeure	demeurions	aie demeuré	ayons demeuré
demeures	demeuriez	aies demeuré	ayez demeuré
demeure	demeurent	ait demeuré	aient demeuré
7　imparfait du subjonctif		14　plus-que-parfait du subjonctif	
demeurasse	demeurassions	eusse demeuré	eussions demeuré
demeurasses	demeurassiez	eusses demeuré	aussiez demeuré
demeurât	demeurassent	eût demeuré	eussent demeuré
		Impératif	
		demeure	
		demeurons	
		demeurez	

—Oú demeurez-vous?
—Je demeure dans un appartement, rue des Jardins.

une demeure dwelling, residence	**demeurer à un hôtel** to stay at a hotel
au demeurant after all	**une personne demeurée** mentally
demeurer couché to stay in bed	retarded person
demeurer court to stop short	

to hurry, to hasten

The Seven Simple Tenses		The Seven Compound Tenses	
Singular	Plural	Singular	Plural
1 présent de l'indicatif		8 passé composé	
me dépêche	nous dépêchons	me suis dépêché(e)	nous sommes dépêché(e)s
te dépêches	vous dépêchez	t'es dépêché(e)	vous êtes dépêché(e)(s)
se dépêche	se dépêchent	s'est dépêché(e)	se sont dépêché(e)s
2 imparfait de l'indicatif		9 plus-que-parfait de l'indicatif	
me dépêchais	nous dépêchions	m'étais dépêché(e)	nous étions dépêché(e)s
te dépêchais	vous dépêchiez	t'étais dépêché(e)	vous étiez dépêché(e)(s)
se dépêchait	se dépêchaient	s'était dépêché(e)	s'étaient dépêché(e)s
3 passé simple		10 passé antérieur	
me dépêchai	nous dépêchâmes	me fus dépêché(e)	nous fûmes dépêché(e)s
te dépêchas	vous dépêchâtes	te fus dépêché(e)	vous fûtes dépêché(e)(s)
se dépêcha	se dépêchèrent	se fut dépêché(e)	se furent dépêché(e)s
4 futur		11 futur antérieur	
me dépêcherai	nous dépêcherons	me serai dépêché(e)	nous serons dépêché(e)s
te dépêcheras	vous dépêcherez	te seras dépêché(e)	vous serez dépêché(e)(s)
se dépêchera	se dépêcheront	se sera dépêché(e)	se seront dépêché(e)s
5 conditionnel		12 conditionnel passé	
me dépêcherais	nous dépêcherions	me serais dépêché(e)	nous serions dépêché(e)s
te dépêcherais	vous dépêcheriez	te serais dépêché(e)	vous seriez dépêché(e)(s)
se dépêcherait	se dépêcheraient	se serait dépêché(e)	se seraient dépêché(e)s
6 présent du subjonctif		13 passé du subjonctif	
me dépêche	nous dépêchions	me sois dépêché(e)	nous soyons dépêché(e)s
te dépêches	vous dépêchiez	te sois dépêché(e)	vous soyez dépêché(e)(s)
se dépêche	se dépêchent	se soit dépêché(e)	se soient dépêché(e)s
7 imparfait du subjonctif		14 plus-que-parfait du subjonctif	
me dépêchasse	nous dépêchassions	me fusse dépêché(e)	nous fussions dépêché(e)s
te dépêchasses	vous dépêchassiez	te fusses dépêché(e)	vous fussiez dépêché(e)(s)
se dépêchât	se dépêchassent	se fût dépêché(e)	se fussent dépêché(e)s

Impératif
dépêche-toi; ne te dépêche pas
dépêchons-nous; ne nous dépêchons pas
dépêchez-vous; ne vous dépêchez pas

En me dépêchant pour attraper l'autobus, je suis tombé et je me suis fait mal au genou. Je me dépêchais de venir chez vous pour vous dire quelque chose de très important.

une dépêche a telegram, a dispatch	**se dépêcher de faire quelque chose** to hurry to do something
dépêcher to dispatch	**Je me dépêche de finir mon travail.** I am hurrying to finish my work.

dépenser	Part. pr. **dépensant**	Part. passé **dépensé**

to spend (money)

The Seven Simple Tenses		The Seven Compound Tenses	
Singular	Plural	Singular	Plural
1 présent de l'indicatif		8 passé composé	
dépense	dépensons	ai dépensé	avons dépensé
dépenses	dépensez	as dépensé	avez dépensé
dépense	dépensent	a dépensé	ont dépensé
2 imparfait de l'indicatif		9 plus-que-parfait de l'indicatif	
dépensais	dépensions	avais dépensé	avions dépensé
dépensais	dépensiez	avais dépensé	aviez dépensé
dépensait	dépensaient	avait dépensé	avaient dépensé
3 passé simple		10 passé antérieur	
dépensai	dépensâmes	eus dépensé	eûmes dépensé
dépensas	dépensâtes	eus dépensé	eûtes dépensé
dépensa	dépensèrent	eut dépensé	eurent dépensé
4 futur		11 futur antérieur	
dépenserai	dépenserons	aurai dépensé	aurons dépensé
dépenseras	dépenserez	auras dépensé	aurez dépensé
dépensera	dépenseront	aura dépensé	auront dépensé
5 conditionnel		12 conditionnel passé	
dépenserais	dépenserions	aurais dépensé	aurions dépensé
dépenserais	dépenseriez	aurais dépensé	auriez dépensé
dépenserait	dépenseraient	aurait dépensé	auraient dépensé
6 présent du subjonctif		13 passé du subjonctif	
dépense	dépensions	aie dépensé	ayons dépensé
dépenses	dépensiez	aies dépensé	ayez dépensé
dépense	dépensent	ait dépensé	aient dépensé
7 imparfait du subjonctif		14 plus-que-parfait du subjonctif	
dépensasse	dépensassions	eusse dépensé	eussions dépensé
dépensasses	dépensassiez	eusses dépensé	eussiez dépensé
dépensât	dépensassent	eût dépensé	eussent dépensé
		Impératif	
		dépense	
		dépensons	
		dépensez	

Mon père m'a dit que je dépense sottement. Je lui ai répondu que je n'ai rien dépensé cette semaine.

dépensier, dépensière extravagant, unthrifty, spendthrift
dépenser sottement to spend money foolishly
aux dépens de quelqu'un at someone's expense

Part. pr. **dérangeant**	Part. passé **dérangé**	**déranger**

to disturb, to derange

The Seven Simple Tenses		The Seven Compound Tenses	
Singular	Plural	Singular	Plural
1 présent de l'indicatif		8 passé composé	
dérange	**dérangeons**	**ai dérangé**	**avons dérangé**
déranges	**dérangez**	**as dérangé**	**avez dérangé**
dérange	**dérangent**	**a dérangé**	**ont dérangé**
2 imparfait de l'indicatif		9 plus-que-parfait de l'indicatif	
dérangeais	**dérangions**	**avais dérangé**	**avions dérangé**
dérangeais	**dérangiez**	**avais dérangé**	**aviez dérangé**
dérangeait	**dérangeaient**	**avait dérangé**	**avaient dérangé**
3 passé simple		10 passé antérieur	
dérangeai	**dérangeâmes**	**eus dérangé**	**eûmes dérangé**
dérangeas	**dérangeâtes**	**eus dérangé**	**eûtes dérangé**
dérangea	**dérangèrent**	**eut dérangé**	**eurent dérangé**
4 futur		11 futur antérieur	
dérangerai	**dérangerons**	**aurai dérangé**	**aurons dérangé**
dérangeras	**dérangerez**	**auras dérangé**	**aurez dérangé**
dérangera	**dérangeront**	**aura dérangé**	**auront dérangé**
5 conditionnel		12 conditionnel passé	
dérangerais	**dérangerions**	**aurais dérangé**	**aurions dérangé**
dérangerais	**dérangeriez**	**aurais dérangé**	**auriez dérangé**
dérangerait	**dérangeraient**	**aurait dérangé**	**auraient dérangé**
6 présent du subjonctif		13 passé du subjonctif	
dérange	**dérangions**	**aie dérangé**	**ayons dérangé**
déranges	**dérangiez**	**aies dérangé**	**ayez dérangé**
dérange	**dérangent**	**ait dérangé**	**aient dérangé**
7 imparfait du subjonctif		14 plus-que-parfait du subjonctif	
dérangeasse	**dérangeassions**	**eusse dérangé**	**eussions dérangé**
dérangeasses	**dérangeassiez**	**eusses dérangé**	**eussiez dérangé**
dérangeât	**dérangeassent**	**eût dérangé**	**eussent dérangé**

Impératif
dérange   dérangeons   dérangez

Le professeur: **Entrez!**
L'élève: **Excusez-moi, monsieur. Est-ce que je vous dérange?**
Le professeur: **Non, tu ne me déranges pas. Qu'est-ce que tu veux?**
L'élève: **Je veux savoir si nous avons un jour de congé demain.**

dérangé, dérangée upset, out of order, broken down
une personne dérangée a deranged person
un dérangement disarrangement, disorder, inconvenience
se déranger to inconvenience oneself
Je vous en prie, ne vous dérangez pas! I beg you (please), don't disturb yourself!

descendre   Part. pr. **descendant**   Part. passé **descendu(e)(s)**

to go down, to descend, to take down, to bring down

The Seven Simple Tenses		The Seven Compound Tenses	
Singular	Plural	Singular	Plural
1 présent de l'indicatif		8 passé composé	
descends	descendons	suis descendu(e)	sommes descendu(e)s
descends	descendez	es descendu(e)	êtes descendu(e)(s)
descend	descendent	est descendu(e)	sont descendu(e)s
2 imparfait de l'indicatif		9 plus-que-parfait de l'indicatif	
descendais	descendions	étais descendu(e)	étions descendu(e)s
descendais	descendiez	étais descendu(e)	étiez descendu(e)(s)
descendait	descendaient	était descendu(e)	étaient descendu(e)s
3 passé simple		10 passé antérieur	
descendis	descendîmes	fus descendu(e)	fûmes descendu(e)s
descendis	descendîtes	fus descendu(e)	fûtes descendu(e)(s)
descendit	descendirent	fut descendu(e)	furent descendu(e)s
4 futur		11 futur antérieur	
descendrai	descendrons	serai descendu(e)	serons descendu(e)s
descendras	descendrez	seras descendu(e)	serez descendu(e)(s)
descendra	descendront	sera descendu(e)	seront descendu(e)s
5 conditionnel		12 conditionnel passé	
descendrais	descendrions	serais descendu(e)	serions descendu(e)s
descendrais	descendriez	serais descendu(e)	seriez descendu(e)(s)
descendrait	descendraient	serait descendu(e)	seraient descendu(e)s
6 présent du subjonctif		13 passé du subjonctif	
descende	descendions	sois descendu(e)	soyons descendu(e)s
descendes	descendiez	sois descendu(e)	soyez descendu(e)(s)
descende	descendent	soit descendu(e)	soient descendu(e)s
7 imparfait du subjonctif		14 plus-que-parfait du subjonctif	
descendisse	descendissions	fusse descendu(e)	fussions descendu(e)s
descendisses	descendissiez	fusses descendu(e)	fussiez descendu(e)(s)
descendît	descendissent	fût descendu(e)	fussent descendu(e)s
		Impératif	
		descends	
		descendons	
		descendez	

This verb is conjugated with *avoir* when it has a direct object.

Examples: **J'ai descendu l'escalier.**   I went down the stairs.
            J'ai descendu les valises.   I brought down the suitcases.

BUT: **Elle est descendue vite.**   She came down quickly.

descendre à un hôtel   to stop (stay over) at a hotel
descendre le store   to pull down the window shade

See also the verb **monter.**

The Seven Simple Tenses		The Seven Compound Tenses	
Singular	Plural	Singular	Plural
1 présent de l'indicatif		8 passé composé	
désire	désirons	ai désiré	avons désiré
désires	désirez	as désiré	avez désiré
désire	désirent	a désiré	ont désiré
2 imparfait de l'indicatif		9 plus-que-parfait de l'indicatif	
désirais	désirions	avais désiré	avions désiré
désirais	désiriez	avais désiré	aviez désiré
désirait	désiraient	avait désiré	avaient désiré
3 passé simple		10 passé antérieur	
désirai	désirâmes	eus désiré	eûmes désiré
désiras	désirâtes	eus désiré	eûtes désiré
désira	désirèrent	eut désiré	eurent désiré
4 futur		11 futur antérieur	
désirerai	désirerons	aurai désiré	aurons désiré
désireras	désirerez	auras désiré	aurez désiré
désirera	désireront	aura désiré	auront désiré
5 conditionnel		12 conditionnel passé	
désirerais	désirerions	aurais désiré	aurions désiré
désirerais	désireriez	aurais désiré	auriez désiré
désirerait	désireraient	aurait désiré	auraient désiré
6 présent du subjonctif		13 passé du subjonctif	
désire	désirions	aie désiré	ayons désiré
désires	désiriez	aies désiré	ayez désiré
désire	désirent	ait désiré	aient désiré
7 imparfait du subjonctif		14 plus-que-parfait du subjonctif	
désirasse	désirassions	eusse désiré	eussions désiré
désirasses	désirassiez	eusses désiré	eussiez désiré
désirât	désirassent	eût désiré	eussent désiré
		Impératif	
		désire	
		désirons	
		désirez	

La vendeuse: **Bonjour, monsieur. Vous désirez?**
Le client: **Je désire acheter une cravate.**
La vendeuse: **Bien, monsieur. Vous pouvez choisir. Voici toutes nos cravates.**

un désir desire, wish   **un désir de plaire** a desire to please
désirable desirable   **laisser à désirer** to leave much to be desired

to detest, to dislike, to hate

The Seven Simple Tenses		The Seven Compound Tenses	
Singular	Plural	Singular	Plural
1 présent de l'indicatif		8 passé composé	
déteste	détestons	ai détesté	avons détesté
détestes	détestez	as détesté	avez détesté
déteste	détestent	a détesté	ont détesté
2 imparfait de l'indicatif		9 plus-que-parfait de l'indicatif	
détestais	détestions	avais détesté	avions détesté
détestais	détestiez	avais détesté	aviez détesté
détestait	détestaient	avait détesté	avaient détesté
3 passé simple		10 passé antérieur	
détestai	détestâmes	eus détesté	eûmes détesté
détestas	détestâtes	eus détesté	eûtes détesté
détesta	détestèrent	eut détesté	eurent détesté
4 futur		11 futur antérieur	
détesterai	détesterons	aurai détesté	aurons détesté
détesteras	détesterez	auras détesté	aurez détesté
détestera	détesteront	aura détesté	auront détesté
5 conditionnel		12 conditionnel passé	
détesterais	détesterions	aurais détesté	aurions détesté
détesterais	détesteriez	aurais détesté	auriez détesté
détesterait	détesteraient	aurait détesté	auraient détesté
6 présent du subjonctif		13 passé du subjonctif	
déteste	détestions	aie détesté	ayons détesté
détestes	détestiez	aies détesté	ayez détesté
déteste	détestent	ait détesté	aient détesté
7 imparfait du subjonctif		14 plus-que-parfait du subjonctif	
détestasse	détestassions	eusse détesté	eussions détesté
détestasses	détestassiez	eusses détesté	eussiez détesté
détestât	détestassent	eût détesté	eussent détesté

Impératif
déteste
détestons
détestez

Je déteste la médiocrité, je déteste le mensonge, et je déteste la calomnie. Ce sont des choses détestables.

détestable loathsome, hateful	**Je déteste attendre.** I hate waiting.	
détestablement detestably	**d'une manière détestable** in a detestable way	

Part. pr. **détruisant** Part. passé **détruit** **détruire**

to destroy

The Seven Simple Tenses		The Seven Compound Tenses	
Singular	Plural	Singular	Plural
1 présent de l'indicatif		8 passé composé	
détruis	**détruisons**	**ai détruit**	**avons détruit**
détruis	**détruisez**	**as détruit**	**avez détruit**
détruit	**détruisent**	**a détruit**	**ont détruit**
2 imparfait de l'indicatif		9 plus-que-parfait de l'indicatif	
détruisais	**détruisions**	**avais détruit**	**avions détruit**
détruisais	**détruisiez**	**avais détruit**	**aviez détruit**
détruisait	**détruisaient**	**avait détruit**	**avaient détruit**
3 passé simple		10 passé antérieur	
détruisis	**détruisîmes**	**eus détruit**	**eûmes détruit**
détruisis	**détruisîtes**	**eus détruit**	**eûtes détruit**
détruisit	**détruisirent**	**eut détruit**	**eurent détruit**
4 futur		11 futur antérieur	
détruirai	**détruirons**	**aurai détruit**	**aurons détruit**
détruiras	**détruirez**	**auras détruit**	**aurez détruit**
détruira	**détruiront**	**aura détruit**	**auront détruit**
5 conditionnel		12 conditionnel passé	
détruirais	**détruirions**	**aurais détruit**	**aurions détruit**
détruirais	**détruiriez**	**aurais détruit**	**auriez détruit**
détruirait	**détruiraient**	**aurait détruit**	**auraient détruit**
6 présent du subjonctif		13 passé du subjonctif	
détruise	**détruisions**	**aie détruit**	**ayons détruit**
détruises	**détruisiez**	**aies détruit**	**ayez détruit**
détruise	**détruisent**	**ait détruit**	**aient détruit**
7 imparfait du subjonctif		14 plus-que-parfait du subjonctif	
détruisisse	**détruisissions**	**eusse détruit**	**eussions détruit**
détruisisses	**détruisissiez**	**eusses détruit**	**eussiez détruit**
détruisît	**détruisissent**	**eût détruit**	**eussent détruit**

Impératif
détruis
détruisons
détruisez

---

la destruction destruction
destructif, destructive destructive
la destructivité destructiveness
destructible destructible

se détruire to destroy (to do away with)
  oneself
Cet homme aime détruire tout.
  This man likes to destroy everything.

devenir	Part. pr. **devenant**	Part.passé **devenu(e)(s)**

to become

The Seven Simple Tenses		The Seven Compound Tenses	
Singular	Plural	Singular	Plural
1 présent de l'indicatif		8 passé composé	
deviens	devenons	suis devenu(e)	sommes devenu(e)s
deviens	devenez	es devenu(e)	êtes devenu(e)(s)
devient	deviennent	est devenu(e)	sont devenu(e)s
2 imparfait de l'indicatif		9 plus-que-parfait de l'indicatif	
devenais	devenions	étais devenu(e)	étions devenu(e)s
devenais	deveniez	étais devenu(e)	étiez devenu(e)s
devenait	devenaient	était devenu(e)	étaient devenu(e)s
3 passé simple		10 passé antérieur	
devins	devînmes	fus devenu(e)	fûmes devenu(e)s
devins	devîntes	fus devenu(e)	fûtes devenu(e)(s)
devint	devinrent	fut devenu(e)	furent devenu(e)s
4 futur		11 futur antérieur	
deviendrai	deviendrons	serai devenu(e)	serons devenu(e)s
deviendras	deviendrez	seras devenu(e)	serez devenu(e)(s)
deviendra	deviendront	sera devenu(e)	seront devenu(e)s
5 conditionnel		12 conditionnel passé	
deviendrais	deviendrions	serais devenu(e)	serions devenu(e)s
deviendrais	deviendriez	serais devenu(e)	seriez devenu(e)(s)
deviendrait	deviendraient	serait devenu(e)	seraient devenu(e)s
6 présent du subjonctif		13 passé du subjonctif	
devienne	devenions	sois devenu(e)	soyons devenu(e)s
deviennes	deveniez	sois devenu(e)	soyez devenu(e)(s)
devienne	deviennent	soit devenu(e)	soient devenu(e)s
7 imparfait du subjonctif		14 plus-que-parfait du subjonctif	
devinsse	devinssions	fusse devenu(e)	fussions devenu(e)s
devinsses	devinssiez	fusses devenu(e)	fussiez devenu(e)(s)
devînt	devinssent	fût devenu(e)	fussent devenu(e)s

Impératif
deviens
devenons
devenez

J'ai entendu dire que Claudette est devenue docteur. Et vous, qu'est-ce que vous voulez devenir?

devenir fou, devenir folle to go mad, crazy
Qu'est devenue votre soeur? What has become of your sister?

to have to, must, ought, owe, should

The Seven Simple Tenses		The Seven Compound Tenses	
Singular	Plural	Singular	Plural
1 présent de l'indicatif		8 passé composé	
dois	devons	ai dû	avons dû
dois	devez	as dû	avez dû
doit	doivent	a dû	ont dû
2 imparfait de l'indicatif		9 plus-que-parfait de l'indicatif	
devais	devions	avais dû	avions dû
devais	deviez	avais dû	aviez dû
devait	devaient	avait dû	avaient dû
3 passé simple		10 passé antérieur	
dus	dûmes	eus dû	eûmes dû
dus	dûtes	eus dû	eûtes dû
dut	durent	eut dû	eurent dû
4 futur		11 futur antérieur	
devrai	devrons	aurai dû	aurons dû
devras	devrez	auras dû	aurez dû
devra	devront	aura dû	auront dû
5 conditionnel		12 conditionnel passé	
devrais	devrions	aurais dû	aurions dû
devrais	devriez	aurais dû	auriez dû
devrait	devraient	aurait dû	auraient dû
6 présent du subjonctif		13 passé du subjonctif	
doive	devions	aie dû	ayons dû
doives	deviez	aies dû	ayez dû
doive	doivent	ait dû	aient dû
7 imparfait du subjonctif		14 plus-que-parfait du subjonctif	
dusse	dussions	eusse dû	eussions dû
dusses	dussiez	eusses dû	eussiez dû
dût	dussent	eût dû	eussent dû

Impératif
dois
devons
devez

Hier soir je suis allé au cinéma avec mes amis. Vous auriez dû venir avec nous. Le film était excellent.

Vous auriez dû venir.   You should have come.

le devoir duty, obligation

les devoirs homework

Cette grosse somme d'argent est due lundi.
This large sum of money is due on Monday.

Mon ami doit arriver demain.
My friend is (due) to arrive tomorrow.

91

dîner	Part. pr. **dînant**	Part. passé **dîné**

to dine, to have dinner

The Seven Simple Tenses		The Seven Compound Tenses	
Singular	Plural	Singular	Plural
1 présent de l'indicatif		**8 passé composé**	
dîne	dînons	ai dîné	avons dîné
dînes	dînez	as dîné	avez dîné
dîne	dînent	a dîné	ont dîné
2 imparfait de l'indicatif		**9 plus-que-parfait de l'indicatif**	
dînais	dînions	avais dîné	avions dîné
dînais	dîniez	avais dîné	aviez dîné
dînait	dînaient	avait dîné	avaient dîné
3 passé simple		**10 passé antérieur**	
dînai	dînâmes	eus dîné	eûmes dîné
dînas	dînâtes	eus dîné	eûtes dîné
dîna	dînèrent	eut dîné	eurent dîné
4 futur		**11 futur antérieur**	
dînerai	dînerons	aurai dîné	aurons dîné
dîneras	dînerez	auras dîné	aurez dîné
dînera	dîneront	aura dîné	auront dîné
5 conditionnel		**12 conditionnel passé**	
dînerais	dînerions	aurais dîné	aurions dîné
dînerais	dîneriez	aurais dîné	auriez dîné
dînerait	dîneraient	aurait dîné	auraient dîné
6 présent du subjonctif		**13 passé du subjonctif**	
dîne	dînions	aie dîné	ayons dîné
dînes	dîniez	aies dîné	ayez dîné
dîne	dînent	ait dîné	aient dîné
7 imparfait du subjonctif		**14 plus-que-parfait du subjonctif**	
dînasse	dînassions	eusse dîné	eussions dîné
dînasses	dînassiez	eusses dîné	eussiez dîné
dînât	dînassent	eût dîné	eussent dîné
		Impératif	
		dîne	
		dînons	
		dînez	

Lundi j'ai dîné chez des amis. Mardi tu as dîné chez moi. Mercredi nous avons dîné chez Pierre. J'aurais dû dîner seul.

le dîner dinner	**un dîneur** diner
une dînette child's dinner party	**donner un dîner** to give a dinner
l'heure du dîner dinner time	**dîner en ville** to dine out
j'aurais dû I should have	**J'aurais dû dîner.** I should have had dinner.

Try reading aloud this play on sounds (the letter **d**) as fast as you can:

    Denis a dîné du dos d'un dindon dodu.
    Dennis dined on (ate) the back of a plump turkey.

to say, to tell

The Seven Simple Tenses		The Seven Compound Tenses	
Singular	Plural	Singular	Plural
1 présent de l'indicatif		8 passé composé	
dis	disons	ai dit	avons dit
dis	dites	as dit	avez dit
dit	disent	a dit	ont dit
2 imparfait de l'indicatif		9 plus-que-parfait de l'indicatif	
disais	disions	avais dit	avions dit
disais	disiez	avais dit	aviez dit
disait	disaient	avait dit	avaient dit
3 passé simple		10 passé antérieur	
dis	dîmes	eus dit	eûmes dit
dis	dîtes	eus dit	eûtes dit
dit	dirent	eut dit	eurent dit
4 futur		11 futur antérieur	
dirai	dirons	aurai dit	aurons dit
diras	direz	auras dit	aurez dit
dira	diront	aura dit	auront dit
5 conditionnel		12 conditionnel passé	
dirais	dirions	aurais dit	aurions dit
dirais	diriez	aurais dit	auriez dit
dirait	diraient	aurait dit	auraient dit
6 présent du subjonctif		13 passé du subjonctif	
dise	disions	aie dit	ayons dit
dises	disiez	aies dit	ayez dit
dise	disent	ait dit	aient dit
7 imparfait du subjonctif		14 plus-que-parfait du subjonctif	
disse	dissions	eusse dit	eussions dit
disses	dissiez	eusses dit	eussiez dit
dît	dissent	eût dit	eussent dit
		Impératif	
		dis	
		disons	
		dites	

—Qu'est-ce que vous avez dit? Je n'ai pas entendu.
—J'ai dit que je ne vous ai pas entendu. Parlez plus fort.

c'est-à-dire that is, that is to say
entendre dire que to hear it said that
vouloir dire to mean
dire du bien de to speak well of

Que voulez-vous dire? What do you mean?
Comment dit-on *je vous aime* en anglais?
  How does one say *I love you* in English?

donner   Part. pr. **donnant**   Part. passé **donné**

to give

The Seven Simple Tenses		The Seven Compound Tenses	
Singular	Plural	Singular	Plural
1 présent de l'indicatif		8 passé composé	
donne	donnons	ai donné	avons donné
donnes	donnez	as donné	avez donné
donne	donnent	a donné	ont donné
2 imparfait de l'indicatif		9 plus-que-parfait de l'indicatif	
donnais	donnions	avais donné	avions donné
donnais	donniez	avais donné	aviez donné
donnait	donnaient	avait donné	avaient donné
3 passé simple		10 passé antérieur	
donnai	donnâmes	eus donné	eûmes donné
donnas	donnâtes	eus donné	eûtes donné
donna	donnèrent	eut donné	eurent donné
4 futur		11 futur antérieur	
donnerai	donnerons	aurai donné	aurons donné
donneras	donnerez	auras donné	aurez donné
donnera	donneront	aura donné	auront donné
5 conditionnel		12 conditionnel passé	
donnerais	donnerions	aurais donné	aurions donné
donnerais	donneriez	aurais donné	auriez donné
donnerait	donneraient	aurait donné	auraient donné
6 présent du subjonctif		13 passé du subjonctif	
donne	donnions	aie donné	ayons donné
donnes	donniez	aies donné	ayez donné
donne	donnent	ait donné	aient donné
7 imparfait du subjonctif		14 plus-que-parfait du subjonctif	
donnasse	donnassions	eusse donné	eussions donné
donnasses	donnassiez	eusses donné	eussiez donné
donnât	donnassent	eût donné	eussent donné
		Impératif	
		donne	
		donnons	
		donnez	

donner rendez-vous à qqn   to make an appointment (a date) with someone
donner sur   to look out upon: **La salle à manger donne sur un joli jardin.**   The
dining room looks out upon (faces) a pretty garden.
donner congé à   to grant leave to
abandonner   to abandon; **ordonner**   to order; **pardonner**   to pardon

to sleep

The Seven Simple Tenses		The Seven Compound Tenses	
Singular	Plural	Singular	Plural
1 présent de l'indicatif		8 passé composé	
dors	dormons	ai dormi	avons dormi
dors	dormez	as dormi	avez dormi
dort	dorment	a dormi	ont dormi
2 imparfait de l'indicatif		9 plus-que-parfait de l'indicatif	
dormais	dormions	avais dormi	avions dormi
dormais	dormiez	avais dormi	aviez dormi
dormait	dormaient	avait dormi	avaient dormi
3 passé simple		10 passé antérieur	
dormis	dormîmes	eus dormi	eûmes dormi
dormis	dormîtes	eus dormi	eûtes dormi
dormit	dormirent	eut dormi	eurent dormi
4 futur		11 futur antérieur	
dormirai	dormirons	aurai dormi	aurons dormi
dormiras	dormirez	auras dormi	aurez dormi
dormira	dormiront	aura dormi	auront dormi
5 conditionnel		12 conditionnel passé	
dormirais	dormirions	aurais dormi	aurions dormi
dormirais	dormiriez	aurais dormi	auriez dormi
dormirait	dormiraient	aurait dormi	auraient dormi
6 présent du subjonctif		13 passé du subjonctif	
dorme	dormions	aie dormi	ayons dormi
dormes	dormiez	aies dormi	ayez dormi
dorme	dorment	ait dormi	aient dormi
7 imparfait du subjonctif		14 plus-que-parfait du subjonctif	
dormisse	dormissions	eusse dormi	eussions dormi
dormisses	dormissiez	eusses dormi	eussiez dormi
dormît	dormissent	eût dormi	eussent dormi
		Impératif	
		dors	
		dormons	
		dormez	

dormir toute la nuit to sleep through the night
parler en dormant to talk in one's sleep
empêcher de dormir to keep from sleeping
la dormition dormition (falling asleep)
le dortoir dormitory
dormir à la belle étoile to sleep outdoors
dormir sur les deux oreilles to sleep soundly

endormir to put to sleep
s'endormir to fall asleep

douter   Part. pr. **doutant**   Part. passé **douté**

to doubt

The Seven Simple Tenses		The Seven Compound Tenses	
Singular	Plural	Singular	Plural
1 présent de l'indicatif		8 passé composé	
doute	**doutons**	**ai douté**	**avons douté**
doutes	**doutez**	**as douté**	**avez douté**
doute	**doutent**	**a douté**	**ont douté**
2 imparfait de l'indicatif		9 plus-que-parfait de l'indicatif	
doutais	**doutions**	**avais douté**	**avions douté**
doutais	**doutiez**	**avais douté**	**aviez douté**
doutait	**doutaient**	**avait douté**	**avaient douté**
3 passé simple		10 passé antérieur	
doutai	**doutâmes**	**eus douté**	**eûmes douté**
doutas	**doutâtes**	**eus douté**	**eûtes douté**
douta	**doutèrent**	**eut douté**	**eurent douté**
4 futur		11 futur antérieur	
douterai	**douterons**	**aurai douté**	**aurons douté**
douteras	**douterez**	**auras douté**	**aurez douté**
doutera	**douteront**	**aura douté**	**auront douté**
5 conditionnel		12 conditionnel passé	
douterais	**douterions**	**aurais douté**	**aurions douté**
douterais	**douteriez**	**aurais douté**	**auriez douté**
douterait	**douteraient**	**aurait douté**	**auraient douté**
6 présent du subjonctif		13 passé du subjonctif	
doute	**doutions**	**aie douté**	**ayons douté**
doutes	**doutiez**	**aies douté**	**ayez douté**
doute	**doutent**	**ait douté**	**aient douté**
7 imparfait du subjonctif		14 plus-que-parfait du subjonctif	
doutasse	**doutassions**	**eusse douté**	**eussions douté**
doutasses	**doutassiez**	**eusses douté**	**eussiez douté**
doutât	**doutassent**	**eût douté**	**eussent douté**
		Impératif	
		doute	
		doutons	
		doutez	

Je doute que cet homme soit coupable. Il n'y a pas de doute qu'il est innocent.

le doute doubt	**ne douter de rien** to doubt nothing,
sans doute no doubt	to be too credulous
sans aucun doute undoubtedly	**ne se douter de rien** to suspect nothing
d'un air de doute dubiously	**se douter de** to suspect
redouter to dread, to fear	

96

to listen (to)

The Seven Simple Tenses		The Seven Compound Tenses	
Singular	Plural	Singular	Plural
1 présent de l'indicatif		8 passé composé	
écoute	**écoutons**	**ai écouté**	**avons écouté**
écoutes	**écoutez**	**as écouté**	**avez écouté**
écoute	**écoutent**	**a écouté**	**ont écouté**
2 imparfait de l'indicatif		9 plus-que-parfait de l'indicatif	
écoutais	**écoutions**	**avais écouté**	**avions écouté**
écoutais	**écoutiez**	**avais écouté**	**aviez écouté**
écoutait	**écoutaient**	**avait écouté**	**avaient écouté**
3 passé simple		10 passé antérieur	
écoutai	**écoutâmes**	**eus écouté**	**eûmes écouté**
écoutas	**écoutâtes**	**eus écouté**	**eûtes écouté**
écouta	**écoutèrent**	**eut écouté**	**eurent écouté**
4 futur		11 futur antérieur	
écouterai	**écouterons**	**aurai écouté**	**aurons écouté**
écouteras	**écouterez**	**auras écouté**	**aurez écouté**
écoutera	**écouteront**	**aura écouté**	**auront écouté**
5 conditionnel		12 conditionnel passé	
écouterais	**écouterions**	**aurais écouté**	**aurions écouté**
écouterais	**écouteriez**	**aurais écouté**	**auriez écouté**
écouterait	**écouteraient**	**aurait écouté**	**auraient écouté**
6 présent du subjonctif		13 passé du subjonctif	
écoute	**écoutions**	**aie écouté**	**ayons écouté**
écoutes	**écoutiez**	**aies écouté**	**ayez écouté**
écoute	**écoutent**	**ait écouté**	**aient écouté**
7 imparfait du subjonctif		14 plus-que-parfait du subjonctif	
écoutasse	**écoutassions**	**eusse écouté**	**eussions écouté**
écoutasses	**écoutassiez**	**eusses écouté**	**eussiez écouté**
écoutât	**écoutassent**	**eût écouté**	**eussent écouté**
		Impératif	
		écoute	
		écoutons	
		écoutez	

   Ecoutez-vous le professeur quand il explique la leçon? L'avez-vous écouté ce matin en classe?

aimer à s'écouter parler   to love to hear one's own voice
un écouteur   telephone receiver (ear piece)
être à l'écoute   to be listening in
n'écouter personne   not to heed anyone
savoir écouter   to be a good listener
écouter aux portes   to eavesdrop, to listen secretly

écrire Part. pr. **écrivant** Part. passé **écrit**

to write

The Seven Simple Tenses		The Seven Compound Tenses	
Singular	Plural	Singular	Plural
1 présent de l'indicatif		8 passé composé	
écris	écrivons	ai écrit	avons écrit
écris	écrivez	as écrit	avez écrit
écrit	écrivent	a écrit	ont écrit
2 imparfait de l'indicatif		9 plus-que-parfait de l'indicatif	
écrivais	écrivions	avais écrit	avions écrit
écrivais	écriviez	avais écrit	aviez écrit
écrivait	écrivaient	avait écrit	avaient écrit
3 passé simple		10 passé antérieur	
écrivis	écrivîmes	eus écrit	eûmes écrit
écrivis	écrivîtes	eus écrit	eûtes écrit
écrivit	écrivirent	eut écrit	eurent écrit
4 futur		11 futur antérieur	
écrirai	écrirons	aurai écrit	aurons écrit
écriras	écrirez	auras écrit	aurez écrit
écrira	écriront	aura écrit	auront écrit
5 conditionnel		12 conditionnel passé	
écrirais	écririons	aurais écrit	aurions écrit
écrirais	écririez	aurais écrit	auriez écrit
écrirait	écriraient	aurait écrit	auraient écrit
6 présent du subjonctif		13 passé du subjonctif	
écrive	écrivions	aie écrit	ayons écrit
écrives	écriviez	aies écrit	ayez écrit
écrive	écrivent	ait écrit	aient écrit
7 imparfait du subjonctif		14 plus-que-parfait du subjonctif	
écrivisse	écrivissions	eusse écrit	eussions écrit
écrivisses	écrivissiez	eusses écrit	eussiez écrit
écrivît	écrivissent	eût écrit	eussent écrit
		Impératif	
		écris	
		écrivons	
		écrivez	

> Jean: **As-tu écrit ta composition pour la classe de français?**
> Jacques: **Non, je ne l'ai pas écrite.**
> Jean: **Écrivons-la ensemble.**

un écrivain writer; **une femme écrivain** woman writer
écriture *(f.)* handwriting, writing
écrire un petit mot à qqn to write a note to someone

See also **décrire**.

to frighten

The Seven Simple Tenses		The Seven Compound Tenses	
Singular	Plural	Singular	Plural
1 présent de l'indicatif		8 passé composé	
effraye	effrayons	ai effrayé	avons effrayé
effrayes	effrayez	as effrayé	avez effrayé
effraye	effrayent	a effrayé	ont effrayé
2 imparfait de l'indicatif		9 plus-que-parfait de l'indicatif	
effrayais	effrayions	avais effrayé	avions effrayé
effrayais	effrayiez	avais effrayé	aviez effrayé
effrayait	effrayaient	avait effrayé	avaient effrayé
3 passé simple		10 passé antérieur	
effrayai	effrayâmes	eus effrayé	eûmes effrayé
effrayas	effrayâtes	eus effrayé	eûtes effrayé
effraya	effrayèrent	eut effrayé	eurent effrayé
4 futur		11 futur antérieur	
effrayerai	effrayerons	aurai effrayé	aurons effrayé
effrayeras	effrayerez	auras effrayé	aurez effrayé
effrayera	effrayeront	aura effrayé	auront effrayé
5 conditionnel		12 conditionnel passé	
effrayerais	effrayerions	aurais effrayé	aurions effrayé
effrayerais	effrayeriez	aurais effrayé	auriez effrayé
effrayerait	effrayeraient	aurait effrayé	auraient effrayé
6 présent du subjonctif		13 passé du subjonctif	
effraye	effrayions	aie effrayé	ayons effrayé
effrayes	effrayiez	aies effrayé	ayez effrayé
effraye	effrayent	ait effrayé	aient effrayé
7 imparfait du subjonctif		14 plus-que-parfait du subjonctif	
effrayasse	effrayassions	eusse effrayé	eussions effrayé
effrayasses	effrayassiez	eusses effrayé	eussiez effrayé
effrayât	effrayassent	eût effrayé	eussent effrayé
		Impératif	
		effraye	
		effrayons	
		effrayez	

Le tigre a effrayé l'enfant. L'enfant a effrayé le singe. Le singe effraiera le bébé. C'est effrayant!

effrayant, effrayante frightful, awful	**effroyable** dreadful, fearful
effrayé, effrayée frightened	**effroyablement** dreadfully, fearfully

Verbs ending in -ayer may change y to i before mute e or may keep y.

to amuse, to cheer up, to enliven, to entertain

The Seven Simple Tenses		The Seven Compound Tenses	
Singular	Plural	Singular	Plural
1 présent de l'indicatif		8 passé composé	
égaye	égayons	ai égayé	avons égayé
égayes	égayez	as égayé	avez égayé
égaye	égayent	a égayé	ont égayé
2 imparfait de l'indicatif		9 plus-que-parfait de l'indicatif	
égayais	égayions	avais égayé	avions égayé
égayais	égayiez	avais égayé	aviez égayé
égayait	égayaient	avait égayé	avaient égayé
3 passé simple		10 passé antérieur	
égayai	égayâmes	eus égayé	eûmes égayé
égayas	égayâtes	eus égayé	eûtes égayé
égaya	égayèrent	eut égayé	eurent égayé
4 futur		11 futur antérieur	
égayerai	égayerons	aurai égayé	aurons égayé
égayeras	égayerez	auras égayé	aurez égayé
égayera	égayeront	aura égayé	auront égayé
5 conditionnel		12 conditionnel passé	
égayerais	égayerions	aurais égayé	aurions égayé
égayerais	égayeriez	aurais égayé	auriez égayé
égayerait	égayeraient	aurait égayé	auraient égayé
6 présent du subjonctif		13 passé du subjonctif	
égaye	égayions	aie égayé	ayons égayé
égayes	égayiez	aies égayé	ayez égayé
égaye	égayent	ait égayé	aient égayé
7 imparfait du subjonctif		14 plus-que-parfait du subjonctif	
égayasse	égayassions	eusse égayé	eussions égayé
égayasses	égayassiez	eusses égayé	eussiez égayé
égayât	égayassent	eût égayé	eussent égayé
		Impératif	
		égaye	
		égayons	
		égayez	

égayant, égayante   lively
s'égayer aux dépens de   to make fun of
gai, gaie   gay, cheerful, merry
gaiment   gaily, cheerfully

Verbs ending in -*ayer* may change *y* to *i* before mute *e* or may keep *y*.

to kiss, to embrace

The Seven Simple Tenses		The Seven Compound Tenses	
Singular	Plural	Singular	Plural
1 présent de l'indicatif		8 passé composé	
embrasse	embrassons	ai embrassé	avons embrassé
embrasses	embrassez	as embrassé	avez embrassé
embrasse	embrassent	a embrassé	ont embrassé
2 imparfait de l'indicatif		9 plus-que-parfait de l'indicatif	
embrassais	embrassions	avais embrassé	avions embrassé
embrassais	embrassiez	avais embrassé	aviez embrassé
embrassait	embrassaient	avait embrassé	avaient embrassé
3 passé simple		10 passé antérieur	
embrassai	embrassâmes	eus embrassé	eûmes embrassé
embrassas	embrassâtes	eus embrassé	eûtes embrassé
embrassa	embrassèrent	eut embrassé	eurent embrassé
4 futur		11 futur antérieur	
embrasserai	embrasserons	aurai embrassé	aurons embrassé
embrasseras	embrasserez	auras embrassé	aurez embrassé
embrassera	embrasseront	aura embrassé	auront embrassé
5 conditionnel		12 conditionnel passé	
embrasserais	embrasserions	aurais embrassé	aurions embrassé
embrasserais	embrasseriez	aurais embrassé	auriez embrassé
embrasserait	embrasseraient	aurait embrassé	auraient embrassé
6 présent du subjonctif		13 passé du subjonctif	
embrasse	embrassions	aie embrassé	ayons embrassé
embrasses	embrassiez	aies embrassé	ayez embrassé
embrasse	embrassent	ait embrassé	aient embrassé
7 imparfait du subjonctif		14 plus-que-parfait du subjonctif	
embrassasse	embrassassions	eusse embrassé	eussions embrassé
embrassasses	embrassassiez	eusses embrassé	eussiez embrassé
embrassât	embrassassent	eût embrassé	eussent embrassé
		Impératif	
		embrasse	
		embrassons	
		embrassez	

—Embrasse-moi. Je t'aime. Ne me laisse pas.
—Je t'embrasse. Je t'aime aussi. Je ne te laisse pas. Embrassons-nous.

le bras arm
un embrassement embracement, embrace
s'embrasser to embrace each other, to hug each other
embrasseur, embrasseuse a person who likes to kiss a lot

emmener	Part. pr. **emmenant**	Part. passé **emmené**

to lead, to lead away, to take away (persons)

The Seven Simple Tenses		The Seven Compound Tenses	
Singular	Plural	Singular	Plural
1 présent de l'indicatif		8 passé composé	
emmène	emmenons	ai emmené	avons emmené
emmènes	emmenez	as emmené	avez emmené
emmène	emmènent	a emmené	ont emmené
2 imparfait de l'indicatif		9 plus-que-parfait de l'indicatif	
emmenais	emmenions	avais emmené	avions emmené
emmenais	emmeniez	avais emmené	aviez emmené
emmenait	emmenaient	avait emmené	avaient emmené
3 passé simple		10 passé antérieur	
emmenai	emmenâmes	eus emmené	eûmes emmené
emmenas	emmenâtes	eus emmené	eûtes emmené
emmena	emmenèrent	eut emmené	eurent emmené
4 futur		11 futur antérieur	
emmènerai	emmènerons	aurai emmené	aurons emmené
emmèneras	emmènerez	auras emmené	aurez emmené
emmènera	emmèneront	aura emmené	auront emmené
5 conditionnel		12 conditionnel passé	
emmènerais	emmènerions	aurais emmené	aurions emmené
emmènerais	emmèneriez	aurais emmené	auriez emmené
emmènerait	emmèneraient	aurait emmené	auraient emmené
6 présent du subjonctif		13 passé du subjonctif	
emmène	emmenions	aie emmené	ayons emmené
emmènes	emmeniez	aies emmené	ayez emmené
emmène	emmènent	ait emmené	aient emmené
7 imparfait du subjonctif		14 plus-que-parfait du subjonctif	
emmenasse	emmenassions	eusse emmené	eussions emmené
emmenasses	emmenassiez	eusses emmené	eussiez emmené
emmenât	emmenassent	eût emmené	eussent emmené
		Impératif	
		emmène	
		emmenons	
		emmenez	

Quand j'emmène une personne d'un lieu dans un autre, je mène cette personne avec moi. Mon père nous emmènera au cinéma lundi prochain. Samedi dernier il nous a emmenés au théâtre.

Le train m'a emmené à Paris.   The train took me to Paris.
Un agent de police a emmené l'assassin.   A policeman took away the assassin.

See also **mener**.

to hinder, to prevent

The Seven Simple Tenses		The Seven Compound Tenses	
Singular	Plural	Singular	Plural
1 présent de l'indicatif		8 passé composé	
empêche	empêchons	ai empêché	avons empêché
empêches	empêchez	as empêché	avez empêché
empêche	empêchent	a empêché	ont empêché
2 imparfait de l'indicatif		9 plus-que-parfait de l'indicatif	
empêchais	empêchions	avais empêché	avions empêché
empêchais	empêchiez	avais empêché	aviez empêché
empêchait	empêchaient	avait empêché	avaient empêché
3 passé simple		10 passé antérieur	
empêchai	empêchâmes	eus empêché	eûmes empêché
empêchas	empêchâtes	eus empêché	eûtes empêché
empêcha	empêchèrent	eut empêché	eurent empêché
4 futur		11 futur antérieur	
empêcherai	empêcherons	aurai empêché	aurons empêché
empêcheras	empêcherez	auras empêché	aurez empêché
empêchera	empêcheront	aura empêché	auront empêché
5 conditionnel		12 conditionnel passé	
empêcherais	empêcherions	aurais empêché	aurions empêché
empêcherais	empêcheriez	aurais empêché	auriez empêché
empêcherait	empêcheraient	aurait empêché	auraient empêché
6 présent du subjonctif		13 passé du subjonctif	
empêche	empêchions	aie empêché	ayons empêché
empêches	empêchiez	aies empêché	ayez empêché
empêche	empêchent	ait empêché	aient empêché
7 imparfait du subjonctif		14 plus-que-parfait du subjonctif	
empêchasse	empêchassions	eusse empêché	eussions empêché
empêchasses	empêchassiez	eusses empêché	eussiez empêché
empêchât	empêchassent	eût empêché	eussent empêché

Impératif
empêche
empêchons
empêchez

Georgette a empêché son frère de finir ses devoirs parce qu'elle jouait des disques en même temps. Le bruit était un vrai empêchement.

un empêchement impediment, hindrance
en cas d'empêchement in case of prevention
empêcher qqn de faire qqch to prevent someone from doing something
empêcher d'entrer to keep from entering
s'empêcher de faire qqch to refrain from doing something

employer	Part. pr. **employant**	Part. passé **employé**

to use, to employ

The Seven Simple Tenses		The Seven Compound Tenses	
Singular	Plural	Singular	Plural
1 présent de l'indicatif		8 passé composé	
emploie	**employons**	**ai employé**	**avons employé**
emploies	**employez**	**as employé**	**avez employé**
emploie	**emploient**	**a employé**	**ont employé**
2 imparfait de l'indicatif		9 plus-que-parfait de l'indicatif	
employais	**employions**	**avais employé**	**avions employé**
employais	**employiez**	**avais employé**	**aviez employé**
employait	**employaient**	**avait employé**	**avaient employé**
3 passé simple		10 passé antérieur	
employai	**employâmes**	**eus employé**	**eûmes employé**
employas	**employâtes**	**eus employé**	**eûtes employé**
employa	**employèrent**	**eut employé**	**eurent employé**
4 futur		11 futur antérieur	
emploierai	**emploierons**	**aurai employé**	**aurons employé**
emploieras	**emploierez**	**auras employé**	**aurez employé**
emploiera	**emploieront**	**aura employé**	**auront employé**
5 conditionnel		12 conditionnel passé	
emploierais	**emploierions**	**aurais employé**	**aurions employé**
emploierais	**emploieriez**	**aurais employé**	**auriez employé**
emploierait	**emploieraient**	**aurait employé**	**auraient employé**
6 présent du subjonctif		13 passé du subjonctif	
emploie	**employions**	**aie employé**	**ayons employé**
emploies	**employiez**	**aies employé**	**ayez employé**
emploie	**emploient**	**ait employé**	**aient employé**
7 imparfait du subjonctif		14 plus-que-parfait du subjonctif	
employasse	**employassions**	**eusse employé**	**eussions employé**
employasses	**employassiez**	**eusses employé**	**eussiez employé**
employât	**employassent**	**eût employé**	**eussent employé**

	Impératif
	emploie
	employons
	employez

un employé, une employée employee	**s'employer à faire qqch** to occupy
employeur employer	oneself doing something
sans emploi jobless	**employer son temps** to spend one's
un emploi employment	time

Verbs ending in -*oyer* must change *y* to *i* before mute *e*.

The Seven Simple Tenses		The Seven Compound Tenses	
Singular	Plural	Singular	Plural
1 présent de l'indicatif		8 passé composé	
emprunte	empruntons	ai emprunté	avons emprunté
empruntes	empruntez	as emprunté	avez emprunté
emprunte	empruntent	a emprunté	ont emprunté
2 imparfait de l'indicatif		9 plus-que-parfait de l'indicatif	
empruntais	empruntions	avais emprunté	avions emprunté
empruntais	empruntiez	avais emprunté	aviez emprunté
empruntait	empruntaient	avait emprunté	avaient emprunté
3 passé simple		10 passé antérieur	
empruntai	empruntâmes	eus emprunté	eûmes emprunté
empruntas	empruntâtes	eus emprunté	eûtes emprunté
emprunta	empruntèrent	eut emprunté	eurent emprunté
4 futur		11 futur antérieur	
emprunterai	emprunterons	aurai emprunté	aurons emprunté
emprunteras	emprunterez	auras emprunté	aurez emprunté
empruntera	emprunteront	aura emprunté	auront emprunté
5 conditionnel		12 conditionnel passé	
emprunterais	emprunterions	aurais emprunté	aurions emprunté
emprunterais	emprunteriez	aurais emprunté	auriez emprunté
emprunterait	emprunteraient	aurait emprunté	auraient emprunté
6 présent du subjonctif		13 passé du subjonctif	
emprunte	empruntions	aie emprunté	ayons emprunté
empruntes	empruntiez	aies emprunté	ayez emprunté
emprunte	empruntent	ait emprunté	aient emprunté
7 imparfait du subjonctif		14 plus-que-parfait du subjonctif	
empruntasse	empruntassions	eusse emprunté	eussions emprunté
empruntasses	empruntassiez	eusses emprunté	eussiez emprunté
empruntât	empruntassent	eût emprunté	eussent emprunté
		Impératif	
		emprunte	
		empruntons	
		empruntez	

emprunteur, emprunteuse   a person who makes a habit of borrowing
un emprunt   loan, borrowing
emprunter qqch à qqn   to borrow something from someone
  Monsieur Leblanc a emprunté de l'argent à mon père.   Mr. Leblanc borrowed
  some money from my father.

| **enlever** | Part. pr. **enlevant** | Part. passé **enlevé** |

to carry away, to take away, to remove

The Seven Simple Tenses		The Seven Compound Tenses	
Singular	Plural	Singular	Plural
1 présent de l'indicatif		8 passé composé	
enlève	enlevons	ai enlevé	avons enlevé
enlèves	enlevez	as enlevé	avez enlevé
enlève	enlèvent	a enlevé	ont enlevé
2 imparfait de l'indicatif		9 plus-que-parfait de l'indicatif	
enlevais	enlevions	avais enlevé	avions enlevé
enlevais	enleviez	avais enlevé	aviez enlevé
enlevait	enlevaient	avait enlevé	avaient enlevé
3 passé simple		10 passé antérieur	
enlevai	enlevâmes	eus enlevé	eûmes enlevé
enlevas	enlevâtes	eus enlevé	eûtes enlevé
enleva	enlevèrent	eut enlevé	eurent enlevé
4 futur		11 futur antérieur	
enlèverai	enlèverons	aurai enlevé	aurons enlevé
enlèveras	enlèverez	auras enlevé	aurez enlevé
enlèvera	enlèveront	aura enlevé	auront enlevé
5 conditionnel		12 conditionnel passé	
enlèverais	enlèverions	aurais enlevé	aurions enlevé
enlèverais	enlèveriez	aurais enlevé	auriez enlevé
enlèverait	enlèveraient	aurait enlevé	auraient enlevé
6 présent du subjonctif		13 passé du subjonctif	
enlève	enlevions	aie enlevé	ayons enlevé
enlèves	enleviez	aies enlevé	ayez enlevé
enlève	enlèvent	ait enlevé	aient enlevé
7 imparfait du subjonctif		14 plus-que-parfait du subjonctif	
enlevasse	enlevassions	eusse enlevé	eussions enlevé
enlevasses	enlevassiez	eusses enlevé	eussiez enlevé
enlevât	enlevassent	eût enlevé	eussent enlevé
		Impératif	
		enlève	
		enlevons	
		enlevez	

Madame Dubac est entrée dans sa maison. Elle a enlevé son chapeau, son manteau et ses gants. Puis, elle est allée directement au salon pour enlever une chaise et la mettre dans la salle à manger. Après cela, elle a enlevé les ordures.

enlever les ordures to take the garbage out
un enlèvement lifting, carrying off, removal
enlèvement d'un enfant baby snatching, kidnapping
un enlevage spurt (sports)

to bore, to annoy, to weary

The Seven Simple Tenses		The Seven Compound Tenses	
Singular	Plural	Singular	Plural
1 présent de l'indicatif		8 passé composé	
ennuie	ennuyons	ai ennuyé	avons ennuyé
ennuies	ennuyez	as ennuyé	avez ennuyé
ennuie	ennuient	a ennuyé	ont ennuyé
2 imparfait de l'indicatif		9 plus-que-parfait de l'indicatif	
ennuyais	ennuyions	avais ennuyé	avions ennuyé
ennuyais	ennuyiez	avais ennuyé	aviez ennuyé
ennuyait	ennuyaient	avait ennuyé	avaient ennuyé
3 passé simple		10 passé antérieur	
ennuyai	ennuyâmes	eus ennuyé	eûmes ennuyé
ennuyas	ennuyâtes	eus ennuyé	eûtes ennuyé
ennuya	ennuyèrent	eut ennuyé	eurent ennuyé
4 futur		11 futur antérieur	
ennuierai	ennuierons	aurai ennuyé	aurons ennuyé
ennuieras	ennuierez	auras ennuyé	aurez ennuyé
ennuiera	ennuieront	aura ennuyé	auront ennuyé
5 conditionnel		12 conditionnel passé	
ennuierais	ennuierions	aurais ennuyé	aurions ennuyé
ennuierais	ennuieriez	aurais ennuyé	auriez ennuyé
ennuierait	ennuieraient	aurait ennuyé	auraient ennuyé
6 présent du subjonctif		13 passé du subjonctif	
ennuie	ennuyions	aie ennuyé	ayons ennuyé
ennuies	ennuyiez	aies ennuyé	ayez ennuyé
ennuie	ennuient	ait ennuyé	aient ennuyé
7 imparfait du subjonctif		14 plus-que-parfait du subjonctif	
ennuyasse	ennuyassions	eusse ennuyé	eussions ennuyé
ennuyasses	ennuyassiez	eusses ennuyé	eussiez ennuyé
ennuyât	ennuyassent	eût ennuyé	eussent ennuyé
		Impératif	
		ennuie	
		ennuyons	
		ennuyez	

—**Est-ce que je vous ennuie?**
—**Oui, vous m'ennuyez. Allez-vous en!**

un ennui   weariness, boredom, ennui
des ennuis   worries, troubles
ennuyeux, ennuyeuse   boring

mourir d'ennui   to be bored to tears
s'ennuyer   to become bored, to get bored

Verbs ending in -*uyer* must change *y* to *i* before mute *e*.

107

enseigner

Part. pr. enseignant **Part. passé enseigné**

to teach

The Seven Simple Tenses		The Seven Compound Tenses	
Singular	Plural	Singular	Plural
1 présent de l'indicatif		8 passé composé	
enseigne	enseignons	ai enseigné	avons enseigné
enseignes	enseignez	as enseigné	avez enseigné
enseigne	enseignent	a enseigné	ont enseigné
2 imparfait de l'indicatif		9 plus-que-parfait de l'indicatif	
enseignais	enseignions	avais enseigné	avions enseigné
enseignais	enseigniez	avais enseigné	aviez enseigné
enseignait	enseignaient	avait enseigné	avaient enseigné
3 passé simple		10 passé antérieur	
enseignai	enseignâmes	eus enseigné	eûmes enseigné
enseignas	enseignâtes	eus enseigné	eûtes enseigné
enseigna	enseignèrent	eut enseigné	eurent enseigné
4 futur		11 futur antérieur	
enseignerai	enseignerons	aurai enseigné	aurons enseigné
enseigneras	enseignerez	auras enseigné	aurez enseigné
enseignera	enseigneront	aura enseigné	auront enseigné
5 conditionnel		12 conditionnel passé	
enseignerais	enseignerions	aurais enseigné	aurions enseigné
enseignerais	enseigneriez	aurais enseigné	auriez enseigné
enseignerait	enseigneraient	aurait enseigné	auraient enseigné
6 présent du subjonctif		13 passé du subjonctif	
enseigne	enseignions	aie enseigné	ayons enseigné
enseignes	enseigniez	aies enseigné	ayez enseigné
enseigne	enseignent	ait enseigné	aient enseigné
7 imparfait du subjonctif		14 plus-que-parfait du subjonctif	
enseignasse	enseignassions	eusse enseigné	eussions enseigné
enseignasses	enseignassiez	eusses enseigné	eussiez enseigné
enseignât	enseignassent	eût enseigné	eussent enseigné
		Impératif	
		enseigne	
		enseignons	
		enseignez	

J'enseigne aux élèves à lire en français. L'enseignement est une profession.

enseigner qqch à qqn to teach something to someone
une enseigne sign, flag
un enseigne ensign
l'enseignement *(m.)* teaching
renseigner qqn de qqch to inform someone about something
se renseigner to get information, to inquire
un renseignement, des renseignements information

108

to hear, to understand

The Seven Simple Tenses		The Seven Compound Tenses	
Singular	Plural	Singular	Plural
1 présent de l'indicatif		8 passé composé	
entends	entendons	ai entendu	avons entendu
entends	entendez	as entendu	avez entendu
entend	entendent	a entendu	ont entendu
2 imparfait de l'indicatif		9 plus-que-parfait de l'indicatif	
entendais	entendions	avais entendu	avions entendu
entendais	entendiez	avais entendu	aviez entendu
entendait	entendaient	avait entendu	avaient entendu
3 passé simple		10 passé antérieur	
entendis	entendîmes	eus entendu	eûmes entendu
entendis	entendîtes	eus entendu	eûtes entendu
entendit	entendirent	eut entendu	eurent entendu
4 futur		11 futur antérieur	
entendrai	entendrons	aurai entendu	aurons entendu
entendras	entendrez	auras entendu	aurez entendu
entendra	entendront	aura entendu	auront entendu
5 conditionnel		12 conditionnel passé	
entendrais	entendrions	aurais entendu	aurions entendu
entendrais	entendriez	aurais entendu	auriez entendu
entendrait	entendraient	aurait entendu	auraient entendu
6 présent du subjonctif		13 passé du subjonctif	
entende	entendions	aie entendu	ayons entendu
entendes	entendiez	aies entendu	ayez entendu
entende	entendent	ait entendu	aient entendu
7 imparfait du subjonctif		14 plus-que-parfait du subjonctif	
entendisse	entendissions	eusse entendu	eussions entendu
entendisses	entendissiez	eusses entendu	eussiez entendu
entendît	entendissent	eût entendu	eussent entendu
		Impératif	
		entends	
		entendons	
		entendez	

—As-tu entendu quelque chose?
—Non, chéri, je n'ai rien entendu.
—J'ai entendu un bruit . . . de la cuisine . . . silence . . . je l'entends encore.
—Oh! Un cambrioleur!

un entendement understanding
sous-entendre to imply
un sous-entendu innuendo
une sous-entente implication
Je m'entends bien avec ma sœur.
I get along very well with my sister.

bien entendu of course
C'est entendu! It's understood! Agreed!
s'entendre avec qqn to get along with
someone, to understand each other

109

to enter, to come in, to go in

The Seven Simple Tenses		The Seven Compound Tenses	
Singular	Plural	Singular	Plural
1 présent de l'indicatif		8 passé composé	
entre	entrons	suis entré(e)	sommes entré(e)s
entres	entrez	es entré(e)	êtes entré(e)s
entre	entrent	est entré(e)	sont entré(e)s
2 imparfait de l'indicatif		9 plus-que-parfait de l'indicatif	
entrais	entrions	étais entré(e)	étions entré(e)s
entrais	entriez	étais entré(e)	étiez entré(e)(s)
entrait	entraient	était entré(e)	étaient entré(e)s
3 passé simple		10 passé antérieur	
entrai	entrâmes	fus entré(e)	fûmes entré(e)s
entras	entrâtes	fus entré(e)	fûtes entré(e)(s)
entra	entrèrent	fut entré(e)	furent entré(e)s
4 futur		11 futur antérieur	
entrerai	entrerons	serai entré(e)	serons entré(e)s
entreras	entrerez	seras entré(e)	serez entré(e)(s)
entrera	entreront	sera entré(e)	seront entré(e)s
5 conditionnel		12 conditionnel passé	
entrerais	entrerions	serais entré(e)	serions entré(e)s
entrerais	entreriez	serais entré(e)	seriez entré(e)(s)
entrerait	entreraient	serait entré(e)	seraient entré(e)s
6 présent du subjonctif		13 passé du subjonctif	
entre	entrions	sois entré(e)	soyons entré(e)s
entres	entriez	sois entré(e)	soyez entré(e)(s)
entre	entrent	soit entré(e)	soient entré(e)s
7 imparfait du subjonctif		14 plus-que-parfait du subjonctif	
entrasse	entrassions	fusse entré(e)	fussions entré(e)s
entrasses	entrassiez	fusses entré(e)	fussiez entré(e)(s)
entrât	entrassent	fût entré(e)	fussent entré(e)s
		Impératif	
		entre	
		entrons	
		entrez	

Mes parents veulent acheter une nouvelle maison. Nous sommes allés voir quelques maisons à vendre. Nous avons vu une jolie maison et nous y sommes entrés. Ma mère est entrée dans la cuisine pour regarder. Mon père est entré dans le garage pour regarder. Ma soeur est entrée dans la salle à manger et moi, je suis entré dans la salle de bains pour voir s'il y avait une douche.

l'entrée *(f.)*   entrance
entrer par la fenêtre   to enter through the window
entrer dans + noun   to enter (into) + noun

See also **rentrer**.

to send

The Seven Simple Tenses		The Seven Compound Tenses	
Singular	Plural	Singular	Plural
1 présent de l'indicatif		8 passé composé	
envoie	envoyons	ai envoyé	avons envoyé
envoies	envoyez	as envoyé	avez envoyé
envoie	envoient	a envoyé	ont envoyé
2 imparfait de l'indicatif		9 plus-que-parfait de l'indicatif	
envoyais	envoyions	avais envoyé	avions envoyé
envoyais	envoyiez	avais envoyé	aviez envoyé
envoyait	envoyaient	avait envoyé	avaient envoyé
3 passé simple		10 passé antérieur	
envoyai	envoyâmes	eus envoyé	eûmes envoyé
envoyas	envoyâtes	eus envoyé	eûtes envoyé
envoya	envoyèrent	eut envoyé	eurent envoyé
4 futur		11 futur antérieur	
enverrai	enverrons	aurai envoyé	aurons envoyé
enverras	enverrez	auras envoyé	aurez envoyé
enverra	enverront	aura envoyé	auront envoyé
5 conditionnel		12 conditionnel passé	
enverrais	enverrions	aurais envoyé	aurions envoyé
enverrais	enverriez	aurais envoyé	auriez envoyé
enverrait	enverraient	aurait envoyé	auraient envoyé
6 présent du subjonctif		13 passé du subjonctif	
envoie	envoyions	aie envoyé	ayons envoyé
envoies	envoyiez	aies envoyé	ayez envoyé
envoie	envoient	ait envoyé	aient envoyé
7 imparfait du subjonctif		14 plus-que-parfait du subjonctif	
envoyasse	envoyassions	eusse envoyé	eussions envoyé
envoyasses	envoyassiez	eusses envoyé	eussiez envoyé
envoyât	envoyassent	eût envoyé	eussent envoyé

Impératif
envoie
envoyons
envoyez

Hier j'ai envoyé une lettre à des amis en France. Demain j'enverrai une lettre à mes amis en Italie. J'enverrais une lettre en Chine mais je ne connais personne dans ce pays.

envoyer chercher to send for; **Mon père a envoyé chercher le docteur parce que mon petit frère est malade.**
un envoi envoy
envoyeur, envoyeuse sender
renvoyer to send away (back), to discharge someone

Verbs ending in *-oyer* must change *y* to *i* before mute *e*.

111

épouser

Part. pr. épousant   **Part. passé épousé**

to marry, to wed

The Seven Simple Tenses		The Seven Compound Tenses	
Singular	Plural	Singular	Plural
1 présent de l'indicatif		**8 passé composé**	
épouse	épousons	ai épousé	avons épousé
épouses	épousez	as épousé	avez épousé
épouse	épousent	a épousé	ont épousé
2 imparfait de l'indicatif		**9 plus-que-parfait de l'indicatif**	
épousais	épousions	avais épousé	avions épousé
épousais	épousiez	avais épousé	aviez épousé
épousait	épousaient	avait épousé	avaient épousé
3 passé simple		**10 passé antérieur**	
épousai	épousâmes	eus épousé	eûmes épousé
épousas	épousâtes	eus épousé	eûtes épousé
épousa	épousèrent	eut épousé	eurent épousé
4 futur		**11 futur antérieur**	
épouserai	épouserons	aurai épousé	aurons épousé
épouseras	épouserez	auras épousé	aurez épousé
épousera	épouseront	aura épousé	auront épousé
5 conditionnel		**12 conditionnel passé**	
épouserais	épouserions	aurais épousé	aurions épousé
épouserais	épouseriez	aurais épousé	auriez épousé
épouserait	épouseraient	aurait épousé	auraient épousé
6 présent du subjonctif		**13 passé du subjonctif**	
épouse	épousions	aie épousé	ayons épousé
épouses	épousiez	aies épousé	ayez épousé
épouse	épousent	ait épousé	aient épousé
7 imparfait du subjonctif		**14 plus-que-parfait du subjonctif**	
épousasse	épousassions	eusse épousé	eussions épousé
épousasses	épousassiez	eusses épousé	eussiez épousé
épousât	épousassent	eût épousé	eussent épousé

Impératif
épouse
épousons
épousez

J'ai trois frères. Le premier a épousé une jolie jeune fille française. Le deuxième a épousé une belle jeune fille italienne, et le troisième a épousé une jolie fille espagnole. Elles sont très intelligentes.

un époux husband
une épouse wife
les nouveaux mariés the newlyweds
se marier avec quelqu'un to get married to someone

The Seven Simple Tenses		The Seven Compound Tenses	
Singular	Plural	Singular	Plural
1 présent de l'indicatif		8 passé composé	
espère	**espérons**	**ai espéré**	**avons espéré**
espères	**espérez**	**as espéré**	**avez espéré**
espère	**espèrent**	**a espéré**	**ont espéré**
2 imparfait de l'indicatif		9 plus-que-parfait de l'indicatif	
espérais	**espérions**	**avais espéré**	**avions espéré**
espérais	**espériez**	**avais espéré**	**aviez espéré**
espérait	**espéraient**	**avait espéré**	**avaient espéré**
3 passé simple		10 passé antérieur	
espérai	**espérâmes**	**eus espéré**	**eûmes espéré**
espéras	**espérâtes**	**eus espéré**	**eûtes espéré**
espéra	**espérèrent**	**eut espéré**	**eurent espéré**
4 futur		11 futur antérieur	
espérerai	**espérerons**	**aurai espéré**	**aurons espéré**
espéreras	**espérerez**	**auras espéré**	**aurez espéré**
espérera	**espéreront**	**aura espéré**	**auront espéré**
5 conditionnel		12 conditionnel passé	
espérerais	**espérerions**	**aurais espéré**	**aurions espéré**
espérerais	**espéreriez**	**aurais espéré**	**auriez espéré**
espérerait	**espéreraient**	**aurait espéré**	**auraient espéré**
6 présent du subjonctif		13 passé du subjonctif	
espère	**espérions**	**aie espéré**	**ayons espéré**
espères	**espériez**	**aies espéré**	**ayez espéré**
espère	**espèrent**	**ait espéré**	**aient espéré**
7 imparfait du subjonctif		14 plus-que-parfait du subjonctif	
espérasse	**espérassions**	**eusse espéré**	**eussions espéré**
espérasses	**espérassiez**	**eusses espéré**	**eussiez espéré**
espérât	**espérassent**	**eût espéré**	**eussent espéré**
		Impératif	
		espère	
		espérons	
		espérez	

J'espère que Paul viendra mais je n'espère pas que son frère vienne.

l'espérance *(f.)* hope, expectation
plein d'espérance hopeful, full of hope
l'espoir *(m.)* hope
avoir bon espoir de réussir   to have good hopes of succeeding
désespérer de to despair of; **se désespérer**   to be in despair
le désespoir despair; **un désespoir d'amour**   disappointed love

to try, to try on

The Seven Simple Tenses		The Seven Compound Tenses	
Singular	Plural	Singular	Plural
1 présent de l'indicatif		8 passé composé	
essaye	essayons	ai essayé	avons essayé
essayes	essayez	as essayé	avez essayé
essaye	essayent	a essayé	ont essayé
2 imparfait de l'indicatif		9 plus-que-parfait de l'indicatif	
essayais	essayions	avais essayé	avions essayé
essayais	essayiez	avais essayé	aviez essayé
essayait	essayaient	avait essayé	avaient essayé
3 passé simple		10 passé antérieur	
essayai	essayâmes	eus essayé	eûmes essayé
essayas	essayâtes	eus essayé	eûtes essayé
essaya	essayèrent	eut essayé	eurent essayé
4 futur		11 futur antérieur	
essayerai	essayerons	aurai essayé	aurons essayé
essayeras	essayerez	auras essayé	aurez essayé
essayera	essayeront	aura essayé	auront essayé
5 conditionnel		12 conditionnel passé	
essayerais	essayerions	aurais essayé	aurions essayé
essayerais	essayeriez	aurais essayé	auriez essayé
essayerait	essayeraient	aurait essayé	auraient essayé
6 présent du subjonctif		13 passé du subjonctif	
essaye	essayions	aie essayé	ayons essayé
essayes	essayiez	aies essayé	ayez essayé
essaye	essayent	ait essayé	aient essayé
7 imparfait du subjonctif		14 plus-que-parfait du subjonctif	
essayasse	essayassions	eusse essayé	eussions essayé
essayasses	essayassiez	eusses essayé	eussiez essayé
essayât	essayassent	eût essayé	eussent essayé

Impératif
essaye
essayons
essayez

Marcel a essayé d'écrire un essai sur la vie des animaux sauvages mais il n'a pas pu réussir à écrire une seule phrase. Alors, il est allé dans la chambre de son grand frère pour travailler ensemble.

un essai essay	essayeur, essayeuse fitter (clothing)
essayiste essayist	essayage *(m.)* fitting (clothing)
essayer de faire qqch to try to do something	

Verbs ending in *-ayer* may change y to *i* before mute *e* or may keep y.

to wipe

The Seven Simple Tenses		The Seven Compound Tenses	
Singular	Plural	Singular	Plural
1 présent de l'indicatif		8 passé composé	
essuie	essuyons	ai essuyé	avons essuyé
essuies	essuyez	as essuyé	avez essuyé
essuie	essuient	a essuyé	ont essuyé
2 imparfait de l'indicatif		9 plus-que-parfait de l'indicatif	
essuyais	essuyions	avais essuyé	avions essuyé
essuyais	essuyiez	avais essuyé	aviez essuyé
essuyait	essuyaient	avait essuyé	avaient essuyé
3 passé simple		10 passé antérieur	
essuyai	essuyâmes	eus essuyé	eûmes essuyé
essuyas	essuyâtes	eus essuyé	eûtes essuyé
essuya	essuyèrent	eut essuyé	eurent essuyé
4 futur		11 futur antérieur	
essuieral	essuierons	aurai essuyé	aurons essuyé
essuieras	essuierez	auras essuyé	aurez essuyé
essuiera	essuieront	aura essuyé	auront essuyé
5 conditionnel		12 conditionnel passé	
essuierais	essuierions	aurais essuyé	aurions essuyé
essuierais	essuieriez	aurais essuyé	auriez essuyé
essuierait	essuieraient	auralt essuyé	auraient essuyé
6 présent du subjonctif		13 passé du subjonctif	
essuie	essuyions	aie essuyé	ayons essuyé
essuies	essuyiez	aies essuyé	ayez essuyé
essuie	essuient	ait essuyé	aient essuyé
7 imparfait du subjonctif		14 plus-que-parfait du subjonctif	
essuyasse	essuyassions	eusse essuyé	eussions essuyé
essuyasses	essuyassiez	eusses essuyé	eussiez essuyé
essuyât	essuyassent	eût essuyé	eussent essuyé

Impératif
essuie
essuyons
essuyez

un essuie-mains hand towel		**un essuie-verres** glass cloth	
un essuie-glace windshield wiper		**s'essuyer** to wipe oneself	
l'essuyage *(m.)* wiping		**s'essuyer le front** to wipe one's brow	

Verbs ending in *-uyer* must change *y* to *i* before mute *e*.

to extinguish

The Seven Simple Tenses		The Seven Compound Tenses	
Singular	Plural	Singular	Plural
1 présent de l'indicatif		8 passé composé	
éteins	**éteignons**	**ai éteint**	**avons éteint**
éteins	**éteignez**	**as éteint**	**avez éteint**
éteint	**éteignent**	**a éteint**	**ont éteint**
2 imparfait de l'indicatif		9 plus-que-parfait de l'indicatif	
éteignais	**éteignions**	**avais éteint**	**avions éteint**
éteignais	**éteigniez**	**avais éteint**	**aviez éteint**
éteignait	**éteignaient**	**avait éteint**	**avaient éteint**
3 passé simple		10 passé antérieur	
éteignis	**éteignîmes**	**eus éteint**	**eûmes éteint**
éteignis	**éteignîtes**	**eus éteint**	**eûtes éteint**
éteignit	**éteignirent**	**eut éteint**	**eurent éteint**
4 futur		11 futur antérieur	
éteindrai	**éteindrons**	**aurai éteint**	**aurons éteint**
éteindras	**éteindrez**	**auras éteint**	**aurez éteint**
éteindra	**éteindront**	**aura éteint**	**auront éteint**
5 conditionnel		12 conditionnel passé	
éteindrais	**éteindrions**	**aurais éteint**	**aurions éteint**
éteindrais	**éteindriez**	**aurais éteint**	**auriez éteint**
éteindrait	**éteindraient**	**aurait éteint**	**auraient éteint**
6 présent du subjonctif		13 passé du subjonctif	
éteigne	**éteignions**	**aie éteint**	**ayons éteint**
éteignes	**éteigniez**	**aies éteint**	**ayez éteint**
éteigne	**éteignent**	**ait éteint**	**aient éteint**
7 imparfait du subjonctif		14 plus-que-parfait du subjonctif	
éteignisse	**éteignissions**	**eusse éteint**	**eussions éteint**
éteignisses	**éteignissiez**	**eusses éteint**	**eussiez éteint**
éteignît	**éteignissent**	**eût éteint**	**eussent éteint**
		Impératif	
		éteins	
		éteignons	
		éteignez	

Il est minuit. Je vais me coucher. Je dois me lever tôt le matin pour aller à l'école. J'éteins la lumière. Bonne nuit!

éteint, éteinte   extinct
un éteignoir   extinguisher, snuffer
s'éteindre   to flicker out, to die out, to die
éteindre le feu   to put out the fire
éteindre la lumière   to turn off the light

to stretch oneself, to stretch out, to lie down

The Seven Simple Tenses		The Seven Compound Tenses	
Singular	Plural	Singular	Plural
1 présent de l'indicatif		8 passé composé	
m'étends	nous étendons	me suis étendu(e)	nous sommes étendu(e)s
t'étends	vous étendez	t'es étendu(e)	vous êtes étendu(e)(s)
s'étend	s'étendent	s'est étendu(e)	se sont étendu(e)s
2 imparfait de l'indicatif		9 plus-que-parfait de l'indicatif	
m'étendais	nous étendions	m'étais étendu(e)	nous étions étendu(e)s
t'étendais	vous étendiez	t'étais étendu(e)	vous étiez étendu(e)(s)
s'étendait	s'étendaient	s'était étendu(e)	s'étaient étendu(e)s
3 passé simple		10 passé antérieur	
m'étendis	nous étendîmes	me fus étendu(e)	nous fûmes étendu(e)s
t'étendis	vous étendîtes	te fus étendu(e)	vous fûtes étendu(e)(s)
s'étendit	s'étendirent	se fut étendu(e)	se furent étendu(e)s
4 futur		11 futur antérieur	
m'étendrai	nous étendrons	me serai étendu(e)	nous serons étendu(e)s
t'étendras	vous étendrez	te seras étendu(e)	vous serez étendu(e)(s)
s'étendra	s'étendront	se sera étendu(e)	se seront étendu(e)s
5 conditionnel		12 conditionnel passé	
m'étendrais	nous étendrions	me serais étendu(e)	nous serions étendu(e)s
t'étendrais	vous étendriez	te serais étendu(e)	vous seriez étendu(e)(s)
s'étendrait	s'étendraient	se serait étendu(e)	se seraient étendu(e)s
6 présent du subjonctif		13 passé du subjonctif	
m'étende	nous étendions	me sois étendu(e)	nous soyons étendu(e)s
t'étendes	vous étendiez	te sois étendu(e)	vous soyez étendu(e)(s)
s'étende	s'étendent	se soit étendu(e)	se soient étendu(e)s
7 imparfait du subjonctif		14 plus-que-parfait du subjonctif	
m'étendisse	nous étendissions	me fusse étendu(e)	nous fussions étendu(e)s
t'étendisses	vous étendissiez	te fusses étendu(e)	vous fussiez étendu(e)(s)
s'étendît	s'étendissent	se fût étendu(e)	se fussent étendu(e)s

Impératif
étends-toi; ne t'étends pas
étendons-nous; ne nous étendons pas
étendez-vous; ne vous étendez pas

Ma mère était si fatiguée quand elle est rentrée à la maison après avoir fait du shopping, qu'elle est allée directement au lit et elle s'est étendue.

étendre le linge   to hang out the wash
étendre la main   to hold out your hand
étendre le bras   to extend your arm
étendre d'eau   to water down
s'étendre sur qqch   to dwell on something

117

| **étonner** | Part. pr. **étonnant** | Part. passé **étonné** |

to amaze, to astonish, to stun, to surprise

The Seven Simple Tenses		The Seven Compound Tenses	
Singular	Plural	Singular	Plural
1 présent de l'indicatif		8 passé composé	
étonne	étonnons	ai étonné	avons étonné
étonnes	étonnez	as étonné	avez étonné
étonne	étonnent	a étonné	ont étonné
2 imparfait de l'indicatif		9 plus-que-parfait de l'indicatif	
étonnais	étonnions	avais étonné	avions étonné
étonnais	étonniez	avais étonné	aviez étonné
étonnait	étonnaient	avait étonné	avaient étonné
3 passé simple		10 passé antérieur	
étonnai	étonnâmes	eus étonné	eûmes étonné
étonnas	étonnâtes	eus étonné	eûtes étonné
étonna	étonnèrent	eut étonné	eurent étonné
4 futur		11 futur antérieur	
étonnerai	étonnerons	aurai étonné	aurons étonné
étonneras	étonnerez	auras étonné	aurez étonné
étonnera	étonneront	aura étonné	auront étonné
5 conditionnel		12 conditionnel passé	
étonnerais	étonnerions	aurais étonné	aurions étonné
étonnerais	étonneriez	aurais étonné	auriez étonné
étonnerait	étonneraient	aurait étonné	auraient étonné
6 présent du subjonctif		13 passé du subjonctif	
étonne	étonnions	aie étonné	ayons étonné
étonnes	étonniez	aies étonné	ayez étonné
étonne	étonnent	ait étonné	aient étonné
7 imparfait du subjonctif		14 plus-que-parfait du subjonctif	
étonnasse	étonnassions	eusse étonné	eussions étonné
étonnasses	étonnassiez	eusses étonné	eussiez étonné
étonnât	étonnassent	eût étonné	eussent étonné
		Impératif	
		étonne	
		étonnons	
		étonnez	

étonnant, étonnante astonishing
C'est bien étonnant! It's quite astonishing!
l'étonnement *(m.)* astonishment, amazement
s'étonner de to be astonished at
Cela m'étonne! That astonishes me!
Cela ne m'étonne pas! That does not surprise me!

to be

The Seven Simple Tenses		The Seven Compound Tenses	
Singular	Plural	Singular	Plural
1 présent de l'indicatif		8 passé composé	
suis	sommes	ai été	avons été
es	êtes	as été	avez été
est	sont	a été	ont été
2 imparfait de l'indicatif		9 plus-que-parfait de l'indicatif	
étais	étions	avais été	avions été
étais	étiez	avais été	aviez été
était	étaient	avait été	avaient été
3 passé simple		10 passé antérieur	
fus	fûmes	eus été	eûmes été
fus	fûtes	eus été	eûtes été
fut	furent	eut été	eurent été
4 futur		11 futur antérieur	
serai	serons	aurai été	aurons été
seras	serez	auras été	aurez été
sera	seront	aura été	auront été
5 conditionnel		12 conditionnel passé	
serais	serions	aurais été	aurions été
serais	seriez	aurais été	auriez été
serait	seraient	aurait été	auraient été
6 présent du subjonctif		13 passé du subjonctif	
sois	soyons	aie été	ayons été
sois	soyez	aies été	ayez été
soit	soient	ait été	aient été
7 imparfait du subjonctif		14 plus-que-parfait du subjonctif	
fusse	fussions	eusse été	eussions été
fusses	fussiez	eusses été	eussiez été
fût	fussent	eût été	eussent été
		Impératif	
		sois	
		soyons	
		soyez	

être en train de + inf. to be in the act of + pres. part., to be in the process of, to be
busy + pres. part.;
Mon père est en train d'écrire une lettre à mes grands-parents.

être à l'heure	to be on time	**Je suis à vous.**	I am at your service.
être à temps	to be in time	**Je suis d'avis que. . .**	I am of the opinion that. . .
être pressé(e)	to be in a hurry	**être ou ne pas être**	to be or not to be

étudier

Part. pr. **étudiant**   Part. passé **étudié**

to study

The Seven Simple Tenses		The Seven Compound Tenses	
Singular	Plural	Singular	Plural
1 présent de l'indicatif		8 passé composé	
étudie	**étudions**	**ai étudié**	**avons étudié**
étudies	**étudiez**	**as étudié**	**avez étudié**
étudie	**étudient**	**a étudié**	**ont étudié**
2 imparfait de l'indicatif		9 plus-que-parfait de l'indicatif	
étudiais	**étudiions**	**avais étudié**	**avions étudié**
étudiais	**étudiiez**	**avais étudié**	**aviez étudié**
étudiait	**étudiaient**	**avait étudié**	**avaient étudié**
3 passé simple		10 passé antérieur	
étudiai	**étudiâmes**	**eus étudié**	**eûmes étudié**
étudias	**étudiâtes**	**eus étudié**	**eûtes étudié**
étudia	**étudièrent**	**eut étudié**	**eurent étudié**
4 futur		11 futur antérieur	
étudierai	**étudierons**	**aurai étudié**	**aurons étudié**
étudieras	**étudierez**	**auras étudié**	**aurez étudié**
étudiera	**étudieront**	**aura étudié**	**auront étudié**
5 conditionnel		12 conditionnel passé	
étudierais	**étudierions**	**aurais étudié**	**aurions étudié**
étudierais	**étudieriez**	**aurais étudié**	**auriez étudié**
étudierait	**étudieraient**	**aurait étudié**	**auraient étudié**
6 présent du subjonctif		13 passé du subjonctif	
étudie	**étudiions**	**aie étudié**	**ayons étudié**
étudies	**étudiiez**	**aies étudié**	**ayez étudié**
étudie	**étudient**	**ait étudié**	**aient étudié**
7 imparfait du subjonctif		14 plus-que-parfait du subjonctif	
étudiasse	**étudiassions**	**eusse étudié**	**eussions étudié**
étudiasses	**étudiassiez**	**eusses étudié**	**eussiez étudié**
étudiât	**étudiassent**	**eût étudié**	**eussent étudié**
		Impératif	
		étudie	
		étudions	
		étudiez	

Je connais une jeune fille qui étudie le piano depuis deux ans. Je connais un garçon qui étudie ses leçons à fond. Je connais un astronome qui étudie les étoiles dans le ciel depuis dix ans.

étudier à fond   to study thoroughly
un étudiant, une étudiante   student
l'étude (*f.*)   study; **les études**   studies
faire ses études   to study, to go to school
à l'étude   under consideration, under study

s'amuser au lieu d'étudier   to have a good time instead of studying
étudier qqch de près   to study something closely
s'étudier   to analyze oneself

to excuse oneself, to apologize

The Seven Simple Tenses		The Seven Compound Tenses	
Singular	Plural	Singular	Plural
1 présent de l'indicatif		8 passé composé	
m'excuse	nous excusons	me suis excusé(e)	nous sommes excusé(e)s
t'excuses	vous excusez	t'es excusé(e)	vous êtes excusé(e)(s)
s'excuse	s'excusent	s'est excusé(e)	se sont excusé(e)s
2 imparfait de l'indicatif		9 plus-que-parfait de l'indicatif	
m'excusais	nous excusions	m'étais excusé(e)	nous étions excusé(e)s
t'excusais	vous excusiez	t'étais excusé(e)	vous étiez excusé(e)(s)
s'excusait	s'excusaient	s'était excusé(e)	s'étaient excusé(e)s
3 passé simple		10 passé antérieur	
m'excusai	nous excusâmes	me fus excusé(e)	nous fûmes excusé(e)s
t'excusas	vous excusâtes	te fus excusé(e)	vous fûtes excusé(e)(s)
s'excusa	s'excusèrent	se fut excusé(e)	se furent excusé(e)s
4 futur		11 futur antérieur	
m'excuserai	nous excuserons	me serai excusé(e)	nous serons excusé(e)s
t'excuseras	vous excuserez	te seras excusé(e)	vous serez excusé(e)(s)
s'excusera	s'excuseront	se sera excusé(e)	se seront excusé(e)s
5 conditionnel		12 conditionnel passé	
m'excuserais	nous excuserions	me serais excusé(e)	nous serions excusé(e)s
t'excuserais	vous excuseriez	te serais excusé(e)	vous seriez excusé(e)(s)
s'excuserait	s'excuseraient	se serait excusé(e)	se seraient excusé(e)s
6 présent du subjonctif		13 passé du subjonctif	
m'excuse	nous excusions	me sois excusé(e)	nous soyons excusé(e)s
t'excuses	vous excusiez	te sois excusé(e)	vous soyez excusé(e)(s)
s'excuse	s'excusent	se soit excusé(e)	se soient excusé(e)s
7 imparfait du subjonctif		14 plus-que-parfait du subjonctif	
m'excusasse	nous excusassions	me fusse excusé(e)	nous fussions excusé(e)s
t'excusasses	vous excusassiez	te fusses excusé(e)	vous fussiez excusé(e)(s)
s'excusât	s'excusassent	se fût excusé(e)	se fussent excusé(e)s

Impératif
excuse-toi; ne t'excuse pas
excusons-nous; ne nous excusons pas
excusez-vous; ne vous excusez pas

L'élève:	**Je m'excuse, madame. Excusez-moi. Je m'excuse de vous déranger. Est-ce que vous m'excusez? Est-ce que je vous dérange?**
La maîtresse:	**Oui, je t'excuse. Non, tu ne me déranges pas. Que veux-tu?**
L'élève:	**Est-ce que je peux quitter la salle de classe pour aller aux toilettes?**
La maîtresse:	**Oui, vas-y.**

s'excuser de   to apologize for
Veuillez m'excuser.   Please (Be good enough to) excuse me.
Qui s'excuse s'accuse.   A guilty conscience needs no accuser.

121

to demand, to require

The Seven Simple Tenses		The Seven Compound Tenses	
Singular	Plural	Singular	Plural
1 présent de l'indicatif		8 passé composé	
exige	exigeons	ai exigé	avons exigé
exiges	exigez	as exigé	avez exigé
exige	exigent	a exigé	ont exigé
2 imparfait de l'indicatif		9 plus-que-parfait de l'indicatif	
exigeais	exigions	avais exigé	avions exigé
exigeais	exigiez	avais exigé	aviez exigé
exigeait	exigeaient	avait exigé	avaient exigé
3 passé simple		10 passé antérieur	
exigeai	exigeâmes	eus exigé	eûmes exigé
exigeas	exigeâtes	eus exigé	eûtes exigé
exigea	exigèrent	eut exigé	eurent exigé
4 futur		11 futur antérieur	
exigerai	exigerons	aurai exigé	aurons exigé
exigeras	exigerez	auras exigé	aurez exigé
exigera	exigeront	aura exigé	auront exigé
5 conditionnel		12 conditionnel passé	
exigerais	exigerions	aurais exigé	aurions exigé
exigerais	exigeriez	aurais exigé	auriez exigé
exigerait	exigeraient	aurait exigé	auraient exigé
6 présent du subjonctif		13 passé du subjonctif	
exige	exigions	aie exigé	ayons exigé
exiges	exigiez	aies exigé	ayez exigé
exige	exigent	ait exigé	aient exigé
7 imparfait du subjonctif		14 plus-que-parfait du subjonctif	
exigeasse	exigeassions	eusse exigé	eussions exigé
exigeasses	exigeassiez	eusses exigé	eussiez exigé
exigeât	exigeassent	eût exigé	eussent exigé
		Impératif	
		exige	
		exigeons	
		exigez	

La maîtresse de français:	Paul, viens ici. Ta composition est pleine de fautes. J'exige que tu la refasses. Rends-la-moi dans dix minutes.
L'élève:	Ce n'est pas de ma faute, madame. C'est mon père qui l'a écrite. Dois-je la refaire?

exigeant, exigeante exacting
l'exigence (*f.*) exigency
exiger des soins attentifs to demand great care
les exigences requirements

to explain

The Seven Simple Tenses		The Seven Compound Tenses	
Singular	Plural	Singular	Plural
1 présent de l'indicatif		8 passé composé	
explique	expliquons	ai expliqué	avons expliqué
expliques	expliquez	as expliqué	avez expliqué
explique	expliquent	a expliqué	ont expliqué
2 imparfait de l'indicatif		9 plus-que-parfait de l'indicatif	
expliquais	expliquions	avais expliqué	avions expliqué
expliquais	expliquiez	avais expliqué	aviez expliqué
expliquait	expliquaient	avait expliqué	avaient expliqué
3 passé simple		10 passé antérieur	
expliquai	expliquâmes	eus expliqué	eûmes expliqué
expliquas	expliquâtes	eus expliqué	eûtes expliqué
expliqua	expliquèrent	eut expliqué	eurent expliqué
4 futur		11 futur antérieur	
expliquerai	expliquerons	aurai expliqué	aurons expliqué
expliqueras	expliquerez	auras expliqué	aurez expliqué
expliquera	expliqueront	aura expliqué	auront expliqué
5 conditionnel		12 conditionnel passé	
expliquerais	expliquerions	aurais expliqué	aurions expliqué
expliquerais	expliqueriez	aurais expliqué	auriez expliqué
expliquerait	expliqueraient	aurait expliqué	auraient expliqué
6 présent du subjonctif		13 passé du subjonctif	
explique	expliquions	aie expliqué	ayons expliqué
expliques	expliquiez	aies expliqué	ayez expliqué
explique	expliquent	ait expliqué	aient expliqué
7 imparfait du subjonctif		14 plus-que-parfait du subjonctif	
expliquasse	expliquassions	eusse expliqué	eussions expliqué
expliquasses	expliquassiez	eusses expliqué	eussiez expliqué
expliquât	expliquassent	eût expliqué	eussent expliqué

	Impératif
	explique
	expliquons
	expliquez

explicite explicit	**explicable** explainable
explicitement explicitly	**explicatif, explicative** explanatory
l'explication (*f.*) explanation	**s'expliciter** to be explicit
explicateur, explicatrice explainer	

Note the difference in meaning in the following two sentences. See p. xxiv (b).

J'ai étudié la leçon que le professeur avait expliquée.   I studied the lesson that the teacher had explained.
J'avais étudié la leçon que le professeur a expliquée.   I had studied the lesson that the teacher explained.

se fâcher   Part. pr. **se fâchant**   Part. passé **fâché(e)(s)**

to become angry, to get angry

The Seven Simple Tenses		The Seven Compound Tenses	
Singular	Plural	Singular	Plural
1 présent de l'indicatif		8 passé composé	
me fâche	nous fâchons	me suis fâché(e)	nous sommes fâché(e)s
te fâches	vous fâchez	t'es fâché(e)	vous êtes fâché(e)(s)
se fâche	se fâchent	s'est fâché(e)	se sont fâché(e)s
2 imparfait de l'indicatif		9 plus-que-parfait de l'indicatif	
me fâchais	nous fâchions	m'étais fâché(e)	nous étions fâché(e)s
te fâchais	vous fâchiez	t'étais fâché(e)	vous étiez fâché(e)(s)
se fâchait	se fâchaient	s'était fâché(e)	s'étaient fâché(e)s
3 passé simple		10 passé antérieur	
me fâchai	nous fâchâmes	me fus fâché(e)	nous fûmes fâché(e)s
te fâchas	vous fâchâtes	te fus fâché(e)	vous fûtes fâché(e)(s)
se fâcha	se fâchèrent	se fut fâché(e)	se furent fâché(e)s
4 futur		11 futur antérieur	
me fâcherai	nous fâcherons	me serai fâché(e)	nous serons fâché(e)s
te fâcheras	vous fâcherez	te seras fâché(e)	vous serez fâché(e)(s)
se fâchera	se fâcheront	se sera fâché(e)	se seront fâché(e)s
5 conditionnel		12 conditionnel passé	
me fâcherais	nous fâcherions	me serais fâché(e)	nous serions fâché(e)s
te fâcherais	vous fâcheriez	te serais fâché(e)	vous seriez fâché(e)(s)
se fâcherait	se fâcheraient	se serait fâché(e)	se seraient fâché(e)s
6 présent du subjonctif		13 passé du subjonctif	
me fâche	nous fâchions	me sois fâché(e)	nous soyons fâché(e)s
te fâches	vous fâchiez	te sois fâché(e)	vous soyez fâché(e)(s)
se fâche	se fâchent	se soit fâché(e)	se soient fâché(e)s
7 imparfait du subjonctif		14 plus-que-parfait du subjonctif	
me fâchasse	nous fâchassions	me fusse fâché(e)	nous fussions fâché(e)s
te fâchasses	vous fâchassiez	te fusses fâché(e)	vous fussiez fâché(e)(s)
se fâchât	se fâchassent	se fût fâché(e)	se fussent fâché(e)s

Impératif
fâche-toi; ne te fâche pas
fâchons-nous; ne nous fâchons pas
fâchez-vous; ne vous fâchez pas

---

fâcher qqn   to anger someone, to offend someone
se fâcher contre qqn   to become angry at someone
une fâcherie   tiff
C'est fâcheux!   It's a nuisance! It's annoying!
fâcheusement   annoyingly
se fâcher tout rouge   to turn red with anger
Ce que vous dites me fâche beaucoup.   What you are saying distresses me very much.

The Seven Simple Tenses		The Seven Compound Tenses	
Singular	Plural	Singular	Plural
1 présent de l'indicatif		8 passé composé	
faux	**faillons**	**ai failli**	**avons failli**
faux	**faillez**	**as failli**	**avez failli**
faut	**faillent**	**a failli**	**ont failli**
2 imparfait de l'indicatif		9 plus-que-parfait de l'indicatif	
faillais	**faillions**	**avais failli**	**avions failli**
faillais	**failliez**	**avais failli**	**aviez failli**
faillait	**faillaient**	**avait failli**	**avaient failli**
3 passé simple		10 passé antérieur	
faillis	**faillîmes**	**eus failli**	**eûmes failli**
faillis	**faillîtes**	**eus failli**	**eûtes failli**
faillit	**faillirent**	**eut failli**	**eurent failli**
4 futur		11 futur antérieur	
faillirai or faudrai	**faillirons or faudrons**	**aurai failli**	**aurons failli**
failliras or faudras	**faillirez or faudrez**	**auras failli**	**aurez failli**
faillira or faudra	**failliront or faudront**	**aura failli**	**auront failli**
5 conditionnel		12 conditionnel passé	
faillirais or faudrais	**faillirions or faudrions**	**aurais failli**	**aurions failli**
faillirais or faudrais	**failliriez or faudriez**	**aurais failli**	**auriez failli**
faillirait or faudrait	**failliraient or faudraient**	**aurait failli**	**auraient failli**
6 présent du subjonctif		13 passé du subjonctif	
faille	**faillions**	**aie failli**	**ayons failli**
failles	**failliez**	**aies failli**	**ayez failli**
faille	**faillent**	**ait failli**	**aient failli**
7 imparfait du subjonctif		14 plus-que-parfait du subjonctif	
faillisse	**faillissions**	**eusse failli**	**eussions failli**
faillisses	**faillissiez**	**eusses failli**	**eussiez failli**
faillît	**faillissent**	**eût failli**	**eussent failli**

Impératif
—

---

la faillite bankruptcy, failure	**défaillir** to weaken, to faint
failli, faillie bankrupt	**défaillant, défaillante** feeble
J'ai failli tomber. I almost fell.	**une défaillance** faint (swoon)
faire faillite to go bankrupt	

faire Part. pr. **faisant** Part. passé **fait**

to do, to make

The Seven Simple Tenses		The Seven Compound Tenses	
Singular	Plural	Singular	Plural
1 présent de l'indicatif		**8 passé composé**	
fais	faisons	ai fait	avons fait
fais	faites	as fait	avez fait
fait	font	a fait	ont fait
2 imparfait de l'indicatif		**9 plus-que-parfait de l'indicatif**	
faisais	faisions	avais fait	avions fait
faisais	faisiez	avais fait	aviez fait
faisait	faisaient	avait fait	avaient fait
3 passé simple		**10 passé antérieur**	
fis	fîmes	eus fait	eûmes fait
fis	fîtes	eus fait	eûtes fait
fit	firent	eut fait	eurent fait
4 futur		**11 futur antérieur**	
ferai	ferons	aurai fait	aurons fait
feras	ferez	auras fait	aurez fait
fera	feront	aura fait	auront fait
5 conditionnel		**12 conditionnel passé**	
ferais	ferions	aurais fait	aurions fait
ferais	feriez	aurais fait	auriez fait
ferait	feraient	aurait fait	auraient fait
6 présent du subjonctif		**13 passé du subjonctif**	
fasse	fassions	aie fait	ayons fait
fasses	fassiez	aies fait	ayez fait
fasse	fassent	ait fait	aient fait
7 imparfait du subjonctif		**14 plus-que-parfait du subjonctif**	
fisse	fissions	eusse fait	eussions fait
fisses	fissiez	eusses fait	eussiez fait
fît	fissent	eût fait	eussent fait

Impératif
fais
faisons
faites

faire beau to be beautiful weather
faire chaud to be warm weather
faire froid to be cold weather
faire de l'autostop to hitchhike
faire attention à qqn ou à qqch to pay
  attention to someone or to something

faire une promenade to take a walk
faire le ménage to do the housework
faire un voyage to take a trip

126

to be necessary, must, to be lacking to (à), to need

The Seven Simple Tenses	The Seven Compound Tenses
Singular	Singular
1 présent de l'indicatif **il faut**	8 passé composé **il a fallu**
2 imparfait de l'indicatif **il fallait**	9 plus-que-parfait de l'indicatif **il avait fallu**
3 passé simple **il fallut**	10 passé antérieur **il eut fallu**
4 futur **il faudra**	11 futur antérieur **il aura fallu**
5 conditionnel **il faudrait**	12 conditionnel passé **il aurait fallu**
6 présent du subjonctif **qu'il faille**	13 passé du subjonctif **qu'il ait fallu**
7 imparfait du subjonctif **qu'il fallût**	14 plus-que-parfait du subjonctif **qu'il eût fallu**

Impératif

Il faut que je fasse mes leçons avant de regarder la télé. Il faut me coucher tôt parce qu'il faut me lever tôt. Il faut faire attention en classe, et il faut être sage. Si je fais toutes ces choses, je serai récompensé.

comme il faut   as is proper
agir comme il faut   to behave properly
Il me faut de l'argent.   I need some money.
Il faut manger pour vivre.   It is necessary to eat in order to live.
Il ne faut pas parler sans politesse.   One must not talk impolitely.

This is an impersonal verb and is used in the tenses given above with the subject *il.*

fermer	Part. pr. **fermant**	Part. passé **fermé**

to close

The Seven Simple Tenses		The Seven Compound Tenses	
Singular	Plural	Singular	Plural
1 présent de l'indicatif		8 passé composé	
ferme	**fermons**	**ai fermé**	**avons fermé**
fermes	**fermez**	**as fermé**	**avez fermé**
ferme	**ferment**	**a fermé**	**ont fermé**
2 imparfait de l'indicatif		9 plus-que-parfait de l'indicatif	
fermais	**fermions**	**avais fermé**	**avions fermé**
fermais	**fermiez**	**avais fermé**	**aviez fermé**
fermait	**fermaient**	**avait fermé**	**avaient fermé**
3 passé simple		10 passé antérieur	
fermai	**fermâmes**	**eus fermé**	**eûmes fermé**
fermas	**fermâtes**	**eus fermé**	**eûtes fermé**
ferma	**fermèrent**	**eut fermé**	**eurent fermé**
4 futur		11 futur antérieur	
fermerai	**fermerons**	**aurai fermé**	**aurons fermé**
fermeras	**fermerez**	**auras fermé**	**aurez fermé**
fermera	**fermeront**	**aura fermé**	**auront fermé**
5 conditionnel		12 conditionnel passé	
fermerais	**fermerions**	**aurais fermé**	**aurions fermé**
fermerais	**fermeriez**	**aurais fermé**	**auriez fermé**
fermerait	**fermeraient**	**aurait fermé**	**auraient fermé**
6 présent du subjonctif		13 passé du subjonctif	
ferme	**fermions**	**aie fermé**	**ayons fermé**
fermes	**fermiez**	**aies fermé**	**ayez fermé**
ferme	**ferment**	**ait fermé**	**aient fermé**
7 imparfait du subjonctif		14 plus-que-parfait du subjonctif	
fermasse	**fermassions**	**eusse fermé**	**eussions fermé**
fermasses	**fermassiez**	**eusses fermé**	**eussiez fermé**
fermât	**fermassent**	**eût fermé**	**eussent fermé**
		Impératif	
		ferme	
		fermons	
		fermez	

Georges est rentré tard hier soir. Il a ouvert la porte, puis il l'a fermée. Il a ouvert la garde-robe pour y mettre son manteau, son chapeau et ses gants et il l'a fermée. Il a ouvert la fenêtre mais il ne l'a pas fermée parce qu'il faisait trop chaud dans sa chambre et il ne peut pas dormir dans une chambre où l'air est lourd.

enfermer to shut in	**renfermer** to enclose
fermer à clef to lock	**une fermeture** closing, shutting
fermer au verrou to bolt	**une fermeture éclair, une**
Ferme-la! Shut up! Zip it!	**fermeture à glissière** zipper
fermer le robinet to turn off the tap	**l'heure de fermer** closing time

to depend on, to rely on, to trust in

The Seven Simple Tenses		The Seven Compound Tenses	
Singular	Plural	Singular	Plural
1 présent de l'indicatif		8 passé composé	
me fie	nous fions	me suis fié(e)	nous sommes fié(e)s
te fies	vous fiez	t'es fié(e)	vous êtes fié(e)(s)
se fie	se fient	s'est fié(e)	se sont fié(e)s
2 imparfait de l'indicatif		9 plus-que-parfait de l'indicatif	
me fiais	nous fiions	m'étais fié(e)	nous étions fié(e)s
te fiais	vous fiiez	t'étais fié(e)	vous étiez fié(e)(s)
se fiait	se fiaient	s'était fié(e)	s'étaient fié(e)s
3 passé simple		10 passé antérieur	
me fiai	nous fiâmes	me fus fié(e)	nous fûmes fié(e)s
te fias	vous fiâtes	te fus fié(e)	vous fûtes fié(e)(s)
se fia	se fièrent	se fut fié(e)	se furent fié(e)s
4 futur		11 futur antérieur	
me fierai	nous fierons	me serai fié(e)	nous serons fié(e)s
te fieras	vous fierez	te seras fié(e)	vous serez fié(e)(s)
se fiera	se fieront	se sera fié(e)	se seront fié(e)s
5 conditionnel		12 conditionnel passé	
me fierais	nous fierions	me serais fié(e)	nous serions fié(e)s
te fierais	vous fieriez	te serais fié(e)	vous seriez fié(e)(s)
se fierait	se fieraient	se serait fié(e)	se seraient fié(e)s
6 présent du subjonctif		13 passé du subjonctif	
me fie	nous fiions	me sois fié(e)	nous soyons fié(e)s
te fies	vous fiiez	te sois fié(e)	vous soyez fié(e)(s)
se fie	se fient	se soit fié(e)	se soient fié(e)s
7 imparfait du subjonctif		14 plus-que-parfait du subjonctif	
me fiasse	nous fiassions	me fusse fié(e)	nous fussions fié(e)s
te fiasses	vous fiassiez	te fusses fié(e)	vous fussiez fié(e)(s)
se fiât	se fiassent	se fût fié(e)	se fussent fié(e)s

Impératif
fie-toi; ne te fie pas
fions-nous; ne nous fions pas
fiez-vous; ne vous fiez pas

la confiance confidence, trust	**se fier à** to depend on, to trust
avoir confiance en soi to be self-confident	in, to rely on
confier à to confide to	**se confier à** to trust to, to
se méfier de to mistrust, to distrust, to beware of	confide in
la méfiance mistrust, distrust	

129

finir Part. pr. **finissant** Part. passé **fini**

to finish, to end, to terminate, to complete

The Seven Simple Tenses		The Seven Compound Tenses	
Singular	Plural	Singular	Plural
1 présent de l'indicatif		8 passé composé	
finis	**finissons**	**ai fini**	**avons fini**
finis	**finissez**	**as fini**	**avez fini**
finit	**finissent**	**a fini**	**ont fini**
2 imparfait de l'indicatif		9 plus-que-parfait de l'indicatif	
finissais	**finissions**	**avais fini**	**avions fini**
finissais	**finissiez**	**avais fini**	**aviez fini**
finissait	**finissaient**	**avait fini**	**avaient fini**
3 passé simple		10 passé antérieur	
finis	**finîmes**	**eus fini**	**eûmes fini**
finis	**finîtes**	**eus fini**	**eûtes fini**
finit	**finirent**	**eut fini**	**eurent fini**
4 futur		11 futur antérieur	
finirai	**finirons**	**aurai fini**	**aurons fini**
finiras	**finirez**	**auras fini**	**aurez fini**
finira	**finiront**	**aura fini**	**auront fini**
5 conditionnel		12 conditionnel passé	
finirais	**finirions**	**aurais fini**	**aurions fini**
finirais	**finiriez**	**aurais fini**	**auriez fini**
finirait	**finiraient**	**aurait fini**	**auraient fini**
6 présent du subjonctif		13 passé du subjonctif	
finisse	**finissions**	**aie fini**	**ayons fini**
finisses	**finissiez**	**aies fini**	**ayez fini**
finisse	**finissent**	**ait fini**	**aient fini**
7 imparfait du subjonctif		14 plus-que-parfait du subjonctif	
finisse	**finissions**	**eusse fini**	**eussions fini**
finisses	**finissiez**	**eusses fini**	**eussiez fini**
finît	**finissent**	**eût fini**	**eussent fini**
		Impératif	
		finis	
		finissons	
		finissez	

finir de + inf. to finish + pr. part.
J'ai fini de travailler pour aujourd'hui. I have finished working for today.

finir par + inf. to end up by + pr. part.
Louis a fini par épouser une femme plus âgée que lui. Louis ended up by marrying a woman older than he.

la fin the end; **la fin de semaine** weekend; **C'est fini!** It's all over!
afin de in order to; **enfin** finally; **finalement** finally
mettre fin à to put an end to; **final, finale** final; **définir** to define

The Seven Simple Tenses		The Seven Compound Tenses	
Singular	Plural	Singular	Plural
1 présent de l'indicatif		8 passé composé	
force	forçons	ai forcé	avons forcé
forces	forcez	as forcé	avez forcé
force	forcent	a forcé	ont forcé
2 imparfait de l'indicatif		9 plus-que-parfait de l'indicatif	
forçais	forcions	avais forcé	avions forcé
forçais	forciez	avais forcé	aviez forcé
forçait	forçaient	avait forcé	avaient forcé
3 passé simple		10 passé antérieur	
forçai	forçâmes	eus forcé	eûmes forcé
forças	forçâtes	eus forcé	eûtes forcé
força	forcèrent	eut forcé	eurent forcé
4 futur		11 futur antérieur	
forcerai	forcerons	aurai forcé	aurons forcé
forceras	forcerez	auras forcé	aurez forcé
forcera	forceront	aura forcé	auront forcé
5 conditionnel		12 conditionnel passé	
forcerais	forcerions	aurais forcé	aurions forcé
forcerais	forceriez	aurais forcé	auriez forcé
forcerait	forceraient	aurait forcé	auraient forcé
6 présent du subjonctif		13 passé du subjonctif	
force	forcions	aie forcé	ayons forcé
forces	forciez	aies forcé	ayez forcé
force	forcent	ait forcé	aient forcé
7 imparfait du subjonctif		14 plus-que-parfait du subjonctif	
forçasse	forçassions	eusse forcé	eussions forcé
forçasses	forçassiez	eusses forcé	eussiez forcé
forçât	forçassent	eût forcé	eussent forcé

	Impératif
	force
	forçons
	forcez

forcer la porte de qqn   to force one's way into someone's house
être forcé de faire qqch   to be obliged to do something
se forcer la voix   to strain one's voice
un forçat   a convict
à force de   by dint of
la force   strength, force; **avec force**   forcefully, with force
forcément   necessarily, inevitably
forcer qqn à faire qqch   to force someone to do something

frapper Part. pr. **frappant** Part. passé **frappé**

to knock, to hit, to frap, to rap, to strike (hit)

The Seven Simple Tenses		The Seven Compound Tenses	
Singular	Plural	Singular	Plural
1 présent de l'indicatif		8 passé composé	
frappe	**frappons**	**ai frappé**	**avons frappé**
frappes	**frappez**	**as frappé**	**avez frappé**
frappe	**frappent**	**a frappé**	**ont frappé**
2 imparfait de l'indicatif		9 plus-que-parfait de l'indicatif	
frappais	**frappions**	**avais frappé**	**avions frappé**
frappais	**frappiez**	**avais frappé**	**aviez frappé**
frappait	**frappaient**	**avait frappé**	**avaient frappé**
3 passé simple		10 passé antérieur	
frappai	**frappâmes**	**eus frappé**	**eûmes frappé**
frappas	**frappâtes**	**eus frappé**	**eûtes frappé**
frappa	**frappèrent**	**eut frappé**	**eurent frappé**
4 futur		11 futur antérieur	
frapperai	**frapperons**	**aurai frappé**	**aurons frappé**
frapperas	**frapperez**	**auras frappé**	**aurez frappé**
frappera	**frapperont**	**aura frappé**	**auront frappé**
5 conditionnel		12 conditionnel passé	
frapperais	**frapperions**	**aurais frappé**	**aurions frappé**
frapperais	**frapperiez**	**aurais frappé**	**auriez frappé**
frapperait	**frapperaient**	**aurait frappé**	**auraient frappé**
6 présent du subjonctif		13 passé du subjonctif	
frappe	**frappions**	**aie frappé**	**ayons frappé**
frappes	**frappiez**	**aies frappé**	**ayez frappé**
frappe	**frappent**	**ait frappé**	**aient frappé**
7 imparfait du subjonctif		14 plus-que-parfait du subjonctif	
frappasse	**frappassions**	**eusse frappé**	**eussions frappé**
frappasses	**frappassiez**	**eusses frappé**	**eussiez frappé**
frappât	**frappassent**	**eût frappé**	**eussent frappé**

	Impératif
	frappe
	frappons
	frappez

---

se frapper la poitrine to beat one's chest
le frappage striking (medals, coins)
une faute de frappe a typing mistake
frapper à la porte to knock on the door
frapper du pied to stamp one's foot
entrer sans frapper enter without knocking
C'est frappant! It's striking!

frappé (frappée) de stricken with
le frappement beating, striking
frappé à mort mortally wounded

to fry

The Seven Simple Tenses		The Seven Compound Tenses	
Singular	Plural	Singular	Plural
1 présent de l'indicatif		8 passé composé	
fris		**ai frit**	**avons frit**
fris		**as frit**	**avez frit**
frit		**a frit**	**ont frit**
		9 plus-que-parfait de l'indicatif	
		avais frit	**avions frit**
		avais frit	**aviez frit**
		avait frit	**avaient frit**
		10 passé antérieur	
		eus frit	**eûmes frit**
		eus frit	**eûtes frit**
		eut frit	**eurent frit**
4 futur		11 futur antérieur	
frirai	**frirons**	**aurai frit**	**aurons frit**
friras	**frirez**	**auras frit**	**aurez frit**
frira	**friront**	**aura frit**	**auront frit**
5 conditionnel		12 conditionnel passé	
frirais	**fririons**	**aurais frit**	**aurions frit**
frirais	**fririez**	**aurais frit**	**auriez frit**
frirait	**friraient**	**aurait frit**	**auraient frit**
		13 passé du subjonctif	
		aie frit	**ayons frit**
		aies frit	**ayez frit**
		ait frit	**aient frit**
		14 plus-que-parfait du subjonctif	
		eusse frit	**eussions frit**
		eusses frit	**eussiez frit**
		eût frit	**eussent frit**

Impératif
fris
faisons frire
faites frire

faire frire to fry (see note below)	**des pommes de terre frites** fried potatoes
pommes frites French fries	(French style)
une friteuse frying basket	**un bifteck frites** steak with French fries
la friture frying	

This verb is generally used only in the persons and tenses given above. To supply the forms that are lacking, use the appropriate form of **faire** plus the infinitive **frire**, e.g., the plural of the present indicative is: **nous faisons frire, vous faites frire, ils font frire.**

133

to flee, to fly off, to shun, to leak

The Seven Simple Tenses		The Seven Compound Tenses	
Singular	Plural	Singular	Plural
1 présent de l'indicatif		8 passé composé	
fuis	fuyons	ai fui	avons fui
fuis	fuyez	as fui	avez fui
fuit	fuient	a fui	ont fui
2 imparfait de l'indicatif		9 plus-que-parfait de l'indicatif	
fuyais	fuyions	avais fui	avions fui
fuyais	fuyiez	avais fui	aviez fui
fuyait	fuyaient	avait fui	avaient fui
3 passé simple		10 passé antérieur	
fuis	fuîmes	eus fui	eûmes fui
fuis	fuîtes	eus fui	eûtes fui
fuit	fuirent	eut fui	eurent fui
4 futur		11 futur antérieur	
fuirai	fuirons	aurai fui	aurons fui
fuiras	fuirez	auras fui	aurez fui
fuira	fuiront	aura fui	auront fui
5 conditionnel		12 conditionnel passé	
fuirais	fuirions	aurais fui	aurions fui
fuirais	fuiriez	aurais fui	auriez fui
fuirait	fuiraient	aurait fui	auraient fui
6 présent du subjonctif		13 passé du subjonctif	
fuie	fuyions	aie fui	ayons fui
fuies	fuyiez	aies fui	ayez fui
fuie	fuient	ait fui	aient fui
7 imparfait du subjonctif		14 plus-que-parfait du subjonctif	
fuisse	fuissions	eusse fui	eussions fui
fuisses	fuissiez	eusses fui	eussiez fui
fuît	fuissent	eût fui	eussent fui
		Impératif	
		fuis	
		fuyons	
		fuyez	

faire fuir to put to flight	**s'enfuir de** to flee from, to run away from
la fuite flight	**fugitif, fugitive** fugitive, fleeting, runaway
prendre la fuite to take to flight	**fugitivement** fugitively

to smoke, to steam

The Seven Simple Tenses		The Seven Compound Tenses	
Singular	Plural	Singular	Plural
1 présent de l'indicatif		8 passé composé	
fume	fumons	ai fumé	avons fumé
fumes	fumez	as fumé	avez fumé
fume	fument	a fumé	ont fumé
2 imparfait de l'indicatif		9 plus-que-parfait de l'indicatif	
fumais	fumions	avais fumé	avions fumé
fumais	fumiez	avais fumé	aviez fumé
fumait	fumaient	avait fumé	avaient fumé
3 passé simple		10 passé antérieur	
fumai	fumâmes	eus fumé	eûmes fumé
fumas	fumâtes	eus fumé	eûtes fumé
fuma	fumèrent	eut fumé	eurent fumé
4 futur		11 futur antérieur	
fumerai	fumerons	aurai fumé	aurons fumé
fumeras	fumerez	auras fumé	aurez fumé
fumera	fumeront	aura fumé	auront fumé
5 conditionnel		12 conditionnel passé	
fumerais	fumerions	aurais fumé	aurions fumé
fumerais	fumeriez	aurais fumé	auriez fumé
fumerait	fumeraient	aurait fumé	auraient fumé
6 présent du subjonctif		13 passé du subjonctif	
fume	fumions	aie fumé	ayons fumé
fumes	fumiez	aies fumé	ayez fumé
fume	fument	ait fumé	aient fumé
7 imparfait du subjonctif		14 plus-que-parfait du subjonctif	
fumasse	fumassions	eusse fumé	eussions fumé
fumasses	fumassiez	eusses fumé	eussiez fumé
fumât	fumassent	eût fumé	eussent fumé

Impératif
fume
fumons
fumez

Le père: **Je te défends de fumer. C'est une mauvaise habitude.**
Le fils: **Alors, pourquoi fumes-tu, papa?**

Défense de fumer No smoking allowed
la fumée smoke
un rideau de fumée smoke screen
parfumer to perfume
compartiment (pour) fumeurs
   smoking car (on a train)

fumeux, fumeuse smoky
un fume-cigare cigar holder
un fume-cigarette cigarette holder
un fumeur, une fumeuse smoker
   (person who smokes)

135

to win, to earn, to gain

The Seven Simple Tenses		The Seven Compound Tenses	
Singular	Plural	Singular	Plural
1 présent de l'indicatif		8 passé composé	
gagne	gagnons	ai gagné	avons gagné
gagnes	gagnez	as gagné	avez gagné
gagne	gagnent	a gagné	ont gagné
2 imparfait de l'indicatif		9 plus-que-parfait de l'indicatif	
gagnais	gagnions	avais gagné	avions gagné
gagnais	gagniez	avais gagné	aviez gagné
gagnait	gagnaient	avait gagné	avaient gagné
3 passé simple		10 passé antérieur	
gagnai	gagnâmes	eus gagné	eûmes gagné
gagnas	gagnâtes	eus gagné	eûtes gagné
gagna	gagnèrent	eut gagné	eurent gagné
4 futur		11 futur antérieur	
gagnerai	gagnerons	aurai gagné	aurons gagné
gagneras	gagnerez	auras gagné	aurez gagné
gagnera	gagneront	aura gagné	auront gagné
5 conditionnel		12 conditionnel passé	
gagnerais	gagnerions	aurais gagné	aurions gagné
gagnerais	gagneriez	aurais gagné	auriez gagné
gagnerait	gagneraient	aurait gagné	auraient gagné
6 présent du subjonctif		13 passé du subjonctif	
gagne	gagnions	aie gagné	ayons gagné
gagnes	gagniez	aies gagné	ayez gagné
gagne	gagnent	ait gagné	aient gagné
7 imparfait du subjonctif		14 plus-que-parfait du subjonctif	
gagnasse	gagnassions	eusse gagné	eussions gagné
gagnasses	gagnassiez	eusses gagné	eussiez gagné
gagnât	gagnassent	eût gagné	eussent gagné
		Impératif	
		gagne	
		gagnons	
		gagnez	

---

gagner sa vie   to earn one's living
gagner du poids   to gain weight
gagner de l'argent   to earn money
gagnable   obtainable
gagner du temps   to save time

regagner   to regain, to recover, to win back
regagner le temps perdu   to make up (to recover) time lost
gagner le gros lot   to win the jackpot
Vous n'y gagnerez rien de bon.   You will get nothing good out of it.

to guard, to keep, to retain

The Seven Simple Tenses		The Seven Compound Tenses	
Singular	Plural	Singular	Plural
1 présent de l'indicatif		8 passé composé	
garde	gardons	ai gardé	avons gardé
gardes	gardez	as gardé	avez gardé
garde	gardent	a gardé	ont gardé
2 imparfait de l'indicatif		9 plus-que-parfait de l'indicatif	
gardais	gardions	avais gardé	avions gardé
gardais	gardiez	avais gardé	aviez gardé
gardait	gardaient	avait gardé	avaient gardé
3 passé simple		10 passé antérieur	
gardai	gardâmes	eus gardé	eûmes gardé
gardas	gardâtes	eus gardé	eûtes gardé
garda	gardèrent	eut gardé	eurent gardé
4 futur		11 futur antérieur	
garderai	garderons	aurai gardé	aurons gardé
garderas	garderez	auras gardé	aurez gardé
gardera	garderont	aura gardé	auront gardé
5 conditionnel		12 conditionnel passé	
garderais	garderions	aurais gardé	aurions gardé
garderais	garderiez	aurais gardé	auriez gardé
garderait	garderaient	aurait gardé	auraient gardé
6 présent du subjonctif		13 passé du subjonctif	
garde	gardions	aie gardé	ayons gardé
gardes	gardiez	aies gardé	ayez gardé
garde	gardent	ait gardé	aient gardé
7 imparfait du subjonctif		14 plus-que-parfait du subjonctif	
gardasse	gardassions	eusse gardé	eussions gardé
gardasses	gardassiez	eusses gardé	eussiez gardé
gardât	gardassent	eût gardé	eussent gardé

Impératif
garde
gardons
gardez

Madame Mimi a mis son enfant chez une gardienne d'enfants parce qu'elle va passer la journée en ville. Elle a besoin d'acheter une nouvelle garde-robe.

se garder to protect oneself
se garder de tomber to take care not to fall
un gardien, une gardienne guardian
prendre garde de to take care not to
une gardienne d'enfants babysitter
une garde-robe wardrobe (closet)
un gardien de but goalie

regarder to look at, to watch, to consider, to regard
un garde-manger pantry
un garde-vue eyeshade (visor)
En garde! On guard!
Dieu m'en garde! God forbid!

137

gâter	Part. pr. **gâtant**	Part. passé **gâté**

to spoil, to damage

The Seven Simple Tenses		The Seven Compound Tenses	
Singular	Plural	Singular	Plural
1 présent de l'indicatif		8 passé composé	
gâte	gâtons	ai gâté	avons gâté
gâtes	gâtez	as gâté	avez gâté
gâte	gâtent	a gâté	ont gâté
2 imparfait de l'indicatif		9 plus-que-parfait de l'indicatif	
gâtais	gâtions	avais gâté	avions gâté
gâtais	gâtiez	avais gâté	aviez gâté
gâtait	gâtaient	avait gâté	avaient gâté
3 passé simple		10 passé antérieur	
gâtai	gâtâmes	eus gâté	eûmes gâté
gâtas	gâtâtes	eus gâté	eûtes gâté
gâta	gâtèrent	eut gâté	eurent gâté
4 futur		11 futur antérieur	
gâterai	gâterons	aurai gâté	aurons gâté
gâteras	gâterez	auras gâté	aurez gâté
gâtera	gâteront	aura gâté	auront gâté
5 conditionnel		12 conditionnel passé	
gâterais	gâterions	aurais gâté	aurions gâté
gâterais	gâteriez	aurais gâté	auriez gâté
gâterait	gâteraient	aurait gâté	auraient gâté
6 présent du subjonctif		13 passé du subjonctif	
gâte	gâtions	aie gâté	ayons gâté
gâtes	gâtiez	aies gâté	ayez gâté
gâte	gâtent	ait gâté	aient gâté
7 imparfait du subjonctif		14 plus-que-parfait du subjonctif	
gâtasse	gâtassions	eusse gâté	eussions gâté
gâtasses	gâtassiez	eusses gâté	eussiez gâté
gâtât	gâtassent	eût gâté	eussent gâté
		Impératif	
		gâte	
		gâtons	
		gâtez	

Marcel est un enfant gâté. Je n'aime pas jouer avec lui. Il gâte tout. Il demande toujours des gâteries.

gâter un enfant to spoil a child		**un enfant gâté** a spoiled child	
se gâter to pamper oneself		**une gâterie** a treat	

to freeze

The Seven Simple Tenses		The Seven Compound Tenses	
Singular	Plural	Singular	Plural
1 présent de l'indicatif		8 passé composé	
gèle	gelons	ai gelé	avons gelé
gèles	gelez	as gelé	avez gelé
gèle	gèlent	a gelé	ont gelé
2 imparfait de l'indicatif		9 plus-que-parfait de l'indicatif	
gelais	gelions	avais gelé	avions gelé
gelais	geliez	avais gelé	aviez gelé
gelait	gelaient	avait gelé	avaient gelé
3 passé simple		10 passé antérieur	
gelai	gelâmes	eus gelé	eûmes gelé
gelas	gelâtes	eus gelé	eûtes gelé
gela	gelèrent	eut gelé	eurent gelé
4 futur		11 futur antérieur	
gèlerai	gèlerons	aurai gelé	aurons gelé
gèleras	gèlerez	auras gelé	aurez gelé
gèlera	gèleront	aura gelé	auront gelé
5 conditionnel		12 conditionnel passé	
gèlerais	gèlerions	aurais gelé	aurions gelé
gèlerais	gèleriez	aurais gelé	auriez gelé
gèlerait	gèleraient	aurait gelé	auraient gelé
6 présent du subjonctif		13 passé du subjonctif	
gèle	gelions	aie gelé	ayons gelé
gèles	geliez	aies gelé	ayez gelé
gèle	gèlent	ait gelé	aient gelé
7 imparfait du subjonctif		14 plus-que-parfait du subjonctif	
gelasse	gelassions	eusse gelé	eussions gelé
gelasses	gelassiez	eusses gelé	eussiez gelé
gelât	gelassent	eût gelé	eussent gelé
		Impératif	
		gèle	
		gelons	
		gelez	

Je ne veux pas sortir aujourd'hui parce qu'il gèle. Quand je me suis levé ce matin, j'ai regardé par la fenêtre et j'ai vu de la gelée partout.

Il gèle! It's freezing!	**congeler** to congeal, to freeze
Qu'il gèle! Let it freeze!	**la congélation** congelation, freezing, icing
le gel frost, freezing	**le point de congélation** freezing point
la gelée frost	**à la gelée** jellied

139

to taste, to have a snack, to enjoy

The Seven Simple Tenses		The Seven Compound Tenses	
Singular	Plural	Singular	Plural
1 présent de l'indicatif		8 passé composé	
goûte	goûtons	ai goûté	avons goûté
goûtes	goûtez	as goûté	avez goûté
goûte	goûtent	a goûté	ont goûté
2 imparfait de l'indicatif		9 plus-que-parfait de l'indicatif	
goûtais	goûtions	avais goûté	avions goûté
goûtais	goûtiez	avais goûté	aviez goûté
goûtait	goûtaient	avait goûté	avaient goûté
3 passé simple		10 passé antérieur	
goûtai	goûtâmes	eus goûté	eûmes goûté
goûtas	goûtâtes	eus goûté	eûtes goûté
goûta	goûtèrent	eut goûté	eurent goûté
4 futur		11 futur antérieur	
goûterai	goûterons	aurai goûté	aurons goûté
goûteras	goûterez	auras goûté	aurez goûté
goûtera	goûteront	aura goûté	auront goûté
5 conditionnel		12 conditionnel passé	
goûterais	goûterions	aurais goûté	aurions goûté
goûterais	goûteriez	aurais goûté	auriez goûté
goûterait	goûteraient	aurait goûté	auraient goûté
6 présent du subjonctif		13 passé du subjonctif	
goûte	goûtions	aie goûté	ayons goûté
goûtes	goûtiez	aies goûté	ayez goûté
goûte	goûtent	ait goûté	aient goûté
7 imparfait du subjonctif		14 plus-que-parfait du subjonctif	
goûtasse	goûtassions	eusse goûté	eussions goûté
goûtasses	goûtassiez	eusses goûté	eussiez goûté
goûtât	goûtassent	eût goûté	eussent goûté

Impératif
goûte
goûtons
goûtez

Quand j'arrive chez moi de l'école l'après-midi, j'ai l'habitude de prendre le goûter à quatre heures.

le goûter snack, bite to eat	**de mauvais goût** in bad taste
goûter sur l'herbe to have a picnic	**avoir un goût de** to taste like
à chacun son goût to each his own	**goûter de** to eat or drink something for the first time
goûter à to drink or eat only a small quantity	**dégoûter** to disgust
le goût taste	**C'est dégoûtant!** It's disgusting!

Part. pr. **grandissant**   Part. passé **grandi**   **grandir**

to grow (up, taller), to increase

The Seven Simple Tenses		The Seven Compound Tenses	
Singular	Plural	Singular	Plural
1 présent de l'indicatif		8 passé composé	
grandis	grandissons	ai grandi	avons grandi
grandis	grandissez	as grandi	avez grandi
grandit	grandissent	a grandi	ont grandi
2 imparfait de l'indicatif		9 plus-que-parfait de l'indicatif	
grandissais	grandissions	avais grandi	avions grandi
grandissais	grandissiez	avais grandi	aviez grandi
grandissait	grandissaient	avait grandi	avaient grandi
3 passé simple		10 passé antérieur	
grandis	grandîmes	eus grandi	eûmes grandi
grandis	grandîtes	eus grandi	eûtes grandi
grandit	grandirent	eut grandi	eurent grandi
4 futur		11 futur antérieur	
grandirai	grandirons	aurai grandi	aurons grandi
grandiras	grandirez	auras grandi	aurez grandi
grandira	grandiront	aura grandi	auront grandi
5 conditionnel		12 conditionnel passé	
grandirais	grandirions	aurais grandi	aurions grandi
grandirais	grandiriez	aurais grandi	auriez grandi
grandirait	grandiraient	aurait grandi	auraient grandi
6 présent du subjonctif		13 passé du subjonctif	
grandisse	grandissions	aie grandi	ayons grandi
grandisses	grandissiez	ales grandi	ayez grandi
grandisse	grandissent	ait grandi	aient grandi
7 imparfait du subjonctif		14 plus-que-parfait du subjonctif	
grandisse	grandissions	eusse grandi	eussions grandi
grandisses	grandissiez	eusses grandi	eussiez grandi
grandît	grandissent	eût grandi	eussent grandi

Impératif
grandis
grandissons
grandissez

Voyez-vous comme Joseph et Joséphine ont grandi? C'est incroyable! Quel âge ont-ils maintenant?

le grandissement   growth
grandiose   grandiose, grand
grand, grande   tall
la grandeur   size, greatness, grandeur
grandiosement   grandiosely

agrandir   to expand, to enlarge
un agrandissement   enlargement, extension, aggrandizement

141

gronder   Part. pr. **grondant**   Part. passé **grondé**

to chide, to reprimand, to scold

The Seven Simple Tenses		The Seven Compound Tenses	
Singular	Plural	Singular	Plural
1 présent de l'indicatif		8 passé composé	
gronde	grondons	ai grondé	avons grondé
grondes	grondez	as grondé	avez grondé
gronde	grondent	a grondé	ont grondé
2 imparfait de l'indicatif		9 plus-que-parfait de l'indicatif	
grondais	grondions	avais grondé	avions grondé
grondais	grondiez	avais grondé	aviez grondé
grondait	grondaient	avait grondé	avaient grondé
3 passé simple		10 passé antérieur	
grondai	grondâmes	eus grondé	eûmes grondé
grondas	grondâtes	eus grondé	eûtes grondé
gronda	grondèrent	eut grondé	eurent grondé
4 futur		11 futur antérieur	
gronderai	gronderons	aurai grondé	aurons grondé
gronderas	gronderez	auras grondé	aurez grondé
grondera	gronderont	aura grondé	auront grondé
5 conditionnel		12 conditionnel passé	
gronderais	gronderions	aurais grondé	aurions grondé
gronderais	gronderiez	aurais grondé	auriez grondé
gronderait	gronderaient	aurait grondé	auraient grondé
6 présent du subjonctif		13 passé du subjonctif	
gronde	grondions	aie grondé	ayons grondé
grondes	grondiez	aies grondé	ayez grondé
gronde	grondent	ait grondé	aient grondé
7 imparfait du subjonctif		14 plus-que-parfait du subjonctif	
grondasse	grondassions	eusse grondé	eussions grondé
grondasses	grondassiez	eusses grondé	eussiez grondé
grondât	grondassent	eût grondé	eussent grondé
		Impératif	
		gronde	
		grondons	
		grondez	

—Victor, pourquoi pleures-tu?

—La maitresse de mathématiques m'a grondé.

—Pourquoi est-ce qu'elle t'a grondé? Qu'est-ce que tu as fait?

—Ce n'est pas parce que j'ai fait quelque chose. C'est parce que je n'ai rien fait. Je n'ai pas préparé la leçon.

—Alors, tu mérites une gronderie et une réprimande.

—C'est une grondeuse. Elle gronde à chaque instant. C'est une criarde.

une grondeuse	a scolder	**une gronderie**	a scolding
une criarde	a nag, nagger	**à chaque instant**	constantly

to cure, to heal, to remedy, to recover

The Seven Simple Tenses		The Seven Compound Tenses	
Singular	Plural	Singular	Plural
1 présent de l'indicatif		8 passé composé	
guéris	guérissons	ai guéri	avons guéri
guéris	guérissez	as guéri	avez guéri
guérit	guérissent	a guéri	ont guéri
2 imparfait de l'indicatif		9 plus-que-parfait de l'indicatif	
guérissais	guérissions	avais guéri	avions guéri
guérissais	guérissiez	avais guéri	aviez guéri
guérissait	guérissaient	avait guéri	avaient guéri
3 passé simple		10 passé antérieur	
guéris	guérîmes	eus guéri	eûmes guéri
guéris	guérîtes	eus guéri	eûtes guéri
guérit	guérirent	eut guéri	eurent guéri
4 futur		11 futur antérieur	
guérirai	guérirons	aurai guéri	aurons guéri
guériras	guérirez	auras guéri	aurez guéri
guérira	guériront	aura guéri	auront guéri
5 conditionnel		12 conditionnel passé	
guérirais	guéririons	aurais guéri	aurions guéri
guérirais	guéririez	aurais guéri	auriez guéri
guérirait	guériraient	aurait guéri	auraient guéri
6 présent du subjonctif		13 passé du subjonctif	
guérisse	guérissions	aie guéri	ayons guéri
guérisses	guérissiez	aies guéri	ayez guéri
guérisse	guérissent	ait guéri	aient guéri
7 imparfait du subjonctif		14 plus-que-parfait du subjonctif	
guérisse	guérissions	eusse guéri	eussions guéri
guérisses	guérissiez	eusses guéri	eussiez guéri
guérît	guérissent	eût guéri	eussent guéri
		Impératif	
		guéris	
		guérissons	
		guérissez	

Madame Gérard est tombée dans l'escalier la semaine dernière et elle a reçu une blessure au genou. Elle est allée chez le médecin et maintenant elle est guérie.

une guérison   healing, cure   **guérir de**   to recover from,
guérisseur, guérisseuse   healer, faith healer   to cure of
guérissable   curable

to get dressed, to dress (oneself)

The Seven Simple Tenses		The Seven Compound Tenses	
Singular	Plural	Singular	Plural

1 présent de l'indicatif

m'habille	nous habillons		
t'habilles	vous habillez		
s'habille	s'habillent		

8 passé composé

me suis habillé(e)	nous sommes habillé(e)s		
t'es habillé(e)	vous êtes habillé(e)(s)		
s'est habillé(e)	se sont habillé(e)s		

2 imparfait de l'indicatif

m'habillais	nous habillions
t'habillais	vous habilliez
s'habillait	s'habillaient

9 plus-que-parfait de l'indicatif

m'étais habillé(e)	nous étions habillé(e)s
t'étais habillé(e)	vous étiez habillé(e)(s)
s'était habillé(e)	s'étaient habillé(e)s

3 passé simple

m'habillai	nous habillâmes
t'habillas	vous habillâtes
s'habilla	s'habillèrent

10 passé antérieur

me fus habillé(e)	nous fûmes habillé(e)s
te fus habillé(e)	vous fûtes habillé(e)(s)
se fut habillé(e)	se furent habillé(e)s

4 futur

m'habillerai	nous habillerons
t'habilleras	vous habillerez
s'habillera	s'habilleront

11 futur antérieur

me serai habillé(e)	nous serons habillé(e)s
te seras habillé(e)	vous serez habillé(e)(s)
se sera habillé(e)	se seront habillé(e)s

5 conditionnel

m'habillerais	nous habillerions
t'habillerais	vous habilleriez
s'habillerait	s'habilleraient

12 conditionnel passé

me serais habillé(e)	nous serions habillé(e)s
te serais habillé(e)	vous seriez habillé(e)(s)
se serait habillé(e)	se seraient habillé(e)s

6 présent du subjonctif

m'habille	nous habillions
t'habilles	vous habilliez
s'habille	s'habillent

13 passé du subjonctif

me sois habillé(e)	nous soyons habillé(e)s
te sois habillé(e)	vous soyez habillé(e)(s)
se soit habillé(e)	se soient habillé(e)s

7 imparfait du subjonctif

m'habillasse	nous habillassions
t'habillasses	vous habillassiez
s'habillât	s'habillassent

14 plus-que-parfait du subjonctif

me fusse habillé(e)	nous fussions habillé(e)s
te fusses habillé(e)	vous fussiez habillé(e)(s)
se fût habillé(e)	se fussent habillé(e)s

Impératif
habille-toi; ne t'habille pas
habillons-nous; ne nous habillons pas
habillez-vous; ne vous habillez pas

---

un habit costume, outfit	**déshabiller** to undress
les habits clothes	**se déshabiller** to undress oneself,
habiller qqn to dress someone	to get undressed
habillement *(m.)* garment, wearing apparel	**habiller de** to clothe with
L'habit ne fait pas le moine. Clothes	
don't make the person (the monk).	

to live(in), to dwell (in), to inhabit

The Seven Simple Tenses		The Seven Compound Tenses	
Singular	Plural	Singular	Plural
1 présent de l'indicatif		8 passé composé	
habite	**habitons**	**ai habité**	**avons habité**
habites	**habitez**	**as habité**	**avez habité**
habite	**habitent**	**a habité**	**ont habité**
2 imparfait de l'indicatif		9 plus-que-parfait de l'indicatif	
habitais	**habitions**	**avais habité**	**avions habité**
habitais	**habitiez**	**avais habité**	**aviez habité**
habitait	**habitaient**	**avait habité**	**avaient habité**
3 passé simple		10 passé antérieur	
habitai	**habitâmes**	**eus habité**	**eûmes habité**
habitas	**habitâtes**	**eus habité**	**eûtes habité**
habita	**habitèrent**	**eut habité**	**eurent habité**
4 futur		11 futur antérieur	
habiterai	**habiterons**	**aurai habité**	**aurons habité**
habiteras	**habiterez**	**auras habité**	**aurez habité**
habitera	**habiteront**	**aura habité**	**auront habité**
5 conditionnel		12 conditionnel passé	
habiterais	**habiterions**	**aurais habité**	**aurions habité**
habiterais	**habiteriez**	**aurais habité**	**auriez habité**
habiterait	**habiteraient**	**aurait habité**	**auraient habité**
6 présent du subjonctif		13 passé du subjonctif	
habite	**habitions**	**aie habité**	**ayons habité**
habites	**habitiez**	**aies habité**	**ayez habité**
habite	**habitent**	**ait habité**	**aient habité**
7 imparfait du subjonctif		14 plus-que-parfait du subjonctif	
habitasse	**habitassions**	**eusse habité**	**eussions habité**
habitasses	**habitassiez**	**eusses habité**	**eussiez habité**
habitât	**habitassent**	**eût habité**	**eussent habité**
		Impératif	
		habite	
		habitons	
		habitez	

—Où habitez-vous?
—J'habite 27 rue Duparc dans une petite maison blanche.
—Avec qui habitez-vous?
—J'habite avec mes parents, mes frères, mes soeurs, et mon chien.

une habitation dwelling, residence, abode
un habitat habitat
un habitant inhabitant
H.L.M. (habitation à loyer modéré)
  lodging at a moderate rental

habitable habitable, inhabitable
l'amélioration de l'habitat
  improvement of living conditions

haïr
Part. pr. **haïssant**　　　　Part. passé **haï**

to hate

The Seven Simple Tenses		The Seven Compound Tenses	
Singular	Plural	Singular	Plural
1　présent de l'indicatif		8　passé composé	
hais	haïssons	ai haï	avons haï
hais	haïssez	as haï	avez haï
hait	haïssent	a haï	ont haï
2　imparfait de l'indicatif		9　plus-que-parfait de l'indicatif	
haïssais	haïssions	avais haï	avions haï
haïssais	haïssiez	avais haï	aviez haï
haïssait	haïssaient	avait haï	avaient haï
3　passé simple		10　passé antérieur	
haïs	haïmes	eus haï	eûmes haï
haïs	haïtes	eus haï	eûtes haï
haït	haïrent	eut haï	eurent haï
4　futur		11　futur antérieur	
haïrai	haïrons	aurai haï	aurons haï
haïras	haïrez	auras haï	aurez haï
haïra	haïront	aura haï	auront haï
5　conditionnel		12　conditionnel passé	
haïrais	haïrions	aurais haï	aurions haï
haïrais	haïriez	aurais haï	auriez haï
haïrait	haïraient	aurait haï	auraient haï
6　présent du subjonctif		13　passé du subjonctif	
haïsse	haïssions	aie haï	ayons haï
haïsses	haïssiez	aies haï	ayez haï
haïsse	haïssent	ait haï	aient haï
7　imparfait du subjonctif		14　plus-que-parfait du subjonctif	
haïsse	haïssions	eusse haï	eussions haï
haïsses	haïssiez	eusses haï	eussiez haï
haït	haïssent	eût haï	eussent haï
		Impératif	
		hais	
		haïssons	
		haïssez	

Je hais le mensonge, je hais la médiocrité, et je hais la calomnie. Ces choses sont haïssables. Je hais Marguerite et Jeanne; elles sont haineuses.

haïssable　detestable, hateful	**haïr qqn comme la peste**
la haine　hatred, hate	to hate somebody like poison
haineux, haineuse　hateful, heinous	

This verb begins with aspirate *h;* make no liaison and use *je* instead of *j'*.

The Seven Simple Tenses		The Seven Compound Tenses	
Singular	Plural	Singular	Plural
1 présent de l'indicatif		8 passé composé	
insiste	insistons	ai insisté	avons insisté
insistes	insistez	as insisté	avez insisté
insiste	insistent	a insisté	ont insisté
2 imparfait de l'indicatif		9 plus-que-parfait de l'indicatif	
insistais	insistions	avais insisté	avions insisté
insistais	insistiez	avais insisté	aviez insisté
insistait	insistaient	avait insisté	avaient insisté
3 passé simple		10 passé antérieur	
insistai	insistâmes	eus insisté	eûmes insisté
insistas	insistâtes	eus insisté	eûtes insisté
insista	insistèrent	eut insisté	eurent insisté
4 futur		11 futur antérieur	
insisterai	insisterons	aurai insisté	aurons insisté
insisteras	insisterez	auras insisté	aurez insisté
insistera	insisteront	aura insisté	auront insisté
5 conditionnel		12 conditionnel passé	
insisterais	insisterions	aurais insisté	aurions insisté
insisterais	insisteriez	aurais insisté	auriez insisté
insisterait	insisteraient	aurait insisté	auraient insisté
6 présent du subjonctif		13 passé du subjonctif	
insiste	insistions	aie insisté	ayons insisté
insistes	insistiez	aies insisté	ayez insisté
insiste	insistent	ait insisté	aient insisté
7 imparfait du subjonctif		14 plus-que-parfait du subjonctif	
insistasse	insistassions	eusse insisté	eussions insisté
insistasses	insistassiez	eusses insisté	eussiez insisté
insistât	insistassent	eût insisté	eussent insisté

	Impératif
	insiste
	insistons
	insistez

Madame Albertine, maîtresse de français, insiste beaucoup sur la discipline dans cette école.

insistant, insistante insistent, persistent	**insister sur** to insist upon
l'insistance (*f.*) insistence	**inutile d'insister sur cela** useless to insist on that

instruire   Part. pr. **instruisant**   Part. passé **instruit**

to instruct

The Seven Simple Tenses		The Seven Compound Tenses	
Singular	Plural	Singular	Plural
1 présent de l'indicatif		8 passé composé	
instruis	**instruisons**	**ai instruit**	**avons instruit**
instruis	**instruisez**	**as instruit**	**avez instruit**
instruit	**instruisent**	**a instruit**	**ont instruit**
2 imparfait de l'indicatif		9 plus-que-parfait de l'indicatif	
instruisais	**instruisions**	**avais instruit**	**avions instruit**
instruisais	**instruisiez**	**avais instruit**	**aviez instruit**
instruisait	**instruisaient**	**avait instruit**	**avaient instruit**
3 passé simple		10 passé antérieur	
instruisis	**instruisîmes**	**eus instruit**	**eûmes instruit**
instruisis	**instruisîtes**	**eus instruit**	**eûtes instruit**
instruisit	**instruisirent**	**eut instruit**	**eurent instruit**
4 futur		11 futur antérieur	
instruirai	**instruirons**	**aurai instruit**	**aurons instruit**
instruiras	**instruirez**	**auras instruit**	**aurez instruit**
instruira	**instruiront**	**aura instruit**	**auront instruit**
5 conditionnel		12 conditionnel passé	
instruirais	**instruirions**	**aurais instruit**	**aurions instruit**
instruirais	**instruiriez**	**aurais instruit**	**auriez instruit**
instruirait	**instruiraient**	**aurait instruit**	**auraient instruit**
6 présent du subjonctif		13 passé du subjonctif	
instruise	**instruisions**	**aie instruit**	**ayons instruit**
instruises	**instruisiez**	**aies instruit**	**ayez instruit**
instruise	**instruisent**	**ait instruit**	**aient instruit**
7 imparfait du subjonctif		14 plus-que-parfait du subjonctif	
instruisisse	**instruisissions**	**eusse instruit**	**eussions instruit**
instruisisses	**instruisissiez**	**eusses instruit**	**eussiez instruit**
instruisît	**instruisissent**	**eût instruit**	**eussent instruit**
		Impératif	
		instruis	
		instruisons	
		instruisez	

---

instruit, instruite   educated
instruction (*f.*)   instruction, teaching
sans instruction   uneducated
instructeur, instructrice   instructor
instructif, instructive   instructive
les instructions   instructions

s'instruire   to teach oneself, to educate oneself
l'instruction publique   public education
bien instruit (instruite), fort instruit (instruite)   well educated

to forbid, to prohibit

The Seven Simple Tenses		The Seven Compound Tenses	
Singular	Plural	Singular	Plural
1 présent de l'indicatif		8 passé composé	
interdis	**interdisons**	**ai interdit**	**avons interdit**
interdis	**interdisez**	**as interdit**	**avez interdit**
interdit	**interdisent**	**a interdit**	**ont interdit**
2 imparfait de l'indicatif		9 plus-que-parfait de l'indicatif	
interdisais	**interdisions**	**avais interdit**	**avions interdit**
interdisais	**interdisiez**	**avais interdit**	**aviez interdit**
interdisait	**interdisaient**	**avait interdit**	**avaient interdit**
3 passé simple		10 passé antérieur	
interdis	**interdîmes**	**eus interdit**	**eûmes interdit**
interdis	**interdîtes**	**eus interdit**	**eûtes interdit**
Interdit	**interdirent**	**eut interdit**	**eurent interdit**
4 futur		11 futur antérieur	
Interdiral	**interdIrons**	**aurai interdit**	**aurons interdit**
interdiras	**interdirez**	**auras interdit**	**aurez interdit**
interdira	**interdiront**	**aura interdit**	**auront interdit**
5 conditionnel		12 conditionnel passé	
interdirais	**interdirions**	**aurais interdit**	**aurions interdit**
inerdirais	**interdiriez**	**aurais interdit**	**auriez interdit**
interdirait	**interdiraient**	**aurait interdit**	**auraient interdit**
6 présent du subjonctif		13 passé du subjonctif	
interdise	**interdisions**	**aie interdit**	**ayons interdit**
interdises	**interdisiez**	**aies interdit**	**ayez interdit**
interdise	**interdisent**	**alt interdit**	**aient interdit**
7 imparfait du subjonctif		14 plus-que-parfait du subjonctif	
interdisse	**interdissions**	**eusse interdit**	**eussions interdit**
interdisses	**Interdissiez**	**eusses interdit**	**eussiez interdit**
interdît	**interdissent**	**eût interdit**	**eussent interdit**

Impératif
interdis
interdisons
interdisez

Je vous **interdis** de m'interrompre constamment, je vous **interdis** d'entrer dans la salle de classe en retard, et je vous **interdis** de quitter la salle sans permission.

interdire qqch à qqn   to forbid someone something
l'interdit *(m.)*   interdict; *(adj.)* **les jeux interdits**   forbidden games
l'interdiction *(f.)*   interdiction, prohibition
Il est interdit de marcher sur l'herbe.   Do not walk on the grass.
interdire à qqn de faire qqch   to forbid someone from doing something
STATIONNEMENT INTERDIT   NO PARKING

interrompre   Part. pr. **interrompant**   Part. passé **interrompu**

to interrupt

The Seven Simple Tenses		The Seven Compound Tenses	
Singular	Plural	Singular	Plural
1 présent de l'indicatif		8 passé composé	
interromps	interrompons	ai interrompu	avons interrompu
interromps	interrompez	as interrompu	avez interrompu
interrompt	interrompent	a interrompu	ont interrompu
2 imparfait de l'indicatif		9 plus-que-parfait de l'indicatif	
interrompais	interrompions	avais interrompu	avions interrompu
interrompais	interrompiez	avais interrompu	aviez interrompu
interrompait	interrompaient	avait interrompu	avaient interrompu
3 passé simple		10 passé antérieur	
interrompis	interrompîmes	eus interrompu	eûmes interrompu
interrompis	interrompîtes	eus interrompu	eûtes interrompu
interrompit	interrompirent	eut interrompu	eurent interrompu
4 futur		11 futur antérieur	
interromprai	interromprons	aurai interrompu	aurons interrompu
interrompras	interromprez	auras interrompu	aurez interrompu
interrompra	interrompront	aura interrompu	auront interrompu
5 conditionnel		12 conditionnel passé	
interromprais	interromprions	aurais interrompu	aurions interrompu
interromprais	interrompriez	aurais interrompu	auriez interrompu
interromprait	interrompraient	aurait interrompu	auraient interrompu
6 présent du subjonctif		13 passé du subjonctif	
interrompe	interrompions	aie interrompu	ayons interrompu
interrompes	interrompiez	aies interrompu	ayez interrompu
interrompe	interrompent	ait interrompu	aient interrompu
7 imparfait du subjonctif		14 plus-que-parfait du subjonctif	
interrompisse	interrompissions	eusse interrompu	eussions interrompu
interrompisses	interrompissiez	eusses interrompu	eussiez interrompu
interrompît	interrompissent	eût interrompu	eussent interrompu

Impératif
interromps
interrompons
interrompez

—Maurice, tu m'interromps à chaque instant. Cesse de m'interrompre, s'il te plaît! C'est une mauvaise habitude et je ne l'aime pas. Est-ce que tu l'aimes quand on t'interrompt continuellement?

une interruption   interruption
interrompu, interrompue   interrupted

un interrupteur, une interruptrice
   interrupter

Part. pr. **introduisant**   Part. passé **introduit**   **introduire**

to introduce, to show in

The Seven Simple Tenses		The Seven Compound Tenses	
Singular	Plural	Singular	Plural
1 présent de l'indicatif		8 passé composé	
introduis	introduisons	ai introduit	avons introduit
introduis	introduisez	as introduit	avez introduit
introduit	introduisent	a introduit	ont introduit
2 imparfait de l'indicatif		9 plus-que-parfait de l'indicatif	
introduisais	introduisions	avais introduit	avions introduit
introduisais	introduisiez	avais introduit	aviez introduit
introduisait	introduisaient	avait introduit	avaient introduit
3 passé simple		10 passé antérieur	
introduisis	introduisîmes	eus introduit	eûmes introduit
introduisis	introduisîtes	eus introduit	eûtes introduit
introduisit	introduisirent	eut introduit	eurent introduit
4 futur		11 futur antérieur	
introduirai	introduirons	aurai introduit	aurons introduit
introduiras	introduirez	auras introduit	aurez introduit
introduira	introduiront	aura introduit	auront introduit
5 conditionnel		12 conditionnel passé	
introduirais	introduirions	aurais introduit	aurions introduit
introduirais	introduiriez	aurais introduit	auriez introduit
introduirait	introduiraient	aurait introduit	auraient introduit
6 présent du subjonctif		13 passé du subjonctif	
introduise	introduisions	aie introduit	ayons introduit
introduises	introduisiez	aies introduit	ayez introduit
introduise	introduisent	ait introduit	aient introduit
7 imparfait du subjonctif		14 plus-que-parfait du subjonctif	
introduisisse	introduisissions	eusse introduit	eussions introduit
introduisisses	introduisissiez	eusses introduit	eussiez introduit
introduisît	introduisissent	eût introduit	eussent introduit

Impératif
introduis
introduisons
introduisez

introductoire introductory	**J'ai introduit la clef dans la serrure.**
introducteur, introductrice introducer	I inserted the key into the lock.
introductif, introductive introductory	
introduction (*f.*) introduction	

151

inviter	Part. pr. **invitant**	Part. passé **invité**

to invite

The Seven Simple Tenses		The Seven Compound Tenses	
Singular	Plural	Singular	Plural
1 présent de l'indicatif		8 passé composé	
invite	**invitons**	**ai invité**	**avons invité**
invites	**invitez**	**as invité**	**avez invité**
invite	**invitent**	**a invité**	**ont invité**
2 imparfait de l'indicatif		9 plus-que-parfait de l'indicatif	
invitais	**invitions**	**avais invité**	**avions invité**
invitais	**invitiez**	**avais invité**	**aviez invité**
invitait	**invitaient**	**avait invité**	**avaient invité**
3 passé simple		10 passé antérieur	
invitai	**invitâmes**	**eus invité**	**eûmes invité**
invitas	**invitâtes**	**eus invité**	**eûtes invité**
invita	**invitèrent**	**eut invité**	**eurent invité**
4 futur		11 futur antérieur	
inviterai	**inviterons**	**aurai invité**	**aurons invité**
inviteras	**inviterez**	**auras invité**	**aurez invité**
invitera	**inviteront**	**aura invité**	**auront invité**
5 conditionnel		12 conditionnel passé	
inviterais	**inviterions**	**aurais invité**	**aurions invité**
inviterais	**inviteriez**	**aurais invité**	**auriez invité**
inviterait	**inviteraient**	**aurait invité**	**auraient invité**
6 présent du subjonctif		13 passé du subjonctif	
invite	**invitions**	**aie invité**	**ayons invité**
invites	**invitiez**	**aies invité**	**ayez invité**
invite	**invitent**	**ait invité**	**aient invité**
7 imparfait du subjonctif		14 plus-que-parfait du subjonctif	
invitasse	**invitassions**	**eusse invité**	**eussions invité**
invitasses	**invitassiez**	**eusses invité**	**eussiez invité**
invitât	**invitassent**	**eût invité**	**eussent invité**

Impératif
invite
invitons
invitez

J'ai reçu une invitation à dîner chez les Martin. C'est pour samedi soir. J'ai accepté avec plaisir et maintenant je vais en ville acheter un cadeau pour eux.

l'invitation *(f.)* invitation	**inviter qqn à faire qqch**
les invités the guests	to invite someone to do something
sur l'invitation de at the invitation of	**J'ai invité mes meilleurs amis à dîner**
sans invitation without invitation,	**chez moi.** I invited my best friends to
uninvited	have dinner at my place.

to throw, to cast

The Seven Simple Tenses		The Seven Compound Tenses	
Singular	Plural	Singular	Plural
1 présent de l'indicatif		**8 passé composé**	
jette	jetons	ai jeté	avons jeté
jettes	jetez	as jeté	avez jeté
jette	jettent	a jeté	ont jeté
2 imparfait de l'indicatif		**9 plus-que-parfait de l'indicatif**	
jetais	jetions	avais jeté	avions jeté
jetais	jetiez	avais jeté	aviez jeté
jetait	jetaient	avait jeté	avaient jeté
3 passé simple		**10 passé antérieur**	
jetai	jetâmes	eus jeté	eûmes jeté
jetas	jetâtes	eus jeté	eûtes jeté
jeta	jetèrent	eut jeté	eurent jeté
4 futur		**11 futur antérieur**	
jetterai	jetterons	aurai jeté	aurons jeté
jetteras	jetterez	auras jeté	aurez jeté
jettera	jetteront	aura jeté	auront jeté
5 conditionnel		**12 conditionnel passé**	
jetterais	jetterions	aurais jeté	aurions jeté
jetterais	jetteriez	aurais jeté	auriez jeté
jetterait	jetteraient	aurait jeté	auraient jeté
6 présent du subjonctif		**13 passé du subjonctif**	
jette	jetions	aie jeté	ayons jeté
jettes	jetiez	aies jeté	ayez jeté
jette	jettent	ait jeté	aient jeté
7 imparfait du subjonctif		**14 plus-que-parfait du subjonctif**	
jetasse	jetassions	eusse jeté	eussions jeté
jetasses	jetassiez	eusses jeté	eussiez jeté
jetât	jetassent	eût jeté	eussent jeté
		Impératif	
		jette	
		jetons	
		jetez	

jeter un cri   to utter a cry
jeter son argent par la fenêtre   to throw one's money out the window
se jeter sur (contre)   to throw oneself at (against)
un jeton de téléphone   telephone slug
une jetée   jetty
un jet d'eau   fountain
jeter un coup d'oeil à   to glance at; **se jeter au cou de qqn**
   to throw oneself at somebody
rejeter   to reject, to throw back; **projeter**   to plan, to project

joindre Part. pr. **joignant** Part. passé **joint**

to join

The Seven Simple Tenses		The Seven Compound Tenses	
Singular	Plural	Singular	Plural
1 présent de l'indicatif		8 passé composé	
joins	joignons	ai joint	avons joint
joins	joignez	as joint	avez joint
joint	joignent	a joint	ont joint
2 imparfait de l'indicatif		9 plus-que-parfait de l'indicatif	
joignais	joignions	avais joint	avions joint
joignais	joigniez	avais joint	aviez joint
joignait	joignaient	avait joint	avaient joint
3 passé simple		10 passé antérieur	
joignis	joignîmes	eus joint	eûmes joint
joignis	joignîtes	eus joint	eûtes joint
joignit	joignirent	eut joint	eurent joint
4 futur		11 futur antérieur	
joindrai	joindrons	aurai joint	aurons joint
joindras	joindrez	auras joint	aurez joint
joindra	joindront	aura joint	auront joint
5 conditionnel		12 conditionnel passé	
joindrais	joindrions	aurais joint	aurions joint
joindrais	joindriez	aurais joint	auriez joint
joindrait	joindraient	aurait joint	auraient joint
6 présent du subjonctif		13 passé du subjonctif	
joigne	joignions	aie joint	ayons joint
joignes	joigniez	aies joint	ayez joint
joigne	joignent	ait joint	aient joint
7 imparfait du subjonctif		14 plus-que-parfait du subjonctif	
joignisse	joignissions	eusse joint	eussions joint
joignisses	joignissiez	eusses joint	eussiez joint
joignît	joignissent	eût joint	eussent joint
		Impératif	
		joins	
		joignons	
		joignez	

joindre les deux bouts to make ends meet
les jointures des doigts knuckles
joint, jointe joined
joignant, joignante adjoining
ci-joint herewith, attached
joindre à to join to, to add to

rejoindre to rejoin,
  to join together
se rejoindre to meet,
  to come together again

154

to play, to act (in a play), to gamble

The Seven Simple Tenses		The Seven Compound Tenses	
Singular	Plural	Singular	Plural
1 présent de l'indicatif		8 passé composé	
joue	jouons	ai joué	avons joué
joues	jouez	as joué	avez joué
joue	jouent	a joué	ont joué
2 imparfait de l'indicatif		9 plus-que-parfait de l'indicatif	
jouais	jouions	avais joué	avions joué
jouais	jouiez	avais joué	aviez joué
jouait	jouaient	avait joué	avaient joué
3 passé simple		10 passé antérieur	
jouai	jouâmes	eus joué	eûmes joué
jouas	jouâtes	eus joué	eûtes joué
joua	jouèrent	eut joué	eurent joué
4 futur		11 futur antérieur	
jouerai	jouerons	aurai joué	aurons joué
joueras	jouerez	auras joué	aurez joué
jouera	joueront	aura joué	auront joué
5 conditionnel		12 conditionnel passé	
jouerais	jouerions	aurais joué	aurions joué
jouerais	joueriez	aurais joué	auriez joué
jouerait	joueraient	aurait joué	auraient joué
6 présent du subjonctif		13 passé du subjonctif	
joue	jouions	aie joué	ayons joué
joues	jouiez	aies joué	ayez joué
joue	jouent	ait joué	aient joué
7 imparfait du subjonctif		14 plus-que-parfait du subjonctif	
jouasse	jouassions	eusse joué	eussions joué
jouasses	jouassiez	eusses joué	eussiez joué
jouât	jouassent	eût joué	eussent joué
		Impératif	
		joue	
		jouons	
		jouez	

---

jouer au tennis to play tennis
jouer aux cartes to play cards
jouer du piano to play the piano
jouer un tour à qqn to play a trick
  on someone
un jouet toy, plaything
joueur, joueuse player, gambler
jouer sur les mots to play with words
déjouer to baffle, to thwart

jouer un rôle to play a part
jouer une partie de qqch to play a game
  of something
jouer de la flûte to play the flute
se jouer de to make fun of, to deride
un joujou, des joujoux toy, toys
  (child's language)

laisser	Part. pr. **laissant**	Part. passé **laissé**

to let, to allow, to leave

The Seven Simple Tenses		The Seven Compound Tenses	
Singular	Plural	Singular	Plural
1 présent de l'indicatif		8 passé composé	
laisse	laissons	ai laissé	avons laissé
laisses	laissez	as laissé	avez laissé
laisse	laissent	a laissé	ont laissé
2 imparfait de l'indicatif		9 plus-que-parfait de l'indicatif	
laissais	laissions	avais laissé	avions laissé
laissais	laissiez	avais laissé	aviez laissé
laissait	laissaient	avait laissé	avaient laissé
3 passé simple		10 passé antérieur	
laissai	laissâmes	eus laissé	eûmes laissé
laissas	laissâtes	eus laissé	eûtes laissé
laissa	laissèrent	eut laissé	eurent laissé
4 futur		11 futur antérieur	
laisserai	laisserons	aurai laissé	aurons laissé
laisseras	laisserez	auras laissé	aurez laissé
laissera	laisseront	aura laissé	auront laissé
5 conditionnel		12 conditionnel passé	
laisserais	laisserions	aurais laissé	aurions laissé
laisserais	laisseriez	aurais laissé	auriez laissé
laisserait	laisseraient	aurait laissé	auraient laissé
6 présent du subjonctif		13 passé du subjonctif	
laisse	laissions	aie laissé	ayons laissé
laisses	laissiez	aies laissé	ayez laissé
laisse	laissent	ait laissé	aient laissé
7 imparfait du subjonctif		14 plus-que-parfait du subjonctif	
laissasse	laissassions	eusse laissé	eussions laissé
laissasses	laissassiez	eusses laissé	eussiez laissé
laissât	laissassent	eût laissé	eussent laissé

	Impératif
	laisse
	laissons
	laissez

Quand j'ai quitté la maison ce matin pour aller à l'école, j'ai laissé mes livres sur la table dans la cuisine. Dans la classe de français, le professeur m'a demandé où étaient mes livres et je lui ai répondu que je les avais laissés sur la table chez moi. C'était fâcheux!

laissez-faire do not interfere; **Laissez-moi faire.** Let me do as I please.
une laisse a leash; **délaisser** to abandon, to forsake
laisser entrer to let in, to allow to enter; **laisser tomber** to drop
laisser aller to let go; **se laisser aller** to let oneself go
C'était fâcheux! (See **se fâcher**)

to hurl, to launch, to throw

The Seven Simple Tenses		The Seven Compound Tenses	
Singular	Plural	Singular	Plural
1 présent de l'indicatif		8 passé composé	
lance	**lançons**	**ai lancé**	**avons lancé**
lances	**lancez**	**as lancé**	**avez lancé**
lance	**lancent**	**a lancé**	**ont lancé**
2 imparfait de l'indicatif		9 plus-que-parfait de l'indicatif	
lançais	**lancions**	**avais lancé**	**avions lancé**
lançais	**lanciez**	**avais lancé**	**aviez lancé**
lançait	**lançaient**	**avait lancé**	**avaient lancé**
3 passé simple		10 passé antérieur	
lançai	**lançâmes**	**eus lancé**	**eûmes lancé**
lanças	**lançâtes**	**eus lancé**	**eûtes lancé**
lança	**lancèrent**	**eut lancé**	**eurent lancé**
4 futur		11 futur antérieur	
lancerai	**lancerons**	**aurai lancé**	**aurons lancé**
lanceras	**lancerez**	**auras lancé**	**aurez lancé**
lancera	**lanceront**	**aura lancé**	**auront lancé**
5 conditionnel		12 conditionnel passé	
lancerais	**lancerions**	**aurais lancé**	**aurions lancé**
lancerais	**lanceriez**	**aurais lancé**	**auriez lancé**
lancerait	**lanceraient**	**aurait lancé**	**auraient lancé**
6 présent du subjonctif		13 passé du subjonctif	
lance	**lancions**	**aie lancé**	**ayons lancé**
lances	**lanciez**	**aies lancé**	**ayez lancé**
lance	**lancent**	**ait lancé**	**aient lancé**
7 imparfait du subjonctif		14 plus-que-parfait du subjonctif	
lançasse	**lançassions**	**eusse lancé**	**eussions lancé**
lançasses	**lançassiez**	**eusses lancé**	**eussiez lancé**
lançât	**lançassent**	**eût lancé**	**eussent lancé**
		Impératif	
		lance	
		lançons	
		lancez	

---

se lancer contre   to throw oneself at, against
un départ lancé   a flying start (sports)
une lance   a spear
lancer une balle en l'air
   to throw a ball in the air
lancer une plaisanterie   to crack a joke

un lancement   hurling, casting
un lanceur   thrower, pitcher (sports)
lancer un cri   to cry out
lancer une idée en l'air
   to toss out an idea

laver   Part. pr. **lavant**   Part. passé **lavé**

to wash

The Seven Simple Tenses		The Seven Compound Tenses	
Singular	Plural	Singular	Plural
1 présent de l'indicatif		8 passé composé	
lave	lavons	ai lavé	avons lavé
laves	lavez	as lavé	avez lavé
lave	lavent	a lavé	ont lavé
2 imparfait de l'indicatif		9 plus-que-parfait de l'indicatif	
lavais	lavions	avais lavé	avions lavé
lavais	laviez	avais lavé	aviez lavé
lavait	lavaient	avait lavé	avaient lavé
3 passé simple		10 passé antérieur	
lavai	lavâmes	eus lavé	eûmes lavé
lavas	lavâtes	eus lavé	eûtes lavé
lava	lavèrent	eut lavé	eurent lavé
4 futur		11 futur antérieur	
laverai	laverons	aurai lavé	aurons lavé
laveras	laverez	auras lavé	aurez lavé
lavera	laveront	aura lavé	auront lavé
5 conditionnel		12 conditionnel passé	
laverais	laverions	aurais lavé	aurions lavé
laverais	laveriez	aurais lavé	auriez lavé
laverait	laveraient	aurait lavé	auraient lavé
6 présent du subjonctif		13 passé du subjonctif	
lave	lavions	aie lavé	ayons lavé
laves	laviez	aies lavé	ayez lavé
lave	lavent	ait lavé	aient lavé
7 imparfait du subjonctif		14 plus-que-parfait du subjonctif	
lavasse	lavassions	eusse lavé	eussions lavé
lavasses	lavassiez	eusses lavé	eussiez lavé
lavât	lavassent	eût lavé	eussent lavé
		Impératif	
		lave	
		lavons	
		lavez	

Samedi après-midi j'ai lavé la voiture de mon père et il m'a donné de l'argent pour mon travail.

le lavage washing		**la lavure** dish water	
le lavement enema		**un laveur, une laveuse** washer	
la lavette dish mop		**une machine à laver** washing machine	

See also **se laver.**

to wash oneself

The Seven Simple Tenses		The Seven Compound Tenses	
Singular	Plural	Singular	Plural
1 présent de l'indicatif		8 passé composé	
me lave	**nous lavons**	**me suis lavé(e)**	**nous sommes lavé(e)s**
te laves	**vous lavez**	**t'es lavé(e)**	**vous êtes lavé(e)(s)**
se lave	**se lavent**	**s'est lavé(e)**	**se sont lavé(e)s**
2 imparfait de l'indicatif		9 plus-que-parfait de l'indicatif	
me lavais	**nous lavions**	**m'étais lavé(e)**	**nous étions lavé(e)s**
te lavais	**vous laviez**	**t'étais lavé(e)**	**vous étiez lavé(e)(s)**
se lavait	**se lavaient**	**s'était lavé(e)**	**s'étaient lavé(e)s**
3 passé simple		10 passé antérieur	
me lavai	**nous lavâmes**	**me fus lavé(e)**	**nous fûmes lavé(e)s**
te lavas	**vous lavâtes**	**te fus lavé(e)**	**vous fûtes lavé(e)(s)**
se lava	**se lavèrent**	**se fut lavé(e)**	**se furent lavé(e)s**
4 futur		11 futur antérieur	
me laverai	**nous laverons**	**me serai lavé(e)**	**nous serons lavé(e)s**
te laveras	**vous laverez**	**te seras lavé(e)**	**vous serez lavé(e)(s)**
se lavera	**se laveront**	**se sera lavé(e)**	**se seront lavé(e)s**
5 conditionnel		12 conditionnel passé	
me laverais	**nous laverions**	**me serais lavé(e)**	**nous serions lavé(e)s**
te laverais	**vous laveriez**	**te serais lavé(e)**	**vous seriez lavé(e)(s)**
se laverait	**se laveraient**	**se serait lavé(e)**	**se seraient lavé(e)s**
6 présent du subjonctif		13 passé du subjonctif	
me lave	**nous lavions**	**me sois lavé(e)**	**nous soyons lavé(e)s**
te laves	**vous laviez**	**te sois lavé(e)**	**vous soyez lavé(e)(s)**
se lave	**se lavent**	**se soit lavé(e)**	**se soient lavé(e)s**
7 imparfait du subjonctif		14 plus-que-parfait du subjonctif	
me lavasse	**nous lavassions**	**me fusse lavé(e)**	**nous fussions lavé(e)s**
te lavasses	**vous lavassiez**	**te fusses lavé(e)**	**vous fussiez lavé(e)(s)**
se lavât	**se lavassent**	**se fût lavé(e)**	**se fussent lavé(e)s**

Impératif
lave-toi; ne te lave pas
lavons-nous; ne nous lavons pas
lavez-vous; ne vous lavez pas

Tous les matins je me lave. Je me lave le visage, je me lave les mains, le cou et les oreilles. Hier soir je me suis lavé les pieds.

Ma mère m'a demandé:—Henriette, est-ce que tu t'es bien lavée?

Je lui ai répondu:—Oui, maman, je me suis lavée! Je me suis bien lavé les mains!

For words related to **se laver,** see the verb **laver.**

to lift, to raise

The Seven Simple Tenses		The Seven Compound Tenses	
Singular	Plural	Singular	Plural
1 présent de l'indicatif		8 passé composé	
lève	**levons**	**ai levé**	**avons levé**
lèves	**levez**	**as levé**	**avez levé**
lève	**lèvent**	**a levé**	**ont levé**
2 imparfait de l'indicatif		9 plus-que-parfait de l'indicatif	
levais	**levions**	**avais levé**	**avions levé**
levais	**leviez**	**avais levé**	**aviez levé**
levait	**levaient**	**avait levé**	**avaient levé**
3 passé simple		10 passé antérieur	
levai	**levâmes**	**eus levé**	**eûmes levé**
levas	**levâtes**	**eus levé**	**eûtes levé**
leva	**levèrent**	**eut levé**	**eurent levé**
4 futur		11 futur antérieur	
lèverai	**lèverons**	**aurai levé**	**aurons levé**
lèveras	**lèverez**	**auras levé**	**aurez levé**
lèvera	**lèveront**	**aura levé**	**auront levé**
5 conditionnel		12 conditionnel passé	
lèverais	**lèverions**	**aurais levé**	**aurions levé**
lèverais	**lèveriez**	**aurais levé**	**auriez levé**
lèverait	**lèveraient**	**aurait levé**	**auraient levé**
6 présent du subjonctif		13 passé du subjonctif	
lève	**levions**	**aie levé**	**ayons levé**
lèves	**leviez**	**aies levé**	**ayez levé**
lève	**lèvent**	**ait levé**	**aient levé**
7 imparfait du subjonctif		14 plus-que-parfait du subjonctif	
levasse	**levassions**	**eusse levé**	**eussions levé**
levasses	**levassiez**	**eusses levé**	**eussiez levé**
levât	**levassent**	**eût levé**	**eussent levé**
		Impératif	
		lève	
		levons	
		levez	

voter à main levée to vote by a show of hands
le levage raising, lifting
faire lever qqn to get someone out of bed
le levant the East
le levain leaven
du pain sans levain unleavened bread
le lever du soleil sunrise

se relever to get up on one's feet
lever la main to raise one's hand
élever to raise, to rear, to bring up
enlever to remove
relever to raise again, to pick up

The Seven Simple Tenses		The Seven Compound Tenses	
Singular	Plural	Singular	Plural
1 présent de l'indicatif		8 passé composé	
me lève	**nous levons**	me suis levé(e)	nous sommes levé(e)s
te lèves	**vous levez**	t'es levé(e)	vous êtes levé(e)s
se lève	**se lèvent**	s'est levé(e)	se sont levé(e)s
2 imparfait de l'indicatif		9 plus-que-parfait de l'indicatif	
me levais	**nous levions**	m'étais levé(e)	nous étions levé(e)s
te levais	**vous leviez**	t'étais levé(e)	vous étiez levé(e)(s)
se levait	**se levaient**	s'était levé(e)	s'étaient levé(e)s
3 passé simple		10 passé antérieur	
me levai	**nous levâmes**	me fus levé(e)	nous fûmes levé(e)s
te levas	**vous levâtes**	te fus levé(e)	vous fûtes levé(e)(s)
se leva	**se levèrent**	se fut levé(e)	se furent levé(e)s
4 futur		11 futur antérieur	
me lèverai	**nous lèverons**	me serai levé(e)	nous serons levé(e)s
te lèveras	**vous lèverez**	te seras levé(e)	vous serez levé(e)(s)
se lèvera	**se lèveront**	se sera levé(e)	se seront levé(e)s
5 conditionnel		12 conditionnel passé	
me lèverais	**nous lèverions**	me serais levé(e)	nous serions levé(e)s
te lèverais	**vous lèveriez**	te serais levé(e)	vous seriez levé(e)(s)
se lèverait	**se lèveraient**	se serait levé(e)	se seraient levé(e)s
6 présent du subjonctif		13 passé du subjonctif	
me lève	**nous levions**	me sois levé(e)	nous soyons levé(e)s
te lèves	**vous leviez**	te sois levé(e)	vous soyez levé(e)(s)
se lève	**se lèvent**	se soit levé(e)	se soient levé(e)s
7 imparfait du subjonctif		14 plus-que-parfait du subjonctif	
me levasse	**nous levassions**	me fusse levé(e)	nous fussions levé(e)s
te levasses	**vous levassiez**	te fusses levé(e)	vous fussiez levé(e)(s)
se levât	**se levassent**	se fût levé(e)	se fussent levé(e)s

Impératif
lève-toi; ne te lève pas
levons-nous; ne nous levons pas
levez-vous; ne vous levez pas

Caroline est entrée dans le salon. Elle s'est assise, puis elle s'est levée. Après s'être levée, elle a quitté la maison.

For words related to **se lever**, see the verb **lever**.

lire	Part. pr. **lisant**	Part. passé **lu**

to read

The Seven Simple Tenses		The Seven Compound Tenses	
Singular	Plural	Singular	Plural

1 présent de l'indicatif		8 passé composé	
lis	lisons	ai lu	avons lu
lis	lisez	as lu	avez lu
lit	lisent	a lu	ont lu

2 imparfait de l'indicatif		9 plus-que-parfait de l'indicatif	
lisais	lisions	avais lu	avions lu
lisais	lisiez	avais lu	aviez lu
lisait	lisaient	avait lu	avaient lu

3 passé simple		10 passé antérieur	
lus	lûmes	eus lu	eûmes lu
lus	lûtes	eus lu	eûtes lu
lut	lurent	eut lu	eurent lu

4 futur		11 futur antérieur	
lirai	lirons	aurai lu	aurons lu
liras	lirez	auras lu	aurez lu
lira	liront	aura lu	auront lu

5 conditionnel		12 conditionnel passé	
lirais	lirions	aurais lu	aurions lu
lirais	liriez	aurais lu	auriez lu
lirait	liraient	aurait lu	auraient lu

6 présent du subjonctif		13 passé du subjonctif	
lise	lisions	aie lu	ayons lu
lises	lisiez	aies lu	ayez lu
lise	lisent	ait lu	aient lu

7 imparfait du subjonctif		14 plus-que-parfait du subjonctif	
lusse	lussions	eusse lu	eussions lu
lusses	lussiez	eusses lu	eussiez lu
lût	lussent	eût lu	eussent lu

	Impératif
	lis
	lisons
	lisez

C'est un livre à lire. It's a book worth reading.
lisible legible, readable
lisiblement legibly
lecteur, lectrice reader (a person who reads)
un lecteur d'épreuves, une lectrice d'épreuves
  proofreader
la lecture reading
lectures pour la jeunesse juvenile reading

lire à haute voix to read aloud
lire à voix basse to read in a
  low voice
lire tout bas to read to oneself
relire to reread
Dans l'espoir de vous lire . . .
  Hoping to receive a letter from
  you soon . . .

to shine

The Seven Simple Tenses	The Seven Compound Tenses
Singular Plural	Singular Plural
1 présent de l'indicatif **il luit**	8 passé composé **il a lui**
2 imparfait de l'indicatif **il luisait**	9 plus-que-parfait de l'indicatif **il avait lui**
3 passé simple —	10 passé antérieur **il eut lui**
4 futur **il luira**	11 futur antérieur **il aura lui**
5 conditionnel **il luirait**	12 conditionnel passé **il aurait lui**
6 présent du subjonctif **qu'il luise**	13 passé du subjonctif **qu'il ait lui**
7 imparfait du subjonctif	14 plus-que-parfait du subjonctif **qu'il eût lui**

Impératif
Qu'il luise!   Let it shine!

---

la lueur   glimmer, gleam, glow | **Le soleil luit.**   The sun is shining.
luisant, luisante   shining | **J'ai le nez qui luit.**   My nose is shiny.

This verb is used ordinarily when referring to the sun.

to reduce (one's weight), to grow thin, to lose weight

The Seven Simple Tenses		The Seven Compound Tenses	
Singular	Plural	Singular	Plural
1 présent de l'indicatif		8 passé composé	
maigris	maigrissons	ai maigri	avons maigri
maigris	maigrissez	as maigri	avez maigri
maigrit	maigrissent	a maigri	ont maigri
2 imparfait de l'indicatif		9 plus-que-parfait de l'indicatif	
maigrissais	maigrissions	avais maigri	avions maigri
maigrissais	maigrissiez	avais maigri	aviez maigri
maigrissait	maigrissaient	avait maigri	avaient maigri
3 passé simple		10 passé antérieur	
maigris	maigrîmes	eus maigri	eûmes maigri
maigris	maigrîtes	eus maigri	eûtes maigri
maigrit	maigrirent	eut maigri	eurent maigri
4 futur		11 futur antérieur	
maigrirai	maigrirons	aurai maigri	aurons maigri
maigriras	maigrirez	auras maigri	aurez maigri
maigrira	maigriront	aura maigri	auront maigri
5 conditionnel		12 conditionnel passé	
maigrirais	maigririons	aurais maigri	aurions maigri
maigrirais	maigririez	aurais maigri	auriez maigri
maigrirait	maigriraient	aurait maigri	auraient maigri
6 présent du subjonctif		13 passé du subjonctif	
maigrisse	maigrissions	aie maigri	ayons maigri
maigrisses	maigrissiez	aies maigri	ayez maigri
maigrisse	maigrissent	ait maigri	aient maigri
7 imparfait du subjonctif		14 plus-que-parfait du subjonctif	
maigrisse	maigrissions	eusse maigri	eussions maigri
maigrisses	maigrissiez	eusses maigri	eussiez maigri
maigrît	maigrissent	eût maigri	eussent maigri
		Impératif	
		maigris	
		maigrissons	
		maigrissez	

maigre thin
la maigreur thinness
maigrement meagerly
se faire maigrir to slim down one's weight
être au régime pour maigrir to be on a diet to lose weight

to eat

The Seven Simple Tenses		The Seven Compound Tenses	
Singular	Plural	Singular	Plural
1 présent de l'indicatif		8 passé composé	
mange	**mangeons**	**ai mangé**	**avons mangé**
manges	**mangez**	**as mangé**	**avez mangé**
mange	**mangent**	**a mangé**	**ont mangé**
2 imparfait de l'indicatif		9 plus-que-parfait de l'indicatif	
mangeais	**mangions**	**avais mangé**	**avions mangé**
mangeais	**mangiez**	**avais mangé**	**aviez mangé**
mangeait	**mangeaient**	**avait mangé**	**avaient mangé**
3 passé simple		10 passé antérieur	
mangeai	**mangeâmes**	**eus mangé**	**eûmes mangé**
mangeas	**mangeâtes**	**eus mangé**	**eûtes mangé**
mangea	**mangèrent**	**eut mangé**	**eurent mangé**
4 futur		11 futur antérieur	
mangerai	**mangerons**	**aurai mangé**	**aurons mangé**
mangeras	**mangerez**	**auras mangé**	**aurez mangé**
mangera	**mangeront**	**aura mangé**	**auront mangé**
5 conditionnel		12 conditionnel passé	
mangerais	**mangerions**	**aurais mangé**	**aurions mangé**
mangerais	**mangeriez**	**aurais mangé**	**auriez mangé**
mangerait	**mangeraient**	**aurait mangé**	**auraient mangé**
6 présent du subjonctif		13 passé du subjonctif	
mange	**mangions**	**aie mangé**	**ayons mangé**
manges	**mangiez**	**aies mangé**	**ayez mangé**
mange	**mangent**	**ait mangé**	**aient mangé**
7 imparfait du subjonctif		14 plus-que-parfait du subjonctif	
mangeasse	**mangeassions**	**eusse mangé**	**eussions mangé**
mangeasses	**mangeassiez**	**eusses mangé**	**eussiez mangé**
mangeât	**mangeassent**	**eût mangé**	**eussent mangé**
		Impératif	
		mange	
		mangeons	
		mangez	

le manger food
gros mangeur big eater
manger de l'argent to spend money foolishly
ne pas manger à sa faim not to have much to eat
un mange-tout spendthrift

manger à sa faim to eat until filled
manger comme quatre to eat like a horse
une mangeoire manger

to miss, to lack

The Seven Simple Tenses		The Seven Compound Tenses	
Singular	Plural	Singular	Plural
1 présent de l'indicatif		8 passé composé	
manque	**manquons**	**ai manqué**	**avons manqué**
manques	**manquez**	**as manqué**	**avez manqué**
manque	**manquent**	**a manqué**	**ont manqué**
2 imparfait de l'indicatif		9 plus-que-parfait de l'indicatif	
manquais	**manquions**	**avais manqué**	**avions manqué**
manquais	**manquiez**	**avais manqué**	**aviez manqué**
manquait	**manquaient**	**avait manqué**	**avaient manqué**
3 passé simple		10 passé antérieur	
manquai	**manquâmes**	**eus manqué**	**eûmes manqué**
manquas	**manquâtes**	**eus manqué**	**eûtes manqué**
manqua	**manquèrent**	**eut manqué**	**eurent manqué**
4 futur		11 futur antérieur	
manquerai	**manquerons**	**aurai manqué**	**aurons manqué**
manqueras	**manquerez**	**auras manqué**	**aurez manqué**
manquera	**manqueront**	**aura manqué**	**auront manqué**
5 conditionnel		12 conditionnel passé	
manquerais	**manquerions**	**aurais manqué**	**aurions manqué**
manquerais	**manqueriez**	**aurais manqué**	**auriez manqué**
manquerait	**manqueraient**	**aurait manqué**	**auraient manqué**
6 présent du subjonctif		13 passé du subjonctif	
manque	**manquions**	**aie manqué**	**ayons manqué**
manques	**manquiez**	**aies manqué**	**ayez manqué**
manque	**manquent**	**ait manqué**	**aient manqué**
7 imparfait du subjonctif		14 plus-que-parfait du subjonctif	
manquasse	**manquassions**	**eusse manqué**	**eussions manqué**
manquasses	**manquassiez**	**eusses manqué**	**eussiez manqué**
manquât	**manquassent**	**eût manqué**	**eussent manqué**

Impératif
manque
manquons
manquez

---

manquer à   to lack; **Le courage lui manque.**   He lacks courage.
Elle me manque.   I miss her.
Est-ce que je te manque?   Do you miss me?
manquer de qqch   to be lacking something; **manquer de sucre**   to be out of sugar
Ne manquez pas de venir.   Don't fail to come.
un mariage manqué   a broken engagement
un héros manqué   a would-be hero
Il me manque un franc.   I am lacking (I need) one franc.

to walk, to march, to run (machine), to function

The Seven Simple Tenses		The Seven Compound Tenses	
Singular	Plural	Singular	Plural
1 présent de l'indicatif		8 passé composé	
marche	marchons	ai marché	avons marché
marches	marchez	as marché	avez marché
marche	marchent	a marché	ont marché
2 imparfait de l'indicatif		9 plus-que-parfait de l'indicatif	
marchais	marchions	avais marché	avions marché
marchais	marchiez	avais marché	aviez marché
marchait	marchaient	avait marché	avaient marché
3 passé simple		10 passé antérieur	
marchai	marchâmes	eus marché	eûmes marché
marchas	marchâtes	eus marché	eûtes marché
marcha	marchèrent	eut marché	eurent marché
4 futur		11 futur antérieur	
marcheral	marcherons	aurai marché	aurons marché
marcheras	marcherez	auras marché	aurez marché
marchera	marcheront	aura marché	auront marché
5 conditionnel		12 conditionnel passé	
marcherais	marcherions	aurais marché	aurions marché
marcherais	marcheriez	aurais marché	auriez marché
marcherait	marcheraient	aurait marché	auraient marché
6 présent du subjonctif		13 passé du subjonctif	
marche	marchions	aie marché	ayons marché
marches	marchiez	aies marché	ayez marché
marche	marchent	ait marché	aient marché
7 imparfait du subjonctif		14 plus-que-parfait du subjonctif	
marchasse	marchassions	eusse marché	eussions marché
marchasses	marchassiez	eusses marché	eussiez marché
marchât	marchassent	eût marché	eussent marché

Impératif
marche
marchons
marchez

---

la marche   march, walking
ralentir sa marche   to slow down one's pace
le marché   market
le marché aux fleurs   flower market
le marché aux puces   flea market
à bon marché   cheap
faire marcher qqn   to put someone on
une démarche   gait, walk
faire une démarche   to take a step

marcher bien   to function (go, run, work) well
marcher sur les pas de qqn   to follow in someone's footsteps
faire marcher qqch   to make something go (run, function)
Ça ne marche plus.   It's out of order.

se méfier   Part. pr. **se méfiant**   Part. passé **méfié(e)(s)**

to beware, to distrust, to mistrust

The Seven Simple Tenses		The Seven Compound Tenses	
Singular	Plural	Singular	Plural
1 présent de l'indicatif		8 passé composé	
me méfie	nous méfions	me suis méfié(e)	nous sommes méfié(e)s
te méfies	vous méfiez	t'es méfié(e)	vous êtes méfié(e)(s)
se méfie	se méfient	s'est méfié(e)	se sont méfié(e)s
2 imparfait de l'indicatif		9 plus-que-parfait de l'indicatif	
me méfiais	nous méfiions	m'étais méfié(e)	nous étions méfié(e)s
te méfiais	vous méfiiez	t'étais méfié(e)	vous étiez méfié(e)(s)
se méfiait	se méfiaient	s'était méfié(e)	s'étaient méfié(e)s
3 passé simple		10 passé antérieur	
me méfiai	nous méfiâmes	me fus méfié(e)	nous fûmes méfié(e)s
te méfias	vous méfiâtes	te fus méfié(e)	vous fûtes méfié(e)(s)
se méfia	se méfièrent	se fut méfié(e)	se furent méfié(e)s
4 futur		11 futur antérieur	
me méfierai	nous méfierons	me serai méfié(e)	nous serons méfié(e)s
te méfieras	vous méfierez	te seras méfié(e)	vous serez méfié(e)(s)
se méfiera	se méfieront	se sera méfié(e)	se seront méfié(e)s
5 conditionnel		12 conditionnel passé	
me méfierais	nous méfierions	me serais méfié(e)	nous serions méfié(e)s
te méfierais	vous méfieriez	te serais méfié(e)	vous seriez méfié(e)(s)
se méfierait	se méfieraient	se serait méfié(e)	se seraient méfié(e)s
6 présent du subjonctif		13 passé du subjonctif	
me méfie	nous méfiions	me sois méfié(e)	nous soyons méfié(e)s
te méfies	vous méfiiez	te sois méfié(e)	vous soyez méfié(e)(s)
se méfie	se méfient	se soit méfié(e)	se soient méfié(e)s
7 imparfait du subjonctif		14 plus-que-parfait du subjonctif	
me méfiasse	nous méfiassions	me fusse méfié(e)	nous fussions méfié(e)s
te méfiasses	vous méfiassiez	te fusses méfié(e)	vous fussiez méfié(e)(s)
se méfiât	se méfiassent	se fût méfié(e)	se fussent méfié(e)s

Impératif
méfie-toi; ne te méfie pas
méfions-nous; ne nous méfions pas
méfiez-vous; ne vous méfiez pas

se méfier de   to distrust, to mistrust
Méfiez-vous!   Watch out!
méfiant, méfiante   distrustful
la méfiance   distrust, mistrust
un méfait   misdeed, wrongdoing

to lead, to control

The Seven Simple Tenses		The Seven Compound Tenses	
Singular	Plural	Singular	Plural
1 présent de l'indicatif		8 passé composé	
mène	menons	ai mené	avons mené
mènes	menez	as mené	avez mené
mène	mènent	a mené	ont mené
2 imparfait de l'indicatif		9 plus-que-parfait de l'indicatif	
menais	menions	avais mené	avions mené
menais	meniez	avais mené	aviez mené
menait	menaient	avait mené	avaient mené
3 passé simple		10 passé antérieur	
menai	menâmes	eus mené	eûmes mené
menas	menâtes	eus mené	eûtes mené
mena	menèrent	eut mené	eurent mené
4 futur		11 futur antérieur	
mènerai	mènerons	aurai mené	aurons mené
mèneras	mènerez	auras mené	aurez mené
mènera	mèneront	aura mené	auront mené
5 conditionnel		12 conditionnel passé	
mènerais	mènerions	aurais mené	aurions mené
mènerais	mèneriez	aurais mené	auriez mené
mènerait	mèneraient	aurait mené	auraient mené
6 présent du subjonctif		13 passé du subjonctif	
mène	menions	aie mené	ayons mené
mènes	meniez	ales mené	ayez mené
mène	mènent	ait mené	aient mené
7 imparfait du subjonctif		14 plus-que-parfait du subjonctif	
menasse	menassions	eusse mené	eussions mené
menasses	menassiez	eusses mené	eussiez mené
menât	menassent	eût mené	eussent mené

	Impératif
	mène
	menons
	menez

un meneur, une meneuse   leader
Cela ne mène à rien.   That leads to nothing
mener qqn par le bout du nez   to lead someone around by the nose
mener une vie vagabonde   to lead a vagabond life
mener tout le monde   to be bossy with everyone
mener la bande   to lead the group
Cela vous mènera loin.   That will take you a long way.

See also **emmener**.

to lie, to tell a lie

The Seven Simple Tenses		The Seven Compound Tenses	
Singular	Plural	Singular	Plural
1 présent de l'indicatif		8 passé composé	
mens	mentons	ai menti	avons menti
mens	mentez	as menti	avez menti
ment	mentent	a menti	ont menti
2 imparfait de l'indicatif		9 plus-que-parfait de l'indicatif	
mentais	mentions	avais menti	avions menti
mentais	mentiez	avais menti	aviez menti
mentait	mentaient	avait menti	avaient menti
3 passé simple		10 passé antérieur	
mentis	mentîmes	eus menti	eûmes menti
mentis	mentîtes	eus menti	eûtes menti
mentit	mentirent	eut menti	eurent menti
4 futur		11 futur antérieur	
mentirai	mentirons	aurai menti	aurons menti
mentiras	mentirez	auras menti	aurez menti
mentira	mentiront	aura menti	auront menti
5 conditionnel		12 conditionnel passé	
mentirais	mentirions	aurais menti	aurions menti
mentirais	mentiriez	aurais menti	auriez menti
mentirait	mentiraient	aurait menti	auraient menti
6 présent du subjonctif		13 passé du subjonctif	
mente	mentions	aie menti	ayons menti
mentes	mentiez	aies menti	ayez menti
mente	mentent	ait menti	aient menti
7 imparfait du subjonctif		14 plus-que-parfait du subjonctif	
mentisse	mentissions	eusse menti	eussions menti
mentisses	mentissiez	eusses menti	eussiez menti
mentît	mentissent	eût menti	eussent menti
		Impératif	
		mens	
		mentons	
		mentez	

---

un mensonge a lie
dire des mensonges to tell lies
un menteur, une menteuse a liar

démentir to belie, to deny, to falsify, to refute
une menterie fib

to put, to place

The Seven Simple Tenses		The Seven Compound Tenses	
Singular	Plural	Singular	Plural
1 présent de l'indicatif		8 passé composé	
mets	mettons	ai mis	avons mis
mets	mettez	as mis	avez mis
met	mettent	a mis	ont mis
2 imparfait de l'indicatif		9 plus-que-parfait de l'indicatif	
mettais	mettions	avais mis	avions mis
mettais	mettiez	avais mis	aviez mis
mettait	mettaient	avait mis	avaient mis
3 passé simple		10 passé antérieur	
mis	mîmes	eus mis	eûmes mis
mis	mîtes	eus mis	eûtes mis
mit	mirent	eut mis	eurent mis
4 futur		11 futur antérieur	
mettrai	mettrons	aurai mis	aurons mis
mettras	mettrez	auras mis	aurez mis
mettra	mettront	aura mis	auront mis
5 conditionnel		12 conditionnel passé	
mettrais	mettrions	aurais mis	aurions mis
mettrais	mettriez	aurais mis	auriez mis
mettrait	mettraient	aurait mis	auraient mis
6 présent du subjonctif		13 passé du subjonctif	
mette	mettions	aie mis	ayons mis
mettes	mettiez	aies mis	ayez mis
mette	mettent	ait mis	aient mis
7 imparfait du subjonctif		14 plus-que-parfait du subjonctif	
misse	missions	eusse mis	eussions mis
misses	missiez	eusses mis	eussiez mis
mît	missent	eût mis	eussent mis

Impératif
mets
mettons
mettez

mettre la table to set the table	**mettre au courant** to inform
mettre de côté to lay aside, to save	**mettre le couvert** to set the table
mettre en cause to question	**mettre au point** to make clear
mettre qqn à la porte to kick somebody out the door	**mettre la télé** to turn on the TV
	mettre la radio to turn on the radio

See also **se mettre**.

Try reading aloud as fast as you can this play on the sound **mi: Mimi a mis ses amis à Miami.** Mimi dropped off her friends in Miami.

se mettre	Part. pr. **se mettant**	Part. passé **mis(e)(es)**

to begin, to start, to place oneself

The Seven Simple Tenses		The Seven Compound Tenses	
Singular	Plural	Singular	Plural
1 présent de l'indicatif		8 passé composé	
me mets	nous mettons	me suis mis(e)	nous sommes mis(es)
te mets	vous mettez	t'es mis(e)	vous êtes mis(e)(es)
se met	se mettent	s'est mis(e)	se sont mis(es)
2 imparfait de l'indicatif		9 plus-que-parfait de l'indicatif	
me mettais	nous mettions	m'étais mis(e)	nous étions mis(es)
te mettais	vous mettiez	t'étais mis(e)	vous étiez mis(e)(es)
se mettait	se mettaient	s'était mis(e)	s'étaient mis(es)
3 passé simple		10 passé antérieur	
me mis	nous mîmes	me fus mis(e)	nous fûmes mis(es)
te mis	vous mîtes	te fus mis(e)	vous fûtes mis(e)(es)
se mit	se mirent	se fut mis(e)	se furent mis(es)
4 futur		11 futur antérieur	
me mettrai	nous mettrons	me serai mis(e)	nous serons mis(es)
te mettras	vous mettrez	te seras mis(e)	vous serez mis(e)(es)
se mettra	se mettront	se sera mis(e)	se seront mis(es)
5 conditionnel		12 conditionnel passé	
me mettrais	nous mettrions	me serais mis(e)	nous serions mis(es)
te mettrais	vous mettriez	te serais mis(e)	vous seriez mis(e)(es)
se mettrait	se mettraient	se serait mis(e)	se seraient mis(es)
6 présent du subjonctif		13 passé du subjonctif	
me mette	nous mettions	me sois mis(e)	nous soyons mis(es)
te mettes	vous mettiez	te sois mis(e)	vous soyez mis(e)(es)
se mette	se mettent	se soit mis(e)	se soient mis(es)
7 imparfait du subjonctif		14 plus-que-parfait du subjonctif	
me misse	nous missions	me fusse mis(e)	nous fussions mis(es)
te misses	vous missiez	te fusses mis(e)	vous fussiez mis(e)(es)
se mît	se missent	se fût mis(e)	se fussent mis(es)

Impératif
mets-toi; ne te mets pas
mettons-nous; ne nous mettons pas
mettez-vous; ne vous mettez pas

---

se mettre à + inf.   to begin, to start + inf.
se mettre à table   to go sit at the table
se mettre en colère   to get angry
mettable   wearable; **se mettre en grande toilette**   to dress for an occasion;
   se mettre en smoking   to put on a dinner jacket
mettre en scène   to stage; **un metteur en scène**   director of a play, film

See also **mettre**.

to go up, to ascend, to take up, to bring up, to mount

The Seven Simple Tenses		The Seven Compound Tenses	
Singular	Plural	Singular	Plural
1 présent de l'indicatif		8 passé composé	
monte	montons	suis monté(e)	sommes monté(e)s
montes	montez	es monté(e)	êtes monté(e)(s)
monte	montent	est monté(e)	sont monté(e)s
2 imparfait de l'indicatif		9 plus-que-parfait de l'indicatif	
montais	montions	étais monté(e)	étions monté(e)s
montais	montiez	étais monté(e)	étiez monté(e)(s)
montait	montaient	était monté(e)	étaient monté(e)s
3 passé simple		10 passé antérieur	
montai	montâmes	fus monté(e)	fûmes monté(e)s
montas	montâtes	fus monté(e)	fûtes monté(e)(s)
monta	montèrent	fut monté(e)	furent monté(e)s
4 futur		11 futur antérieur	
monterai	monterons	serai monté(e)	serons monté(e)s
monteras	monterez	seras monté(e)	serez monté(e)(s)
montera	monteront	sera monté(e)	seront monté(e)s
5 conditionnel		12 conditionnel passé	
monterais	monterions	serais monté(e)	serions monté(e)s
monterais	monteriez	serais monté(e)	seriez monté(e)(s)
monterait	monteraient	serait monté(e)	seraient monté(e)s
6 présent du subjonctif		13 passé du subjonctif	
monte	montions	sois monté(e)	soyons monté(e)s
montes	montiez	sois monté(e)	soyez monté(e)(s)
monte	montent	soit monté(e)	soient monté(e)s
7 imparfait du subjonctif		14 plus-que-parfait du subjonctif	
montasse	montassions	fusse monté(e)	fussions monté(e)s
montasses	montassiez	fusses monté(e)	fussiez monté(e)(s)
montât	montassent	fût monté(e)	fussent monté(e)s

	Impératif
	monte
	montons
	montez

This verb is conjugated with *avoir* when it has a direct object.

Examples: **J'ai monté l'escalier.**   I went up the stairs.
                     J'ai monté les valises.   I brought up the suitcases.

BUT: **Elle est montée vite.**   She went up quickly.

See also the verb **descendre**.

monter à bicyclette   to ride a bicycle
monter dans un train   to get on a train
monter une pièce de théâtre   to stage a play

montrer	Part. pr. **montrant**	Part. passé **montré**

to show, to display, to exhibit, to point out

The Seven Simple Tenses		The Seven Compound Tenses	
Singular	Plural	Singular	Plural
1 présent de l'indicatif		8 passé composé	
montre	montrons	ai montré	avons montré
montres	montrez	as montré	avez montré
montre	montrent	a montré	ont montré
2 imparfait de l'indicatif		9 plus-que-parfait de l'indicatif	
montrais	montrions	avais montré	avions montré
montrais	montriez	avais montré	aviez montré
montrait	montraient	avait montré	avaient montré
3 passé simple		10 passé antérieur	
montrai	montrâmes	eus montré	eûmes montré
montras	montrâtes	eus montré	eûtes montré
montra	montrèrent	eut montré	eurent montré
4 futur		11 futur antérieur	
montrerai	montrerons	aurai montré	aurons montré
montreras	montrerez	auras montré	aurez montré
montrera	montreront	aura montré	auront montré
5 conditionnel		12 conditionnel passé	
montrerais	montrerions	aurais montré	aurions montré
montrerais	montreriez	aurais montré	auriez montré
montrerait	montreraient	aurait montré	auraient montré
6 présent du subjonctif		13 passé du subjonctif	
montre	montrions	aie montré	ayons montré
montres	montriez	aies montré	ayez montré
montre	montrent	ait montré	aient montré
7 imparfait du subjonctif		14 plus-que-parfait du subjonctif	
montrasse	montrassions	eusse montré	eussions montré
montrasses	montrassiez	eusses montré	eussiez montré
montrât	montrassent	eût montré	eussent montré
		Impératif	
		montre	
		montrons	
		montrez	

une montre a watch, display
une montre-bracelet wristwatch
faire montre de sa richesse to display, to show off one's wealth
Quelle heure est-il à votre montre? What time is it on your watch?
se faire montrer la porte to be put out the door
démontrer to demonstrate
se démontrer to be proved
se montrer to show oneself, to appear

The Seven Simple Tenses		The Seven Compound Tenses	
Singular	Plural	Singular	Plural
1 présent de l'indicatif		8 passé composé	
mords	**mordons**	**ai mordu**	**avons mordu**
mords	**mordez**	**as mordu**	**avez mordu**
mord	**mordent**	**a mordu**	**ont mordu**
2 imparfait de l'indicatif		9 plus-que-parfait de l'indicatif	
mordais	**mordions**	**avais mordu**	**avions mordu**
mordais	**mordiez**	**avais mordu**	**aviez mordu**
mordait	**mordaient**	**avait mordu**	**avaient mordu**
3 passé simple		10 passé antérieur	
mordis	**mordîmes**	**eus mordu**	**eûmes mordu**
mordis	**mordîtes**	**eus mordu**	**eûtes mordu**
mordit	**mordirent**	**eut mordu**	**eurent mordu**
4 futur		11 futur antérieur	
mordrai	**mordrons**	**aurai mordu**	**aurons mordu**
mordras	**mordrez**	**auras mordu**	**aurez mordu**
mordra	**mordront**	**aura mordu**	**auront mordu**
5 conditionnel		12 conditionnel passé	
mordrais	**mordrions**	**aurais mordu**	**aurions mordu**
mordrais	**mordriez**	**aurais mordu**	**auriez mordu**
mordrait	**mordraient**	**aurait mordu**	**auraient mordu**
6 présent du subjonctif		13 passé du subjonctif	
morde	**mordions**	**aie mordu**	**ayons mordu**
mordes	**mordiez**	**aies mordu**	**ayez mordu**
morde	**mordent**	**ait mordu**	**aient mordu**
7 imparfait du subjonctif		14 plus-que-parfait du subjonctif	
mordisse	**mordissions**	**eusse mordu**	**eussions mordu**
mordisses	**mordissiez**	**eusses mordu**	**eussiez mordu**
mordît	**mordissent**	**eût mordu**	**eussent mordu**

	Impératif
	mords
	mordons
	mordez

Chien qui aboie ne mord pas. A barking dog does not bite. (**aboyer,** to bark)
Tous les chiens qui aboient ne mordent pas. All dogs that bark do not bite.
mordre la poussière to bite the dust
se mordre les lèvres to bite one's lips

mordeur, mordeuse biter (one who bites)
mordiller to bite playfully, to nibble
mordant, mordante biting, trenchant
une morsure bite

mourir	Part. pr. **mourant**	Part. passé **mort(e)(s)**

to die

The Seven Simple Tenses		The Seven Compound Tenses	
Singular	Plural	Singular	Plural
1 présent de l'indicatif		8 passé composé	
meurs	mourons	suis mort(e)	sommes mort(e)s
meurs	mourez	es mort(e)	êtes mort(e)(s)
meurt	meurent	est mort(e)	sont mort(e)s
2 imparfait de l'indicatif		9 plus-que-parfait de l'indicatif	
mourais	mourions	étais mort(e)	étions mort(e)s
mourais	mouriez	étais mort(e)	étiez mort(e)(s)
mourait	mouraient	était mort(e)	étaient mort(e)s
3 passé simple		10 passé antérieur	
mourus	mourûmes	fus mort(e)	fûmes mort(e)s
mourus	mourûtes	fus mort(e)	fûtes mort(e)(s)
mourut	moururent	fut mort(e)	furent mort(e)s
4 futur		11 futur antérieur	
mourrai	mourrons	serai mort(e)	serons mort(e)s
mourras	mourrez	seras mort(e)	serez mort(e)(s)
mourra	mourront	sera mort(e)	seront mort(e)s
5 conditionnel		12 conditionnel passé	
mourrais	mourrions	serais mort(e)	serions mort(e)s
mourrais	mourriez	serais mort(e)	seriez mort(e)(s)
mourrait	mourraient	serait mort(e)	seraient mort(e)s
6 présent du subjonctif		13 passé du subjonctif	
meure	mourions	sois mort(e)	soyons mort(e)s
meures	mouriez	sois mort(e)	soyez mort(e)(s)
meure	meurent	soit mort(e)	soient mort(e)s
7 imparfait du subjonctif		14 plus-que-parfait du subjonctif	
mourusse	mourussions	fusse mort(e)	fussions mort(e)s
mourusses	mourussiez	fusses mort(e)	fussiez mort(e)(s)
mourût	mourussent	fût mort(e)	fussent mort(e)s
		Impératif	
		meurs	
		mourons	
		mourez	

mourir de faim   to starve to death
la mort   death
Elle est mourante.   She is dying. **Elle se meurt.**   She is dying.
mourir d'ennui   to be bored to death
mourir de chagrin   to die of a broken heart
mourir de soif   to die of thirst
mourir de rire   to die laughing
mourir d'envie de faire qqch   to be very eager to do something

to move

The Seven Simple Tenses		The Seven Compound Tenses	
Singular	Plural	Singular	Plural
1 présent de l'indicatif		8 passé composé	
meus	**mouvons**	**ai mû**	**avons mû**
meus	**mouvez**	**as mû**	**avez mû**
meut	**meuvent**	**a mû**	**ont mû**
2 imparfait de l'indicatif		9 plus-que-parfait de l'indicatif	
mouvais	**mouvions**	**avais mû**	**avions mû**
mouvais	**mouviez**	**avais mû**	**aviez mû**
mouvait	**mouvaient**	**avait mû**	**avaient mû**
3 passé simple		10 passé antérieur	
mus	**mûmes**	**eus mû**	**eûmes mû**
mus	**mûtes**	**eus mû**	**eûtes mû**
mut	**murent**	**eut mû**	**eurent mû**
4 futur		11 futur antérieur	
mouvrai	**mouvrons**	**aurai mû**	**aurons mû**
mouvras	**mouvrez**	**auras mû**	**aurez mû**
mouvra	**mouvront**	**aura mû**	**auront mû**
5 conditionnel		12 conditionnel passé	
mouvrais	**mouvrions**	**aurais mû**	**aurions mû**
mouvrais	**mouvriez**	**aurais mû**	**auriez mû**
mouvrait	**mouvraient**	**aurait mû**	**auraient mû**
6 présent du subjonctif		13 passé du subjonctif	
meuve	**mouvions**	**aie mû**	**ayons mû**
meuves	**mouviez**	**aies mû**	**ayez mû**
meuve	**meuvent**	**ait mû**	**aient mû**
7 imparfait du subjonctif		14 plus-que-parfait du subjonctif	
musse	**mussions**	**eusse mû**	**eussions mû**
musses	**mussiez**	**eusses mû**	**eussiez mû**
mût	**mussent**	**eût mû**	**eussent mû**
		Impératif	
		meus	
		mouvons	
		mouvez	

émouvoir   to move, to affect (emotionally)
s'émouvoir   to be moved, to be touched, to be affected (emotionally)
faire mouvoir   to move, to set in motion

Do not confuse this verb with **déménager,** which means to move from one dwelling to another or from one city to another.

nager	Part. pr. **nageant**	Part. passé **nagé**

to swim

The Seven Simple Tenses		The Seven Compound Tenses	
Singular	Plural	Singular	Plural
1 présent de l'indicatif		8 passé composé	
nage	nageons	ai nagé	avons nagé
nages	nagez	as nagé	avez nagé
nage	nagent	a nagé	ont nagé
2 imparfait de l'indicatif		9 plus-que-parfait de l'indicatif	
nageais	nagions	avais nagé	avions nagé
nageais	nagiez	avais nagé	aviez nagé
nageait	nageaient	avait nagé	avaient nagé
3 passé simple		10 passé antérieur	
nageai	nageâmes	eus nagé	eûmes nagé
nageas	nageâtes	eus nagé	eûtes nagé
nagea	nagèrent	eut nagé	eurent nagé
4 futur		11 futur antérieur	
nagerai	nagerons	aurai nagé	aurons nagé
nageras	nagerez	auras nagé	aurez nagé
nagera	nageront	aura nagé	auront nagé
5 conditionnel		12 conditionnel passé	
nagerais	nagerions	aurais nagé	aurions nagé
nagerais	nageriez	aurais nagé	auriez nagé
nagerait	nageraient	aurait nagé	auraient nagé
6 présent du subjonctif		13 passé du subjonctif	
nage	nagions	aie nagé	ayons nagé
nages	nagiez	aies nagé	ayez nagé
nage	nagent	ait nagé	aient nagé
7 imparfait du subjonctif		14 plus-que-parfait du subjonctif	
nageasse	nageassions	eusse nagé	eussions nagé
nageasses	nageassiez	eusses nagé	eussiez nagé
nageât	nageassent	eût nagé	eussent nagé
		Impératif	
		nage	
		nageons	
		nagez	

---

un nageur, une nageuse   swimmer
la piscine   swimming pool
savoir nager   to know how to swim
la natation   swimming
nager entre deux eaux   to sit on the fence; to avoid a commitment
la nage   swimming; **la nage libre**   freestyle swimming
se sauver à la nage   to swim to safety

to be born

The Seven Simple Tenses		The Seven Compound Tenses	
Singular	Plural	Singular	Plural
1 présent de l'indicatif		8 passé composé	
nais	naissons	suis né(e)	sommes né(e)s
nais	naissez	es né(e)	êtes né(e)(s)
naît	naissent	est né(e)	sont né(e)s
2 imparfait de l'indicatif		9 plus-que-parfait de l'indicatif	
naissais	naissions	étais né(e)	étions né(e)s
naissais	naissiez	étais né(e)	étiez né(e)(s)
naissait	naissaient	était né(e)	étaient né(e)s
3 passé simple		10 passé antérieur	
naquis	naquîmes	fus né(e)	fûmes né(e)s
naquis	naquîtes	fus né(e)	fûtes né(e)(s)
naquit	naquirent	fut né(e)	furent né(e)s
4 futur		11 futur antérieur	
naîtrai	naîtrons	serai né(e)	serons né(e)s
naîtras	naîtrez	seras né(e)	serez né(e)(s)
naîtra	naîtront	sera né(e)	seront né(e)s
5 conditionnel		12 conditionnel passé	
naîtrais	naîtrions	serais né(e)	serions né(e)s
naîtrais	naîtriez	serais né(e)	seriez né(e)(s)
naîtrait	naîtraient	serait né(e)	seraient né(e)s
6 présent du subjonctif		13 passé du subjonctif	
naisse	naissions	sois né(e)	soyons né(e)s
naisses	naissiez	sois né(e)	soyez né(e)(s)
naisse	naissent	soit né(e)	soient né(e)s
7 imparfait du subjonctif		14 plus-que-parfait du subjonctif	
naquisse	naquissions	fusse né(e)	fussions né(e)s
naquisses	naquissiez	fusses né(e)	fussiez né(e)(s)
naquît	naquissent	fût né(e)	fussent né(e)s
		Impératif	
		nais	
		naissons	
		naissez	

la naissance   birth
un anniversaire de naissance   a birthday anniversary
donner naissance à   to give birth to; **la naissance du monde**   beginning of the world
Anne est Française de naissance.   Anne was born French.
renaître   to be born again
faire naître   to cause, to give rise to
Je ne suis pas né(e) d'hier!   I wasn't born yesterday!

neiger   Part. pr. **neigeant**   Part. passé **neigé**

to snow

The Seven Simple Tenses	The Seven Compound Tenses
Singular	Singular
1 présent de l'indicatif **il neige**	8 passé composé **il a neigé**
2 imparfait de l'indicatif **il neigeait**	9 plus-que-parfait de l'indicatif **il avait neigé**
3 passé simple **il neigea**	10 passé antérieur **il eut neigé**
4 futur **il neigera**	11 futur antérieur **il aura neigé**
5 conditionnel **il neigerait**	12 conditionnel passé **il aurait neigé**
6 présent du subjonctif **qu'il neige**	13 passé du subjonctif **qu'il ait neigé**
7 imparfait du subjonctif **qu'il neigeât**	14 plus-que-parfait du subjonctif **qu'il eût neigé**

Impératif
Qu'il neige! (Let it snow!)

la neige   snow
un bonhomme de neige   a snowman
neige fondue   slush
neigeux, neigeuse   snowy
Blanche-Neige   Snow-White
une boule de neige   snowball
lancer des boules de neige   to throw snowballs
une chute de neige   snowfall

to clean

The Seven Simple Tenses		The Seven Compound Tenses	
Singular	Plural	Singular	Plural
1 présent de l'indicatif		8 passé composé	
nettoie	nettoyons	ai nettoyé	avons nettoyé
nettoies	nettoyez	as nettoyé	avez nettoyé
nettoie	nettoient	a nettoyé	ont nettoyé
2 imparfait de l'indicatif		9 plus-que-parfait de l'indicatif	
nettoyais	nettoyions	avais nettoyé	avions nettoyé
nettoyais	nettoyiez	avais nettoyé	aviez nettoyé
nettoyait	nettoyaient	avait nettoyé	avaient nettoyé
3 passé simple		10 passé antérieur	
nettoyai	nettoyâmes	eus nettoyé	eûmes nettoyé
nettoyas	nettoyâtes	eus nettoyé	eûtes nettoyé
nettoya	nettoyèrent	eut nettoyé	eurent nettoyé
4 futur		11 futur antérieur	
nettoierai	nettoierons	aurai nettoyé	aurons nettoyé
nettoieras	nettoierez	auras nettoyé	aurez nettoyé
nettoiera	nettoieront	aura nettoyé	auront nettoyé
5 conditionnel		12 conditionnel passé	
nettoierais	nettoierions	aurais nettoyé	aurions nettoyé
nettoierais	nettoieriez	aurais nettoyé	auriez nettoyé
nettoierait	nettoieraient	aurait nettoyé	auraient nettoyé
6 présent du subjonctif		13 passé du subjonctif	
nettoie	nettoyions	aie nettoyé	ayons nettoyé
nettoies	nettoyiez	aies nettoyé	ayez nettoyé
nettoie	nettoient	ait nettoyé	aient nettoyé
7 imparfait du subjonctif		14 plus-que-parfait du subjonctif	
nettoyasse	nettoyassions	eusse nettoyé	eussions nettoyé
nettoyasses	nettoyassiez	eusses nettoyé	eussiez nettoyé
nettoyât	nettoyassent	eût nettoyé	eussent nettoyé
		Impératif	
		nettoie	
		nettoyons	
		nettoyez	

le nettoyage   cleaning; **le nettoyage à sec**   dry cleaning
nettoyer à sec   to dry clean
une nettoyeuse   cleaning machine
un nettoyeur de fenêtres   window cleaner

Verbs ending in *-oyer* must change *y* to *i* before mute *e*.

nourrir   Part. pr. **nourrissant**   Part. passé **nourri**

to feed, to nourish

The Seven Simple Tenses		The Seven Compound Tenses	
Singular	Plural	Singular	Plural
1 présent de l'indicatif		8 passé composé	
nourris	**nourrissons**	**ai nourri**	**avons nourri**
nourris	**nourrissez**	**as nourri**	**avez nourri**
nourrit	**nourrissent**	**a nourri**	**ont nourri**
2 imparfait de l'indicatif		9 plus-que-parfait de l'indicatif	
nourrissais	**nourrissions**	**avais nourri**	**avions nourri**
nourrissais	**nourrissiez**	**avais nourri**	**aviez nourri**
nourrissait	**nourrissaient**	**avait nourri**	**avaient nourri**
3 passé simple		10 passé antérieur	
nourris	**nourrîmes**	**eus nourri**	**eûmes nourri**
nourris	**nourrîtes**	**eus nourri**	**eûtes nourri**
nourrit	**nourrirent**	**eut nourri**	**eurent nourri**
4 futur		11 futur antérieur	
nourrirai	**nourrirons**	**aurai nourri**	**aurons nourri**
nourriras	**nourrirez**	**auras nourri**	**aurez nourri**
nourrira	**nourriront**	**aura nourri**	**auront nourri**
5 conditionnel		12 conditionnel passé	
nourrirais	**nourririons**	**aurais nourri**	**aurions nourri**
nourrirais	**nourririez**	**aurais nourri**	**auriez nourri**
nourrirait	**nourriraient**	**aurait nourri**	**auraient nourri**
6 présent du subjonctif		13 passé du subjonctif	
nourrisse	**nourrissions**	**aie nourri**	**ayons nourri**
nourrisses	**nourrissiez**	**aies nourri**	**ayez nourri**
nourrisse	**nourrissent**	**ait nourri**	**aient nourri**
7 imparfait du subjonctif		14 plus-que-parfait du subjonctif	
nourrisse	**nourrissions**	**eusse nourri**	**eussions nourri**
nourrisses	**nourrissiez**	**eusses nourri**	**eussiez nourri**
nourrît	**nourrissent**	**eût nourri**	**eussent nourri**

Impératif
nourris
nourrissons
nourrissez

---

la nourriture nourishment, food
une nourrice wet nurse
bien nourri well fed; **mal nourri** poorly fed
nourrissant, nourrissante nourishing

un nourrisson infant
nourricier, nourricière nutritious
une mère nourricière foster mother
un père nourricier foster father

to harm, to hinder

The Seven Simple Tenses		The Seven Compound Tenses	
Singular	Plural	Singular	Plural
1 présent de l'indicatif		8 passé composé	
nuis	nuisons	ai nui	avons nui
nuis	nuisez	as nui	avez nui
nuit	nuisent	a nui	ont nui
2 imparfait de l'indicatif		9 plus-que-parfait de l'indicatif	
nuisais	nuisions	avais nui	avions nui
nuisais	nuisiez	avais nui	aviez nui
nuisait	nuisaient	avait nui	avaient nui
3 passé simple		10 passé antérieur	
nuisis	nuisîmes	eus nui	eûmes nui
nuisis	nuisîtes	eus nui	eûtes nui
nuisit	nuisirent	eut nui	eurent nui
4 futur		11 futur antérieur	
nuirai	nuirons	aurai nui	aurons nui
nuiras	nuirez	auras nui	aurez nui
nuira	nuiront	aura nui	auront nui
5 conditionnel		12 conditionnel passé	
nuirais	nuirions	aurais nui	aurions nui
nuirais	nuiriez	aurais nui	auriez nui
nuirait	nuiraient	aurait nui	auraient nui
6 présent du subjonctif		13 passé du subjonctif	
nuise	nuisions	aie nui	ayons nui
nuises	nuisiez	aies nui	ayez nui
nuise	nuisent	ait nui	aient nui
7 imparfait du subjonctif		14 plus-que-parfait du subjonctif	
nuisisse	nuisissions	eusse nul	eussions nui
nuisisses	nuisissiez	eusses nui	eussiez nui
nuisît	nuisissent	eût nui	eussent nui
		Impératif	
		nuis	
		nuisons	
		nuisez	

la **nuisance** nuisance
la **nuisibilité** harmfulness
nuisible harmful

nuire à to do harm to, to be injurious to,
  to be harmful to
Cela peut nuire à la réputation de votre famille.
  That may harm the reputation of your family.

to obey

The Seven Simple Tenses		The Seven Compound Tenses	
Singular	Plural	Singular	Plural
1 présent de l'indicatif		8 passé composé	
obéis	obéissons	ai obéi	avons obéi
obéis	obéissez	as obéi	avez obéi
obéit	obéissent	a obéi	ont obéi
2 imparfait de l'indicatif		9 plus-que-parfait de l'indicatif	
obéissais	obéissions	avais obéi	avions obéi
obéissais	obéissiez	avais obéi	aviez obéi
obéissait	obéissaient	avait obéi	avaient obéi
3 passé simple		10 passé antérieur	
obéis	obéîmes	eus obéi	eûmes obéi
obéis	obéîtes	eus obéi	eûtes obéi
obéit	obéirent	eut obéi	eurent obéi
4 futur		11 futur antérieur	
obéirai	obéirons	aurai obéi	aurons obéi
obéiras	obéirez	auras obéi	aurez obéi
obéira	obéiront	aura obéi	auront obéi
5 conditionnel		12 conditionnel passé	
obéirais	obéirions	aurais obéi	aurions obéi
obéirais	obéiriez	aurais obéi	auriez obéi
obéirait	obéiraient	aurait obéi	auraient obéi
6 présent du subjonctif		13 passé du subjonctif	
obéisse	obéissions	aie obéi	ayons obéi
obéisses	obéissiez	aies obéi	ayez obéi
obéisse	obéissent	ait obéi	aient obéi
7 imparfait du subjonctif		14 plus-que-parfait du subjonctif	
obéisse	obéissions	eusse obéi	eussions obéi
obéisses	obéissiez	eusses obéi	eussiez obéi
obéît	obéissent	eût obéi	eussent obéi

Impératif
obéis
obéissons
obéissez

---

obéir à qqn   to obey someone
désobéir à qqn   to disobey someone
l'obéissance *(f.)*   obedience

obéissant, obéissante   obedient
désobéissant, désobéissante   disobedient

to oblige

The Seven Simple Tenses		The Seven Compound Tenses	
Singular	Plural	Singular	Plural
1 présent de l'indicatif		8 passé composé	
oblige	obligeons	ai obligé	avons obligé
obliges	obligez	as obligé	avez obligé
oblige	obligent	a obligé	ont obligé
2 imparfait de l'indicatif		9 plus-que-parfait de l'indicatif	
obligeais	obligions	avais obligé	avions obligé
obligeais	obligiez	avais obligé	aviez obligé
obligeait	obligeaient	avait obligé	avaient obligé
3 passé simple		10 passé antérieur	
obligeai	obligeâmes	eus obligé	eûmes obligé
obligeas	obligeâtes	eus obligé	eûtes obligé
obligea	obligèrent	eut obligé	eurent obligé
4 futur		11 futur antérieur	
obligerai	obligerons	aurai obligé	aurons obligé
obligeras	obligerez	auras obligé	aurez obligé
obligera	obligeront	aura obligé	auront obligé
5 conditionnel		12 conditionnel passé	
obligerais	obligerions	aurais obligé	aurions obligé
obligerais	obligeriez	aurais obligé	auriez obligé
obligerait	obligeraient	aurait obligé	auraient obligé
6 présent du subjonctif		13 passé du subjonctif	
oblige	obligions	aie obligé	ayons obligé
obliges	obligiez	aies obligé	ayez obligé
oblige	obligent	ait obligé	aient obligé
7 imparfait du subjonctif		14 plus-que-parfait du subjonctif	
obligeasse	obligeassions	eusse obligé	eussions obligé
obligeasses	obligeassiez	eusses obligé	eussiez obligé
obligeât	obligeassent	eût obligé	eussent obligé
		Impératif	
		oblige	
		obligeons	
		obligez	

obligatoire   obligatory
obligation (f.)   obligation
avoir beaucoup d'obligation à qqn   to be much obliged to someone
obligeant, obligeante   obliging
se montrer obligeant envers qqn   to show kindness to someone
obligé, obligée   obliged
Noblesse oblige.   Nobility obliges. (i.e., the moral obligation of a highborn person is to show honorable conduct)

185

to obtain, to get

The Seven Simple Tenses		The Seven Compound Tenses	
Singular	Plural	Singular	Plural
1 présent de l'indicatif		8 passé composé	
obtiens	obtenons	ai obtenu	avons obtenu
obtiens	obtenez	as obtenu	avez obtenu
obtient	obtiennent	a obtenu	ont obtenu
2 imparfait de l'indicatif		9 plus-que-parfait de l'indicatif	
obtenais	obtenions	avais obtenu	avions obtenu
obtenais	obteniez	avais obtenu	aviez obtenu
obtenait	obtenaient	avait obtenu	avaient obtenu
3 passé simple		10 passé antérieur	
obtins	obtînmes	eus obtenu	eûmes obtenu
obtins	obtîntes	eus obtenu	eûtes obtenu
obtint	obtinrent	eut obtenu	eurent obtenu
4 futur		11 futur antérieur	
obtiendrai	obtiendrons	aurai obtenu	aurons obtenu
obtiendras	obtiendrez	auras obtenu	aurez obtenu
obtiendra	obtiendront	aura obtenu	auront obtenu
5 conditionnel		12 conditionnel passé	
obtiendrais	obtiendrions	aurais obtenu	aurions obtenu
obtiendrais	obtiendriez	aurais obtenu	auriez obtenu
obtiendrait	obtiendraient	aurait obtenu	auraient obtenu
6 présent du subjonctif		13 passé du subjonctif	
obtienne	obtenions	aie obtenu	ayons obtenu
obtiennes	obteniez	aies obtenu	ayez obtenu
obtienne	obtiennent	ait obtenu	aient obtenu
7 imparfait du subjonctif		14 plus-que-parfait du subjonctif	
obtinsse	obtinssions	eusse obtenu	eussions obtenu
obtinsses	obtinssiez	eusses obtenu	eussiez obtenu
obtînt	obtinssent	eût obtenu	eussent obtenu
		Impératif	
		obtiens	
		obtenons	
		obtenez	

l'obtention obtainment
obtenir de qqn qqch de force to get something out of someone by force
s'obtenir de to be obtained from

See also **tenir.**

to occupy

The Seven Simple Tenses		The Seven Compound Tenses	
Singular	Plural	Singular	Plural
1 présent de l'indicatif		8 passé composé	
occupe	occupons	ai occupé	avons occupé
occupes	occupez	as occupé	avez occupé
occupe	occupent	a occupé	ont occupé
2 imparfait de l'indicatif		9 plus-que-parfait de l'indicatif	
occupais	occupions	avais occupé	avions occupé
occupais	occupiez	avais occupé	aviez occupé
occupait	occupaient	avait occupé	avaient occupé
3 passé simple		10 passé antérieur	
occupai	occupâmes	eus occupé	eûmes occupé
occupas	occupâtes	eus occupé	eûtes occupé
occupa	occupèrent	eut occupé	eurent occupé
4 futur		11 futur antérieur	
occuperai	occuperons	aurai occupé	aurons occupé
occuperas	occuperez	auras occupé	aurez occupé
occupera	occuperont	aura occupé	auront occupé
5 conditionnel		12 conditionnel passé	
occuperais	occuperions	aurais occupé	aurions occupé
occuperais	occuperiez	aurais occupé	auriez occupé
occuperait	occuperaient	aurait occupé	auraient occupé
6 présent du subjonctif		13 passé du subjonctif	
occupe	occupions	aie occupé	ayons occupé
occupes	occupiez	aies occupé	ayez occupé
occupe	occupent	ait occupé	aient occupé
7 imparfait du subjonctif		14 plus-que-parfait du subjonctif	
occupasse	occupassions	eusse occupé	eussions occupé
occupasses	occupassiez	eusses occupé	eussiez occupé
occupât	occupassent	eût occupé	eussent occupé
		Impératif	
		occupe	
		occupons	
		occupez	

occupation (*f.*)   occupation
être occupé(e)   to be busy
occuper qqn   to keep someone busy
occuper trop de place   to take up too much room
occupant, occupante   occupying; **du travail occupant**   engrossing work
occuper l'attention de qqn   to hold someone's attention
préoccuper   to preoccupy; **une préoccupation**   preoccupation

to be busy, to keep oneself busy

The Seven Simple Tenses		The Seven Compound Tenses	
Singular	Plural	Singular	Plural
1 présent de l'indicatif		8 passé composé	
m'occupe	nous occupons	me suis occupé(e)	nous sommes occupé(e)s
t'occupes	vous occupez	t'es occupé(e)	vous êtes occupé(e)s
s'occupe	s'occupent	s'est occupé(e)	se sont occupé(e)s
2 imparfait de l'indicatif		9 plus-que-parfait de l'indicatif	
m'occupais	nous occupions	m'étais occupé(e)	nous étions occupé(e)s
t'occupais	vous occupiez	t'étais occupé(e)	vous étiez occupé(e)(s)
s'occupait	s'occupaient	s'était occupé(e)	s'étaient occupé(e)s
3 passé simple		10 passé antérieur	
m'occupai	nous occupâmes	me fus occupé(e)	nous fûmes occupé(e)s
t'occupas	vous occupâtes	te fus occupé(e)	vous fûtes occupé(e)(s)
s'occupa	s'occupèrent	se fut occupé(e)	se furent occupé(e)s
4 futur		11 futur antérieur	
m'occuperai	nous occuperons	me serai occupé(e)	nous serons occupé(e)s
t'occuperas	vous occuperez	te seras occupé(e)	vous serez occupé(e)(s)
s'occupera	s'occuperont	se sera occupé(e)	se seront occupé(e)s
5 conditionnel		12 conditionnel passé	
m'occuperais	nous occuperions	me serais occupé(e)	nous serions occupé(e)s
t'occuperais	vous occuperiez	te serais occupé(e)	vous seriez occupé(e)(s)
s'occuperait	s'occuperaient	se serait occupé(e)	se seraient occupé(e)s
6 présent du subjonctif		13 passé du subjonctif	
m'occupe	nous occupions	me sois occupé(e)	nous soyons occupé(e)s
t'occupes	vous occupiez	te sois occupé(e)	vous soyez occupé(e)(s)
s'occupe	s'occupent	se soit occupé(e)	se soient occupé(e)s
7 imparfait du subjonctif		14 plus-que-parfait du subjonctif	
m'occupasse	nous occupassions	me fusse occupé(e)	nous fussions occupé(e)s
t'occupasses	vous occupassiez	te fusses occupé(e)	vous fussiez occupé(e)(s)
s'occupât	s'occupassent	se fût occupé(e)	se fussent occupé(e)s

	Impératif
	occupe-toi; ne t'occupe pas
	occupons-nous; ne nous occupons pas
	occupez-vous; ne vous occupez pas

s'occuper de ses affaires   to mind one's own business

Je m'occupe de mes affaires.   I mind my own business.

s'occuper des enfants   to look after children

s'occuper de   to look after, to tend to

s'occuper à   to be engaged in

Occupez-vous de vos affaires!   Mind your own business!

Ne vous occupez pas de mes affaires!   Don't mind my business!

Est-ce qu'on s'occupe de vous?   Is someone helping you?

See also the verb **occuper.**

to offer

The Seven Simple Tenses		The Seven Compound Tenses	
Singular	Plural	Singular	Plural
1 présent de l'indicatif		8 passé composé	
offre	**offrons**	**ai offert**	**avons offert**
offres	**offrez**	**as offert**	**avez offert**
offre	**offrent**	**a offert**	**ont offert**
2 imparfait de l'indicatif		9 plus-que-parfait de l'indicatif	
offrais	**offrions**	**avais offert**	**avions offert**
offrais	**offriez**	**avais offert**	**aviez offert**
offrait	**offraient**	**avait offert**	**avaient offert**
3 passé simple		10 passé antérieur	
offris	**offrîmes**	**eus offert**	**eûmes offert**
offris	**offrîtes**	**eus offert**	**eûtes offert**
offrit	**offrirent**	**eut offert**	**eurent offert**
4 futur		11 futur antérieur	
offrirai	**offrirons**	**aurai offert**	**aurons offert**
offriras	**offrirez**	**auras offert**	**aurez offert**
offrira	**offriront**	**aura offert**	**auront offert**
5 conditionnel		12 conditionnel passé	
offrirais	**offririons**	**aurais offert**	**aurions offert**
offrirais	**offririez**	**aurais offert**	**auriez offert**
offrirait	**offriraient**	**aurait offert**	**auraient offert**
6 présent du subjonctif		13 passé du subjonctif	
offre	**offrions**	**aie offert**	**ayons offert**
offres	**offriez**	**aies offert**	**ayez offert**
offre	**offrent**	**ait offert**	**aient offert**
7 imparfait du subjonctif		14 plus-que-parfait du subjonctif	
offrisse	**offrissions**	**eusse offert**	**eussions offert**
offrisses	**offrissiez**	**eusses offert**	**eussiez offert**
offrît	**offrissent**	**eût offert**	**eussent offert**

Impératif
offre
offrons
offrez

---

offrir qqch à qqn   to offer (to present)   **C'est pour offrir?**   Is it to give as a gift?
  something to someone   **une offre d'emploi**   a job offer
une offre   an offer, a proposal
une offrande   gift, offering
l'offre et la demande   supply and demand

omettre	Part. pr. **omettant**	Part. passé **omis**

to omit

The Seven Simple Tenses		The Seven Compound Tenses	
Singular	Plural	Singular	Plural
1 présent de l'indicatif		8 passé composé	
omets	omettons	ai omis	avons omis
omets	omettez	as omis	avez omis
omet	omettent	a omis	ont omis
2 imparfait de l'indicatif		9 plus-que-parfait de l'indicatif	
omettais	omettions	avais omis	avions omis
omettais	omettiez	avais omis	aviez omis
omettait	omettaient	avait omis	avaient omis
3 passé simple		10 passé antérieur	
omis	omîmes	eus omis	eûmes omis
omis	omîtes	eus omis	eûtes omis
omit	omirent	eut omis	eurent omis
4 futur		11 futur antérieur	
omettrai	omettrons	aurai omis	aurons omis
omettras	omettrez	auras omis	aurez omis
omettra	omettront	aura omis	auront omis
5 conditionnel		12 conditionnel passé	
omettrais	omettrions	aurais omis	aurions omis
omettrais	omettriez	aurais omis	auriez omis
omettrait	omettraient	aurait omis	auraient omis
6 présent du subjonctif		13 passé du subjonctif	
omette	omettions	aie omis	ayons omis
omettes	omettiez	aies omis	ayez omis
omette	omettent	ait omis	aient omis
7 imparfait du subjonctif		14 plus-que-parfait du subjonctif	
omisse	omissions	eusse omis	eussions omis
omisses	omissiez	eusses omis	eussiez omis
omît	omissent	eût omis	eussent omis

	Impératif
	omets
	omettons
	omettez

omettre de faire qqch to neglect to do something
une omission an omission
omis, omise omitted
commettre to commit

190

The Seven Simple Tenses		The Seven Compound Tenses	
Singular	Plural	Singular	Plural
1 présent de l'indicatif		8 passé composé	
oublie	oublions	ai oublié	avons oublié
oublies	oubliez	as oublié	avez oublié
oublie	oublient	a oublié	ont oublié
2 imparfait de l'indicatif		9 plus-que-parfait de l'indicatif	
oubliais	oubliions	avais oublié	avions oublié
oubliais	oubliiez	avais oublié	aviez oublié
oubliait	oubliaient	avait oublié	avaient oublié
3 passé simple		10 passé antérieur	
oubliai	oubliâmes	eus oublié	eûmes oublié
oublias	oubliâtes	eus oublié	eûtes oublié
oublia	oublièrent	eut oublié	eurent oublié
4 futur		11 futur antérieur	
oublierai	oublierons	aurai oublié	aurons oublié
oublieras	oublierez	auras oublié	aurez oublié
oubliera	oublieront	aura oublié	auront oublié
5 conditionnel		12 conditionnel passé	
oublierais	oublierions	aurais oublié	aurions oublié
oublierais	oublieriez	aurais oublié	auriez oublié
oublierait	oublieraient	aurait oublié	auraient oublié
6 présent du subjonctif		13 passé du subjonctif	
oublie	oubliions	aie oublié	ayons oublié
oublies	oubliiez	aies oublié	ayez oublié
oublie	oublient	ait oublié	aient oublié
7 imparfait du subjonctif		14 plus-que-parfait du subjonctif	
oubliasse	oubliassions	eusse oublié	eussions oublié
oubliasses	oubliassiez	eusses oublié	eussiez oublié
oubliât	oubliassent	eût oublié	eussent oublié
		Impératif	
		oublie	
		oublions	
		oubliez	

---

un oubli oversight; oblivion
oubliable forgettable
inoubliable unforgettable
s'oublier to forget oneself, to be
  unmindful of oneself

oublier de faire qqch to forget
  to do something
oublieux, oublieuse oblivious; **oublieux de**
  unmindful of

ouvrir　　　　　Part. pr. **ouvrant**　　　　　Part. passé **ouvert**

to open

The Seven Simple Tenses		The Seven Compound Tenses	
Singular	Plural	Singular	Plural
1　présent de l'indicatif		8　passé composé	
ouvre	ouvrons	ai ouvert	avons ouvert
ouvres	ouvrez	as ouvert	avez ouvert
ouvre	ouvrent	a ouvert	ont ouvert
2　imparfait de l'indicatif		9　plus-que-parfait de l'indicatif	
ouvrais	ouvrions	avais ouvert	avions ouvert
ouvrais	ouvriez	avais ouvert	aviez ouvert
ouvrait	ouvraient	avait ouvert	avaient ouvert
3　passé simple		10　passé antérieur	
ouvris	ouvrîmes	eus ouvert	eûmes ouvert
ouvris	ouvrîtes	eus ouvert	eûtes ouvert
ouvrit	ouvrirent	eut ouvert	eurent ouvert
4　futur		11　futur antérieur	
ouvrirai	ouvrirons	aurai ouvert	aurons ouvert
ouvriras	ouvrirez	auras ouvert	aurez ouvert
ouvrira	ouvriront	aura ouvert	auront ouvert
5　conditionnel		12　conditionnel passé	
ouvrirais	ouvririons	aurais ouvert	aurions ouvert
ouvrirais	ouvririez	aurais ouvert	auriez ouvert
ouvrirait	ouvriraient	aurait ouvert	auraient ouvert
6　présent du subjonctif		13　passé du subjonctif	
ouvre	ouvrions	aie ouvert	ayons ouvert
ouvres	ouvriez	aies ouvert	ayez ouvert
ouvre	ouvrent	ait ouvert	aient ouvert
7　imparfait du subjonctif		14　plus-que-parfait du subjonctif	
ouvrisse	ouvrissions	eusse ouvert	eussions ouvert
ouvrisses	ouvrissiez	eusses ouvert	eussiez ouvert
ouvrît	ouvrissent	eût ouvert	eussent ouvert

Impératif
ouvre
ouvrons
ouvrez

---

ouvert, ouverte　open
ouverture (*f.*)　opening
ouvrir le gaz　to turn on the gas
ouvrir de force　to force open

rouvrir　to reopen, to open again
entrouvrir　to open just a bit
s'ouvrir à　to confide in

to appear, to seem

The Seven Simple Tenses		The Seven Compound Tenses	
Singular	Plural	Singular	Plural
1 présent de l'indicatif		8 passé composé	
parais	**paraissons**	**ai paru**	**avons paru**
parais	**paraissez**	**as paru**	**avez paru**
paraît	**paraissent**	**a paru**	**ont paru**
2 imparfait de l'indicatif		9 plus-que-parfait de l'indicatif	
paraissais	**paraissions**	**avais paru**	**avions paru**
paraissais	**paraissiez**	**avais paru**	**aviez paru**
paraissait	**paraissaient**	**avait paru**	**avaient paru**
3 passé simple		10 passé antérieur	
parus	**parûmes**	**eus paru**	**eûmes paru**
parus	**parûtes**	**eus paru**	**eûtes paru**
parut	**parurent**	**eut paru**	**eurent paru**
4 futur		11 futur antérieur	
paraîtrai	**paraîtrons**	**aurai paru**	**aurons paru**
paraîtras	**paraîtrez**	**auras paru**	**aurez paru**
paraîtra	**paraîtront**	**aura paru**	**auront paru**
5 conditionnel		12 conditionnel passé	
paraîtrais	**paraîtrions**	**aurais paru**	**aurions paru**
paraîtrais	**paraîtriez**	**aurais paru**	**auriez paru**
paraîtrait	**paraîtraient**	**aurait paru**	**auraient paru**
6 présent du subjonctif		13 passé du subjonctif	
paraisse	**paraissions**	**aie paru**	**ayons paru**
paraisses	**paraissiez**	**aies paru**	**ayez paru**
paraisse	**paraissent**	**ait paru**	**aient paru**
7 imparfait du subjonctif		14 plus-que-parfait du subjonctif	
parusse	**parussions**	**eusse paru**	**eussions paru**
parusses	**parussiez**	**eusses paru**	**eussiez paru**
parût	**parussent**	**eût paru**	**eussent paru**
		Impératif	
		parais	
		paraissons	
		paraissez	

apparition (*f.*)   apparition, appearance
Cela me paraît incroyable.   That seems unbelievable to me.
Le jour paraît.   Day is breaking.
apparaître   to appear, to come into view
disparaître   to disappear
réapparaître   to reappear
Ce livre vient de paraître.   This book has just been published.

pardonner	Part. pr. **pardonnant**	Part. passé **pardonné**

to pardon, to forgive

The Seven Simple Tenses		The Seven Compound Tenses	
Singular	Plural	Singular	Plural
1 présent de l'indicatif		8 passé composé	
pardonne	pardonnons	ai pardonné	avons pardonné
pardonnes	pardonnez	as pardonné	avez pardonné
pardonne	pardonnent	a pardonné	ont pardonné
2 imparfait de l'indicatif		9 plus-que-parfait de l'indicatif	
pardonnais	pardonnions	avais pardonné	avions pardonné
pardonnais	pardonniez	avais pardonné	aviez pardonné
pardonnait	pardonnaient	avait pardonné	avaient pardonné
3 passé simple		10 passé antérieur	
pardonnai	pardonnâmes	eus pardonné	eûmes pardonné
pardonnas	pardonnâtes	eus pardonné	eûtes pardonné
pardonna	pardonnèrent	eut pardonné	eurent pardonné
4 futur		11 futur antérieur	
pardonnerai	pardonnerons	aurai pardonné	aurons pardonné
pardonneras	pardonnerez	auras pardonné	aurez pardonné
pardonnera	pardonneront	aura pardonné	auront pardonné
5 conditionnel		12 conditionnel passé	
pardonnerais	pardonnerions	aurais pardonné	aurions pardonné
pardonnerais	pardonneriez	aurais pardonné	auriez pardonné
pardonnerait	pardonneraient	aurait pardonné	auraient pardonné
6 présent du subjonctif		13 passé du subjonctif	
pardonne	pardonnions	aie pardonné	ayons pardonné
pardonnes	pardonniez	aies pardonné	ayez pardonné
pardonne	pardonnent	ait pardonné	aient pardonné
7 imparfait du subjonctif		14 plus-que-parfait du subjonctif	
pardonnasse	pardonnassions	eusse pardonné	eussions pardonné
pardonnasses	pardonnassiez	eusses pardonné	eussiez pardonné
pardonnât	pardonnassent	eût pardonné	eussent pardonné

Impératif
pardonne
pardonnons
pardonnez

---

pardonner à qqn de qqch to forgive someone for something
J'ai pardonné à mon ami d'être arrivé en retard. I forgave my friend for
having arrived late.
un pardon forgiveness, pardon
un don gift
pardonnable forgivable, pardonable
Pardonnez-moi. Pardon me.

to talk, to speak

The Seven Simple Tenses		The Seven Compound Tenses	
Singular	Plural	Singular	Plural
1 présent de l'indicatif		8 passé composé	
parle	parlons	ai parlé	avons parlé
parles	parlez	as parlé	avez parlé
parle	parlent	a parlé	ont parlé
2 imparfait de l'indicatif		9 plus-que-parfait de l'indicatif	
parlais	parlions	avais parlé	avions parlé
parlais	parliez	avais parlé	aviez parlé
parlait	parlaient	avait parlé	avaient parlé
3 passé simple		10 passé antérieur	
parlai	parlâmes	eus parlé	eûmes parlé
parlas	parlâtes	eus parlé	eûtes parlé
parla	parlèrent	eut parlé	eurent parlé
4 futur		11 futur antérieur	
parlerai	parlerons	aurai parlé	aurons parlé
parleras	parlerez	auras parlé	aurez parlé
parlera	parleront	aura parlé	auront parlé
5 conditionnel		12 conditionnel passé	
parlerais	parlerions	aurais parlé	aurions parlé
parlerais	parleriez	aurais parlé	auriez parlé
parlerait	parleraient	aurait parlé	auraient parlé
6 présent du subjonctif		13 passé du subjonctif	
parle	parlions	aie parlé	ayons parlé
parles	parliez	aies parlé	ayez parlé
parle	parlent	ait parlé	aient parlé
7 imparfait du subjonctif		14 plus-que-parfait du subjonctif	
parlasse	parlassions	eusse parlé	eussions parlé
parlasses	parlassiez	eusses parlé	eussiez parlé
parlât	parlassent	eût parlé	eussent parlé
		Impératif	
		parle	
		parlons	
		parlez	

parler à haute voix   to speak in a loud voice; **parler haut**   to speak loudly
parler à voix basse   to speak in a soft voice; **parler bas**   to speak softly
la parole   spoken word; **parler à**   to talk to; **parler de**   to talk about (of)
selon la parole du Christ   according to Christ's words
le don de la parole   the gift of gab
parler affaires   to talk business, to talk shop
sans parler de . . .   not to mention . . .
parler pour qqn   to speak for someone; **parler contre qqn**   to speak against
   someone
un parloir   parlor (room where people talk)

partir		Part. pr. **partant**	Part. passé **parti(e)(s)**

partir

to leave, to depart

The Seven Simple Tenses		The Seven Compound Tenses	
Singular	Plural	Singular	Plural
1 présent de l'indicatif		8 passé composé	
pars	**partons**	**suis parti(e)**	**sommes parti(e)s**
pars	**partez**	**es parti(e)**	**êtes parti(e)(s)**
part	**partent**	**est parti(e)**	**sont parti(e)s**
2 imparfait de l'indicatif		9 plus-que-parfait de l'indicatif	
partais	**partions**	**étais parti(e)**	**étions parti(e)s**
partais	**partiez**	**étais parti(e)**	**étiez parti(e)(s)**
partait	**partaient**	**était parti(e)**	**étaient parti(e)s**
3 passé simple		10 passé antérieur	
partis	**partîmes**	**fus parti(e)**	**fûmes parti(e)s**
partis	**partîtes**	**fus parti(e)**	**fûtes parti(e)(s)**
partit	**partirent**	**fut parti(e)**	**furent parti(e)s**
4 futur		11 futur antérieur	
partirai	**partirons**	**serai parti(e)**	**serons parti(e)s**
partiras	**partirez**	**seras parti(e)**	**serez parti(e)(s)**
partira	**partiront**	**sera parti(e)**	**seront parti(e)s**
5 conditionnel		12 conditionnel passé	
partirais	**partirions**	**serais parti(e)**	**serions parti(e)s**
partirais	**partiriez**	**serais parti(e)**	**seriez parti(e)(s)**
partirait	**partiraient**	**serait parti(e)**	**seraient parti(e)s**
6 présent du subjonctif		13 passé du subjonctif	
parte	**partions**	**sois parti(e)**	**soyons parti(e)s**
partes	**partiez**	**sois parti(e)**	**soyez parti(e)(s)**
parte	**partent**	**soit parti(e)**	**soient parti(e)s**
7 imparfait du subjonctif		14 plus-que-parfait du subjonctif	
partisse	**partissions**	**fusse parti(e)**	**fussions parti(e)s**
partisses	**partissiez**	**fusses parti(e)**	**fussiez parti(e)(s)**
partît	**partissent**	**fût parti(e)**	**fussent parti(e)s**
		Impératif	
		pars	
		partons	
		partez	

A quelle heure part le train pour Paris?   At what time does the train for Paris leave?
à partir de maintenant   from now on; **à partir d'aujourd'hui**   from today on
le départ   departure
partir en voyage   to go on a trip
partir en vacances   to leave for a vacation
repartir   to leave again, to set out again

to pass, to spend (time)

The Seven Simple Tenses		The Seven Compound Tenses	
Singular	Plural	Singular	Plural
1 présent de l'indicatif		8 passé composé	
passe	passons	ai passé	avons passé
passes	passez	as passé	avez passé
passe	passent	a passé	ont passé
2 imparfait de l'indicatif		9 plus-que-parfait de l'indicatif	
passais	passions	avais passé	avions passé
passais	passiez	avais passé	aviez passé
passait	passaient	avait passé	avaient passé
3 passé simple		10 passé antérieur	
passai	passâmes	eus passé	eûmes passé
passas	passâtes	eus passé	eûtes passé
passa	passèrent	eut passé	eurent passé
4 futur		11 futur antérieur	
passerai	passerons	aurai passé	aurons passé
passeras	passerez	auras passé	aurez passé
passera	passeront	aura passé	auront passé
5 conditionnel		12 conditionnel passé	
passerais	passerions	aurais passé	aurions passé
passerais	passeriez	aurais passé	auriez passé
passerait	passeraient	aurait passé	auraient passé
6 présent du subjonctif		13 passé du subjonctif	
passe	passions	aie passé	ayons passé
passes	passiez	aies passé	ayez passé
passe	passent	ait passé	aient passé
7 imparfait du subjonctif		14 plus-que-parfait du subjonctif	
passasse	passassions	eusse passé	eussions passé
passasses	passassiez	eusses passé	eussiez passé
passât	passassent	eût passé	eussent passé
		Impératif	
		passe	
		passons	
		passez	

This verb is conjugated with **être** to indicate a state.

Example: **Ses soupçons sont passés en certitudes.**

This verb is conjugated with **être** when it means *to pass by, go by:*
Example: **Elle est passée chez moi.**   She came by my house.

BUT: This verb is conjugated with **avoir** when it has a direct object:
Examples: **Elle m'a passé le sel.**   She passed me the salt.
               Elle a passé un examen.   She took an exam.

repasser to pass again; to iron
dépasser to protrude, to exceed, to surpass

See also **se passer**.

se passer	Part. pr. **se passant**	Part. passé **passé**

to happen, to take place

The Seven Simple Tenses	The Seven Compound Tenses
Singular	Singular
1 présent de l'indicatif	8 passé composé
il se passe	**il s'est passé**
2 imparfait de l'indicatif	9 plus-que-parfait de l'indicatif
il se passait	**il s'était passé**
3 passé simple	10 passé antérieur
il se passa	**il se fut passé**
4 futur	11 futur antérieur
il se passera	**il se sera passé**
5 conditionnel	12 conditionnel passé
il se passerait	**il se serait passé**
6 présent du subjonctif	13 passé du subjonctif
qu'il se passe	**qu'il se soit passé**
7 imparfait du subjonctif	14 plus-que-parfait du subjonctif
qu'il se passât	**qu'il se fût passé**

Impératif
Qu'il se passe! (Let it happen!)

Que se passe-t-il? What's going on? What's happening?
Qu'est-ce qui se passe? What's going on? What's happening?
Qu'est-ce qui s'est passé? What happened?
se passer de qqch to do without something
Je peux me passer de fumer. I can do without smoking.

This verb is impersonal and is generally used in the 3rd person sing. only.

See also **passer**.

to skate

The Seven Simple Tenses		The Seven Compound Tenses	
Singular	Plural	Singular	Plural
1 présent de l'indicatif		8 passé composé	
patine	patinons	ai patiné	avons patiné
patines	patinez	as patiné	avez patiné
patine	patinent	a patiné	ont patiné
2 imparfait de l'indicatif		9 plus-que-parfait de l'indicatif	
patinais	patinions	avais patiné	avions patiné
patinais	patiniez	avais patiné	aviez patiné
patinait	patinaient	avait patiné	avaient patiné
3 passé simple		10 passé antérieur	
patinai	patinâmes	eus patiné	eûmes patiné
patinas	patinâtes	eus patiné	eûtes patiné
patina	patinèrent	eut patiné	eurent patiné
4 futur		11 futur antérieur	
patinerai	patinerons	aurai patiné	aurons patiné
patineras	patinerez	auras patiné	aurez patiné
patinera	patineront	aura patiné	auront patiné
5 conditionnel		12 conditionnel passé	
patinerais	patinerions	aurais patiné	aurions patiné
patinerais	patineriez	aurais patiné	auriez patiné
patinerait	patineraient	aurait patiné	auraient patiné
6 présent du subjonctif		13 passé du subjonctif	
patine	patinions	aie patiné	ayons patiné
patines	patiniez	aies patiné	ayez patiné
patine	patinent	ait patiné	aient patiné
7 imparfait du subjonctif		14 plus-que-parfait du subjonctif	
patinasse	patinassions	eusse patiné	eussions patiné
patinasses	patinassiez	eusses patiné	eussiez patiné
patinât	patinassent	eût patiné	eussent patiné
		Impératif	
		patine	
		patinons	
		patinez	

patiner sur glace   to skate on ice
une patinette   scooter
un patineur, une patineuse   skater

une patinoire   skating rink
patiner sur roulettes, patiner à
    roulettes   to roller skate
le patinage à roulettes   roller skating

199

payer   Part. pr. **payant**   Part. passé **payé**

to pay (for)

The Seven Simple Tenses		The Seven Compound Tenses	
Singular	Plural	Singular	Plural
1 présent de l'indicatif		8 passé composé	
paye	payons	ai payé	avons payé
payes	payez	as payé	avez payé
paye	payent	a payé	ont payé
2 imparfait de l'indicatif		9 plus-que-parfait de l'indicatif	
payais	payions	avais payé	avions payé
payais	payiez	avais payé	aviez payé
payait	payaient	avait payé	avaient payé
3 passé simple		10 passé antérieur	
payai	payâmes	eus payé	eûmes payé
payas	payâtes	eus payé	eûtes payé
paya	payèrent	eut payé	eurent payé
4 futur		11 futur antérieur	
payerai	payerons	aurai payé	aurons payé
payeras	payerez	auras payé	aurez payé
payera	payeront	aura payé	auront payé
5 conditionnel		12 conditionnel passé	
payerais	payerions	aurais payé	aurions payé
payerais	payeriez	aurais payé	auriez payé
payerait	payeraient	aurait payé	auraient payé
6 présent du subjonctif		13 passé du subjonctif	
paye	payions	aie payé	ayons payé
payes	payiez	aies payé	ayez payé
paye	payent	ait payé	aient payé
7 imparfait du subjonctif		14 plus-que-parfait du subjonctif	
payasse	payassions	eusse payé	eussions payé
payasses	payassiez	eusses payé	eussiez payé
payât	payassent	eût payé	eussent payé
		Impératif	
		paye	
		payons	
		payez	

Payez à la caisse, s'il vous plaît.   Pay at the cashier, please.
un payement (or paiement)   payment
avoir de quoi payer   to have the means to pay
payable   payable
se faire payer à dîner par qqn   to get your dinner paid for by someone
payer cher   to pay a lot
payer peu   to pay little
payer comptant   to pay in cash

Verbs ending in *-ayer* may change *y* to *i* before mute *e* or may keep *y*.

to sin, to commit a sin

The Seven Simple Tenses		The Seven Compound Tenses	
Singular	Plural	Singular	Plural
1 présent de l'indicatif		8 passé composé	
pèche	**péchons**	**ai péché**	**avons péché**
pèches	**péchez**	**as péché**	**avez péché**
pèche	**pèchent**	**a péché**	**ont péché**
2 imparfait de l'indicatif		9 plus-que-parfait de l'indicatif	
péchais	**péchions**	**avais péché**	**avions péché**
péchais	**péchiez**	**avais péché**	**aviez péché**
péchait	**péchaient**	**avait péché**	**avaient péché**
3 passé simple		10 passé antérieur	
péchai	**péchâmes**	**eus péché**	**eûmes péché**
péchas	**péchâtes**	**eus péché**	**eûtes péché**
pécha	**péchèrent**	**eut péché**	**eurent péché**
4 futur		11 futur antérieur	
pécherai	**pécherons**	**aurai péché**	**aurons péché**
pécheras	**pécherez**	**auras péché**	**aurez péché**
péchera	**pécheront**	**aura péché**	**auront péché**
5 conditionnel		12 conditionnel passé	
pécherais	**pécherions**	**aurais péché**	**aurions péché**
pécherais	**pécheriez**	**aurais péché**	**auriez péché**
pécherait	**pécheraient**	**aurait péché**	**auraient péché**
6 présent du subjonctif		13 passé du subjonctif	
pèche	**péchions**	**aie péché**	**ayons péché**
pèches	**péchiez**	**aies péché**	**ayez péché**
pèche	**pèchent**	**ait péché**	**aient péché**
7 imparfait du subjonctif		14 plus-que-parfait du subjonctif	
péchasse	**péchassions**	**eusse péché**	**eussions péché**
péchasses	**péchassiez**	**eusses péché**	**eussiez péché**
péchât	**péchassent**	**eût péché**	**eussent péché**

Impératif

---

le péché   sin
un pécheur, une pécheresse   sinner
à tout péché miséricorde   forgiveness for every sin
commettre, faire un péché   to commit sin

Do not confuse this verb with **pêcher,** *to fish.*

pêcher	Part. pr. **pêchant**	Part. passé **pêché**

to fish

The Seven Simple Tenses		The Seven Compound Tenses	
Singular	Plural	Singular	Plural
1 présent de l'indicatif		8 passé composé	
pêche	pêchons	ai pêché	avons pêché
pêches	pêchez	as pêché	avez pêché
pêche	pêchent	a pêché	ont pêché
2 imparfait de l'indicatif		9 plus-que-parfait de l'indicatif	
pêchais	pêchions	avais pêché	avions pêché
pêchais	pêchiez	avais pêché	aviez pêché
pêchait	pêchaient	avait pêché	avaient pêché
3 passé simple		10 passé antérieur	
pêchai	pêchâmes	eus pêché	eûmes pêché
pêchas	pêchâtes	eus pêché	eûtes pêché
pêcha	pêchèrent	eut pêché	eurent pêché
4 futur		11 futur antérieur	
pêcherai	pêcherons	aurai pêché	aurons pêché
pêcheras	pêcherez	auras pêché	aurez pêché
pêchera	pêcheront	aura pêché	auront pêché
5 conditionnel		12 conditionnel passé	
pêcherais	pêcherions	aurais pêché	aurions pêché
pêcherais	pêcheriez	aurais pêché	auriez pêché
pêcherait	pêcheraient	aurait pêché	auraient pêché
6 présent du subjonctif		13 passé du subjonctif	
pêche	pêchions	aie pêché	ayons pêché
pêches	pêchiez	aies pêché	ayez pêché
pêche	pêchent	ait pêché	aient pêché
7 imparfait du subjonctif		14 plus-que-parfait du subjonctif	
pêchasse	pêchassions	eusse pêché	eussions pêché
pêchasses	pêchassiez	eusses pêché	eussiez pêché
pêchât	pêchassent	eût pêché	eussent pêché
		Impératif	
		pêche	
		pêchons	
		pêchez	

Samedi nous irons à la pêche. Je connais un lac à la campagne où il y a beaucoup de poissons.

aller à la pêche to go fishing	**la pêche au filet** net fishing
un pêcheur fisherman; **une pêcheuse**	**un pêcheur de perles** pearl diver
un bateau pêcheur fishing boat	

Do not confuse this verb with **pécher,** *to sin.* And do not confuse **une pêche** (peach), which is a fruit, with a verb form of **pêcher** and with the noun **la pêche,** which means *fishing,* the sport.

Part. pr. **se peignant**   Part. passé **peigné(e)(s)**   **se peigner**

to comb one's hair

The Seven Simple Tenses		The Seven Compound Tenses	
Singular	Plural	Singular	Plural
1 présent de l'indicatif		8 passé composé	
me peigne	nous peignons	me suis peigné(e)	nous sommes peigné(e)s
te peignes	vous peignez	t'es peigné(e)	vous êtes peigné(e)(s)
se peigne	se peignent	s'est peigné(e)	se sont peigné(e)s
2 imparfait de l'indicatif		9 plus-que-parfait de l'indicatif	
me peignais	nous peignions	m'étais peigné(e)	nous étions peigné(e)s
te peignais	vous peigniez	t'étais peigné(e)	vous étiez peigné(e)(s)
se peignait	se peignaient	s'était peigné(e)	s'étaient peigné(e)s
3 passé simple		10 passé antérieur	
me peignai	nous peignâmes	me fus peigné(e)	nous fûmes peigné(e)s
te peignas	vous peignâtes	te fus peigné(e)	vous fûtes peigné(e)(s)
se peigna	se peignèrent	se fut peigné(e)	se furent peigné(e)s
4 futur		11 futur antérieur	
me peignerai	nous peignerons	me serai peigné(e)	nous serons peigné(e)s
te peigneras	vous peignerez	te seras peigné(e)	vous serez peigné(e)(s)
se peignera	se peigneront	se sera peigné(e)	se seront peigné(e)s
5 conditionnel		12 conditionnel passé	
me peignerais	nous peignerions	me serais peigné(e)	nous serions peigné(e)s
te peignerais	vous peigneriez	te serais peigné(e)	vous seriez peigné(e)(s)
se peignerait	se peigneraient	se serait peigné(e)	se seraient peigné(e)s
6 présent du subjonctif		13 passé du subjonctif	
me peigne	nous peignions	me sois peigné(e)	nous soyons peigné(e)s
te peignes	vous peigniez	te sois peigné(e)	vous soyez peigné(e)(s)
se peigne	se peignent	se soit peigné(e)	se soient peigné(e)s
7 imparfait du subjonctif		14 plus-que-parfait du subjonctif	
me peignasse	nous peignassions	me fusse peigné(e)	nous fussions peigné(e)s
te peignasses	vous peignassiez	te fusses peigné(e)	vous fussiez peigné(e)(s)
se peignât	se peignassent	se fût peigné(e)	se fussent peigné(e)s

Impératif
peigne-toi; ne te peigne pas
peignons-nous; ne nous peignons pas
peignez-vous; ne vous peignez pas

Mon frère a peigné notre petit chien. Ma mère a lavé les cheveux de ma petite sœur et elle l'a peignée. Après cela, elle s'est lavé les cheveux et elle s'est peignée.

peigner qqn	to comb someone	**mal peigné(e)(s)**	untidy hair, disheveled
un peigne	a comb	**bien peigné(e)(s)**	well combed
un peignoir	dressing gown	**un peignoir de bain**	bathrobe

203

peindre   Part. pr. **peignant**   Part. passé **peint**

to paint, to portray

The Seven Simple Tenses		The Seven Compound Tenses	
Singular	Plural	Singular	Plural
1 présent de l'indicatif		8 passé composé	
peins	peignons	ai peint	avons peint
peins	peignez	as peint	avez peint
peint	peignent	a peint	ont peint
2 imparfait de l'indicatif		9 plus-que-parfait de l'indicatif	
peignais	peignions	avais peint	avions peint
peignais	peigniez	avais peint	aviez peint
peignait	peignaient	avait peint	avaient peint
3 passé simple		10 passé antérieur	
peignis	peignîmes	eus peint	eûmes peint
peignis	peignîtes	eus peint	eûtes peint
peignit	peignirent	eut peint	eurent peint
4 futur		11 futur antérieur	
peindrai	peindrons	aurai peint	aurons peint
peindras	peindrez	auras peint	aurez peint
peindra	peindront	aura peint	auront peint
5 conditionnel		12 conditionnel passé	
peindrais	peindrions	aurais peint	aurions peint
peindrais	peindriez	aurais peint	auriez peint
peindrait	peindraient	aurait peint	auraient peint
6 présent du subjonctif		13 passé du subjonctif	
peigne	peignions	aie peint	ayons peint
peignes	peigniez	aies peint	ayez peint
peigne	peignent	ait peint	aient peint
7 imparfait du subjonctif		14 plus-que-parfait du subjonctif	
peignisse	peignissions	eusse peint	eussions peint
peignisses	peignissiez	eusses peint	eussiez peint
peignît	peignissent	eût peint	eussent peint
		Impératif	
		peins	
		peignons	
		peignez	

—Qui a peint ce tableau? Mon fils. Il est artiste peintre.
—Est-ce que Renoir a jamais peint une reine noire?

une peinture painting, picture	**un peintre** painter
un tableau painting, picture	**un artiste peintre** artist
une peinture à l'huile oil painting	**une femme peintre** woman artist
peintre en bâtiments house painter	**une palette de peintre** artist's palette
dépeindre to depict, to describe	**se faire peindre** to have one's portrait painted

The Seven Simple Tenses		The Seven Compound Tenses	
Singular	Plural	Singular	Plural
1 présent de l'indicatif		8 passé composé	
pense	pensons	ai pensé	avons pensé
penses	pensez	as pensé	avez pensé
pense	pensent	a pensé	ont pensé
2 imparfait de l'indicatif		9 plus-que-parfait de l'indicatif	
pensais	pensions	avais pensé	avions pensé
pensais	pensiez	avais pensé	aviez pensé
pensait	pensaient	avait pensé	avaient pensé
3 passé simple		10 passé antérieur	
pensai	pensâmes	eus pensé	eûmes pensé
pensas	pensâtes	eus pensé	eûtes pensé
pensa	pensèrent	eut pensé	eurent pensé
4 futur		11 futur antérieur	
penserai	penserons	aurai pensé	aurons pensé
penseras	penserez	auras pensé	aurez pensé
pensera	penseront	aura pensé	auront pensé
5 conditionnel		12 conditionnel passé	
penserais	penserions	aurais pensé	aurions pensé
penserais	penseriez	aurais pensé	auriez pensé
penserait	penseraient	aurait pensé	auraient pensé
6 présent du subjonctif		13 passé du subjonctif	
pense	pensions	aie pensé	ayons pensé
penses	pensiez	aies pensé	ayez pensé
pense	pensent	ait pensé	aient pensé
7 imparfait du subjonctif		14 plus-que-parfait du subjonctif	
pensasse	pensassions	eusse pensé	eussions pensé
pensasses	pensassiez	eusses pensé	eussiez pensé
pensât	pensassent	eût pensé	eussent pensé
		Impératif	
		pense	
		pensons	
		pensez	

—Robert, tu as l'air pensif; à quoi penses-tu?
—Je pense à mon examen de français.
—Moi, je pense aux vacances de Noël.
—Que penses-tu de cette classe de français?
—Je trouve que cette classe est excellente.
—Penses-tu continuer à étudier le français l'année prochaine?
—Certainement.

penser à   to think of, to think about;   **penser de**   to think about (i.e., to have an opinion about)

perdre	Part. pr. **perdant**	Part. passé **perdu**

to lose

The Seven Simple Tenses		The Seven Compound Tenses	
Singular	Plural	Singular	Plural
1 présent de l'indicatif		8 passé composé	
perds	perdons	ai perdu	avons perdu
perds	perdez	as perdu	avez perdu
perd	perdent	a perdu	ont perdu
2 imparfait de l'indicatif		9 plus-que-parfait de l'indicatif	
perdais	perdions	avais perdu	avions perdu
perdais	perdiez	avais perdu	aviez perdu
perdait	perdaient	avait perdu	avaient perdu
3 passé simple		10 passé antérieur	
perdis	perdîmes	eus perdu	eûmes perdu
perdis	perdîtes	eus perdu	eûtes perdu
perdit	perdirent	eut perdu	eurent perdu
4 futur		11 futur antérieur	
perdrai	perdrons	aurai perdu	aurons perdu
perdras	perdrez	auras perdu	aurez perdu
perdra	perdront	aura perdu	auront perdu
5 conditionnel		12 conditionnel passé	
perdrais	perdrions	aurais perdu	aurions perdu
perdrais	perdriez	aurais perdu	auriez perdu
perdrait	perdraient	aurait perdu	auraient perdu
6 présent du subjonctif		13 passé du subjonctif	
perde	perdions	aie perdu	ayons perdu
perdes	perdiez	aies perdu	ayez perdu
perde	perdent	ait perdu	aient perdu
7 imparfait du subjonctif		14 plus-que-parfait du subjonctif	
perdisse	perdissions	eusse perdu	eussions perdu
perdisses	perdissiez	eusses perdu	eussiez perdu
perdît	perdissent	eût perdu	eussent perdu

Impératif
perds
perdons
perdez

Je n'ai pas d'argent sur moi. Je l'ai laissé à la maison parce que si je l'avais pris avec moi je sais que je l'aurais perdu dans la rue. Puis-je vous demander deux dollars? Je vous les rendrai la semaine prochaine.

se perdre to lose oneself, to lose one's way, to be ruined
perdre son temps to waste one's time
perdre son chemin to lose one's way
perdre pied to lose one's footing
perdre l'esprit to go out of one's mind

Vous n'avez rien à perdre. You have nothing to lose.
une perte a loss
perdre de vue to lose sight of
perdre la raison to take leave of one's senses

206

to perish, to die

The Seven Simple Tenses		The Seven Compound Tenses	
Singular	Plural	Singular	Plural
1 présent de l'indicatif		8 passé composé	
péris	périssons	ai péri	avons péri
péris	périssez	as péri	avez péri
périt	périssent	a péri	ont péri
2 imparfait de l'indicatif		9 plus-que-parfait de l'indicatif	
périssais	périssions	avais péri	avions péri
périssais	périssiez	avais péri	aviez péri
périssait	périssaient	avait péri	avaient péri
3 passé simple		10 passé antérieur	
péris	pérîmes	eus péri	eûmes péri
péris	pérîtes	eus péri	eûtes péri
périt	périrent	eut péri	eurent péri
4 futur		11 futur antérieur	
périrai	périrons	aurai péri	aurons péri
périras	périrez	auras péri	aurez péri
périra	périront	aura péri	auront péri
5 conditionnel		12 conditionnel passé	
périrais	péririons	aurais péri	aurions péri
périrais	péririez	aurais péri	auriez péri
périrait	périraient	aurait péri	auraient péri
6 présent du subjonctif		13 passé du subjonctif	
périsse	périssions	aie péri	ayons péri
périsses	périssiez	aies péri	ayez péri
périsse	périssent	ait péri	aient péri
7 imparfait du subjonctif		14 plus-que-parfait du subjonctif	
périsse	périssions	eusse péri	eussions péri
périsses	périssiez	eusses péri	eussiez péri
pérît	périssent	eût péri	eussent péri

Impératif
péris
périssons
périssez

---

faire périr to kill	**péri en mer** lost at sea
s'ennuyer à périr to be bored to death	**périr de froid** to freeze to death
périssable perishable	
périr d'ennui to be bored to death	

permettre   Part. pr. **permettant**   Part. passé **permis**

to permit, to allow, to let

The Seven Simple Tenses		The Seven Compound Tenses	
Singular	Plural	Singular	Plural
1 présent de l'indicatif		8 passé composé	
permets	**permettons**	**ai permis**	**avons permis**
permets	**permettez**	**as permis**	**avez permis**
permet	**permettent**	**a permis**	**ont permis**
2 imparfait de l'indicatif		9 plus-que-parfait de l'indicatif	
permettais	**permettions**	**avais permis**	**avions permis**
permettais	**permettiez**	**avais permis**	**aviez permis**
permettait	**permettaient**	**avait permis**	**avaient permis**
3 passé simple		10 passé antérieur	
permis	**permîmes**	**eus permis**	**eûmes permis**
permis	**permîtes**	**eus permis**	**eûtes permis**
permit	**permirent**	**eut permis**	**eurent permis**
4 futur		11 futur antérieur	
permettrai	**permettrons**	**aurai permis**	**aurons permis**
permettras	**permettrez**	**auras permis**	**aurez permis**
permettra	**permettront**	**aura permis**	**auront permis**
5 conditionnel		12 conditionnel passé	
permettrais	**permettrions**	**aurais permis**	**aurions permis**
permettrais	**permettriez**	**aurais permis**	**auriez permis**
permettrait	**permettraient**	**aurait permis**	**auraient permis**
6 présent du subjonctif		13 passé du subjonctif	
permette	**permettions**	**aie permis**	**ayons permis**
permettes	**permettiez**	**aies permis**	**ayez permis**
permette	**permettent**	**ait permis**	**aient permis**
7 imparfait du subjonctif		14 plus-que-parfait du subjonctif	
permisse	**permissions**	**eusse permis**	**eussions permis**
permisses	**permissiez**	**eusses permis**	**eussiez permis**
permît	**permissent**	**eût permis**	**eussent permis**
		Impératif	
		permets	
		permettons	
		permettez	

La maîtresse de français a permis à l'élève de quitter la salle de classe quelques minutes avant la fin de la leçon.

permettre à qqn de faire qqch to permit (to allow) someone to do something
Vous permettez? May I? Do you mind?   **se permettre de faire qqch** to take
s'il est permis if it is allowed, permitted   the liberty to do something;
un permis permit   to venture to do something
un permis de conduire driving license
la permission permission

to place, to put

The Seven Simple Tenses		The Seven Compound Tenses	
Singular	Plural	Singular	Plural
1 présent de l'indicatif		8 passé composé	
place	plaçons	ai placé	avons placé
places	placez	as placé	avez placé
place	placent	a placé	ont placé
2 imparfait de l'indicatif		9 plus-que-parfait de l'indicatif	
plaçais	placions	avais placé	avions placé
plaçais	placiez	avais placé	aviez placé
plaçait	plaçaient	avait placé	avaient placé
3 passé simple		10 passé antérieur	
plaçai	plaçâmes	eus placé	eûmes placé
plaças	plaçâtes	eus placé	eûtes placé
plaça	placèrent	eut placé	eurent placé
4 futur		11 futur antérieur	
placerai	placerons	aurai placé	aurons placé
placeras	placerez	auras placé	aurez placé
placera	placeront	aura placé	auront placé
5 conditionnel		12 conditionnel passé	
placerais	placerions	aurais placé	aurions placé
placerais	placeriez	aurais placé	auriez placé
placerait	placeraient	aurait placé	auraient placé
6 présent du subjonctif		13 passé du subjonctif	
place	placions	aie placé	ayons placé
places	placiez	aies placé	ayez placé
place	placent	ait placé	aient placé
7 imparfait du subjonctif		14 plus-que-parfait du subjonctif	
plaçasse	plaçassions	eusse placé	eussions placé
plaçasses	plaçassiez	eusses placé	eussiez placé
plaçât	plaçassent	eût placé	eussent placé

	Impératif
	place
	plaçons
	placez

Nous pouvons déjeuner maintenant. Ma place est ici près de la fenêtre, ta place est là-bas près de la porte. Marie, place-toi à côté de Pierre. Combien de places y a-t-il? Y a-t-il assez de places pour tout le monde?

une place   a seat, a place
chaque chose à sa place   everything in its place
un placement   placing
un bureau de placement   employment agency
se placer   to place oneself, to take a seat, to find employment
remplacer   to replace

plaindre　　　Part. pr. **plaignant**　　　Part. passé **plaint**

to pity

The Seven Simple Tenses		The Seven Compound Tenses	
Singular	Plural	Singular	Plural
1　présent de l'indicatif		8　passé composé	
plains	plaignons	ai plaint	avons plaint
plains	plaignez	as plaint	avez plaint
plaint	plaignent	a plaint	ont plaint
2　imparfait de l'indicatif		9　plus-que-parfait de l'indicatif	
plaignais	plaignions	avais plaint	avions plaint
plaignais	plaigniez	avais plaint	aviez plaint
plaignait	plaignaient	avait plaint	avaient plaint
3　passé simple		10　passé antérieur	
plaignis	plaignîmes	eus plaint	eûmes plaint
plaignis	plaignîtes	eus plaint	eûtes plaint
plaignit	plaignirent	eut plaint	eurent plaint
4　futur		11　futur antérieur	
plaindrai	plaindrons	aurai plaint	aurons plaint
plaindras	plaindrez	auras plaint	aurez plaint
plaindra	plaindront	aura plaint	auront plaint
5　conditionnel		12　conditionnel passé	
plaindrais	plaindrions	aurais plaint	aurions plaint
plaindrais	plaindriez	aurais plaint	auriez plaint
plaindrait	plaindraient	aurait plaint	auraient plaint
6　présent du subjonctif		13　passé du subjonctif	
plaigne	plaignions	aie plaint	ayons plaint
plaignes	plaigniez	aies plaint	ayez plaint
plaigne	plaignent	ait plaint	aient plaint
7　imparfait du subjonctif		14　plus-que-parfait du subjonctif	
plaignisse	plaignissions	eusse plaint	eussions plaint
plaignisses	plaignissiez	eusses plaint	eussiez plaint
plaignît	plaignissent	eût plaint	eussent plaint
		Impératif	
		plains	
		plaignons	
		plaignez	

Pauvre Madame Bayou! Elle a des ennuis et je la plains.

une plainte　groan, moan, protest, complaint	**Je te plains.**　I feel for you; I feel sorry for you; I pity you.
porter plainte contre　to bring charges against	**être à plaindre**　to be pitied
plaintif, plaintive　plaintive	**Elle est à plaindre.**　She is to be pitied.
plaintivement　plaintively, mournfully	

For additional related words, see **se plaindre.**

to complain, to lament, to moan

The Seven Simple Tenses		The Seven Compound Tenses	
Singular	Plural	Singular	Plural
1 présent de l'indicatif		**8 passé composé**	
me plains	nous plaignons	me suis plaint(e)	nous sommes plaint(e)s
te plains	vous plaignez	t'es plaint(e)	vous êtes plaint(e)(s)
se plaint	se plaignent	s'est plaint(e)	se sont plaint(e)s
2 imparfait de l'indicatif		**9 plus-que-parfait de l'indicatif**	
me plaignais	nous plaignions	m'étais plaint(e)	nous étions plaint(e)s
te plaignais	vous plaigniez	t'étais plaint(e)	vous étiez plaint(e)(s)
se plaignait	se plaignaient	s'était plaint(e)	s'étaient plaint(e)s
3 passé simple		**10 passé antérieur**	
me plaignis	nous plaignîmes	me fus plaint(e)	nous fûmes plaint(e)s
te plaignis	vous plaignîtes	te fus plaint(e)	vous fûtes plaint(e)(s)
se plaignit	se plaignirent	se fut plaint(e)	se furent plaint(e)s
4 futur		**11 futur antérieur**	
me plaindrai	nous plaindrons	me serai plaint(e)	nous serons plaint(e)s
te plaindras	vous plaindrez	te seras plaint(e)	vous serez plaint(e)(s)
se plaindra	se plaindront	se sera plaint(e)	se seront plaint(e)s
5 conditionnel		**12 conditionnel passé**	
me plaindrais	nous plaindrions	me serais plaint(e)	nous serions plaint(e)s
te plaindrais	vous plaindriez	te serais plaint(e)	vous seriez plaint(e)(s)
se plaindrait	se plaindraient	se serait plaint(e)	se seraient plaint(e)s
6 présent du subjonctif		**13 passé du subjonctif**	
me plaigne	nous plaignions	me sois plaint(e)	nous soyons plaint(e)s
te plaignes	vous plaigniez	te sois plaint(e)	vous soyez plaint(e)(s)
se plaigne	se plaignent	se soit plaint(e)	se soient plaint(e)s
7 imparfait du subjonctif		**14 plus-que-parfait du subjonctif**	
me plaignisse	nous plaignissions	me fusse plaint(e)	nous fussions plaint(e)s
te plaignisses	vous plaignissiez	te fusses plaint(e)	vous fussiez plaint(e)(s)
se plaignît	se plaignissent	se fût plaint(e)	se fussent plaint(e)s

Impératif
plains-toi; ne te plains pas
plaignons-nous; ne nous plaignons pas
plaignez-vous; ne vous plaignez pas

Quelle jeune fille! Elle se plaint toujours de tout! Hier elle s'est plainte de son professeur de français, aujourd'hui elle se plaint de ses devoirs, et je suis certain que demain elle se plaindra du temps.

se plaindre du temps   to complain about the weather
se plaindre de qqn ou de qqch   to complain of, to find fault with someone or something
avoir bonne raison de se plaindre   to have good reason to complain

For other words related to this verb, see **plaindre**.

plaire	Part. pr. **plaisant**	Part. passé **plu**

to please

The Seven Simple Tenses		The Seven Compound Tenses	
Singular	Plural	Singular	Plural

1 présent de l'indicatif		8 passé composé	
plais	plaisons	ai plu	avons plu
plais	plaisez	as plu	avez plu
plaît	plaisent	a plu	ont plu

2 imparfait de l'indicatif		9 plus-que-parfait de l'indicatif	
plaisais	plaisions	avais plu	avions plu
plaisais	plaisiez	avais plu	aviez plu
plaisait	plaisaient	avait plu	avaient plu

3 passé simple		10 passé antérieur	
plus	plûmes	eus plu	eûmes plu
plus	plûtes	eus plu	eûtes plu
plut	plurent	eut plu	eurent plu

4 futur		11 futur antérieur	
plairai	plairons	aurai plu	aurons plu
plairas	plairez	auras plu	aurez plu
plaira	plairont	aura plu	auront plu

5 conditionnel		12 conditionnel passé	
plairais	plairions	aurais plu	aurions plu
plairais	plairiez	aurais plu	auriez plu
plairait	plairaient	aurait plu	auraient plu

6 présent du subjonctif		13 passé du subjonctif	
plaise	plaisions	aie plu	ayons plu
plaises	plaisiez	aies plu	ayez plu
plaise	plaisent	ait plu	aient plu

7 imparfait du subjonctif		14 plus-que-parfait du subjonctif	
plusse	plussions	eusse plu	eussions plu
plusses	plussiez	eusses plu	eussiez plu
plût	plussent	eût plu	eussent plu

	Impératif
	plais
	plaisons
	plaisez

plaire à qqn   to please, to be pleasing to someone; **Son mariage a plu à sa famille.**
   Her (his) marriage pleased her (his) family. **Est-ce que ce cadeau lui plaira?**
   Will this present please her (him)? Will this gift be pleasing to her (to him)?
se plaire à   to take pleasure in; **Robert se plaît à ennuyer son petit frère.**   Robert
   takes pleasure in bothering his little brother.
le plaisir   delight, pleasure; **complaire à**   to please; **déplaire à**   to displease
s'il vous plaît; s'il te plaît   please (if it is pleasing to you)
Il a beaucoup plu hier et cela m'a beaucoup plu.   It rained a lot yesterday and that
   pleased me a great deal. (See **pleuvoir**)

to cry, to weep, to mourn

The Seven Simple Tenses		The Seven Compound Tenses	
Singular	Plural	Singular	Plural
1 présent de l'indicatif		**8 passé composé**	
pleure	pleurons	ai pleuré	avons pleuré
pleures	pleurez	as pleuré	avez pleuré
pleure	pleurent	a pleuré	ont pleuré
2 imparfait de l'indicatif		**9 plus-que-parfait de l'indicatif**	
pleurais	pleurions	avais pleuré	avions pleuré
pleurais	pleuriez	avais pleuré	aviez pleuré
pleurait	pleuraient	avait pleuré	avaient pleuré
3 passé simple		**10 passé antérieur**	
pleurai	pleurâmes	eus pleuré	eûmes pleuré
pleuras	pleurâtes	eus pleuré	eûtes pleuré
pleura	pleurèrent	eut pleuré	eurent pleuré
4 futur		**11 futur antérieur**	
pleurerai	pleurerons	aurai pleuré	aurons pleuré
pleureras	pleurerez	auras pleuré	aurez pleuré
pleurera	pleureront	aura pleuré	auront pleuré
5 conditionnel		**12 conditionnel passé**	
pleurerais	pleurerions	aurais pleuré	aurions pleuré
pleurerais	pleureriez	aurais pleuré	auriez pleuré
pleurerait	pleureraient	aurait pleuré	auraient pleuré
6 présent du subjonctif		**13 passé du subjonctif**	
pleure	pleurions	aie pleuré	ayons pleuré
pleures	pleuriez	aies pleuré	ayez pleuré
pleure	pleurent	ait pleuré	aient pleuré
7 imparfait du subjonctif		**14 plus-que-parfait du subjonctif**	
pleurasse	pleurassions	eusse pleuré	eussions pleuré
pleurasses	pleurassiez	eusses pleuré	eussiez pleuré
pleurât	pleurassent	eût pleuré	eussent pleuré

Impératif
pleure
pleurons
pleurez

---

pleurer toutes les larmes de son corps   to cry one's eyes out
une larme   a tear
un pleur   a tear
pleurard, pleurarde   whimpering person
une pièce pleurnicharde   soap opera
larmoyant, larmoyante   tearful, lachrymose

pleuvoir	Part. pr. **pleuvant**	Part. passé **plu**

to rain

The Seven Simple Tenses	The Seven Compound Tenses
Singular	Singular
1 présent de l'indicatif **il pleut**	8 passé composé **il a plu**
2 imparfait de l'indicatif **il pleuvait**	9 plus-que-parfait de l'indicatif **il avait plu**
3 passé simple **il plut**	10 passé antérieur **il eut plu**
4 futur **il pleuvra**	11 futur antérieur **il aura plu**
5 conditionnel **il pleuvrait**	12 conditionnel passé **il aurait plu**
6 présent du subjonctif **qu'il pleuve**	13 passé du subjonctif **qu'il ait plu**
7 imparfait du subjonctif **qu'il plût**	14 plus-que-parfait du subjonctif **qu'il eût plu**

Impératif
Qu'il pleuve! (Let it rain!)

Hier il a plu, il pleut maintenant, et je suis certain qu'il pleuvra demain.

la pluie the rain	**bruiner** to drizzle
pluvieux, pluvieuse rainy	**Il pleut à seaux.** It's raining buckets.
pleuvoter to drizzle	**Il pleut à verse.** It's raining hard.

Il a beaucoup plu hier et cela m'a beaucoup plu. It rained a lot yesterday and that pleased me a great deal. (See **plaire**)

Do not confuse the past part. of this verb with the past part. of **plaire,** which is identical.

to wear, to carry

The Seven Simple Tenses		The Seven Compound Tenses	
Singular	Plural	Singular	Plural
1 présent de l'indicatif		8 passé composé	
porte	portons	ai porté	avons porté
portes	portez	as porté	avez porté
porte	portent	a porté	ont porté
2 imparfait de l'indicatif		9 plus-que-parfait de l'indicatif	
portais	portions	avais porté	avions porté
portais	portiez	avais porté	aviez porté
portait	portaient	avait porté	avaient porté
3 passé simple		10 passé antérieur	
portai	portâmes	eus porté	eûmes porté
portas	portâtes	eus porté	eûtes porté
porta	portèrent	eut porté	eurent porté
4 futur		11 futur antérieur	
porterai	porterons	aurai porté	aurons porté
porteras	porterez	auras porté	aurez porté
portera	porteront	aura porté	auront porté
5 conditionnel		12 conditionnel passé	
porterais	porterions	aurais porté	aurions porté
porterais	porteriez	aurais porté	auriez porté
porterait	porteraient	aurait porté	auraient porté
6 présent du subjonctif		13 passé du subjonctif	
porte	portions	aie porté	ayons porté
portes	portiez	aies porté	ayez porté
porte	portent	ait porté	aient porté
7 imparfait du subjonctif		14 plus-que-parfait du subjonctif	
portasse	portassions	eusse porté	eussions porté
portasses	portassiez	eusses porté	eussiez porté
portât	portassent	eût porté	eussent porté

Impératif
porte
portons
portez

---

porter la main sur qqn   to raise one's hand against someone
porter son âge   to look one's age
se porter   to feel (health); **Comment vous portez-vous aujourd'hui?**   How do you feel today?

apporter to bring	**comporter** to comprise
exporter to export	**déporter** to deport
importer to import; to matter, to be of importance	**se comporter** to behave
un porte-monnaie change purse (**des porte-monnaie**)	**emporter** to carry away; **Autant en emporte le vent** (*Gone with the Wind*)

to push, to grow

The Seven Simple Tenses		The Seven Compound Tenses	
Singular	Plural	Singular	Plural
1 présent de l'indicatif		**8 passé composé**	
pousse	poussons	ai poussé	avons poussé
pousses	poussez	as poussé	avez poussé
pousse	poussent	a poussé	ont poussé
2 imparfait de l'indicatif		**9 plus-que-parfait de l'indicatif**	
poussais	poussions	avais poussé	avions poussé
poussais	poussiez	avais poussé	aviez poussé
poussait	poussaient	avait poussé	avaient poussé
3 passé simple		**10 passé antérieur**	
poussai	poussâmes	eus poussé	eûmes poussé
poussas	poussâtes	eus poussé	eûtes poussé
poussa	poussèrent	eut poussé	eurent poussé
4 futur		**11 futur antérieur**	
pousserai	pousserons	aurai poussé	aurons poussé
pousseras	pousserez	auras poussé	aurez poussé
poussera	pousseront	aura poussé	auront poussé
5 conditionnel		**12 conditionnel passé**	
pousserais	pousserions	aurais poussé	aurions poussé
pousserais	pousseriez	aurais poussé	auriez poussé
pousserait	pousseraient	aurait poussé	auraient poussé
6 présent du subjonctif		**13 passé du subjonctif**	
pousse	poussions	aie poussé	ayons poussé
pousses	poussiez	aies poussé	ayez poussé
pousse	poussent	ait poussé	aient poussé
7 imparfait du subjonctif		**14 plus-que-parfait du subjonctif**	
poussasse	poussassions	eusse poussé	eussions poussé
poussasses	poussassiez	eusses poussé	eussiez poussé
poussât	poussassent	eût poussé	eussent poussé
		Impératif	
		pousse	
		poussons	
		poussez	

---

une poussée   a push, a thrust
pousser qqn à faire qqch   to egg someone on to do something
Robert pousse une barbe.   Robert is growing a beard.
pousser un cri   to utter a cry; **pousser un soupir**   to heave a sigh
une poussette   a stroller
repousser   to repulse, to drive back; to grow in again, to grow back in
se pousser   to push oneself; to push each other
un pousse-pousse   rickshaw
pousser qqn à bout   to corner someone

to be able, can

The Seven Simple Tenses		The Seven Compound Tenses	
Singular	Plural	Singular	Plural
1 présent de l'indicatif		8 passé composé	
peux *or* **puis**	**pouvons**	**ai pu**	**avons pu**
peux	**pouvez**	**as pu**	**avez pu**
peut	**peuvent**	**a pu**	**ont pu**
2 imparfait de l'indicatif		9 plus-que-parfait de l'indicatif	
pouvais	**pouvions**	**avais pu**	**avions pu**
pouvais	**pouviez**	**avais pu**	**aviez pu**
pouvait	**pouvaient**	**avait pu**	**avaient pu**
3 passé simple		10 passé antérieur	
pus	**pûmes**	**eus pu**	**eûmes pu**
pus	**pûtes**	**eus pu**	**eûtes pu**
put	**purent**	**eut pu**	**eurent pu**
4 futur		11 futur antérieur	
pourrai	**pourrons**	**aurai pu**	**aurons pu**
pourras	**pourrez**	**auras pu**	**aurez pu**
pourra	**pourront**	**aura pu**	**auront pu**
5 conditionnel		12 conditionnel passé	
pourrais	**pourrions**	**aurais pu**	**aurions pu**
pourrais	**pourriez**	**aurais pu**	**auriez pu**
pourrait	**pourraient**	**aurait pu**	**auraient pu**
6 présent du subjonctif		13 passé du subjonctif	
puisse	**puissions**	**aie pu**	**ayons pu**
puisses	**puissiez**	**aies pu**	**ayez pu**
puisse	**puissent**	**ait pu**	**aient pu**
7 imparfait du subjonctif		14 plus-que-parfait du subjonctif	
pusse	**pussions**	**eusse pu**	**eussions pu**
pusses	**pussiez**	**eusses pu**	**eussiez pu**
pût	**pussent**	**eût pu**	**eussent pu**
		Impératif	

---

si l'on peut dire   if one may say so
se pouvoir: Cela se peut.   That may be.
le pouvoir   power
avoir du pouvoir sur soi-même   to have self-control
n'y pouvoir rien   not to be able to do anything about it; **Que me voulez-vous?**
   What do you want from me? **Je n'y peux rien.**   I can't help it; I can't do anything
   about it.
Puis-je entrer? Est-ce que je peux entrer?   May I come in?

217

préférer   Part. pr. **préférant**   Part. passé **préféré**

to prefer

The Seven Simple Tenses		The Seven Compound Tenses	
Singular	Plural	Singular	Plural
1 présent de l'indicatif		8 passé composé	
préfère	préférons	ai préféré	avons préféré
préfères	préférez	as préféré	avez préféré
préfère	préfèrent	a préféré	ont préféré
2 imparfait de l'indicatif		9 plus-que-parfait de l'indicatif	
préférais	préférions	avais préféré	avions préféré
préférais	préfériez	avais préféré	aviez préféré
préférait	préféraient	avait préféré	avaient préféré
3 passé simple		10 passé antérieur	
préférai	préférâmes	eus préféré	eûmes préféré
préféras	préférâtes	eus préféré	eûtes préféré
préféra	préférèrent	eut préféré	eurent préféré
4 futur		11 futur antérieur	
préférerai	préférerons	aurai préféré	aurons préféré
préféreras	préférerez	auras préféré	aurez préféré
préférera	préféreront	aura préféré	auront préféré
5 conditionnel		12 conditionnel passé	
préférerais	préférerions	aurais préféré	aurions préféré
préférerais	préféreriez	aurais préféré	auriez préféré
préférerait	préféreraient	aurait préféré	auraient préféré
6 présent du subjonctif		13 passé du subjonctif	
préfère	préférions	aie préféré	ayons préféré
préfères	préfériez	aies préféré	ayez préféré
préfère	préfèrent	ait préféré	aient préféré
7 imparfait du subjonctif		14 plus-que-parfait de subjonctif	
préférasse	préférassions	eusse préféré	eussions préféré
préférasses	préférassiez	eusses préféré	eussiez préféré
préférât	préférassent	eût préféré	eussent préféré

Impératif
préfère
préférons
préférez

—Qu'est-ce que vous préférez faire ce soir?
—Je préfère aller voir un bon film. Et vous?
—Je préfère rester à la maison. Ne préféreriez-vous pas rester ici avec moi?

une préférence a preference
préférentiel, préférentielle preferential
préférable preferable
préférablement preferably

de préférence à in preference to
Je n'ai pas de préférence.
   I have no preference.

to take

The Seven Simple Tenses		The Seven Compound Tenses	
Singular	Plural	Singular	Plural
1 présent de l'indicatif		8 passé composé	
prends	prenons	ai pris	avons pris
prends	prenez	as pris	avez pris
prend	prennent	a pris	ont pris
2 imparfait de l'indicatif		9 plus-que-parfait de l'indicatif	
prenais	prenions	avais pris	avions pris
prenais	preniez	avais pris	aviez pris
prenait	prenaient	avait pris	avaient pris
3 passé simple		10 passé antérieur	
pris	prîmes	eus pris	eûmes pris
pris	prîtes	eus pris	eûtes pris
prit	prirent	eut pris	eurent pris
4 futur		11 futur antérieur	
prendrai	prendrons	aurai pris	aurons pris
prendras	prendrez	auras pris	aurez pris
prendra	prendront	aura pris	auront pris
5 conditionnel		12 conditionnel passé	
prendrais	prendrions	aurais pris	aurions pris
prendrais	prendriez	aurais pris	auriez pris
prendrait	prendraient	aurait pris	auraient pris
6 présent du subjonctif		13 passé du subjonctif	
prenne	prenions	aie pris	ayons pris
prennes	preniez	aies pris	ayez pris
prenne	prennent	ait pris	aient pris
7 imparfait du subjonctif		14 plus-que-parfait du subjonctif	
prisse	prissions	eusse pris	eussions pris
prisses	prissiez	eusses pris	eussiez pris
prît	prissent	eût pris	eussent pris
		Impératif	
		prends	
		prenons	
		prenez	

—Qui a pris les fleurs qui étaient sur la table?
—C'est moi qui les ai prises.

à tout prendre   on the whole, all in all
un preneur, une preneuse   taker, purchaser
s'y prendre   to go about it, to handle it, to set about it
Je ne sais comment m'y prendre.   I don't know how to go about it.
C'est à prendre ou à laisser.   Take it or leave it.
prendre à témoin   to call to witness

See also **reprendre**.

préparer	Part. pr. **préparant**	Part. passé **préparé**

to prepare

The Seven Simple Tenses		The Seven Compound Tenses	
Singular	Plural	Singular	Plural
1 présent de l'indicatif		8 passé composé	
prépare	préparons	ai préparé	avons préparé
prépares	préparez	as préparé	avez préparé
prépare	préparent	a préparé	ont préparé
2 imparfait de l'indicatif		9 plus-que-parfait de l'indicatif	
préparais	préparions	avais préparé	avions préparé
préparais	prépariez	avais préparé	aviez préparé
préparait	préparaient	avait préparé	avaient préparé
3 passé simple		10 passé antérieur	
préparai	préparâmes	eus préparé	eûmes préparé
préparas	préparâtes	eus préparé	eûtes préparé
prépara	préparèrent	eut préparé	eurent préparé
4 futur		11 futur antérieur	
préparerai	préparerons	aurai préparé	aurons préparé
prépareras	préparerez	auras préparé	aurez préparé
préparera	prépareront	aura préparé	auront préparé
5 conditionnel		12 conditionnel passé	
préparerais	préparerions	aurais préparé	aurions préparé
préparerais	prépareriez	aurais préparé	auriez préparé
préparerait	prépareraient	aurait préparé	auraient préparé
6 présent du subjonctif		13 passé du subjonctif	
prépare	préparions	aie préparé	ayons préparé
prépares	prépariez	aies préparé	ayez préparé
prépare	préparent	ait préparé	aient préparé
7 imparfait du subjonctif		14 plus-que-parfait du subjonctif	
préparasse	préparassions	eusse préparé	eussions préparé
préparasses	préparassiez	eusses préparé	eussiez préparé
préparât	préparassent	eût préparé	eussent préparé

Impératif
prépare
préparons
préparez

Si Albert avait préparé sa leçon, il aurait reçu une bonne note. Il prépare toujours ses leçons mais cette fois il ne les a pas préparées.

la **préparation** preparation
les **préparatifs** *(m.)* preparations
préparatoire preparatory
se **préparer** to prepare oneself
préparer un examen to study for an exam

The Seven Simple Tenses		The Seven Compound Tenses	
Singular	Plural	Singular	Plural
1 présent de l'indicatif		8 passé composé	
prête	**prêtons**	**ai prêté**	**avons prêté**
prêtes	**prêtez**	**as prêté**	**avez prêté**
prête	**prêtent**	**a prêté**	**ont prêté**
2 imparfait de l'indicatif		9 plus-que-parfait de l'indicatif	
prêtais	**prêtions**	**avais prêté**	**avions prêté**
prêtais	**prêtiez**	**avais prêté**	**aviez prêté**
prêtait	**prêtaient**	**avait prêté**	**avaient prêté**
3 passé simple		10 passé antérieur	
prêtai	**prêtâmes**	**eus prêté**	**eûmes prêté**
prêtas	**prêtâtes**	**eus prêté**	**eûtes prêté**
prêta	**prêtèrent**	**eut prêté**	**eurent prêté**
4 futur		11 futur antérieur	
prêterai	**prêterons**	**aurai prêté**	**aurons prêté**
prêteras	**prêterez**	**auras prêté**	**aurez prêté**
prêtera	**prêteront**	**aura prêté**	**auront prêté**
5 conditionnel		12 conditionnel passé	
prêterais	**prêterions**	**aurais prêté**	**aurions prêté**
prêterais	**prêteriez**	**aurais prêté**	**auriez prêté**
prêterait	**prêteraient**	**aurait prêté**	**auraient prêté**
6 présent du subjonctif		13 passé du subjonctif	
prête	**prêtions**	**aie prêté**	**ayons prêté**
prêtes	**prêtiez**	**ales prêté**	**ayez prêté**
prête	**prêtent**	**ait prêté**	**aient prêté**
7 imparfait du subjonctif		14 plus-que-parfait du subjonctif	
prêtasse	**prêtassions**	**eusse prêté**	**eussions prêté**
prêtasses	**prêtassiez**	**eusses prêté**	**eussiez prêté**
prêtât	**prêtassent**	**eût prêté**	**eussent prêté**
		Impératif	
		prête	
		prêtons	
		prêtez	

prêter à intérêt   to lend at interest
prêter attention à qqn ou à qqch   to pay attention to someone or something
un prêteur sur gages   pawnbroker
prêter la main à qqn   to give a helping hand to someone
prêter secours à qqn   to go to someone's rescue (help)
apprêter   to prepare, to get (something) ready
s'apprêter   to get oneself ready

produire   Part. pr. **produisant**   Part. passé **produit**

to produce

The Seven Simple Tenses		The Seven Compound Tenses	
Singular	Plural	Singular	Plural
1 présent de l'indicatif		8 passé composé	
produis	produisons	ai produit	avons produit
produis	produisez	as produit	avez produit
produit	produisent	a produit	ont produit
2 imparfait de l'indicatif		9 plus-que-parfait de l'indicatif	
produisais	produisions	avais produit	avions produit
produisais	produisiez	avais produit	aviez produit
produisait	produisaient	avait produit	avaient produit
3 passé simple		10 passé antérieur	
produisis	produisîmes	eus produit	eûmes produit
produisis	produisîtes	eus produit	eûtes produit
produisit	produisirent	eut produit	eurent produit
4 futur		11 futur antérieur	
produirai	produirons	aurai produit	aurons produit
produiras	produirez	auras produit	aurez produit
produira	produiront	aura produit	auront produit
5 conditionnel		12 conditionnel passé	
produirais	produirions	aurais produit	aurions produit
produirais	produiriez	aurais produit	auriez produit
produirait	produiraient	aurait produit	auraient produit
6 présent du subjonctif		13 passé du subjonctif	
produise	produisions	aie produit	ayons produit
produises	produisiez	ales produit	ayez produit
produise	produisent	ait produit	aient produit
7 imparfait du subjonctif		14 plus-que-parfait du subjonctif	
produisisse	produisissions	eusse produit	eussions produit
produisisses	produisissiez	eusses produit	eussiez produit
produisît	produisissent	eût produit	eussent produit
		Impératif	
		produis	
		produisons	
		produisez	

---

un produit product
la production production
productible producible
productif, productive productive

la productivité productivity
se produire to happen, to occur, to be brought about

Part. pr. **se promenant**   Part. passé **promené(e)(s)**   **se promener**

to take a walk

The Seven Simple Tenses		The Seven Compound Tenses	
Singular	Plural	Singular	Plural

1   présent de l'indicatif

me promène	nous promenons
te promènes	vous promenez
se promène	se promènent

8   passé composé

me suis	nous sommes	
t'es	vous êtes	+ promené(e)(s)
s'est	se sont	

2   imparfait de l'indicatif

me promenais	nous promenions
te promenais	vous promeniez
se promenait	se promenaient

9   plus-que-parfait de l'indicatif

m'étais	nous étions	
t'étais	vous étiez	+ promené(e)(s)
s'était	s'étaient	

3   passé simple

me promenai	nous promenâmes
te promenas	vous promenâtes
se promena	se promenèrent

10   passé antérieur

me fus	nous fûmes	
te fus	vous fûtes	+ promené(e)(s)
se fut	se furent	

4   futur

me promènerai	nous promènerons
te promèneras	vous promènerez
se promènera	se promèneront

11   futur antérieur

me serai	nous serons	
te seras	vous serez	+ promené(e)(s)
se sera	se seront	

5   conditionnel

me promènerais	nous promènerions
te promènerais	vous promèneriez
se promènerait	se promèneraient

12   conditionnel passé

me serais	nous serions	
te serais	vous seriez	+ promené(e)(s)
se serait	se seraient	

6   présent du subjonctif

me promène	nous promenions
te promènes	vous promeniez
se promène	se promènent

13   passé du subjonctif

me sois	nous soyons	
te sois	vous soyez	+ promené(e)(s)
se soit	se soient	

7   imparfait du subjonctif

me promenasse	nous promenassions
te promenasses	vous promenassiez
se promenât	se promenassent

14   plus-que-parfait du subjonctif

me fusse	nous fussions	
te fusses	vous fussiez	+ promené(e)(s)
se fût	se fussent	

Impératif
promène-toi; ne te promène pas
promenons-nous; ne nous promenons pas
promenez-vous; ne vous promenez pas

Je me promène tous les matins.   I take a walk every morning.
Cette promenade est merveilleuse.   This walk is marvelous.
Janine et Robert se sont promenés dans le parc.   Janine and Robert took a walk in the park.
Faire une promenade   to take a walk
Faire une promenade en voiture   to go for a drive
promener son chien   to take one's dog out for a walk
promener ses regards sur   to cast one's eyes on, to look over
un promenoir   indoor mall for walking, strolling

to promise

The Seven Simple Tenses		The Seven Compound Tenses	
Singular	Plural	Singular	Plural
1 présent de l'indicatif		8 passé composé	
promets	**promettons**	**ai promis**	**avons promis**
promets	**promettez**	**as promis**	**avez promis**
promet	**promettent**	**a promis**	**ont promis**
2 imparfait de l'indicatif		9 plus-que-parfait de l'indicatif	
promettais	**promettions**	**avais promis**	**avions promis**
promettais	**promettiez**	**avais promis**	**aviez promis**
promettait	**promettaient**	**avait promis**	**avaient promis**
3 passé simple		10 passé antérieur	
promis	**promîmes**	**eus promis**	**eûmes promis**
promis	**promîtes**	**eus promis**	**eûtes promis**
promit	**promirent**	**eut promis**	**eurent promis**
4 futur		11 futur antérieur	
promettrai	**promettrons**	**aurai promis**	**aurons promis**
promettras	**promettrez**	**auras promis**	**aurez promis**
promettra	**promettront**	**aura promis**	**auront promis**
5 conditionnel		12 conditionnel passé	
promettrais	**promettrions**	**aurais promis**	**aurions promis**
promettrais	**promettriez**	**aurais promis**	**auriez promis**
promettrait	**promettraient**	**aurait promis**	**auraient promis**
6 présent du subjonctif		13 passé du subjonctif	
promette	**promettions**	**aie promis**	**ayons promis**
promettes	**promettiez**	**aies promis**	**ayez promis**
promette	**promettent**	**ait promis**	**aient promis**
7 imparfait du subjonctif		14 plus-que-parfait du subjonctif	
promisse	**promissions**	**eusse promis**	**eussions promis**
promisses	**promissiez**	**eusses promis**	**eussiez promis**
promît	**promissent**	**eût promis**	**eussent promis**
		Impératif	
		promets	
		promettons	
		promettez	

promettre de faire qqch   to promise to do something
une promesse   promise
tenir sa promesse   to keep one's promise
promettre à qqn de faire qqch   to promise someone to do something
Ça promet!   It looks promising!
se promettre   to promise oneself

See also **mettre** and compounds of **mettre**, e.g., **permettre**.

to pronounce, to declare

The Seven Simple Tenses		The Seven Compound Tenses	
Singular	Plural	Singular	Plural
1 présent de l'indicatif		8 passé composé	
prononce	prononçons	ai prononcé	avons prononcé
prononces	prononcez	as prononcé	avez prononcé
prononce	prononcent	a prononcé	ont prononcé
2 imparfait de l'indicatif		9 plus-que-parfait de l'indicatif	
prononçais	prononcions	avais prononcé	avions prononcé
prononçais	prononciez	avais prononcé	aviez prononcé
prononçait	prononçaient	avait prononcé	avaient prononcé
3 passé simple		10 passé antérieur	
prononçai	prononçâmes	eus prononcé	eûmes prononcé
prononças	prononçâtes	eus prononcé	eûtes prononcé
prononça	prononcèrent	eut prononcé	eurent prononcé
4 futur		11 futur antérieur	
prononcerai	prononcerons	aurai prononcé	aurons prononcé
prononceras	prononcerez	auras prononcé	aurez prononcé
prononcera	prononceront	aura prononcé	auront prononcé
5 conditionnel		12 conditionnel passé	
prononcerais	prononcerions	aurais prononcé	aurions prononcé
prononcerais	prononceriez	aurais prononcé	auriez prononcé
prononcerait	prononceraient	aurait prononcé	auraient prononcé
6 présent du subjonctif		13 passé du subjonctif	
prononce	prononcions	aie prononcé	ayons prononcé
prononces	prononciez	aies prononcé	ayez prononcé
prononce	prononcent	ait prononcé	aient prononcé
7 imparfait du subjonctif		14 plus-que-parfait du subjonctif	
prononçasse	prononçassions	eusse prononcé	eussions prononcé
prononçasses	prononçassiez	eusses prononcé	eussiez prononcé
prononçât	prononçassent	eût prononcé	eussent prononcé

Impératif
prononce
prononçons
prononcez

prononcer un discours to deliver a speech	**annoncer** to announce
la prononciation pronunciation	**dénoncer** to denounce
prononçable pronounceable	**se prononcer** to declare, to be
se prononcer pour to decide in favor of	pronounced (as a word)
énoncer to enunciate	**se prononcer contre** to decide
	against

prouver   Part. pr. **prouvant**   Part. passé **prouvé**

to prove

The Seven Simple Tenses		The Seven Compound Tenses	
Singular	Plural	Singular	Plural
1 présent de l'indicatif		8 passé composé	
prouve	prouvons	ai prouvé	avons prouvé
prouves	prouvez	as prouvé	avez prouvé
prouve	prouvent	a prouvé	ont prouvé
2 imparfait de l'indicatif		9 plus-que-parfait de l'indicatif	
prouvais	prouvions	avais prouvé	avions prouvé
prouvais	prouviez	avais prouvé	aviez prouvé
prouvait	prouvaient	avait prouvé	avaient prouvé
3 passé simple		10 passé antérieur	
prouvai	prouvâmes	eus prouvé	eûmes prouvé
prouvas	prouvâtes	eus prouvé	eûtes prouvé
prouva	prouvèrent	eut prouvé	eurent prouvé
4 futur		11 futur antérieur	
prouverai	prouverons	aurai prouvé	aurons prouvé
prouveras	prouverez	auras prouvé	aurez prouvé
prouvera	prouveront	aura prouvé	auront prouvé
5 conditionnel		12 conditionnel passé	
prouverais	prouverions	aurais prouvé	aurions prouvé
prouverais	prouveriez	aurais prouvé	auriez prouvé
prouverait	prouveraient	aurait prouvé	auraient prouvé
6 présent du subjonctif		13 passé du subjonctif	
prouve	prouvions	aie prouvé	ayons prouvé
prouves	prouviez	aies prouvé	ayez prouvé
prouve	prouvent	ait prouvé	aient prouvé
7 imparfait du subjonctif		14 plus-que-parfait du subjonctif	
prouvasse	prouvassions	eusse prouvé	eussions prouvé
prouvasses	prouvassiez	eusses prouvé	eussiez prouvé
prouvât	prouvassent	eût prouvé	eussent prouvé
		Impératif	
		prouve	
		prouvons	
		prouvez	

---

une preuve proof	**éprouver** to test, to try, to experience
comme preuve by way of proof	**éprouver de la sympathie pour** to feel
prouvable provable	sympathy for
une épreuve test, proof	**mettre à l'épreuve** to put to the test
approuver to approve of	
désapprouver to disapprove of	

to stink

The Seven Simple Tenses

Singular	Plural
1 présent de l'indicatif	
pue	**puons**
pues	**puez**
pue	**puent**
2 imparfait de l'indicatif	
puais	**puions**
puais	**puiez**
puait	**puaient**
4 futur	
puerai	**puerons**
pueras	**puerez**
puera	**pueront**
5 conditionnel	
puerais	**puerions**
puerais	**pueriez**
puerait	**pueraient**

---

puant, puante   stinking; conceited
la puanteur   stink, foul smell
Robert est un type puant.   Robert is a stinker.
Cet ivrogne pue l'alcool; je me bouche le nez.   This drunkard stinks of alcohol;
   I'm blocking my nose.
Joseph, ta chambre pue la porcherie.   Joseph, your room smells like a pigsty.

This verb is used mainly in the above tenses.

227

punir	Part. pr. **punissant**	Part. passé **puni**

to punish

The Seven Simple Tenses		The Seven Compound Tenses	
Singular	Plural	Singular	Plural
1 présent de l'indicatif		8 passé composé	
punis	**punissons**	**ai puni**	**avons puni**
punis	**punissez**	**as puni**	**avez puni**
punit	**punissent**	**a puni**	**ont puni**
2 imparfait de l'indicatif		9 plus-que-parfait de l'indicatif	
punissais	**punissions**	**avais puni**	**avions puni**
punissais	**punissiez**	**avais puni**	**aviez puni**
punissait	**punissaient**	**avait puni**	**avaient puni**
3 passé simple		10 passé antérieur	
punis	**punîmes**	**eus puni**	**eûmes puni**
punis	**punîtes**	**eus puni**	**eûtes puni**
punit	**punirent**	**eut puni**	**eurent puni**
4 futur		11 futur antérieur	
punirai	**punirons**	**aurai puni**	**aurons puni**
puniras	**punirez**	**auras puni**	**aurez puni**
punira	**puniront**	**aura puni**	**auront puni**
5 conditionnel		12 conditionnel passé	
punirais	**punirions**	**aurais puni**	**aurions puni**
punirais	**puniriez**	**aurais punl**	**auriez puni**
punirait	**puniraient**	**aurait puni**	**auraient puni**
6 présent du subjonctif		13 passé du subjonctif	
punisse	**punissions**	**aie puni**	**ayons puni**
punisses	**punissiez**	**aies puni**	**ayez puni**
punisse	**punissent**	**ait puni**	**aient puni**
7 imparfait du subjonctif		14 plus-que-parfait du subjonctif	
punisse	**punissions**	**eusse puni**	**eussions puni**
punisses	**punissiez**	**eusses puni**	**eussiez puni**
punît	**punissent**	**eût puni**	**eussent puni**
		Impératif	
		punis	
		punissons	
		punissez	

---

punisseur, punisseuse punisher
punissable punishable
punition *(f.)* punishment
punitif, punitive punitive

échapper à la punition to escape punishment

La maîtresse de biologie: **Pierre, si tu continues à venir dans cette classe sans avoir fait tes devoirs, je téléphonerai à tes parents pour te punir. Mérites-tu une punition? Oui ou non? Aimes-tu les mesures disciplinaires? Aimes-tu les mesures punitives? Je ne le pense pas. Compris?**

to leave

The Seven Simple Tenses		The Seven Compound Tenses	
Singular	Plural	Singular	Plural
1 présent de l'indicatif		8 passé composé	
quitte	quittons	ai quitté	avons quitté
quittes	quittez	as quitté	avez quitté
quitte	quittent	a quitté	ont quitté
2 imparfait de l'indicatif		9 plus-que-parfait de l'indicatif	
quittais	quittions	avais quitté	avions quitté
quittais	quittiez	avais quitté	aviez quitté
quittait	quittaient	avait quitté	avaient quitté
3 passé simple		10 passé antérieur	
quittai	quittâmes	eus quitté	eûmes quitté
quittas	quittâtes	eus quitté	eûtes quitté
quitta	quittèrent	eut quitté	eurent quitté
4 futur		11 futur antérieur	
quitterai	quitterons	aurai quitté	aurons quitté
quitteras	quitterez	auras quitté	aurez quitté
quittera	quitteront	aura quitté	auront quitté
5 conditionnel		12 conditionnel passé	
quitterais	quitterions	aurais quitté	aurions quitté
quitterais	quitteriez	aurais quitté	auriez quitté
quitterait	quitteraient	aurait quitté	auraient quitté
6 présent du subjonctif		13 passé du subjonctif	
quitte	quittions	aie quitté	ayons quitté
quittes	quittiez	ales quitté	ayez quitté
quitte	quittent	ait quitté	aient quitté
7 imparfait du subjonctif		14 plus-que-parfait du subjonctif	
quittasse	quittassions	eusse quitté	eussions quitté
quittasses	quittassiez	eusses quitté	eussiez quitté
quittât	quittassent	eût quitté	eussent quitté
		Impératif	
		quitte	
		quittons	
		quittez	

---

une quittance acquittance, discharge	**acquitter** to acquit
quitter son chapeau to take off one's hat	**s'acquitter de** to fulfill
se quitter to separate, to leave each other	**un acquittement** acquittal
Ne quittez pas, s'il vous plaît. Hold the line, please! (on the phone)	**Je vous ai payé la dette; maintenant nous sommes quittes!** I paid you the debt; now we're even!
être quitte to be free of an obligation	

| **raconter** | Part. pr. **racontant** | Part. passé **raconté** |

to relate, to tell about, to narrate

The Seven Simple Tenses		The Seven Compound Tenses	
Singular	Plural	Singular	Plural
1 présent de l'indicatif		8 passé composé	
raconte	racontons	ai raconté	avons raconté
racontes	racontez	as raconté	avez raconté
raconte	racontent	a raconté	ont raconté
2 imparfait de l'indicatif		9 plus-que-parfait de l'indicatif	
racontais	racontions	avais raconté	avions raconté
racontais	racontiez	avais raconté	aviez raconté
racontait	racontaient	avait raconté	avaient raconté
3 passé simple		10 passé antérieur	
racontai	racontâmes	eus raconté	eûmes raconté
racontas	racontâtes	eus raconté	eûtes raconté
raconta	racontèrent	eut raconté	eurent raconté
4 futur		11 futur antérieur	
raconterai	raconterons	aurai raconté	aurons raconté
raconteras	raconterez	auras raconté	aurez raconté
racontera	raconteront	aura raconté	auront raconté
5 conditionnel		12 conditionnel passé	
raconterais	raconterions	aurais raconté	aurions raconté
raconterais	raconteriez	aurais raconté	auriez raconté
raconterait	raconteraient	aurait raconté	auraient raconté
6 présent du subjonctif		13 passé du subjonctif	
raconte	racontions	aie raconté	ayons raconté
racontes	racontiez	aies raconté	ayez raconté
raconte	racontent	ait raconté	aient raconté
7 imparfait du subjonctif		14 plus-que-parfait du subjonctif	
racontasse	racontassions	eusse raconté	eussions raconté
racontasses	racontassiez	eusses raconté	eussiez raconté
racontât	racontassent	eût raconté	eussent raconté
		Impératif	
		raconte	
		racontons	
		racontez	

Mon professeur de français aime nous raconter des anecdotes en français dans la classe de français. C'est un bon raconteur.

un raconteur   storyteller
Qu'est-ce que vous racontez?   What are you talking about?
le racontar   gossip

See also **conter**.

to call again, to call back, to recall, to remind

The Seven Simple Tenses		The Seven Compound Tenses	
Singular	Plural	Singular	Plural
1 présent de l'indicatif		**8 passé composé**	
rappelle	rappelons	ai rappelé	avons rappelé
rappelles	rappelez	as rappelé	avez rappelé
rappelle	rappellent	a rappelé	ont rappelé
2 imparfait de l'indicatif		**9 plus-que-parfait de l'indicatif**	
rappelais	rappelions	avais rappelé	avions rappelé
rappelais	rappeliez	avais rappelé	aviez rappelé
rappelait	rappelaient	avait rappelé	avaient rappelé
3 passé simple		**10 passé antérieur**	
rappelai	rappelâmes	eus rappelé	eûmes rappelé
rappelas	rappelâtes	eus rappelé	eûtes rappelé
rappela	rappelèrent	eut rappelé	eurent rappelé
4 futur		**11 futur antérieur**	
rappellerai	rappellerons	aurai rappelé	aurons rappelé
rappelleras	rappellerez	auras rappelé	aurez rappelé
rappellera	rappelleront	aura rappelé	auront rappelé
5 conditionnel		**12 conditionnel passé**	
rappellerais	rappellerions	aurais rappelé	aurions rappelé
rappellerais	rappelleriez	aurais rappelé	auriez rappelé
rappellerait	rappelleraient	aurait rappelé	auraient rappelé
6 présent du subjonctif		**13 passé du subjonctif**	
rappelle	rappelions	aie rappelé	ayons rappelé
rappelles	rappeliez	aies rappelé	ayez rappelé
rappelle	rappellent	ait rappelé	aient rappelé
7 imparfait du subjonctif		**14 plus-que-parfait du subjonctif**	
rappelasse	rappelassions	eusse rappelé	eussions rappelé
rappelasses	rappelassiez	eusses rappelé	eussiez rappelé
rappelât	rappelassent	eût rappelé	eussent rappelé

	Impératif
	rappelle
	rappelons
	rappelez

—**Je ne peux pas vous parler maintenant. Rappelez-moi demain.**
—**D'accord. Je vous rappellerai demain.**

un rappel   recall, callback, recalling
rappeler à la vie   to restore to life
Rappelez-moi votre nom.   Remind me of your name.
rappeler qqn à l'ordre   to call someone to order

See also **appeler, s'appeler,** and **se rappeler.**

se rappeler   Part. pr. **se rappelant**   Part. passé **rappelé(e)(s)**

to remember, to recall, to recollect

The Seven Simple Tenses		The Seven Compound Tenses		
Singular	Plural	Singular	Plural	
1 présent de l'indicatif		8 passé composé		
me rappelle	nous rappelons	me suis	nous sommes	
te rappelles	vous rappelez	t'es	vous êtes	+ rappelé(e)(s)
se rappelle	se rappellent	s'est	se sont	
2 imparfait de l'indicatif		9 plus-que-parfait de l'indicatif		
me rappelais	nous rappelions	m'étais	nous étions	
te rappelais	vous rappeliez	t'étais	vous étiez	+ rappelé(e)(s)
se rappelait	se rappelaient	s'était	s'étaient	
3 passé simple		10 passé antérieur		
me rappelai	nous rappelâmes	me fus	nous fûmes	
te rappelas	vous rappelâtes	te fus	vous fûtes	+ rappelé(e)(s)
se rappela	se rappelèrent	se fut	se furent	
4 futur		11 futur antérieur		
me rappellerai	nous rappellerons	me serai	nous serons	
te rappelleras	vous rappellerez	te seras	vous serez	+ rappelé(e)(s)
se rappellera	se rappelleront	se sera	se seront	
5 conditionnel		12 conditionnel passé		
me rappellerais	nous rappellerions	me serais	nous serions	
te rappellerais	vous rappelleriez	te serais	vous seriez	+ rappelé(e)(s)
se rappellerait	se rappelleraient	se serait	se seraient	
6 présent du subjonctif		13 passé du subjonctif		
me rappelle	nous rappelions	me sois	nous soyons	
te rappelles	vous rappeliez	te sois	vous soyez	+ rappelé(e)(s)
se rappelle	se rappellent	se soit	se soient	
7 imparfait du subjonctif		14 plus-que-parfait du subjonctif		
me rappelasse	nous rappelassions	me fusse	nous fussions	
te rappelasses	vous rappelassiez	te fusses	vous fussiez +	rappelé(e)(s)
se rappelât	se rappelassent	se fût	se fussent	

	Impératif
	rappelle-toi; ne te rappelle pas
	rappelons-nous; ne nous rappelons pas
	rappelez-vous; ne vous rappelez pas

Je me rappelle bien le premier jour quand j'ai vu la belle Hélène. C'était un jour inoubliable.

See also **appeler**, **s'appeler**, and **rappeler**.

to receive, to get

The Seven Simple Tenses		The Seven Compound Tenses	
Singular	Plural	Singular	Plural
1 présent de l'indicatif		8 passé composé	
reçois	**recevons**	**ai reçu**	**avons reçu**
reçois	**recevez**	**as reçu**	**avez reçu**
reçoit	**reçoivent**	**a reçu**	**ont reçu**
2 imparfait de l'indicatif		9 plus-que-parfait de l'indicatif	
recevais	**recevions**	**avais reçu**	**avions reçu**
recevais	**receviez**	**avais reçu**	**aviez reçu**
recevait	**recevaient**	**avait reçu**	**avaient reçu**
3 passé simple		10 passé antérieur	
reçus	**reçûmes**	**eus reçu**	**eûmes reçu**
reçus	**reçûtes**	**eus reçu**	**eûtes reçu**
reçut	**reçurent**	**eut reçu**	**eurent reçu**
4 futur		11 futur antérieur	
recevrai	**recevrons**	**aurai reçu**	**aurons reçu**
recevras	**recevrez**	**auras reçu**	**aurez reçu**
recevra	**recevront**	**aura reçu**	**auront reçu**
5 conditionnel		12 conditionnel passé	
recevrais	**recevrions**	**aurais reçu**	**aurions reçu**
recevrais	**recevriez**	**aurais reçu**	**auriez reçu**
recevrait	**recevraient**	**aurait reçu**	**auraient reçu**
6 présent du subjonctif		13 passé du subjonctif	
reçoive	**recevions**	**aie reçu**	**ayons reçu**
reçoives	**receviez**	**aies reçu**	**ayez reçu**
reçoive	**reçoivent**	**ait reçu**	**aient reçu**
7 imparfait du subjonctif		14 plus-que-parfait du subjonctif	
reçusse	**reçussions**	**eusse reçu**	**eussions reçu**
reçusses	**reçussiez**	**eusses reçu**	**eussiez reçu**
reçût	**reçussent**	**eût reçu**	**eussent reçu**

Impératif
reçois
recevons
recevez

---

réceptif, réceptive receptive
une réception reception, welcome
un, une réceptionniste receptionist
un reçu a receipt
au reçu de on receipt of

recevable receivable
un receveur, une receveuse receiver
être reçu à un examen
    to pass an exam

réfléchir   Part. pr. **réfléchissant**   Part. passé **réfléchi**

to think, to meditate, to reflect, to ponder

The Seven Simple Tenses		The Seven Compound Tenses	
Singular	Plural	Singular	Plural
1 présent de l'indicatif		8 passé composé	
réfléchis	**réfléchissons**	**ai réfléchi**	**avons réfléchi**
réfléchis	**réfléchissez**	**as réfléchi**	**avez réfléchi**
réfléchit	**réfléchissent**	**a réfléchi**	**ont réfléchi**
2 imparfait de l'indicatif		9 plus-que-parfait de l'indicatif	
réfléchissais	**réfléchissions**	**avais réfléchi**	**avions réfléchi**
réfléchissais	**réfléchissiez**	**avais réfléchi**	**aviez réfléchi**
réfléchissait	**réfléchissaient**	**avait réfléchi**	**avaient réfléchi**
3 passé simple		10 passé antérieur	
réfléchis	**réfléchîmes**	**eus réfléchi**	**eûmes réfléchi**
réfléchis	**réfléchîtes**	**eus réfléchi**	**eûtes réfléchi**
réfléchit	**réfléchirent**	**eut réfléchi**	**eurent réfléchi**
4 futur		11 futur antérieur	
réfléchirai	**réfléchirons**	**aurai réfléchi**	**aurons réfléchi**
réfléchiras	**réfléchirez**	**auras réfléchi**	**aurez réfléchi**
réfléchira	**réfléchiront**	**aura réfléchi**	**auront réfléchi**
5 conditionnel		12 conditionnel passé	
réfléchirais	**réfléchirions**	**aurais réfléchi**	**aurions réfléchi**
réfléchirais	**réfléchiriez**	**aurais réfléchi**	**auriez réfléchi**
réfléchirait	**réfléchiraient**	**aurait réfléchi**	**auraient réfléchi**
6 présent du subjonctif		13 passé du subjonctif	
réfléchisse	**réfléchissions**	**aie réfléchi**	**ayons réfléchi**
réfléchisses	**réfléchissiez**	**aies réfléchi**	**ayez réfléchi**
réfléchisse	**réfléchissent**	**ait réfléchi**	**aient réfléchi**
7 imparfait du subjonctif		14 plus-que-parfait du subjonctif	
réfléchisse	**réfléchissions**	**eusse réfléchi**	**eussions réfléchi**
réfléchisses	**réfléchissiez**	**eusses réfléchi**	**eussiez réfléchi**
réfléchît	**réfléchissent**	**eût réfléchi**	**eussent réfléchi**

	Impératif
	réfléchis
	réfléchissons
	réfléchissez

Mathilde: **Yvette, vas-tu au bal samedi soir?**
Yvette: **Je ne sais pas si j'y vais. Je demande à réfléchir.**
Mathilde: **Bon, alors, réfléchis avant de me donner ta réponse.**

réfléchir à qqch   to think over (ponder) something
réfléchir avant de parler   to think before speaking
La mer réfléchit le ciel.   The sea reflects the sky.

to refuse, to withhold

The Seven Simple Tenses		The Seven Compound Tenses	
Singular	Plural	Singular	Plural
1 présent de l'indicatif		8 passé composé	
refuse	refusons	ai refusé	avons refusé
refuses	refusez	as refusé	avez refusé
refuse	refusent	a refusé	ont refusé
2 imparfait de l'indicatif		9 plus-que-parfait de l'indicatif	
refusais	refusions	avais refusé	avions refusé
refusais	refusiez	avais refusé	aviez refusé
refusait	refusaient	avait refusé	avaient refusé
3 passé simple		10 passé antérieur	
refusai	refusâmes	eus refusé	eûmes refusé
refusas	refusâtes	eus refusé	eûtes refusé
refusa	refusèrent	eut refusé	eurent refusé
4 futur		11 futur antérieur	
refuserai	refuserons	aurai refusé	aurons refusé
refuseras	refuserez	auras refusé	aurez refusé
refusera	refuseront	aura refusé	auront refusé
5 conditionnel		12 conditionnel passé	
refuserais	refuserions	aurais refusé	aurions refusé
refuserais	refuseriez	aurais refusé	auriez refusé
refuserait	refuseraient	aurait refusé	auraient refusé
6 présent du subjonctif		13 passé du subjonctif	
refuse	refusions	aie refusé	ayons refusé
refuses	refusiez	aies refusé	ayez refusé
refuse	refusent	ait refusé	aient refusé
7 imparfait du subjonctif		14 plus-que-parfait du subjonctif	
refusasse	refusassions	eusse refusé	eussions refusé
refusasses	refusassiez	eusses refusé	eussiez refusé
refusât	refusassent	eût refusé	eussent refusé
		Impératif	
		refuse	
		refusons	
		refusez	

**Je refuse absolument de vous écouter. Sortez, s'il vous plaît! Si vous refusez,
vous le regretterez.**

refuser de faire qqch to refuse to do something
se refuser qqch to deny oneself something
refusable refusable
un refus refusal

regarder   Part. pr. **regardant**   Part. passé **regardé**

to look (at), to watch

The Seven Simple Tenses		The Seven Compound Tenses	
Singular	Plural	Singular	Plural
1 présent de l'indicatif		8 passé composé	
regarde	regardons	ai regardé	avons regardé
regardes	regardez	as regardé	avez regardé
regarde	regardent	a regardé	ont regardé
2 imparfait de l'indicatif		9 plus-que-parfait de l'indicatif	
regardais	regardions	avais regardé	avions regardé
regardais	regardiez	avais regardé	aviez regardé
regardait	regardaient	avait regardé	avaient regardé
3 passé simple		10 passé antérieur	
regardai	regardâmes	eus regardé	eûmes regardé
regardas	regardâtes	eus regardé	eûtes regardé
regarda	regardèrent	eut regardé	eurent regardé
4 futur		11 futur antérieur	
regarderai	regarderons	aurai regardé	aurons regardé
regarderas	regarderez	auras regardé	aurez regardé
regardera	regarderont	aura regardé	auront regardé
5 conditionnel		12 conditionnel passé	
regarderais	regarderions	aurais regardé	aurions regardé
regarderais	regarderiez	aurais regardé	auriez regardé
regarderait	regarderaient	aurait regardé	auraient regardé
6 présent du subjonctif		13 passé du subjonctif	
regarde	regardions	aie regardé	ayons regardé
regardes	regardiez	aies regardé	ayez regardé
regarde	regardent	ait regardé	aient regardé
7 imparfait du subjonctif		14 plus-que-parfait du subjonctif	
regardasse	regardassions	eusse regardé	eussions regardé
regardasses	regardassiez	eusses regardé	eussiez regardé
regardât	regardassent	eût regardé	eussent regardé
		Impératif	
		regarde	
		regardons	
		regardez	

—Qu'est-ce que tu regardes, Bernard?
—Je regarde le ciel. Il est beau et clair.
—Pourquoi ne me regardes-tu pas?

regarder qqch   to look at (to watch) something
un regard   glance, look; **au regard de**   compared to, with regard to

236

Part. pr. **remarquant**   Part. passé **remarqué**   **remarquer**

to remark, to notice, to observe, to distinguish

The Seven Simple Tenses		The Seven Compound Tenses	
Singular	Plural	Singular	Plural
1 présent de l'indicatif		8 passé composé	
remarque	remarquons	ai remarqué	avons remarqué
remarques	remarquez	as remarqué	avez remarqué
remarque	remarquent	a remarqué	ont remarqué
2 imparfait de l'indicatif		9 plus-que-parfait de l'indicatif	
remarquais	remarquions	avais remarqué	avions remarqué
remarquais	remarquiez	avais remarqué	aviez remarqué
remarquait	remarquaient	avait remarqué	avaient remarqué
3 passé simple		10 passé antérieur	
remarquai	remarquâmes	eus remarqué	eûmes remarqué
remarquas	remarquâtes	eus remarqué	eûtes remarqué
remarqua	remarquèrent	eut remarqué	eurent remarqué
4 futur		11 futur antérieur	
remarquerai	remarquerons	aurai remarqué	aurons remarqué
remarqueras	remarquerez	auras remarqué	aurez remarqué
remarquera	remarqueront	aura remarqué	auront remarqué
5 conditionnel		12 conditionnel passé	
remarquerais	remarquerions	aurais remarqué	aurions remarqué
remarquerais	remarqueriez	aurais remarqué	auriez remarqué
remarquerait	remarqueraient	aurait remarqué	auraient remarqué
6 présent du subjonctif		13 passé du subjonctif	
remarque	remarquions	aie remarqué	ayons remarqué
remarques	remarquiez	aies remarqué	ayez remarqué
remarque	remarquent	ait remarqué	aient remarqué
7 imparfait du subjonctif		14 plus-que-parfait du subjonctif	
remarquasse	remarquassions	eusse remarqué	eussions remarqué
remarquasses	remarquassiez	eusses remarqué	eussiez remarqué
remarquât	remarquassent	eût remarqué	eussent remarqué
		Impératif	
		remarque	
		remarquons	
		remarquez	

un remarque   remark, observation, comment; **marquer**   to mark
faire remarquer qqch à qqn   to bring something to someone's attention, to point
out something to someone

Erich Maria Remarque, romancier, est l'auteur du roman *All Quiet on the Western
Front.* **Son nom de famille est d'origine française.**

remettre	Part. pr. **remettant**	Part. passé **remis**

to put (on) again, to replace, to put back, to give back, to postpone

The Seven Simple Tenses		The Seven Compound Tenses	
Singular	Plural	Singular	Plural
1 présent de l'indicatif		8 passé composé	
remets	remettons	ai remis	avons remis
remets	remettez	as remis	avez remis
remet	remettent	a remis	ont remis
2 imparfait de l'indicatif		9 plus-que-parfait de l'indicatif	
remettais	remettions	avais remis	avions remis
remettais	remettiez	avais remis	aviez remis
remettait	remettaient	avait remis	avaient remis
3 passé simple		10 passé antérieur	
remis	remîmes	eus remis	eûmes remis
remis	remîtes	eus remis	eûtes remis
remit	remirent	eut remis	eurent remis
4 futur		11 futur antérieur	
remettrai	remettrons	aurai remis	aurons remis
remettras	remettrez	auras remis	aurez remis
remettra	remettront	aura remis	auront remis
5 conditionnel		12 conditionnel passé	
remettrais	remettrions	aurais remis	aurions remis
remettrais	remettriez	aurais remis	auriez remis
remettrait	remettraient	aurait remis	auraient remis
6 présent du subjonctif		13 passé du subjonctif	
remette	remettions	aie remis	ayons remis
remettes	remettiez	ales remis	ayez remis
remette	remettent	ait remis	aient remis
7 imparfait du subjonctif		14 plus-que-parfait du subjonctif	
remisse	remissions	eusse remis	eussions remis
remisses	remissiez	eusses remis	eussiez remis
remît	remissent	eût remis	eussent remis

	Impératif
	remets
	remettons
	remettez

—Où avez-vous remis les fleurs que je vous ai données?
—Je les ai remises là-bas. Ne les voyez-vous pas?

se remettre de   to recover from
se remettre à faire qqch   to start to do something again
s'en remettre à   to depend on, to rely on
Remettez-vous!   Pull yourself together!
une remise   remittance, postponement, discount

See also **mettre** and compounds of **mettre,** e.g., **promettre.**

to replace

The Seven Simple Tenses		The Seven Compound Tenses	
Singular	Plural	Singular	Plural
1 présent de l'indicatif		8 passé composé	
remplace	remplaçons	ai remplacé	avons remplacé
remplaces	remplacez	as remplacé	avez remplacé
remplace	remplacent	a remplacé	ont remplacé
2 imparfait de l'indicatif		9 plus-que-parfait de l'indicatif	
remplaçais	remplacions	avais remplacé	avions remplacé
remplaçais	remplaciez	avais remplacé	aviez remplacé
remplaçait	remplaçaient	avait remplacé	avaient remplacé
3 passé simple		10 passé antérieur	
remplaçai	remplaçâmes	eus remplacé	eûmes remplacé
remplaças	remplaçâtes	eus remplacé	eûtes remplacé
remplaça	remplacèrent	eut remplacé	eurent remplacé
4 futur		11 futur antérieur	
remplacerai	remplacerons	aurai remplacé	aurons remplacé
remplaceras	remplacerez	auras remplacé	aurez remplacé
remplacera	remplaceront	aura remplacé	auront remplacé
5 conditionnel		12 conditionnel passé	
remplacerais	remplacerions	aurais remplacé	aurions remplacé
remplacerais	remplaceriez	aurais remplacé	auriez remplacé
remplacerait	remplaceraient	aurait remplacé	auraient remplacé
6 présent du subjonctif		13 passé du subjonctif	
remplace	remplacions	aie remplacé	ayons remplacé
remplaces	remplaciez	aies remplacé	ayez remplacé
remplace	remplacent	ait remplacé	aient remplacé
7 imparfait du subjonctif		14 plus-que-parfait du subjonctif	
remplaçasse	remplaçassions	eusse remplacé	eussions remplacé
remplaçasses	remplaçassiez	eusses remplacé	eussiez remplacé
remplaçât	remplaçassent	eût remplacé	eussent remplacé

Impératif
remplace
remplaçons
remplacez

remplacer par   to replace with
un remplacement   replacement (thing)
un remplaçant, une remplaçante   replacement (person), substitute
remplaçable   replaceable
en remplacement de   in place of

See also **placer.**

remplir	Part. pr. **remplissant**	Part.passé **rempli**

to fill, to fulfill, to fill in, to fill out

The Seven Simple Tenses		The Seven Compound Tenses	
Singular	Plural	Singular	Plural
1 présent de l'indicatif		8 passé composé	
remplis	**remplissons**	**ai rempli**	**avons rempli**
remplis	**remplissez**	**as rempli**	**avez rempli**
remplit	**remplissent**	**a rempli**	**ont rempli**
2 imparfait de l'indicatif		9 plus-que-parfait de l'indicatif	
remplissais	**remplissions**	**avais rempli**	**avions rempli**
remplissais	**remplissiez**	**avais rempli**	**aviez rempli**
remplissait	**remplissaient**	**avait rempli**	**avaient rempli**
3 passé simple		10 passé antérieur	
remplis	**remplîmes**	**eus rempli**	**eûmes rempli**
remplis	**remplîtes**	**eus rempli**	**eûtes rempli**
remplit	**remplirent**	**eut rempli**	**eurent rempli**
4 futur		11 futur antérieur	
remplirai	**remplirons**	**aurai rempli**	**aurons rempli**
rempliras	**remplirez**	**auras rempli**	**aurez rempli**
remplira	**rempliront**	**aura rempli**	**auront rempli**
5 conditionnel		12 conditionnel passé	
remplirais	**remplirions**	**aurais rempli**	**aurions rempli**
remplirais	**rempliriez**	**aurais rempli**	**auriez rempli**
remplirait	**rempliraient**	**aurait rempli**	**auraient rempli**
6 présent du subjonctif		13 passé du subjonctif	
remplisse	**remplissions**	**aie rempli**	**ayons rempli**
remplisses	**remplissiez**	**aies rempli**	**ayez rempli**
remplisse	**remplissent**	**ait rempli**	**aient rempli**
7 imparfait du subjonctif		14 plus-que-parfait du subjonctif	
remplisse	**remplissions**	**eusse rempli**	**eussions rempli**
remplisses	**remplissiez**	**eusses rempli**	**eussiez rempli**
remplît	**remplissent**	**eût rempli**	**eussent rempli**

Impératif
remplis
remplissons
remplissez

---

remplir de to fill with
remplir qqch de qqch to fill something
  with something
se remplir to fill up
un remplissage filling up

remplir des conditions to fulfill
  requirements, conditions
remplir une tâche to carry out
  (perform) a task

to meet, to encounter

The Seven Simple Tenses		The Seven Compound Tenses	
Singular	Plural	Singular	Plural
1 présent de l'indicatif		8 passé composé	
rencontre	**rencontrons**	**ai rencontré**	**avons rencontré**
rencontres	**rencontrez**	**as rencontré**	**avez rencontré**
rencontre	**rencontrent**	**a rencontré**	**ont rencontré**
2 imparfait de l'indicatif		9 plus-que-parfait de l'indicatif	
rencontrais	**rencontrions**	**avais rencontré**	**avions rencontré**
rencontrais	**rencontriez**	**avais rencontré**	**aviez rencontré**
rencontrait	**rencontraient**	**avait rencontré**	**avaient rencontré**
3 passé simple		10 passé antérieur	
rencontrai	**rencontrâmes**	**eus rencontré**	**eûmes rencontré**
rencontras	**rencontrâtes**	**eus rencontré**	**eûtes rencontré**
rencontra	**rencontrèrent**	**eut rencontré**	**eurent rencontré**
4 futur		11 futur antérieur	
rencontrerai	**rencontrerons**	**aurai rencontré**	**aurons rencontré**
rencontreras	**rencontrerez**	**auras rencontré**	**aurez rencontré**
rencontrera	**rencontreront**	**aura rencontré**	**auront rencontré**
5 conditionnel		12 conditionnel passé	
rencontrerais	**rencontrerions**	**aurais rencontré**	**aurions rencontré**
rencontrerais	**rencontreriez**	**aurais rencontré**	**auriez rencontré**
rencontrerait	**rencontreraient**	**aurait rencontré**	**auraient rencontré**
6 présent du subjonctif		13 passé du subjonctif	
rencontre	**rencontrions**	**aie rencontré**	**ayons rencontré**
rencontres	**rencontriez**	**aies rencontré**	**ayez rencontré**
rencontre	**rencontrent**	**ait rencontré**	**aient rencontré**
7 imparfait du subjonctif		14 plus-que-parfait du subjonctif	
recontrasse	**rencontrassions**	**eusse rencontré**	**eussions rencontré**
rencontrasses	**rencontrassiez**	**eusses rencontré**	**eussiez rencontré**
rencontrât	**rencontrassent**	**eût rencontré**	**eussent rencontré**
		Impératif	
		rencontre	
		rencontrons	
		rencontrez	

se rencontrer   to meet each other
une rencontre   encounter, meeting
aller à la rencontre de qqn   to go to meet someone
rencontrer par hasard   to meet someone by chance (bump into)

rendre	Part. pr. **rendant**	Part.passé **rendu**

to give back, to return (something), to render; to vomit

The Seven Simple Tenses		The Seven Compound Tenses	

Singular	Plural	Singular	Plural
1 présent de l'indicatif		8 passé composé	
rends	rendons	ai rendu	avons rendu
rends	rendez	as rendu	avez rendu
rend	rendent	a rendu	ont rendu
2 imparfait de l'indicatif		9 plus-que-parfait de l'indicatif	
rendais	rendions	avais rendu	avions rendu
rendais	rendiez	avais rendu	aviez rendu
rendait	rendaient	avait rendu	avaient rendu
3 passé simple		10 passé antérieur	
rendis	rendîmes	eus rendu	eûmes rendu
rendis	rendîtes	eus rendu	eûtes rendu
rendit	rendirent	eut rendu	euront rendu
4 futur		11 futur antérieur	
rendrai	rendrons	aurai rendu	aurons rendu
rendras	rendrez	auras rendu	aurez rendu
rendra	rendront	aura rendu	auront rendu
5 conditionnel		12 conditionnel passé	
rendrais	rendrions	aurais rendu	aurions rendu
rendrais	rendriez	aurais rendu	auriez rendu
rendrait	rendraient	aurait rendu	auraient rendu
6 présent du subjonctif		13 passé du subjonctif	
rende	rendions	aie rendu	ayons rendu
rendes	rendiez	aies rendu	ayez rendu
rende	rendent	ait rendu	aient rendu
7 imparfait du subjonctif		14 plus-que-parfait du subjonctif	
rendisse	rendissions	eusse rendu	eussions rendu
rendisses	rendissiez	eusses rendu	eussiez rendu
rendît	rendissent	eût rendu	eussent rendu
		Impératif	
		rends	
		rendons	
		rendez	

---

un rendez-vous appointment, date
un compte rendu report, account
se rendre à to surrender to
se rendre compte de to realize
rendre un service à qqn to do someone a favor
rendre qqn + adj. to make someone + adj.

rendre grâce à qqn to give thanks to someone
rendre service à qqn to be of service to someone
rendre compte de qqch to give an account of something
rendre justice to uphold justice
rendre qqch to return something

to return

The Seven Simple Tenses		The Seven Compound Tenses	
Singular	Plural	Singular	Plural
1 présent de l'indicatif		8 passé composé	
rentre	rentrons	suis rentré(e)	sommes rentré(e)s
rentres	rentrez	es rentré(e)	êtes rentré(e)(s)
rentre	rentrent	est rentré(e)	sont rentré(e)s
2 imparfait de l'indicatif		9 plus-que-parfait de l'indicatif	
rentrais	rentrions	étais rentré(e)	étions rentré(e)s
rentrais	rentriez	étais rentré(e)	étiez rentré(e)(s)
rentrait	rentraient	était rentré(e)	étaient rentré(e)s
3 passé simple		10 passé antérieur	
rentrai	rentrâmes	fus rentré(e)	fûmes rentré(e)s
rentras	rentrâtes	fus rentré(e)	fûtes rentré(e)(s)
rentra	rentrèrent	fut rentré(e)	furent rentré(e)s
4 futur		11 futur antérieur	
rentrerai	rentrerons	serai rentré(e)	serons rentré(e)s
rentreras	rentrerez	seras rentré(e)	serez rentré(e)(s)
rentrera	rentreront	sera rentré(e)	seront rentré(e)s
5 conditionnel		12 conditionnel passé	
rentrerais	rentrerions	serais rentré(e)	serions rentré(e)s
rentrerais	rentreriez	serais rentré(e)	seriez rentré(e)(s)
rentrerait	rentreraient	serait rentré(e)	seraient rentré(e)s
6 présent du subjonctif		13 passé du subjonctif	
rentre	rentrions	sois rentré(e)	soyons rentré(e)s
rentres	rentriez	sois rentré(e)	soyez rentré(e)(s)
rentre	rentrent	soit rentré(e)	soient rentré(e)s
7 imparfait du subjonctif		14 plus-que-parfait du subjonctif	
rentrasse	rentrassions	fusse rentré(e)	fussions rentré(e)s
rentrasses	rentrassiez	fusses rentré(e)	fussiez rentré(e)(s)
rentrât	rentrassent	fût rentré(e)	fussent rentré(e)s

	Impératif
	rentre
	rentrons
	rentrez

This verb is conjugated with **avoir** when it has a direct object.

Example: **Elle a rentré le chat dans la maison.**   She brought (took) the cat into the house.

BUT: **Elle est rentrée tôt.**   She returned home early.

rentrer chez soi   to go back home
rentrer les enfants   to take the children home
rentrer ses larmes   to hold back one's tears
la rentrée   return, homecoming
la rentrée des classes   back to school

répéter   Part. pr. **répétant**   Part.passé **répété**

to repeat, to rehearse

The Seven Simple Tenses		The Seven Compound Tenses	
Singular	Plural	Singular	Plural
1 présent de l'indicatif		8 passé composé	
répète	répétons	ai répété	avons répété
répètes	répétez	as répété	avez répété
répète	répètent	a répété	ont répété
2 imparfait de l'indicatif		9 plus-que-parfait de l'indicatif	
répétais	répétions	avais répété	avions répété
répétais	répétiez	avais répété	aviez répété
répétait	répétaient	avait répété	avaient répété
3 passé simple		10 passé antérieur	
répétai	répétâmes	eus répété	eûmes répété
répétas	répétâtes	eus répété	eûtes répété
répéta	répétèrent	eut répété	eurent répété
4 futur		11 futur antérieur	
répéterai	répéterons	aurai répété	aurons répété
répéteras	répéterez	auras répété	aurez répété
répétera	répéteront	aura répété	auront répété
5 conditionnel		12 conditionnel passé	
répéterais	répéterions	aurais répété	aurions répété
répéterais	répéteriez	aurais répété	auriez répété
répéterait	répéteraient	aurait répété	auraient répété
6 présent du subjonctif		13 passé du subjonctif	
répète	répétions	aie répété	ayons répété
répètes	répétiez	ales répété	ayez répété
répète	répètent	ait répété	aient répété
7 imparfait du subjonctif		14 plus-que-parfait du subjonctif	
répétasse	répétassions	eusse répété	eussions répété
répétasses	répétassiez	eusses répété	eussiez répété
répétât	répétassent	eût répété	eussent répété

Impératif
répète
répétons
répétez

---

répéter une pièce de théâtre   to rehearse a play
une répétition   repetition
La pièce est en répétition.   The play is in rehearsal.
se répéter   to repeat oneself; to recur
répétailler   to keep on repeating

to respond, to reply, to answer

The Seven Simple Tenses		The Seven Compound Tenses	
Singular	Plural	Singular	Plural
1 présent de l'indicatif		8 passé composé	
réponds	**répondons**	**ai répondu**	**avons répondu**
réponds	**répondez**	**as répondu**	**avez répondu**
répond	**répondent**	**a répondu**	**ont répondu**
2 imparfait de l'indicatif		9 plus-que-parfait de l'indicatif	
répondais	**répondions**	**avais répondu**	**avions répondu**
répondais	**répondiez**	**avais répondu**	**aviez répondu**
répondait	**répondaient**	**avait répondu**	**avaient répondu**
3 passé simple		10 passé antérieur	
répondis	**répondîmes**	**eus répondu**	**eûmes répondu**
répondis	**répondîtes**	**eus répondu**	**eûtes répondu**
répondit	**répondirent**	**eut répondu**	**eurent répondu**
4 futur		11 futur antérieur	
répondrai	**répondrons**	**aurai répondu**	**aurons répondu**
répondras	**répondrez**	**auras répondu**	**aurez répondu**
répondra	**répondront**	**aura répondu**	**auront répondu**
5 conditionnel		12 conditionnel passé	
répondrais	**répondrions**	**aurais répondu**	**aurions répondu**
répondrais	**répondriez**	**aurais répondu**	**auriez répondu**
répondrait	**répondraient**	**aurait répondu**	**auraient répondu**
6 présent du subjonctif		13 passé du subjonctif	
réponde	**répondions**	**aie répondu**	**ayons répondu**
répondes	**répondiez**	**aies répondu**	**ayez répondu**
réponde	**répondent**	**ait répondu**	**aient répondu**
7 imparfait du subjonctif		14 plus-que-parfait du subjonctif	
répondisse	**répondissions**	**eusse répondu**	**eussions répondu**
répondisses	**répondissiez**	**eusses répondu**	**eussiez répondu**
répondît	**répondissent**	**eût répondu**	**eussent répondu**
		Impératif	
		réponds	
		répondons	
		répondez	

répondre à qqn   to answer someone; to reply to someone
répondre de qqn   to be responsible for, to vouch for someone
répondre de qqch   to vouch for something, to guarantee something
une réponse   answer, reply; **en réponse à votre lettre . . .**   in reply to your letter . . .
pour répondre à la question de . . .   in answer to the question of . . .

se reposer	Part. pr. **se reposant**	Part. passé **reposé(e)(s)**

to rest

The Seven Simple Tenses		The Seven Compound Tenses	
Singular	Plural	Singular	Plural
1 présent de l'indicatif		8 passé composé	
me repose	nous reposons	me suis reposé(e)	nous sommes reposé(e)s
te reposes	vous reposez	t'es reposé(e)	vous êtes reposé(e)(s)
se repose	se reposent	s'est reposé(e)	se sont reposé(e)s
2 imparfait de l'indicatif		9 plus-que-parfait de l'indicatif	
me reposais	nous reposions	m'étais reposé(e)	nous étions reposé(e)s
te reposais	vous reposiez	t'étais reposé(e)	vous étiez reposé(e)(s)
se reposait	se reposaient	s'était reposé(e)	s'étaient reposé(e)s
3 passé simple		10 passé antérieur	
me reposai	nous reposâmes	me fus reposé(e)	nous fûmes reposé(e)s
te reposas	vous reposâtes	te fus reposé(e)	vous fûtes reposé(e)(s)
se reposa	se reposèrent	se fut reposé(e)	se furent reposé(e)s
4 futur		11 futur antérieur	
me reposerai	nous reposerons	me serai reposé(e)	nous serons reposé(e)s
te reposeras	vous reposerez	te seras reposé(e)	vous serez reposé(e)(s)
se reposera	se reposeront	se sera reposé(e)	se seront reposé(e)s
5 conditionnel		12 conditionnel passé	
me reposerais	nous reposerions	me serais reposé(e)	nous serions reposé(e)s
te reposerais	vous reposeriez	te serais reposé(e)	vous seriez reposé(e)(s)
se reposerait	se reposeraient	se serait reposé(e)	se seraient reposé(e)s
6 présent du subjonctif		13 passé du subjonctif	
me repose	nous reposions	me sois reposé(e)	nous soyons reposé(e)s
te reposes	vous reposiez	te sois reposé(e)	vous soyez reposé(e)(s)
se repose	se reposent	se soit reposé(e)	se soient reposé(e)s
7 imparfait du subjonctif		14 plus-que-parfait du subjonctif	
me reposasse	nous reposassions	me fusse reposé(e)	nous fussions reposé(e)s
te reposasses	vous reposassiez	te fusses reposé(e)	vous fussiez reposé(e)(s)
se reposât	se reposassent	se fût reposé(e)	se fussent reposé(e)s

Impératif
repose-toi; ne te repose pas
reposons-nous; ne nous reposons pas
reposez-vous; ne vous reposez pas

---

reposer to put down again; **reposer la tête sur** to rest one's head on; **reposer sur**
to be based on
le repos rest, repose; **Au repos!** At ease!
se reposer sur qqn, qqch to put one's trust in someone, something
un repose-pied footrest; **un repose-bras** armrest
Je suis fatigué; je vais me reposer. I'm tired; I'm going to rest.

to take again, to take back, to recover, to resume

The Seven Simple Tenses		The Seven Compound Tenses	
Singular	Plural	Singular	Plural
1 présent de l'indicatif		8 passé composé	
reprends	**reprenons**	**ai repris**	**avons repris**
reprends	**reprenez**	**as repris**	**avez repris**
reprend	**reprennent**	**a repris**	**ont repris**
2 imparfait de l'indicatif		9 plus-que-parfait de l'indicatif	
reprenais	**reprenions**	**avais repris**	**avions repris**
reprenais	**repreniez**	**avais repris**	**aviez repris**
reprenait	**reprenaient**	**avait repris**	**avaient repris**
3 passé simple		10 passé antérieur	
repris	**reprîmes**	**eus repris**	**eûmes repris**
repris	**reprîtes**	**eus repris**	**eûtes repris**
reprit	**reprirent**	**eut repris**	**eurent repris**
4 futur		11 futur antérieur	
reprendrai	**reprendrons**	**aurai repris**	**aurons repris**
reprendras	**reprendrez**	**auras repris**	**aurez repris**
reprendra	**reprendront**	**aura repris**	**auront repris**
5 conditionnel		12 conditionnel passé	
reprendrais	**reprendrions**	**aurais repris**	**aurions repris**
reprendrais	**reprendriez**	**aurais repris**	**auriez repris**
reprendrait	**reprendraient**	**aurait repris**	**auraient repris**
6 présent du subjonctif		13 passé du subjonctif	
reprenne	**reprenions**	**aie repris**	**ayons repris**
reprennes	**repreniez**	**aies repris**	**ayez repris**
reprenne	**reprennent**	**ait repris**	**aient repris**
7 imparfait du subjonctif		14 plus-que-parfait du subjonctif	
reprisse	**reprissions**	**eusse repris**	**eussions repris**
reprisses	**reprissiez**	**eusses repris**	**eussiez repris**
reprît	**reprissent**	**eût repris**	**eussent repris**

Impératif
reprends
reprenons
reprenez

---

reprendre froid   to catch cold again
reprendre ses esprits   to recover one's senses
reprendre le dessus   to regain the upper hand
reprendre ses forces   to recover one's strength
se reprendre   to take hold of oneself, to recover oneself
une reprise   resumption, renewal, repetition
à maintes reprises   over and over again

See also **prendre**.

résoudre   Part. pr. **résolvant**   Part. passé **résolu (résous)**

to resolve, to solve

The Seven Simple Tenses		The Seven Compound Tenses	
Singular	Plural	Singular	Plural
1 présent de l'indicatif		8 passé composé	
résous	résolvons	ai résolu	avons résolu
résous	résolvez	as résolu	avez résolu
résout	résolvent	a résolu	ont résolu
2 imparfait de l'indicatif		9 plus-que-parfait de l'indicatif	
résolvais	résolvions	avais résolu	avions résolu
résolvais	résolviez	avais résolu	aviez résolu
résolvait	résolvaient	avait résolu	avaient résolu
3 passé simple		10 passé antérieur	
résolus	résolûmes	eus résolu	eûmes résolu
résolus	résolûtes	eus résolu	eûtes résolu
résolut	résolurent	eut résolu	eurent résolu
4 futur		11 futur antérieur	
résoudrai	résoudrons	aurai résolu	aurons résolu
résoudras	résoudrez	auras résolu	aurez résolu
résoudra	résoudront	aura résolu	auront résolu
5 conditionnel		12 conditionnel passé	
résoudrais	résoudrions	aurais résolu	aurions résolu
résoudrais	résoudriez	aurais résolu	auriez résolu
résoudrait	résoudraient	aurait résolu	auraient résolu
6 présent du subjonctif		13 passé du subjonctif	
résolve	résolvions	aie résolu	ayons résolu
résolves	résolviez	aies résolu	ayez résolu
résolve	résolvent	ait résolu	aient résolu
7 imparfait du subjonctif		14 plus-que-parfait du subjonctif	
résolusse	résolussions	eusse résolu	eussions résolu
résolusses	résolussiez	eusses résolu	eussiez résolu
résolût	résolussent	eût résolu	eussent résolu

Impératif
résous
résolvons
résolvez

se résoudre à   to make up one's mind to
résoudre qqn à faire qqch   to induce someone to do something
résoudre un problème mathématique   to solve a math problem
une résolution   resolution
être résolu(e) à faire qqch   to be resolved to doing something
Le feu a résous le bois en cendres.   The fire has changed the wood into ashes.
   (The past part. **résous** is used for things that have undergone a physical change.)

248

Part. pr. **ressemblant**   Part. passé **ressemblé**   **ressembler**

to resemble, to be like, to look like

The Seven Simple Tenses		The Seven Compound Tenses	
Singular	Plural	Singular	Plural
1 présent de l'indicatif		8 passé composé	
ressemble	ressemblons	ai ressemblé	avons ressemblé
ressembles	ressemblez	as ressemblé	avez ressemblé
ressemble	ressemblent	a ressemblé	ont ressemblé
2 imparfait de l'indicatif		9 plus-que-parfait de l'indicatif	
ressemblais	ressemblions	avais ressemblé	avions ressemblé
ressemblais	ressembliez	avais ressemblé	aviez ressemblé
ressemblait	ressemblaient	avait ressemblé	avaient ressemblé
3 passé simple		10 passé antérieur	
ressemblai	ressemblâmes	eus ressemblé	eûmes ressemblé
ressemblas	ressemblâtes	eus ressemblé	eûtes ressemblé
ressembla	ressemblèrent	eut ressemblé	eurent ressemblé
4 futur		11 futur antérieur	
ressemblerai	ressemblerons	aurai ressemblé	aurons ressemblé
ressembleras	ressemblerez	auras ressemblé	aurez ressemblé
ressemblera	ressembleront	aura ressemblé	auront ressemblé
5 conditionnel		12 conditionnel passé	
ressemblerais	ressemblerions	aurais ressemblé	aurions ressemblé
ressemblerais	ressembleriez	aurais ressemblé	auriez ressemblé
ressemblerait	ressembleraient	aurait ressemblé	auraient ressemblé
6 présent du subjonctif		13 passé du subjonctif	
ressemble	ressemblions	aie ressemblé	ayons ressemblé
ressembles	ressembliez	aies ressemblé	ayez ressemblé
ressemble	ressemblent	ait ressemblé	aient ressemblé
7 imparfait du subjonctif		14 plus-que-parfait du subjonctif	
ressemblasse	ressemblassions	eusse ressemblé	eussions ressemblé
ressemblasses	ressemblassiez	eusses ressemblé	eussiez ressemblé
ressemblât	ressemblassent	eût ressemblé	eussent ressemblé

Impératif
ressemble
ressemblons
ressemblez

---

ressembler à qqn   to resemble someone
Paulette ressemble beaucoup à sa mère.   Paulette looks very much like her mother.
se ressembler   to resemble each other, to look alike
Qui se ressemble s'assemble.   Birds of a feather flock together.
sembler   to seem, to appear
une ressemblance   resemblance

249

rester	Part. pr. **restant**	Part. passé **resté(e)(s)**

to remain, to stay; to be left (over)

The Seven Simple Tenses		The Seven Compound Tenses	
Singular	Plural	Singular	Plural
1 présent de l'indicatif		8 passé composé	
reste	restons	suis resté(e)	sommes resté(e)s
restes	restez	es resté(e)	êtes resté(e)(s)
reste	restent	est resté(e)	sont resté(e)s
2 imparfait de l'indicatif		9 plus-que-parfait de l'indicatif	
restais	restions	étais resté(e)	étions resté(e)s
restais	restiez	étais resté(e)	étiez resté(e)(s)
restait	restaient	était resté(e)	étaient resté(e)s
3 passé simple		10 passé antérieur	
restai	restâmes	fus resté(e)	fûmes resté(e)s
restas	restâtes	fus resté(e)	fûtes resté(e)(s)
resta	restèrent	fut resté(e)	furent resté(e)s
4 futur		11 futur antérieur	
resterai	resterons	serai resté(e)	serons resté(e)s
resteras	resterez	seras resté(e)	serez resté(e)(s)
restera	resteront	sera resté(e)	seront resté(e)s
5 conditionnel		12 conditionnel passé	
resterais	resterions	serais resté(e)	serions resté(e)s
resterais	resteriez	serais resté(e)	seriez resté(e)(s)
resterait	resteraient	serait resté(e)	seraient resté(e)s
6 présent du subjonctif		13 passé du subjonctif	
reste	restions	sois resté(e)	soyons resté(e)s
restes	restiez	sois resté(e)	soyez resté(e)(s)
reste	restent	soit resté(e)	soient resté(e)s
7 imparfait du subjonctif		14 plus-que-parfait du subjonctif	
restasse	restassions	fusse resté(e)	fussions resté(e)s
restasses	restassiez	fusses resté(e)	fussiez resté(e)(s)
restât	restassent	fût resté(e)	fussent resté(e)s

Impératif
reste
restons
restez

Combien d'argent vous reste-t-il?   How much money do you have left (over)?
Il me reste deux cents francs.   I have two hundred francs left.
rester au lit   to stay in bed
Restez là; je reviens tout de suite.   Stay there; I'll be right back.

Do not confuse **rester** with **se reposer.**

to return, to go back, to turn again

The Seven Simple Tenses		The Seven Compound Tenses	
Singular	Plural	Singular	Plural
1 présent de l'indicatif		8 passé composé	
retourne	retournons	suis retourné(e)	sommes retourné(e)s
retournes	retournez	es retourné(e)	êtes retourné(e)(s)
retourne	retournent	est retourné(e)	sont retourné(e)s
2 imparfait de l'indicatif		9 plus-que-parfait de l'indicatif	
retournais	retournions	étais retourné(e)	étions retourné(e)s
retournais	retourniez	étais retourné(e)	étiez retourné(e)(s)
retournait	retournaient	était retourné(e)	étaient retourné(e)s
3 passé simple		10 passé antérieur	
retournai	retournâmes	fus retourné(e)	fûmes retourné(e)s
retournas	retournâtes	fus retourné(e)	fûtes retourné(e)(s)
retourna	retournèrent	fut retourné(e)	furent retourné(e)s
4 futur		11 futur antérieur	
retournerai	retournerons	serai retourné(e)	serons retourné(e)s
retourneras	retournerez	seras retourné(e)	serez retourné(e)(s)
retournera	retourneront	sera retourné(e)	seront retourné(e)s
5 conditionnel		12 conditionnel passé	
retournerais	retournerions	serais retourné(e)	serions retourné(e)s
retournerais	retourneriez	serais retourné(e)	seriez retourné(e)(s)
retournerait	retourneraient	serait retourné(e)	seraient retourné(e)s
6 présent du subjonctif		13 passé du subjonctif	
retourne	retournions	sois retourné(e)	soyons retourné(e)s
retournes	retourniez	sois retourné(e)	soyez retourné(e)(s)
retourne	retournent	soit retourné(e)	soient retourné(e)s
7 imparfait du subjonctif		14 plus-que-parfait du subjonctif	
retournasse	retournassions	fusse retourné(e)	fussions retourné(e)s
retournasses	retournassiez	fusses retourné(e)	fussiez retourné(e)(s)
retournât	retournassent	fût retourné(e)	fussent retourné(e)s

Impératif
retourne
retournons
retournez

retourner une chaussette   to turn a sock inside out
retourner un matelas   to turn over a mattress
retourner qqn   to change someone's mind
se retourner   to turn around; **se retourner sur le dos**   to turn over on one's back
un retour   return; **un billet de retour**   return ticket
un billet d'aller et retour   a round-trip ticket
être de retour   to be back; **Madame Dupin sera de retour demain.**

to succeed, to result

The Seven Simple Tenses		The Seven Compound Tenses	
Singular	Plural	Singular	Plural
1 présent de l'indicatif		8 passé composé	
réussis	**réussissons**	**ai réussi**	**avons réussi**
réussis	**réussissez**	**as réussi**	**avez réussi**
réussit	**réussissent**	**a réussi**	**ont réussi**
2 imparfait de l'indicatif		9 plus-que-parfait de l'indicatif	
réussissais	**réussissions**	**avais réussi**	**avions réussi**
réussissais	**réussissiez**	**avais réussi**	**aviez réussi**
réussissait	**réussissaient**	**avait réussi**	**avaient réussi**
3 passé simple		10 passé antérieur	
réussis	**réussîmes**	**eus réussi**	**eûmes réussi**
réussis	**réussîtes**	**eus réussi**	**eûtes réussi**
réussit	**réussirent**	**eut réussi**	**eurent réussi**
4 futur		11 futur antérieur	
réussirai	**réussirons**	**aurai réussi**	**aurons réussi**
réussiras	**réussirez**	**auras réussi**	**aurez réussi**
réussira	**réussiront**	**aura réussi**	**auront réussi**
5 conditionnel		12 conditionnel passé	
réussirais	**réussirions**	**aurais réussi**	**aurions réussi**
réussirais	**réussiriez**	**aurais réussi**	**auriez réussi**
réussirait	**réussiraient**	**aurait réussi**	**auraient réussi**
6 présent du subjonctif		13 passé du subjonctif	
réussisse	**réussissions**	**aie réussi**	**ayons réussi**
réussisses	**réussissiez**	**aies réussi**	**ayez réussi**
réussisse	**réussissent**	**ait réussi**	**aient réussi**
7 imparfait du subjonctif		14 plus-que-parfait du subjonctif	
réussisse	**réussissions**	**eusse réussi**	**eussions réussi**
réussisses	**réussissiez**	**eusses réussi**	**eussiez réussi**
réussît	**réussissent**	**eût réussi**	**eussent réussi**
		Impératif	
		réussis	
		réussissons	
		réussissez	

réussir à qqch   to succeed in something
réussir à un examen   to pass an exam
une réussite   success; **une réussite sociale**   social success
réussir   to result; **Le projet a mal réussi.**   The plan turned out badly; **Le projet a bien réussi.**   The plan turned out well.

The Seven Simple Tenses		The Seven Compound Tenses	
Singular	Plural	Singular	Plural
1 présent de l'indicatif		8 passé composé	
me réveille	nous réveillons	me suis réveillé(e)	nous sommes réveillé(e)s
te réveilles	vous réveillez	t'es réveillé(e)	vous êtes réveillé(e)(s)
se réveille	se réveillent	s'est réveillé(e)	se sont réveillé(e)s
2 imparfait de l'indicatif		9 plus-que-parfait de l'indicatif	
me réveillais	nous réveillions	m'étais réveillé(e)	nous étions réveillé(e)s
te réveillais	vous réveilliez	t'étais réveillé(e)	vous étiez réveillé(e)(s)
se réveillait	se réveillaient	s'était réveillé(e)	s'étaient réveillé(e)s
3 passé simple		10 passé antérieur	
me réveillai	nous réveillâmes	me fus réveillé(e)	nous fûmes réveillé(e)s
te réveillas	vous réveillâtes	te fus réveillé(e)	vous fûtes réveillé(e)(s)
se réveilla	se réveillèrent	se fut réveillé(e)	se furent réveillé(e)s
4 futur		11 futur antérieur	
me réveillerai	nous réveillerons	me serai réveillé(e)	nous serons réveillé(e)s
te réveilleras	vous réveillerez	te seras réveillé(e)	vous serez réveillé(e)(s)
se réveillera	se réveilleront	se sera réveillé(e)	se seront réveillé(e)s
5 conditionnel		12 conditionnel passé	
me réveillerais	nous réveillerions	me serais réveillé(e)	nous serions réveillé(e)s
te réveillerais	vous réveilleriez	te serais réveillé(e)	vous seriez réveillé(e)(s)
se réveillerait	se réveilleraient	se serait réveillé(e)	se seraient réveillé(e)s
6 présent du subjonctif		13 passé du subjonctif	
me réveille	nous réveillions	me sois réveillé(e)	nous soyons réveillé(e)s
te réveilles	vous réveilliez	te sois réveillé(e)	vous soyez réveillé(e)(s)
se réveille	se réveillent	se soit réveillé(e)	se soient réveillé(e)s
7 imparfait du subjonctif		14 plus-que-parfait du subjonctif	
me réveillasse	nous réveillassions	me fusse réveillé(e)	nous fussions réveillé(e)s
te réveillasses	vous réveillassiez	te fusses réveillé(e)	vous fussiez réveillé(e)(s)
se réveillât	se réveillassent	se fût réveillé(e)	se fussent réveillé(e)s

Impératif
réveille-toi; ne te réveille pas
réveillons-nous; ne nous réveillons pas
réveillez-vous; ne vous réveillez pas

---

le réveillon   Christmas or New Year's Eve party
faire réveillon   to see the New Year in, to see Christmas in on Christmas Eve
un réveille-matin   alarm clock
éveiller (réveiller) qqn   to wake up, awaken someone; **éveiller**   implies to awaken
  or wake up gently; **réveiller**   suggests with some effort
veiller   to stay awake; **veiller à**   to look after
veiller sur   to watch over; **surveiller**   to keep an eye on
la veille de Noël   Christmas Eve

to come back

The Seven Simple Tenses		The Seven Compound Tenses	
Singular	Plural	Singular	Plural
1 présent de l'indicatif		8 passé composé	
reviens	revenons	suis revenu(e)	sommes revenu(e)s
reviens	revenez	es revenu(e)	êtes revenu(e)(s)
revient	reviennent	est revenu(e)	sont revenu(e)s
2 imparfait de l'indicatif		9 plus-que-parfait de l'indicatif	
revenais	revenions	étais revenu(e)	étions revenu(e)s
revenais	reveniez	étais revenu(e)	étiez revenu(e)(s)
revenait	revenaient	était revenu(e)	étaient revenu(e)s
3 passé simple		10 passé antérieur	
revins	revînmes	fus revenu(e)	fûmes revenu(e)s
revins	revîntes	fus revenu(e)	fûtes revenu(e)(s)
revint	revinrent	fut revenu(e)	furent revenu(e)s
4 futur		11 futur antérieur	
reviendrai	reviendrons	serai revenu(e)	serons revenu(e)s
reviendras	reviendrez	seras revenu(e)	serez revenu(e)(s)
reviendra	reviendront	sera revenu(e)	seront revenu(e)s
5 conditionnel		12 conditionnel passé	
reviendrais	reviendrions	serais revenu(e)	serions revenu(e)s
reviendrais	reviendriez	serais revenu(e)	seriez revenu(e)(s)
reviendrait	reviendraient	serait revenu(e)	seraient revenu(e)s
6 présent du subjonctif		13 passé du subjonctif	
revienne	revenions	sois revenu(e)	soyons revenu(e)s
reviennes	reveniez	sois revenu(e)	soyez revenu(e)(s)
revienne	reviennent	soit revenu(e)	soient revenu(e)s
7 imparfait du subjonctif		14 plus-que-parfait du subjonctif	
revinsse	revinssions	fusse revenu(e)	fussions revenu(e)s
revinsses	revinssiez	fusses revenu(e)	fussiez revenu(e)(s)
revînt	revinssent	fût revenu(e)	fussent revenu(e)s
		Impératif	
		reviens	
		revenons	
		revenez	

le revenu   revenue, income
à revenu fixe   fixed interest
revenir d'une erreur   to realize one's mistake
revenir au même   to amount to the same thing
revenir sur ses pas   to retrace one's steps
revenir sur le sujet   to get back to the subject
revenir sur sa parole   to go back on one's word
Tout revient à ceci . . .   It all boils down to this . . .

to see again, to see once more

The Seven Simple Tenses		The Seven Compound Tenses	
Singular	Plural	Singular	Plural
1 présent de l'indicatif		8 passé composé	
revois	revoyons	ai revu	avons revu
revois	revoyez	as revu	avez revu
revoit	revoient	a revu	ont revu
2 imparfait de l'indicatif		9 plus-que-parfait de l'indicatif	
revoyais	revoyions	avais revu	avions revu
revoyais	revoyiez	avais revu	aviez revu
revoyait	revoyaient	avait revu	avaient revu
3 passé simple		10 passé antérieur	
revis	revîmes	eus revu	eûmes revu
revis	revîtes	eus revu	eûtes revu
revit	revirent	eut revu	eurent revu
4 futur		11 futur antérieur	
reverrai	reverrons	aurai revu	aurons revu
reverras	reverrez	auras revu	aurez revu
reverra	reverront	aura revu	auront revu
5 conditionnel		12 conditionnel passé	
reverrais	reverrions	aurais revu	aurions revu
reverrais	reverriez	aurais revu	auriez revu
reverrait	reverraient	aurait revu	auraient revu
6 présent du subjonctif		13 passé du subjonctif	
revoie	revoyions	aie revu	ayons revu
revoies	revoyiez	aies revu	ayez revu
revoie	revoient	ait revu	aient revu
7 imparfait du subjonctif		14 plus-que-parfait du subjonctif	
revisse	revissions	eusse revu	eussions revu
revisses	revissiez	eusses revu	eussiez revu
revît	revissent	eût revu	eussent revu
		Impératif	
		revois	
		revoyons	
		revoyez	

au revoir   good-bye, see you again, until we meet again
se revoir   to see each other again
une revue   review, magazine
un, une revuiste   a writer of reviews
une révision   revision;   **à revoir**   to be revised

See also **voir.**

255

rire   Part. pr. **riant**   Part. passé **ri**

to laugh

The Seven Simple Tenses		The Seven Compound Tenses	
Singular	Plural	Singular	Plural
1 présent de l'indicatif		8 passé composé	
ris	**rions**	**ai ri**	**avons ri**
ris	**riez**	**as ri**	**avez ri**
rit	**rient**	**a ri**	**ont ri**
2 imparfait de l'indicatif		9 plus-que-parfait de l'indicatif	
riais	**riions**	**avais ri**	**avions ri**
riais	**riiez**	**avais ri**	**aviez ri**
riait	**riaient**	**avait ri**	**avaient ri**
3 passé simple		10 passé antérieur	
ris	**rîmes**	**eus ri**	**eûmes ri**
ris	**rîtes**	**eus ri**	**eûtes ri**
rit	**rirent**	**eut ri**	**eurent ri**
4 futur		11 futur antérieur	
rirai	**rirons**	**aurai ri**	**aurons ri**
riras	**rirez**	**auras ri**	**aurez ri**
rira	**riront**	**aura ri**	**auront ri**
5 conditionnel		12 conditionnel passé	
rirais	**ririons**	**aurais ri**	**aurions ri**
rirais	**ririez**	**aurais ri**	**auriez ri**
rirait	**riraient**	**aurait ri**	**auraient ri**
6 présent du subjonctif		13 passé du subjonctif	
rie	**riions**	**aie ri**	**ayons ri**
ries	**riiez**	**aies ri**	**ayez ri**
rie	**rient**	**ait ri**	**aient ri**
7 imparfait du subjonctif		14 plus-que-parfait du subjonctif	
risse	**rissions**	**eusse ri**	**eussions ri**
risses	**rissiez**	**eusses ri**	**eussiez ri**
rît	**rissent**	**eût ri**	**eussent ri**
		Impératif	
		ris	
		rions	
		riez	

éclater de rire to burst out laughing; **rire de** to laugh at
dire qqch pour rire to say something just for a laugh
rire au nez de qqn to laugh in someone's face
rire de bon coeur to laugh heartily
le rire laughter; **un sourire** smile; **risible** laughable

See also **sourire**.

256

to break, to burst, to shatter, to break off

The Seven Simple Tenses		The Seven Compound Tenses	
Singular	Plural	Singular	Plural
1 présent de l'indicatif		8 passé composé	
romps	rompons	ai rompu	avons rompu
romps	rompez	as rompu	avez rompu
rompt	rompent	a rompu	ont rompu
2 imparfait de l'indicatif		9 plus-que-parfait de l'indicatif	
rompais	rompions	avais rompu	avions rompu
rompais	rompiez	avais rompu	aviez rompu
rompait	rompaient	avait rompu	avaient rompu
3 passé simple		10 passé antérieur	
rompis	rompîmes	eus rompu	eûmes rompu
rompis	rompîtes	eus rompu	eûtes rompu
rompit	rompirent	eut rompu	eurent rompu
4 futur		11 futur antérieur	
romprai	romprons	aurai rompu	aurons rompu
rompras	romprez	auras rompu	aurez rompu
rompra	rompront	aura rompu	auront rompu
5 conditionnel		12 conditionnel passé	
romprais	romprions	aurais rompu	aurions rompu
romprais	rompriez	aurais rompu	auriez rompu
romprait	rompraient	aurait rompu	auraient rompu
6 présent du subjonctif		13 passé du subjonctif	
rompe	rompions	aie rompu	ayons rompu
rompes	rompiez	aies rompu	ayez rompu
rompe	rompent	ait rompu	aient rompu
7 imparfait du subjonctif		14 plus-que-parfait du subjonctif	
rompisse	rompissions	eusse rompu	eussions rompu
rompisses	rompissiez	eusses rompu	eussiez rompu
rompît	rompissent	eût rompu	eussent rompu
		Impératif	
		romps	
		rompons	
		rompez	

rompu de fatigue worn out	**corrompre** to corrupt
rompu aux affaires experienced in business	**interrompre** to interrupt
se rompre à to get used to	**une rupture** rupture, bursting
se rompre la tête to rack one's brains	**un rupteur** circuit breaker
une rupture de contrat breach of	**rompre avec qqn** to have a falling
contract	out with someone

to seize, to grasp, to comprehend

The Seven Simple Tenses		The Seven Compound Tenses	
Singular	Plural	Singular	Plural
1 présent de l'indicatif		8 passé composé	
saisis	saisissons	ai saisi	avons saisi
saisis	saisissez	as saisi	avez saisi
saisit	saisissent	a saisi	ont saisi
2 imparfait de l'indicatif		9 plus-que-parfait de l'indicatif	
saisissais	saisissions	avais saisi	avions saisi
saisissais	saisissiez	avais saisi	aviez saisi
saisissait	saisissaient	avait saisi	avaient saisi
3 passé simple		10 passé antérieur	
saisis	saisîmes	eus saisi	eûmes saisi
saisis	saisîtes	eus saisi	eûtes saisi
saisit	saisirent	eut saisi	eurent saisi
4 futur		11 futur antérieur	
saisirai	saisirons	aurai saisi	aurons saisi
saisiras	saisirez	auras saisi	aurez saisi
saisira	saisiront	aura saisi	auront saisi
5 conditionnel		12 conditionnel passé	
saisirais	saisirions	aurais saisi	aurions saisi
saisirais	saisiriez	aurais saisi	auriez saisi
saisirait	saisiraient	aurait saisi	auraient saisi
6 présent du subjonctif		13 passé du subjonctif	
saisisse	saisissions	aie saisi	ayons saisi
saisisses	saisissiez	aies saisi	ayez saisi
saisisse	saisissent	ait saisi	aient saisi
7 imparfait du subjonctif		14 plus-que-parfait du subjonctif	
saisisse	saisissions	eusse saisi	eussions saisi
saisisses	saisissiez	eusses saisi	eussiez saisi
saisît	saisissent	eût saisi	eussent saisi
		Impératif	
		saisis	
		saisissons	
		saisissez	

un saisissement shock	**saisir l'occasion** to seize the
saisissable seizable	opportunity
saisissant, saisissante thrilling, piercing	**saisir la signification de qqch** to
une saisie seizure	grasp the meaning of something
se saisir de to take possession of	

to soil, to dirty

The Seven Simple Tenses		The Seven Compound Tenses	
Singular	Plural	Singular	Plural
1 présent de l'indicatif		8 passé composé	
salis	salissons	ai sali	avons sali
salis	salissez	as sali	avez sali
salit	salissent	a sali	ont sali
2 imparfait de l'indicatif		9 plus-que-parfait de l'indicatif	
salissais	salissions	avais sali	avions sali
salissais	salissiez	avais sali	aviez sali
salissait	salissaient	avait sali	avaient sali
3 passé simple		10 passé antérieur	
salis	salîmes	eus sali	eûmes sali
salis	salîtes	eus sali	eûtes sali
salit	salirent	eut sali	eurent sali
4 futur		11 futur antérieur	
salirai	salirons	aurai sali	aurons sali
saliras	salirez	auras sali	aurez sali
salira	saliront	aura sali	auront sali
5 conditionnel		12 conditionnel passé	
salirais	salirions	aurais sali	aurions sali
salirais	saliriez	aurais sali	auriez sali
salirait	saliraient	aurait sali	auraient sali
6 présent du subjonctif		13 passé du subjonctif	
salisse	salissions	aie sali	ayons sali
salisses	salissiez	aies sali	ayez sali
salisse	salissent	ait sali	aient sali
7 imparfait du subjonctif		14 plus-que-parfait du subjonctif	
salisse	salissions	eusse sali	eussions sali
salisses	salissiez	eusses sali	eussiez sali
salît	salissent	eût sali	eussent sali
		Impératif	
		salis	
		salissons	
		salissez	

sale dirty, soiled		**dire des saletés** to use filthy language
salement disgustingly		**un saligaud, une saligaude** filthy beast
la saleté filth		

Avez-vous jamais lu ou vu la pièce de théâtre *Les mains sales* de Jean-Paul Sartre?

sauter   Part. pr. **sautant**   Part. passé **sauté**

to jump, to leap

The Seven Simple Tenses		The Seven Compound Tenses	
Singular	Plural	Singular	Plural
1 présent de l'indicatif		8 passé composé	
saute	sautons	ai sauté	avons sauté
sautes	sautez	as sauté	avez sauté
saute	sautent	a sauté	ont sauté
2 imparfait de l'indicatif		9 plus-que-parfait de l'indicatif	
sautais	sautions	avais sauté	avions sauté
sautais	sautiez	avais sauté	aviez sauté
sautait	sautaient	avait sauté	avaient sauté
3 passé simple		10 passé antérieur	
sautai	sautâmes	eus sauté	eûmes sauté
sautas	sautâtes	eus sauté	eûtes sauté
sauta	sautèrent	eut sauté	eurent sauté
4 futur		11 futur antérieur	
sauterai	sauterons	aurai sauté	aurons sauté
sauteras	sauterez	auras sauté	aurez sauté
sautera	sauteront	aura sauté	auront sauté
5 conditionnel		12 conditionnel passé	
sauterais	sauterions	aurais sauté	aurions sauté
sauterais	sauteriez	aurais sauté	auriez sauté
sauterait	sauteraient	aurait sauté	auraient sauté
6 présent du subjonctif		13 passé du subjonctif	
saute	sautions	aie sauté	ayons sauté
sautes	sautiez	aies sauté	ayez sauté
saute	sautent	ait sauté	aient sauté
7 imparfait du subjonctif		14 plus-que-parfait du subjonctif	
sautasse	sautassions	eusse sauté	eussions sauté
sautasses	sautassiez	eusses sauté	eussiez sauté
sautât	sautassent	eût sauté	eussent sauté
		Impératif	
		saute	
		sautons	
		sautez	

---

un saut   leap, jump
une sauterelle   grasshopper
sautiller   to skip, to hop
sauter à la corde   to jump (skip) rope

sauter au bas du lit   to jump out of bed
faire sauter une crêpe   to toss a pancake
Cela saute aux yeux.   That's obvious.

to rescue, to save

The Seven Simple Tenses		The Seven Compound Tenses	
Singular	Plural	Singular	Plural
1 présent de l'indicatif		**8 passé composé**	
sauve	sauvons	ai sauvé	avons sauvé
sauves	sauvez	as sauvé	avez sauvé
sauve	sauvent	a sauvé	ont sauvé
2 imparfait de l'indicatif		**9 plus-que-parfait de l'indicatif**	
sauvais	sauvions	avais sauvé	avions sauvé
sauvais	sauviez	avais sauvé	aviez sauvé
sauvait	sauvaient	avait sauvé	avaient sauvé
3 passé simple		**10 passé antérieur**	
sauvai	sauvâmes	eus sauvé	eûmes sauvé
sauvas	sauvâtes	eus sauvé	eûtes sauvé
sauva	sauvèrent	eut sauvé	eurent sauvé
4 futur		**11 futur antérieur**	
sauverai	sauverons	aurai sauvé	aurons sauvé
sauveras	sauverez	auras sauvé	aurez sauvé
sauvera	sauveront	aura sauvé	auront sauvé
5 conditionnel		**12 conditionnel passé**	
sauverais	sauverions	aurais sauvé	aurions sauvé
sauverais	sauveriez	aurais sauvé	auriez sauvé
sauverait	sauveraient	aurait sauvé	auraient sauvé
6 présent du subjonctif		**13 passé du subjonctif**	
sauve	sauvions	aie sauvé	ayons sauvé
sauves	sauviez	aies sauvé	ayez sauvé
sauve	sauvent	ait sauvé	aient sauvé
7 imparfait du subjonctif		**14 plus-que-parfait du subjonctif**	
sauvasse	sauvassions	eusse sauvé	eussions sauvé
sauvasses	sauvassiez	eusses sauvé	eussiez sauvé
sauvât	sauvassent	eût sauvé	eussent sauvé
		Impératif	
		sauve	
		sauvons	
		sauvez	

sauvegarder to safeguard
le sauvetage life-saving, rescue
sauve-qui-peut run for your life
sauver les apparences to preserve
  appearances

See also **se sauver.**

se sauver to run away, to escape,
  to rush off
sauver la vie à qqn to save someone's life
une échelle de sauvetage fire escape,
  escape ladder

se sauver Part. pr. **se sauvant** Part. passé **sauvé(e)(s)**

to run away, to rush off, to escape

The Seven Simple Tenses		The Seven Compound Tenses	
Singular	Plural	Singular	Plural

1 présent de l'indicatif
me sauve	nous sauvons		
te sauves	vous sauvez		
se sauve	se sauvent		

8 passé composé
me suis sauvé(e)	nous sommes sauvé(e)s
t'es sauvé(e)	vous êtes sauvé(e)(s)
s'est sauvé(e)	se sont sauvé(e)s

2 imparfait de l'indicatif
me sauvais	nous sauvions
te sauvais	vous sauviez
se sauvait	se sauvaient

9 plus-que-parfait de l'indicatif
m'étais sauvé(e)	nous étions sauvé(e)s
t'étais sauvé(e)	vous étiez sauvé(e)(s)
s'était sauvé(e)	s'étaient sauvé(e)s

3 passé simple
me sauvai	nous sauvâmes
te sauvas	vous sauvâtes
se sauva	se sauvèrent

10 passé antérieur
me fus sauvé(e)	nous fûmes sauvé(e)s
te fus sauvé(e)	vous fûtes sauvé(e)(s)
se fut sauvé(e)	se furent sauvé(e)s

4 futur
me sauverai	nous sauverons
te sauveras	vous sauverez
se sauvera	se sauveront

11 futur antérieur
me serai sauvé(e)	nous serons sauvé(e)s
te seras sauvé(e)	vous serez sauvé(e)(s)
se sera sauvé(e)	se seront sauvé(e)s

5 conditionnel
me sauverais	nous sauverions
te sauverais	vous sauveriez
se sauverait	se sauveraient

12 conditionnel passé
me serais sauvé(e)	nous serions sauvé(e)s
te serais sauvé(e)	vous seriez sauvé(e)(s)
se serait sauvé(e)	se seraient sauvé(e)s

6 présent du subjonctif
me sauve	nous sauvions
te sauves	vous sauviez
se sauve	se sauvent

13 passé du subjonctif
me sois sauvé(e)	nous soyons sauvé(e)s
te sois sauvé(e)	vous soyez sauvé(e)(s)
se soit sauvé(e)	se soient sauvé(e)s

7 imparfait du subjonctif
me sauvasse	nous sauvassions
te sauvasses	vous sauvassiez
se sauvât	se sauvassent

14 plus-que-parfait du subjonctif
me fusse sauvé(e)	nous fussions sauvé(e)s
te fusses sauvé(e)	vous fussiez sauvé(e)(s)
se fût sauvé(e)	se fussent sauvé(e)s

Impératif
sauve-toi; ne te sauve pas
sauvons-nous; ne nous sauvons pas
sauvez-vous; ne vous sauvez pas

---

se sauver de prison to escape from prison	**sauver** to rescue, to save
sauvegarder to safeguard	**sauver la vie à qqn** to save
le sauvetage life-saving, rescue	someone's life
sauve-qui-peut run for your life	

to know (how)

The Seven Simple Tenses		The Seven Compound Tenses	
Singular	Plural	Singular	Plural
1 présent de l'indicatif		8 passé composé	
sais	savons	ai su	avons su
sais	savez	as su	avez su
sait	savent	a su	ont su
2 imparfait de l'indicatif		9 plus-que-parfait de l'indicatif	
savais	savions	avais su	avions su
savais	saviez	avais su	aviez su
savait	savaient	avait su	avaient su
3 passé simple		10 passé antérieur	
sus	sûmes	eus su	eûmes su
sus	sûtes	eus su	eûtes su
sut	surent	eut su	eurent su
4 futur		11 futur antérieur	
saurai	saurons	aurai su	aurons su
sauras	saurez	auras su	aurez su
saura	sauront	aura su	auront su
5 conditionnel		12 conditionnel passé	
saurais	saurions	aurais su	aurions su
saurais	sauriez	aurais su	auriez su
saurait	sauraient	aurait su	auraient su
6 présent du subjonctif		13 passé du subjonctif	
sache	sachions	aie su	ayons su
saches	sachiez	aies su	ayez su
sache	sachent	ait su	aient su
7 imparfait du subjonctif		14 plus-que-parfait du subjonctif	
susse	sussions	eusse su	eussions su
susses	sussiez	eusses su	eussiez su
sût	sussent	eût su	eussent su
		Impératif	
		sache	
		sachons	
		sachez	

---

le savoir   knowledge
le savoir-faire   know-how, tact, ability
le savoir-vivre   to be well-mannered, well-bred
faire savoir   to inform
Pas que je sache.   Not to my knowledge.

savoir faire qqch   to know how to do something; **Savez-vous jouer du piano?**
Autant que je sache . . .
   As far as I know . . .
C'est à savoir.   That remains to be seen.

sembler   Part. pr. —   Part. passé **semblé**

to seem

The Seven Simple Tenses	The Seven Compound Tenses
Singular	Singular
1 présent de l'indicatif **il semble**	8 passé composé **il a semblé**
2 imparfait de l'indicatif **il semblait**	9 plus-que-parfait de l'indicatif **il avait semblé**
3 passé simple **il sembla**	10 passé antérieur **il eut semblé**
4 futur **il semblera**	11 futur antérieur **il aura semblé**
5 conditionnel **il semblerait**	12 conditionnel passé **il aurait semblé**
6 présent du subjonctif **qu'il semble**	13 passé du subjonctif **qu'il ait semblé**
7 imparfait du subjonctif **qu'il semblât**	14 plus-que-parfait du subjonctif **qu'il eût semblé**

Impératif
—

This verb has regular forms in all the tenses (like **ressembler** among the 301 verbs in this book) but much of the time it is used impersonally in the forms given above with **il** (it) as the subject.

Il me semble difficile.
  It seems difficult to me.

C'est ce qui me semble.
  That's what it looks like to me.

to feel, to smell, to perceive

The Seven Simple Tenses		The Seven Compound Tenses	
Singular	Plural	Singular	Plural
1 présent de l'indicatif		8 passé composé	
sens	sentons	al senti	avons senti
sens	sentez	as senti	avez senti
sent	sentent	a senti	ont senti
2 imparfait de l'indicatif		9 plus-que-parfait de l'indicatif	
sentais	sentions	avais senti	avions senti
sentais	sentiez	avais senti	aviez senti
sentait	sentaient	avait senti	avaient senti
3 passé simple		10 passé antérieur	
sentis	sentîmes	eus senti	eûmes senti
sentis	sentîtes	eus senti	eûtes senti
sentit	sentirent	eut senti	eurent senti
4 futur		11 futur antérieur	
sentirai	sentirons	aurai senti	aurons senti
sentiras	sentirez	auras senti	aurez senti
sentira	sentiront	aura senti	auront senti
5 conditionnel		12 conditionnel passé	
sentirais	sentirions	aurais senti	aurions senti
sentirais	sentiriez	aurais senti	auriez senti
sentirait	sentiraient	aurait senti	auraient senti
6 présent du subjonctif		13 passé du subjonctif	
sente	sentions	aie senti	ayons senti
sentes	sentiez	ales senti	ayez senti
sente	sentent	ait senti	aient senti
7 imparfait du subjonctif		14 plus-que-parfait du subjonctif	
sentisse	sentissions	eusse senti	eussions senti
sentisses	sentissiez	eusses senti	eussiez senti
sentît	sentissent	eût senti	eussent senti

Impératif
sens
sentons
sentez

---

un sentiment   feeling, sense, impression
sentimental, sentimentale   sentimental
la sentimentalité   sentimentality
sentir le chagrin   to feel sorrow
se sentir + adj.   to feel + adj.;
   Je me sens malade.   I feel sick.

sentir bon   to smell good
sentir mauvais   to smell bad
faire sentir qqch à qqn   to make someone feel something
se faire sentir   to make itself felt
ne se sentir pas bien   not to feel well; **Je ne me sens pas bien.**   I don't feel well.

servir	Part. pr. **servant**	Part. passé **servi**

to serve, to be useful

The Seven Simple Tenses		The Seven Compound Tenses	
Singular	Plural	Singular	Plural
1 présent de l'indicatif		8 passé composé	
sers	servons	ai servi	avons servi
sers	servez	as servi	avez servi
sert	servent	a servi	ont servi
2 imparfait de l'indicatif		9 plus-que-parfait de l'indicatif	
servais	servions	avais servi	avions servi
servais	serviez	avais servi	aviez servi
servait	servaient	avait servi	avaient servi
3 passé simple		10 passé antérieur	
servis	servîmes	eus servi	eûmes servi
servis	servîtes	eus servi	eûtes servi
servit	servirent	eut servi	eurent servi
4 futur		11 futur antérieur	
servirai	servirons	aurai servi	aurons servi
serviras	servirez	auras servi	aurez servi
servira	serviront	aura servi	auront servi
5 conditionnel		12 conditionnel passé	
servirais	servirions	aurais servi	aurions servi
servirais	serviriez	aurais servi	auriez servi
servirait	serviraient	aurait servi	auraient servi
6 présent du subjonctif		13 passé du subjonctif	
serve	servions	aie servi	ayons servi
serves	serviez	aies servi	ayez servi
serve	servent	ait servi	aient servi
7 imparfait du subjonctif		14 plus-que-parfait du subjonctif	
servisse	servissions	eusse servi	eussions servi
servisses	servissiez	eusses servi	eussiez servi
servît	servissent	eût servi	eussent servi

Impératif
sers
servons
servez

---

le serveur waiter	**se servir** to serve oneself, to help oneself
la serveuse waitress	**se servir de qqch** to use something, to
le service service	avail oneself of something, to
une serviette napkin	make use of something
un serviteur servant	**servir à qqch** to be of some use
la servitude servitude	**servir à rien** to be of no use; **Cela**
desservir to clear off the table	**ne sert à rien.** That serves no purpose.

to serve oneself, to help oneself (to food and drink)

The Seven Simple Tenses		The Seven Compound Tenses	
Singular	Plural	Singular	Plural
1 présent de l'indicatif		8 passé composé	
me sers	nous servons	me suis servi(e)	nous sommes servi(e)s
te sers	vous servez	t'es servi(e)	vous êtes servi(e)(s)
se sert	se servent	s'est servi(e)	se sont servi(e)s
2 imparfait de l'indicatif		9 plus-que-parfait de l'indicatif	
me servais	nous servions	m'étais servi(e)	nous étions servi(e)s
te servais	vous serviez	t'étais servi(e)	vous étiez servi(e)(s)
se servait	se servaient	s'était servi(e)	s'étaient servi(e)s
3 passé simple		10 passé antérieur	
me servis	nous servîmes	me fus servi(e)	nous fûmes servi(e)s
te servis	vous servîtes	te fus servi(e)	vous fûtes servi(e)(s)
se servit	se servirent	se fut servi(e)	se furent servi(e)s
4 futur		11 futur antérieur	
me servirai	nous servirons	me serai servi(e)	nous serons servi(e)s
te serviras	vous servirez	te seras servi(e)	vous serez servi(e)(s)
se servira	se serviront	se sera servi(e)	se seront servi(e)s
5 conditionnel		12 conditionnel passé	
me servirais	nous servirions	me serais servi(e)	nous serions servi(e)s
te servirais	vous serviriez	te serais servi(e)	vous seriez servi(e)(s)
se servirait	se serviraient	se serait servi(e)	se seraient servi(e)s
6 présent du subjonctif		13 passé du subjonctif	
me serve	nous servions	me sois servi(e)	nous soyons servi(e)s
te serves	vous serviez	te sois servi(e)	vous soyez servi(e)(s)
se serve	se servent	se soit servi(e)	se soient servi(e)s
7 imparfait du subjonctif		14 plus-que-parfait du subjonctif	
me servisse	nous servissions	me fusse servi(e)	nous fussions servi(e)s
te servisses	vous servissiez	te fusses servi(e)	vous fussiez servi(e)(s)
se servît	se servissent	se fût servi(e)	se fussent servi(e)s

	Impératif
	sers-toi; ne te sers pas
	servons-nous; ne nous servons pas
	servez-vous; ne vous servez pas

un serviteur servant	se servir de qqch to use something, to
la servitude servitude	make use of something
le serveur waiter	se servir to serve oneself, to help
la serveuse waitress	oneself; **Servez-vous, je vous en**
le service service	**prie!** Help yourself, please!
une serviette napkin	**Est-ce qu'on se sert seul dans ce restaurant?**
	—Oui, c'est un restaurant self-service.

See also **servir**.

songer Part. pr. **songeant** Part. passé **songé**

to dream, to think

The Seven Simple Tenses		The Seven Compound Tenses	
Singular	Plural	Singular	Plural
1 présent de l'indicatif		8 passé composé	
songe	songeons	ai songé	avons songé
songes	songez	as songé	avez songé
songe	songent	a songé	ont songé
2 imparfait de l'indicatif		9 plus-que-parfait de l'indicatif	
songeais	songions	avais songé	avions songé
songeais	songiez	avais songé	aviez songé
songeait	songeaient	avait songé	avaient songé
3 passé simple		10 passé antérieur	
songeai	songeâmes	eus songé	eûmes songé
songeas	songeâtes	eus songé	eûtes songé
songea	songèrent	eut songé	eurent songé
4 futur		11 futur antérieur	
songerai	songerons	aurai songé	aurons songé
songeras	songerez	auras songé	aurez songé
songera	songeront	aura songé	auront songé
5 conditionnel		12 conditionnel passé	
songerais	songerions	aurais songé	aurions songé
songerais	songeriez	aurais songé	auriez songé
songerait	songeraient	aurait songé	auraient songé
6 présent du subjonctif		13 passé du subjonctif	
songe	songions	aie songé	ayons songé
songes	songiez	aies songé	ayez songé
songe	songent	ait songé	aient songé
7 imparfait du subjonctif		14 plus-que-parfait du subjonctif	
songeasse	songeassions	eusse songé	eussions songé
songeasses	songeassiez	eusses songé	eussiez songé
songeât	songeassent	eût songé	eussent songé
		Impératif	
		songe	
		songeons	
		songez	

un songe dream	**songer à** to think of something, to
un songeur, une songeuse dreamer	give thought to something
songer à l'avenir to think of the future	**Songez-y bien!** Think it over carefully!
faire un songe to have a dream	

268

to ring

The Seven Simple Tenses		The Seven Compound Tenses	
Singular	Plural	Singular	Plural
1 présent de l'indicatif		8 passé composé	
sonne	sonnons	ai sonné	avons sonné
sonnes	sonnez	as sonné	avez sonné
sonne	sonnent	a sonné	ont sonné
2 imparfait de l'indicatif		9 plus-que-parfait de l'indicatif	
sonnais	sonnions	avais sonné	avions sonné
sonnais	sonniez	avais sonné	aviez sonné
sonnait	sonnaient	avait sonné	avaient sonné
3 passé simple		10 passé antérieur	
sonnai	sonnâmes	eus sonné	eûmes sonné
sonnas	sonnâtes	eus sonné	eûtes sonné
sonna	sonnèrent	eut sonné	eurent sonné
4 futur		11 futur antérieur	
sonnerai	sonnerons	aurai sonné	aurons sonné
sonneras	sonnerez	auras sonné	aurez sonné
sonnera	sonneront	aura sonné	auront sonné
5 conditionnel		12 conditionnel passé	
sonnerais	sonnerions	aurais sonné	aurions sonné
sonnerais	sonneriez	aurais sonné	auriez sonné
sonnerait	sonneraient	aurait sonné	auraient sonné
6 présent du subjonctif		13 passé du subjonctif	
sonne	sonnions	aie sonné	ayons sonné
sonnes	sonniez	aies sonné	ayez sonné
sonne	sonnent	ait sonné	aient sonné
7 imparfait du subjonctif		14 plus-que-parfait du subjonctif	
sonnasse	sonnassions	eusse sonné	eussions sonné
sonnasses	sonnassiez	eusses sonné	eussiez sonné
sonnât	sonnassent	eût sonné	eussent sonné

Impératif
sonne
sonnons
sonnez

une sonnerie ringing, chiming	**sonner creux** to sound hollow
une sonnette house bell, hand bell	**une sonnerie d'alarme** alarm bell
une sonnette électrique electric bell	**faire sonner un mot** to emphasize a word
le son sound, ringing	

sortir	Part. pr. **sortant**	Part. passé **sorti(e)(s)**

to go out, to leave

The Seven Simple Tenses		The Seven Compound Tenses	
Singular	Plural	Singular	Plural
1 présent de l'indicatif		8 passé composé	
sors	sortons	suis sorti(e)	sommes sorti(e)s
sors	sortez	es sorti(e)	êtes sorti(e)(s)
sort	sortent	est sorti(e)	sont sorti(e)s
2 imparfait de l'indicatif		9 plus-que-parfait de l'indicatif	
sortais	sortions	étais sorti(e)	étions sorti(e)s
sortais	sortiez	étais sorti(e)	étiez sorti(e)(s)
sortait	sortaient	était sorti(e)	étaient sorti(e)s
3 passé simple		10 passé antérieur	
sortis	sortîmes	fus sorti(e)	fûmes sorti(e)s
sortis	sortîtes	fus sorti(e)	fûtes sorti(e)(s)
sortit	sortirent	fut sorti(e)	furent sorti(e)s
4 futur		11 futur antérieur	
sortirai	sortirons	serai sorti(e)	serons sorti(e)s
sortiras	sortirez	seras sorti(e)	serez sorti(e)(s)
sortira	sortiront	sera sorti(e)	seront sorti(e)s
5 conditionnel		12 conditionnel passé	
sortirais	sortirions	serais sorti(e)	serions sorti(e)s
sortirais	sortiriez	serais sorti(e)	seriez sorti(e)(s)
sortirait	sortiraient	serait sorti(e)	seraient sorti(e)s
6 présent du subjonctif		13 passé du subjonctif	
sorte	sortions	sois sorti(e)	soyons sorti(e)s
sortes	sortiez	sois sorti(e)	soyez sorti(e)(s)
sorte	sortent	soit sorti(e)	soient sorti(e)s
7 imparfait du subjonctif		14 plus-que-parfait du subjonctif	
sortisse	sortissions	fusse sorti(e)	fussions sorti(e)s
sortisses	sortissiez	fusses sorti(e)	fussiez sorti(e)(s)
sortît	sortissent	fût sorti(e)	fussent sorti(e)s
		Impératif	
		sors	
		sortons	
		sortez	

This verb is conjugated with **avoir** when it has a direct object.

Example: **Elle a sorti son mouchoir.** She took out her handkerchief.
BUT: **Elle est sortie hier soir.** She went out last night.

ressortir to go out again
une sortie exit;
  une sortie de secours
  emergency exit

sortir du lit to get out of bed
se sortir d'une situation to get
  oneself out of a situation

to blow, to pant, to prompt (an actor/actress with a cue)

The Seven Simple Tenses		The Seven Compound Tenses	
Singular	Plural	Singular	Plural
1 présent de l'indicatif		8 passé composé	
souffle	soufflons	ai soufflé	avons soufflé
souffles	soufflez	as soufflé	avez soufflé
souffle	soufflent	a soufflé	ont soufflé
2 imparfait de l'indicatif		9 plus-que-parfait de l'indicatif	
soufflais	soufflions	avais soufflé	avions soufflé
soufflais	souffliez	avais soufflé	aviez soufflé
soufflait	soufflaient	avait soufflé	avaient soufflé
3 passé simple		10 passé antérieur	
soufflai	soufflâmes	eus soufflé	eûmes soufflé
soufflas	soufflâtes	eus soufflé	eûtes soufflé
souffla	soufflèrent	eut soufflé	eurent soufflé
4 futur		11 futur antérieur	
soufflerai	soufflerons	aurai soufflé	aurons soufflé
souffleras	soufflerez	auras soufflé	aurez soufflé
soufflera	souffleront	aura soufflé	auront soufflé
5 conditionnel		12 conditionnel passé	
soufflerais	soufflerions	aurais soufflé	aurions soufflé
soufflerais	souffleriez	aurais soufflé	auriez soufflé
soufflerait	souffleraient	aurait soufflé	auraient soufflé
6 présent du subjonctif		13 passé du subjonctif	
souffle	soufflions	aie soufflé	ayons soufflé
souffles	souffliez	aies soufflé	ayez soufflé
souffle	soufflent	ait soufflé	aient soufflé
7 imparfait du subjonctif		14 plus-que-parfait du subjonctif	
soufflasse	soufflassions	eusse soufflé	eussions soufflé
soufflasses	soufflassiez	eusses soufflé	eussiez soufflé
soufflât	soufflassent	eût soufflé	eussent soufflé
		Impératif	
		souffle	
		soufflons	
		soufflez	

le souffle   breath, breathing
à bout de souffle   out of breath
retenir son souffle   to hold one's breath
couper le souffle à qqn   to take someone's breath away

souffrir	Part. pr. **souffrant**	Part. passé **souffert**

to suffer, to endure

The Seven Simple Tenses		The Seven Compound Tenses	
Singular	Plural	Singular	Plural
1 présent de l'indicatif		8 passé composé	
souffre	souffrons	ai souffert	avons souffert
souffres	souffrez	as souffert	avez souffert
souffre	souffrent	a souffert	ont souffert
2 imparfait de l'indicatif		9 plus-que-parfait de l'indicatif	
souffrais	souffrions	avais souffert	avions souffert
souffrais	souffriez	avais souffert	aviez souffert
souffrait	souffraient	avait souffert	avaient souffert
3 passé simple		10 passé antérieur	
souffris	souffrîmes	eus souffert	eûmes souffert
souffris	souffrîtes	eus souffert	eûtes souffert
souffrit	souffrirent	eut souffert	eurent souffert
4 futur		11 futur antérieur	
souffrirai	souffrirons	aurai souffert	aurons souffert
souffriras	souffrirez	auras souffert	aurez souffert
souffrira	souffriront	aura souffert	auront souffert
5 conditionnel		12 conditionnel passé	
souffrirais	souffririons	aurais souffert	aurions souffert
souffrirais	souffririez	aurais souffert	auriez souffert
souffrirait	souffriraient	aurait souffert	auraient souffert
6 présent du subjonctif		13 passé du subjonctif	
souffre	souffrions	aie souffert	ayons souffert
souffres	souffriez	aies souffert	ayez souffert
souffre	souffrent	ait souffert	aient souffert
7 imparfait du subjonctif		14 plus-que-parfait du subjonctif	
souffrisse	souffrissions	eusse souffert	eussions souffert
souffrisses	souffrissiez	eusses souffert	eussiez souffert
souffrît	souffrissent	eût souffert	eussent souffert

	Impératif
	souffre
	souffrons
	souffrez

la souffrance suffering
souffrant, souffrante ailing, sick
souffreteux, souffreteuse sickly, feeble

souffrir le froid to withstand the cold
Cela me fait souffrir. That hurts me.

to wish

The Seven Simple Tenses		The Seven Compound Tenses	
Singular	Plural	Singular	Plural
1 présent de l'indicatif		**8 passé composé**	
souhaite	souhaitons	ai souhaité	avons souhaité
souhaites	souhaitez	as souhaité	avez souhaité
souhaite	souhaitent	a souhaité	ont souhaité
2 imparfait de l'indicatif		**9 plus-que-parfait de l'indicatif**	
souhaitais	souhaitions	avais souhaité	avions souhaité
souhaitais	souhaitiez	avais souhaité	aviez souhaité
souhaitait	souhaitaient	avait souhaité	avaient souhaité
3 passé simple		**10 passé antérieur**	
souhaitai	souhaitâmes	eus souhaité	eûmes souhaité
souhaltas	souhaitâtes	eus souhaité	eûtes souhaité
souhaita	souhaitèrent	eut souhaité	eurent souhaité
4 futur		**11 futur antérieur**	
souhaiteral	souhaiterons	aurai souhaité	aurons souhaité
souhaiteras	souhaiterez	auras souhaité	aurez souhaité
souhaitera	souhaiteront	aura souhaité	auront souhaité
5 conditionnel		**12 conditionnel passé**	
souhaiterais	souhaiterions	aurais souhaité	aurions souhaité
souhaiterais	souhaiteriez	aurais souhaité	auriez souhaité
souhaiterait	souhaiteraient	aurait souhaité	auraient souhaité
6 présent du subjonctif		**13 passé du subjonctif**	
souhaite	souhaitions	aie souhaité	ayons souhaité
souhaites	souhaitiez	aies souhaité	ayez souhalté
souhaite	souhaitent	ait souhaité	aient souhaité
7 imparfait du subjonctif		**14 plus-que-parfait du subjonctif**	
souhaitasse	souhaitassions	eusse souhaité	eussions souhaité
souhaitasses	souhaitassiez	eusses souhaité	eussiez souhaité
souhaitât	souhaitassent	eût souhaité	eussent souhaité
		Impératif	
		souhaite	
		souhaitons	
		souhaitez	

---

un souhait   a wish
à souhait   to one's liking
souhaits de bonne année   New Year's greetings
souhaiter bon voyage à qqn   to wish someone a good trip

souhaiter la bienvenue à qqn   to welcome someone
souhaiter le bonjour à qqn   to greet someone
souhaitable   desirable

to submit

The Seven Simple Tenses		The Seven Compound Tenses	
Singular	Plural	Singular	Plural
1 présent de l'indicatif		8 passé composé	
soumets	soumettons	ai soumis	avons soumis
soumets	soumettez	as soumis	avez soumis
soumet	soumettent	a soumis	ont soumis
2 imparfait de l'indicatif		9 plus-que-parfait de l'indicatif	
soumettais	soumettions	avais soumis	avions soumis
soumettais	soumettiez	avais soumis	aviez soumis
soumettait	soumettaient	avait soumis	avaient soumis
3 passé simple		10 passé antérieur	
soumis	soumîmes	eus soumis	eûmes soumis
soumis	soumîtes	eus soumis	eûtes soumis
soumit	soumirent	eut soumis	eurent soumis
4 futur		11 futur antérieur	
soumettrai	soumettrons	aurai soumis	aurons soumis
soumettras	soumettrez	auras soumis	aurez soumis
soumettra	soumettront	aura soumis	auront soumis
5 conditionnel		12 conditionnel passé	
soumettrais	soumettrions	aurais soumis	aurions soumis
soumettrais	soumettriez	aurais soumis	auriez soumis
soumettrait	soumettraient	aurait soumis	auraient soumis
6 présent du subjonctif		13 passé du subjonctif	
soumette	soumettions	aie soumis	ayons soumis
soumettes	soumettiez	aies soumis	ayez soumis
soumette	soumettent	ait soumis	aient soumis
7 imparfait du subjonctif		14 plus-que-parfait du subjonctif	
soumisse	soumissions	eusse soumis	eussions soumis
soumisses	soumissiez	eusses soumis	eussiez soumis
soumît	soumissent	eût soumis	eussent soumis
		Impératif	
		soumets	
		soumettons	
		soumettez	

se soumettre à   to give in to, to comply with
se soumettre à une décision   to comply with a decision
la soumission   submission

See also **mettre** and compounds of **mettre,** e.g., **promettre.**

to smile

The Seven Simple Tenses		The Seven Compound Tenses	
Singular	Plural	Singular	Plural
1 présent de l'indicatif		8 passé composé	
souris	**sourions**	**ai souri**	**avons souri**
souris	**souriez**	**as souri**	**avez souri**
sourit	**sourient**	**a souri**	**ont souri**
2 imparfait de l'indicatif		9 plus-que-parfait de l'indicatif	
souriais	**souriions**	**avais souri**	**avions souri**
souriais	**souriiez**	**avais souri**	**aviez souri**
souriait	**souriaient**	**avait souri**	**avaient souri**
3 passé simple		10 passé antérieur	
souris	**sourîmes**	**eus souri**	**eûmes souri**
souris	**sourîtes**	**eus souri**	**eûtes souri**
sourit	**sourirent**	**eut souri**	**eurent souri**
4 futur		11 futur antérieur	
sourirai	**sourirons**	**aurai souri**	**aurons souri**
souriras	**sourirez**	**auras souri**	**aurez souri**
sourira	**souriront**	**aura souri**	**auront souri**
5 conditionnel		12 conditionnel passé	
sourirais	**souririons**	**aurais souri**	**aurions souri**
sourirais	**souririez**	**aurais souri**	**auriez souri**
sourirait	**souriraient**	**aurait souri**	**auraient souri**
6 présent du subjonctif		13 passé du subjonctif	
sourie	**souriions**	**aie souri**	**ayons souri**
souries	**souriiez**	**aies souri**	**ayez souri**
sourie	**sourient**	**ait souri**	**aient souri**
7 imparfait du subjonctif		14 plus-que-parfait du subjonctif	
sourisse	**sourissions**	**eusse souri**	**eussions souri**
sourisses	**sourissiez**	**eusses souri**	**eussiez souri**
sourît	**sourissent**	**eût souri**	**eussent souri**
		Impératif	
		souris	
		sourions	
		souriez	

un sourire a smile
Gardez le sourire!   Keep smiling!
un large sourire a broad smile
le rire laughter

See also **rire**.

sourire à   to favor, to be favorable to, to smile on; **Claudine est heureuse; la vie lui sourit.**

se souvenir   Part. pr. **se souvenant**   Part. passé **souvenu(e)(s)**

to remember, to recall

The Seven Simple Tenses		The Seven Compound Tenses	
Singular	Plural	Singular	Plural
1 présent de l'indicatif		8 passé composé	
me souviens	nous souvenons	me suis	nous sommes
te souviens	vous souvenez	t'es	vous êtes + souvenu(e)(s)
se souvient	se souviennent	s'est	se sont
2 imparfait de l'indicatif		9 plus-que-parfait de l'indicatif	
me souvenais	nous souvenions	m'étais	nous étions
te souvenais	vous souveniez	t'étais	vous étiez + souvenu(e)(s)
se souvenait	se souvenaient	s'était	s'étaient
3 passé simple		10 passé antérieur	
me souvins	nous souvînmes	me fus	nous fûmes
te souvins	vous souvîntes	te fus	vous fûtes + souvenu(e)(s)
se souvint	se souvinrent	se fut	se furent
4 futur		11 futur antérieur	
me souviendrai	nous souviendrons	me serai	nous serons
te souviendras	vous souviendrez	te seras	vous serez + souvenu(e)(s)
se souviendra	se souviendront	se sera	se seront
5 conditionnel		12 conditionnel passé	
me souviendrais	nous souviendrions	me serais	nous serions
te souviendrais	vous souviendriez	te serais	vous seriez + souvenu(e)(s)
se souviendrait	se souviendraient	se serait	se seraient
6 présent du subjonctif		13 passé du subjonctif	
me souvienne	nous souvenions	me sois	nous soyons
te souviennes	vous souveniez	te sois	vous soyez + souvenu(e)(s)
se souvienne	se souviennent	se soit	se soient
7 imparfait du subjonctif		14 plus-que-parfait du subjonctif	
me souvinsse	nous souvinssions	me fusse	nous fussions
te souvinsses	vous souvinssiez	te fusses	vous fussiez + souvenu(e)(s)
se souvînt	se souvinssent	se fût	se fussent

Impératif
souviens-toi; ne te souviens pas
souvenons-nous; ne nous souvenons pas
souvenez-vous; ne vous souvenez pas

---

un souvenir   souvenir, remembrance
Je m'en souviendrai!   I'll remember that! I won't forget that!
se souvenir de qqn ou de qqch   to remember someone or something

to suffice, to be sufficient, to be enough

The Seven Simple Tenses	The Seven Compound Tenses
Singular	Singular
1 présent de l'indicatif **il suffit**	8 passé composé **il a suffi**
2 imparfait de l'indicatif **il suffisait**	9 plus-que-parfait de l'indicatif **il avait suffi**
3 passé simple **il suffit**	10 passé antérieur **il eut suffi**
4 futur **il suffira**	11 futur antérieur **il aura suffi**
5 conditionnel **il suffirait**	12 conditionnel passé **il aurait suffi**
6 présent du subjonctif **qu'il suffise**	13 passé du subjonctif **qu'il ait suffi**
7 imparfait du subjonctif **qu'il suffît**	14 plus-que-parfait du subjonctif **qu'il eût suffi**

Impératif
Qu'il suffise!   (Enough!)

---

la suffisance sufficiency
suffisamment sufficiently
Cela suffit!   That's quite enough!
Suffit!   Enough! Stop it!

Ma famille suffit à mon bonheur.
   My family is enough for my happiness.

suivre	Part. pr. **suivant**	Part. passé **suivi**

to follow

The Seven Simple Tenses		The Seven Compound Tenses	
Singular	Plural	Singular	Plural
1 présent de l'indicatif		8 passé composé	
suis	suivons	ai suivi	avons suivi
suis	suivez	as suivi	avez suivi
suit	suivent	a suivi	ont suivi
2 imparfait de l'indicatif		9 plus-que-parfait de l'indicatif	
suivais	suivions	avais suivi	avions suivi
suivais	suiviez	avais suivi	aviez suivi
suivait	suivaient	avait suivi	avaient suivi
3 passé simple		10 passé antérieur	
suivis	suivîmes	eus suivi	eûmes suivi
suivis	suivîtes	eus suivi	eûtes suivi
suivit	suivirent	eut suivi	eurent suivi
4 futur		11 futur antérieur	
suivrai	suivrons	aurai suivi	aurons suivi
suivras	suivrez	auras suivi	aurez suivi
suivra	suivront	aura suivi	auront suivi
5 conditionnel		12 conditionnel passé	
suivrais	suivrions	aurais suivi	aurions suivi
suivrais	suivriez	aurais suivi	auriez suivi
suivrait	suivraient	aurait suivi	auraient suivi
6 présent du subjonctif		13 passé du subjonctif	
suive	suivions	aie suivi	ayons suivi
suives	suiviez	aies suivi	ayez suivi
suive	suivent	ait suivi	aient suivi
7 imparfait du subjonctif		14 plus-que-parfait du subjonctif	
suivisse	suivissions	eusse suivi	eussions suivi
suivisses	suivissiez	eusses suivi	eussiez suivi
suivît	suivissent	eût suivi	eussent suivi

Impératif
suis
suivons
suivez

---

suivant according to
suivant que. . . according as. . .
la suite continuation
à la suite de coming after
de suite in succession, right away
à suivre to be continued

le jour suivant on the following day
les questions suivantes the following questions
tout de suite immediately
suivre un cours to take a course

to be silent, to be quiet, not to speak

The Seven Simple Tenses		The Seven Compound Tenses	
Singular	Plural	Singular	Plural
1 présent de l'indicatif		8 passé composé	
me tais	nous taisons	me suis tu(e)	nous sommes tu(e)s
te tais	vous taisez	t'es tu(e)	vous êtes tu(e)(s)
se tait	se taisent	s'est tu(e)	se sont tu(e)s
2 imparfait de l'indicatif		9 plus-que-parfait de l'indicatif	
me taisais	nous taisions	m'étais tu(e)	nous étions tu(e)s
te taisais	vous taisiez	t'étais tu(e)	vous étiez tu(e)(s)
se taisait	se taisaient	s'était tu(e)	s'étaient tu(e)s
3 passé simple		10 passé antérieur	
me tus	nous tûmes	me fus tu(e)	nous fûmes tu(e)s
te tus	vous tûtes	te fus tu(e)	vous fûtes tu(e)(s)
se tut	se turent	se fut tu(e)	se furent tu(e)s
4 futur		11 futur antérieur	
me tairai	nous tairons	me serai tu(e)	nous serons tu(e)s
te tairas	vous tairez	te seras tu(e)	vous serez tu(e)(s)
se taira	se tairont	se sera tu(e)	se seront tu(e)s
5 conditionnel		12 conditionnel passé	
me tairais	nous tairions	me serais tu(e)	nous serions tu(e)s
te tairais	vous tairiez	te serais tu(e)	vous seriez tu(e)(s)
se tairait	se tairaient	se serait tu(e)	se seraient tu(e)s
6 présent du subjonctif		13 passé du subjonctif	
me taise	nous taisions	me sois tu(e)	nous soyons tu(e)s
te taises	vous taisiez	te sois tu(e)	vous soyez tu(e)(s)
se taise	se taisent	se soit tu(e)	se soient tu(e)s
7 imparfait du subjonctif		14 plus-que-parfait du subjonctif	
me tusse	nous tussions	me fusse tu(e)	nous fussions tu(e)s
te tusses	vous tussiez	te fusses tu(e)	vous fussiez tu(e)(s)
se tût	se tussent	se fût tu(e)	se fussent tu(e)s

Impératif
tais-toi; ne te tais pas
taisons-nous; ne nous taisons pas
taisez-vous; ne vous taisez pas

—Marie, veux-tu te taire! Tu es trop bavarde. Et toi, Hélène, tais-toi aussi.
Les deux élèves ne se taisent pas. La maîtresse de chimie continue:
—Taisez-vous, je vous dis, toutes les deux; autrement, vous resterez dans cette salle après la classe.
Les deux jeunes filles se sont tues.

See also **bavarder** and **cesser**.

to telephone

The Seven Simple Tenses		The Seven Compound Tenses	
Singular	Plural	Singular	Plural
1 présent de l'indicatif		8 passé composé	
téléphone	téléphonons	ai téléphoné	avons téléphoné
téléphones	téléphonez	as téléphoné	avez téléphoné
téléphone	téléphonent	a téléphoné	ont téléphoné
2 imparfait de l'indicatif		9 plus-que-parfait de l'indicatif	
téléphonais	téléphonions	avais téléphoné	avions téléphoné
téléphonais	téléphoniez	avais téléphoné	aviez téléphoné
téléphonait	téléphonaient	avait téléphoné	avaient téléphoné
3 passé simple		10 passé antérieur	
téléphonai	téléphonâmes	eus téléphoné	eûmes téléphoné
téléphonas	téléphonâtes	eus téléphoné	eûtes téléphoné
téléphona	téléphonèrent	eut téléphoné	eurent téléphoné
4 futur		11 futur antérieur	
téléphonerai	téléphonerons	aurai téléphoné	aurons téléphoné
téléphoneras	téléphonerez	auras téléphoné	aurez téléphoné
téléphonera	téléphoneront	aura téléphoné	auront téléphoné
5 conditionnel		12 conditionnel passé	
téléphonerais	téléphonerions	aurais téléphoné	aurions téléphoné
téléphonerais	téléphoneriez	aurais téléphoné	auriez téléphoné
téléphonerait	téléphoneraient	aurait téléphoné	auraient téléphoné
6 présent du subjonctif		13 passé du subjonctif	
téléphone	téléphonions	aie téléphoné	ayons téléphoné
téléphones	téléphoniez	aies téléphoné	ayez téléphoné
téléphone	téléphonent	ait téléphoné	aient téléphoné
7 imparfait du subjonctif		14 plus-que-parfait du subjonctif	
téléphonasse	téléphonassions	eusse téléphoné	eussions téléphoné
téléphonasses	téléphonassiez	eusses téléphoné	eussiez téléphoné
téléphonât	téléphonassent	eût téléphoné	eussent téléphoné

Impératif
téléphone
téléphonons
téléphonez

---

le téléphone   telephone
téléphonique   telephonic
téléphoniquement   telephonically
  (by telephone)
un, une téléphoniste   telephone operator

téléphoner à qqn
  to telephone someone
Marie? Je lui ai téléphoné hier.
  Mary? I telephoned her yesterday.

to hold, to grasp

The Seven Simple Tenses		The Seven Compound Tenses	
Singular	Plural	Singular	Plural
1 présent de l'indicatif		8 passé composé	
tiens	**tenons**	**ai tenu**	**avons tenu**
tiens	**tenez**	**as tenu**	**avez tenu**
tient	**tiennent**	**a tenu**	**ont tenu**
2 imparfait de l'indicatif		9 plus-que-parfait de l'indicatif	
tenais	**tenions**	**avais tenu**	**avions tenu**
tenais	**teniez**	**avais tenu**	**aviez tenu**
tenait	**tenaient**	**avait tenu**	**avaient tenu**
3 passé simple		10 passé antérieur	
tins	**tînmes**	**eus tenu**	**eûmes tenu**
tins	**tîntes**	**eus tenu**	**eûtes tenu**
tint	**tinrent**	**eut tenu**	**eurent tenu**
4 futur		11 futur antérieur	
tiendrai	**tiendrons**	**aurai tenu**	**aurons tenu**
tiendras	**tiendrez**	**auras tenu**	**aurez tenu**
tiendra	**tiendront**	**aura tenu**	**auront tenu**
5 conditionnel		12 conditionnel passé	
tiendrais	**tiendrions**	**aurais tenu**	**aurions tenu**
tiendrais	**tiendriez**	**aurais tenu**	**auriez tenu**
tiendrait	**tiendraient**	**aurait tenu**	**auraient tenu**
6 présent du subjonctif		13 passé du subjonctif	
tienne	**tenions**	**aie tenu**	**ayons tenu**
tiennes	**teniez**	**aies tenu**	**ayez tenu**
tienne	**tiennent**	**ait tenu**	**aient tenu**
7 imparfait du subjonctif		14 plus-que-parfait du subjonctif	
tinsse	**tinssions**	**eusse tenu**	**eussions tenu**
tinsses	**tinssiez**	**eusses tenu**	**eussiez tenu**
tînt	**tinssent**	**eût tenu**	**eussent tenu**

	Impératif
	tiens
	tenons
	tenez

---

tenir de qqn   to take after (to favor) someone;
   Robert tient de son père.   Robert takes
   after his father.
tenir de bonne source   to have on good authority
tenir à qqch   to cherish something

tenir le pari   to take on the bet
Tiens! Voilà Bob!
   Look! There's Bob!

terminer   Part. pr. **terminant**   Part. passé **terminé**

to terminate, to finish, to end

The Seven Simple Tenses		The Seven Compound Tenses	
Singular	Plural	Singular	Plural
1 présent de l'indicatif		8 passé composé	
termine	terminons	ai terminé	avons teminé
termines	terminez	as terminé	avez terminé
termine	terminent	a terminé	ont terminé
2 imparfait de l'indicatif		9 plus-que-parfait de l'indicatif	
terminais	terminions	avais terminé	avions terminé
terminais	terminiez	avais terminé	aviez terminé
terminait	terminaient	avait terminé	avaient terminé
3 passé simple		10 passé antérieur	
terminai	terminâmes	eus terminé	eûmes terminé
terminas	terminâtes	eus terminé	eûtes terminé
termina	terminèrent	eut terminé	eurent terminé
4 futur		11 futur antérieur	
terminerai	terminerons	aurai terminé	aurons terminé
termineras	terminerez	auras terminé	aurez terminé
terminera	termineront	aura terminé	auront terminé
5 conditionnel		12 conditionnel passé	
terminerais	terminerions	aurais terminé	aurions terminé
terminerais	termineriez	aurais terminé	auriez terminé
terminerait	termineraient	aurait terminé	auraient terminé
6 présent du subjonctif		13 passé du subjonctif	
termine	terminions	aie terminé	ayons terminé
termines	terminiez	aies terminé	ayez terminé
termine	terminent	ait terminé	aient terminé
7 imparfait du subjonctif		14 plus-que-parfait du subjonctif	
terminasse	terminassions	eusse terminé	eussions terminé
terminasses	terminassiez	eusses terminé	eussiez terminé
terminât	terminassent	eût terminé	eussent terminé
		Impératif	
		termine	
		terminons	
		terminez	

---

terminal, terminale terminal
la terminaison ending, termination
terminable terminable
interminable interminable, endless
exterminer to exterminate

se terminer to end (itself)
se terminer en to end in; **un verbe qui se termine en** *er. . .* a verb that ends in *er. . .*

to fall

The Seven Simple Tenses		The Seven Compound Tenses	
Singular	Plural	Singular	Plural
1 présent de l'indicatif		8 passé composé	
tombe	tombons	suis tombé(e)	sommes tombé(e)s
tombes	tombez	es tombé(e)	êtes tombé(e)(s)
tombe	tombent	est tombé(e)	sont tombé(e)s
2 imparfait de l'indicatif		9 plus-que-parfait de l'indicatif	
tombais	tombions	étais tombé(e)	étions tombé(e)s
tombais	tombiez	étais tombé(e)	étiez tombé(e)(s)
tombait	tombaient	était tombé(e)	étaient tombé(e)s
3 passé simple		10 passé antérieur	
tombai	tombâmes	fus tombé(e)	fûmes tombé(e)s
tombas	tombâtes	fus tombé(e)	fûtes tombé(e)(s)
tomba	tombèrent	fut tombé(e)	furent tombé(e)s
4 futur		11 futur antérieur	
tomberai	tomberons	serai tombé(e)	serons tombé(e)s
tomberas	tomberez	seras tombé(e)	serez tombé(e)(s)
tombera	tomberont	sera tombé(e)	seront tombé(e)s
5 conditionnel		12 conditionnel passé	
tomberais	tomberions	serais tombé(e)	serions tombé(e)s
tomberais	tomberiez	serais tombé(e)	seriez tombé(e)(s)
tomberait	tomberaient	serait tombé(e)	seraient tombé(e)s
6 présent du subjonctif		13 passé du subjonctif	
tombe	tombions	sois tombé(e)	soyons tombé(e)s
tombes	tombiez	sois tombé(e)	soyez tombé(e)(s)
tombe	tombent	soit tombé(e)	soient tombé(e)s
7 imparfait du subjonctif		14 plus-que-parfait du subjonctif	
tombasse	tombassions	fusse tombé(e)	fussions tombé(e)s
tombasses	tombassiez	fusses tombé(e)	fussiez tombé(e)(s)
tombât	tombassent	fût tombé(e)	fussent tombé(e)s

Impératif
tombe
tombons
tombez

---

tomber amoureux (amoureuse) de qqn
  to fall in love with someone
tomber sur to run into, to come across
laisser tomber to drop

tomber malade to fall sick
faire tomber to knock down
retomber to fall again

283

toucher   Part. pr. **touchant**   Part. passé **touché**

to touch, to affect

The Seven Simple Tenses		The Seven Compound Tenses	
Singular	Plural	Singular	Plural
1 présent de l'indicatif		8 passé composé	
touche	touchons	ai touché	avons touché
touches	touchez	as touché	avez touché
touche	touchent	a touché	ont touché
2 imparfait de l'indicatif		9 plus-que-parfait de l'indicatif	
touchais	touchions	avais touché	avions touché
touchais	touchiez	avais touché	aviez touché
touchait	touchaient	avait touché	avaient touché
3 passé simple		10 passé antérieur	
touchai	touchâmes	eus touché	eûmes touché
touchas	touchâtes	eus touché	eûtes touché
toucha	touchèrent	eut touché	eurent touché
4 futur		11 futur antérieur	
toucherai	toucherons	aurai touché	aurons touché
toucheras	toucherez	auras touché	aurez touché
touchera	toucheront	aura touché	auront touché
5 conditionnel		12 conditionnel passé	
toucherais	toucherions	aurais touché	aurions touché
toucherais	toucheriez	aurais touché	auriez touché
toucherait	toucheraient	aurait touché	auraient touché
6 présent du subjonctif		13 passé du subjonctif	
touche	touchions	aie touché	ayons touché
touches	touchiez	aies touché	ayez touché
touche	touchent	ait touché	aient touché
7 imparfait du subjonctif		14 plus-que-parfait du subjonctif	
touchasse	touchassions	eusse touché	eussions touché
touchasses	touchassiez	eusses touché	eussiez touché
touchât	touchassent	eût touché	eussent touché
		Impératif	
		touche	
		touchons	
		touchez	

Une personne qui touche à tout
  a meddlesome person
Touchez là!   Put it there! Shake!
toucher à qqch   to touch something
N'y touchez pas!   Don't touch!

le toucher   touch, feeling
toucher de l'argent   to get some money
Cela me touche profondément.
  That touches me deeply.

to turn

The Seven Simple Tenses		The Seven Compound Tenses	
Singular	Plural	Singular	Plural
1 présent de l'indicatif		8 passé composé	
tourne	**tournons**	**ai tourné**	**avons tourné**
tournes	**tournez**	**as tourné**	**avez tourné**
tourne	**tournent**	**a tourné**	**ont tourné**
2 imparfait de l'indicatif		9 plus-que-parfait de l'indicatif	
tournais	**tournions**	**avais tourné**	**avions tourné**
tournais	**tourniez**	**avais tourné**	**aviez tourné**
tournait	**tournaient**	**avait tourné**	**avaient tourné**
3 passé simple		10 passé antérieur	
tournai	**tournâmes**	**eus tourné**	**eûmes tourné**
tournas	**tournâtes**	**eus tourné**	**eûtes tourné**
tourna	**tournèrent**	**eut tourné**	**eurent tourné**
4 futur		11 futur antérieur	
tournerai	**tournerons**	**aurai tourné**	**aurons tourné**
tourneras	**tournerez**	**auras tourné**	**aurez tourné**
tournera	**tourneront**	**aura tourné**	**auront tourné**
5 conditionnel		12 conditionnel passé	
tournerais	**tournerions**	**aurais tourné**	**aurions tourné**
tournerais	**tourneriez**	**aurais tourné**	**auriez tourné**
tournerait	**tourneraient**	**aurait tourné**	**auraient tourné**
6 présent du subjonctif		13 passé du subjonctif	
tourne	**tournions**	**aie tourné**	**ayons tourné**
tournes	**tourniez**	**aies tourné**	**ayez tourné**
tourne	**tournent**	**ait tourné**	**aient tourné**
7 imparfait du subjonctif		14 plus-que-parfait du subjonctif	
tournasse	**tournassions**	**eusse tourné**	**eussions tourné**
tournasses	**tournassiez**	**eusses tourné**	**eussiez tourné**
tournât	**tournassent**	**eût tourné**	**eussent tourné**

Impératif
tourne
tournons
tournez

---

se tourner to turn around	**retourner** to return
tourner qqn en ridicule to ridicule someone	**tourner l'estomac à qqn** to turn someone's stomach
un tourne-disque record player **(des tourne-disques)**	**faire une tournée** to go on a tour **tourner autour du pot** to beat around the bush

traduire   Part. pr. **traduisant**   Part. passé **traduit**

to translate

The Seven Simple Tenses		The Seven Compound Tenses	
Singular	Plural	Singular	Plural
1 présent de l'indicatif		8 passé composé	
traduis	traduisons	ai traduit	avons traduit
traduis	traduisez	as traduit	avez traduit
traduit	traduisent	a traduit	ont traduit
2 imparfait de l'indicatif		9 plus-que-parfait de l'indicatif	
traduisais	traduisions	avais traduit	avions traduit
traduisais	traduisiez	avais traduit	aviez traduit
traduisait	traduisaient	avait traduit	avaient traduit
3 passé simple		10 passé antérieur	
traduisis	traduisîmes	eus traduit	eûmes traduit
traduisis	traduisîtes	eus traduit	eûtes traduit
traduisit	traduisirent	eut traduit	eurent traduit
4 futur		11 futur antérieur	
traduirai	traduirons	aurai traduit	aurons traduit
traduiras	traduirez	auras traduit	aurez traduit
traduira	traduiront	aura traduit	auront traduit
5 conditionnel		12 conditionnel passé	
traduirais	traduirions	aurais traduit	aurions traduit
traduirais	traduiriez	aurais traduit	auriez traduit
traduirait	traduiraient	aurait traduit	auraient traduit
6 présent du subjonctif		13 passé du subjonctif	
traduise	traduisions	aie traduit	ayons traduit
traduises	traduisiez	aies traduit	ayez traduit
traduise	traduisent	ait traduit	aient traduit
7 imparfait du subjonctif		14 plus-que-parfait du subjonctif	
traduisisse	traduisissions	eusse traduit	eussions traduit
traduisisses	traduisissiez	eusses traduit	eussiez traduit
traduisît	traduisissent	eût traduit	eussent traduit
		Impératif	
		traduis	
		traduisons	
		traduisez	

---

un traducteur, une traductrice   translator
une **traduction**   a translation
traduisible   translatable
une **traduction littérale**   a literal translation
une **traduction libre**   a free translation

se traduire   to be translated; **Cette phrase se traduit facilement.**
This sentence is easily translated.
une **traduction fidèle**   a faithful translation

to work

The Seven Simple Tenses		The Seven Compound Tenses	
Singular	Plural	Singular	Plural
1 présent de l'indicatif		8 passé composé	
travaille	travaillons	ai travaillé	avons travaillé
travailles	travaillez	as travaillé	avez travaillé
travaille	travaillent	a travaillé	ont travaillé
2 imparfait de l'indicatif		9 plus-que-parfait de l'indicatif	
travaillais	travaillions	avais travaillé	avions travaillé
travaillais	travailliez	avais travaillé	aviez travaillé
travaillait	travaillaient	avait travaillé	avaient travaillé
3 passé simple		10 passé antérieur	
travaillai	travaillâmes	eus travaillé	eûmes travaillé
travaillas	travaillâtes	eus travaillé	eûtes travaillé
travailla	travaillèrent	eut travaillé	eurent travaillé
4 futur		11 futur antérieur	
travaillerai	travaillerons	aurai travaillé	aurons travaillé
travailleras	travaillerez	auras travaillé	aurez travaillé
travaillera	travailleront	aura travaillé	auront travaillé
5 conditionnel		12 conditionnel passé	
travaillerais	travaillerions	aurais travaillé	aurions travaillé
travaillerais	travailleriez	aurais travaillé	auriez travaillé
travaillerait	travailleraient	aurait travaillé	auraient travaillé
6 présent du subjonctif		13 passé du subjonctif	
travaille	travaillions	aie travaillé	ayons travaillé
travailles	travailliez	aies travaillé	ayez travaillé
travaille	travaillent	ait travaillé	aient travaillé
7 imparfait du subjonctif		14 plus-que-parfait du subjonctif	
travaillasse	travaillassions	eusse travaillé	eussions travaillé
travaillasses	travaillassiez	eusses travaillé	eussiez travaillé
travaillât	travaillassent	eût travaillé	eussent travaillé

Impératif
travaille
travaillons
travaillez

---

travailleur, travailleuse industrious;
  worker
être sans travail to be out of work
faire travailler son argent to put one's
  money to work (to earn interest)

le travail work, labor,
  travail (**les travaux**)
les travaux publics public works
les vêtements de travail work clothes

traverser   Part. pr. **traversant**   Part. passé **traversé**

to traverse, to cross

The Seven Simple Tenses		The Seven Compound Tenses	
Singular	Plural	Singular	Plural
1 présent de l'indicatif		**8 passé composé**	
traverse	traversons	ai traversé	avons traversé
traverses	traversez	as traversé	avez traversé
traverse	traversent	a traversé	ont traversé
2 imparfait de l'indicatif		**9 plus-que-parfait de l'indicatif**	
traversais	traversions	avais traversé	avions traversé
traversais	traversiez	avais traversé	aviez traversé
traversait	traversaient	avait traversé	avaient traversé
3 passé simple		**10 passé antérieur**	
traversai	traversâmes	eus traversé	eûmes traversé
traversas	traversâtes	eus traversé	eûtes traversé
traversa	traversèrent	eut traversé	eurent traversé
4 futur		**11 futur antérieur**	
traverserai	traverserons	aurai traversé	aurons traversé
traverseras	traverserez	auras traversé	aurez traversé
traversera	traverseront	aura traversé	auront traversé
5 conditionnel		**12 conditionnel passé**	
traverserais	traverserions	aurais traversé	aurions traversé
traverserais	traverseriez	aurais traversé	auriez traversé
traverserait	traverseraient	aurait traversé	auraient traversé
6 présent du subjonctif		**13 passé du subjonctif**	
traverse	traversions	aie traversé	ayons traversé
traverses	traversiez	aies traversé	ayez traversé
traverse	traversent	ait traversé	aient traversé
7 imparfait du subjonctif		**14 plus-que-parfait du subjonctif**	
traversasse	traversassions	eusse traversé	eussions traversé
traversasses	traversassiez	eusses traversé	eussiez traversé
traversât	traversassent	eût traversé	eussent traversé
		Impératif	
		traverse	
		traversons	
		traversez	

la traversée the crossing	**une traversée de voie** railroad crossing
à travers through	**traverser la foule** to make one's way
de travers askew, awry, crooked	through the crowd

to find

The Seven Simple Tenses		The Seven Compound Tenses	
Singular	Plural	Singular	Plural
1 présent de l'indicatif		8 passé composé	
trouve	trouvons	ai trouvé	avons trouvé
trouves	trouvez	as trouvé	avez trouvé
trouve	trouvent	a trouvé	ont trouvé
2 imparfait de l'indicatif		9 plus-que-parfait de l'indicatif	
trouvais	trouvions	avais trouvé	avions trouvé
trouvais	trouviez	avais trouvé	aviez trouvé
trouvait	trouvaient	avait trouvé	avaient trouvé
3 passé simple		10 passé antérieur	
trouvai	trouvâmes	eus trouvé	eûmes trouvé
trouvas	trouvâtes	eus trouvé	eûtes trouvé
trouva	trouvèrent	eut trouvé	eurent trouvé
4 futur		11 futur antérieur	
trouverai	trouverons	aurai trouvé	aurons trouvé
trouveras	trouverez	auras trouvé	aurez trouvé
trouvera	trouveront	aura trouvé	auront trouvé
5 conditionnel		12 conditionnel passé	
trouverais	trouverions	aurais trouvé	aurions trouvé
trouverais	trouveriez	aurais trouvé	auriez trouvé
trouverait	trouveraient	aurait trouvé	auraient trouvé
6 présent du subjonctif		13 passé du subjonctif	
trouve	trouvions	aie trouvé	ayons trouvé
trouves	trouviez	aies trouvé	ayez trouvé
trouve	trouvent	ait trouvé	aient trouvé
7 imparfait du subjonctif		14 plus-que-parfait du subjonctif	
trouvasse	trouvassions	eusse trouvé	eussions trouvé
trouvasses	trouvassiez	eusses trouvé	eussiez trouvé
trouvât	trouvassent	eût trouvé	eussent trouvé

Impératif
trouve
trouvons
trouvez

J'ai une nouvelle voiture; comment la trouvez-vous?
   I have a new car; how do you like it?
trouver un emploi   to find a job
trouver bon de faire qqch   to think fit to do something
retrouver   to find again, to recover, to retrieve
trouver porte close   not to find anyone answering the door after knocking

See also **se trouver.**

se trouver Part. pr. **se trouvant** Part. passé **trouvé(e)(s)**

to be located, to be situated

The Seven Simple Tenses		The Seven Compound Tenses	
Singular	Plural	Singular	Plural
1 présent de l'indicatif		**8 passé composé**	
me trouve	nous trouvons	me suis trouvé(e)	nous sommes trouvé(e)s
te trouves	vous trouvez	t'es trouvé(e)	vous êtes trouvé(e)(s)
se trouve	se trouvent	s'est trouvé(e)	se sont trouvé(e)s
2 imparfait de l'indicatif		**9 plus-que-parfait de l'indicatif**	
me trouvais	nous trouvions	m'étais trouvé(e)	nous étions trouvé(e)s
te trouvais	vous trouviez	t'étais trouvé(e)	vous étiez trouvé(e)(s)
se trouvait	se trouvaient	s'était trouvé(e)	s'étaient trouvé(e)s
3 passé simple		**10 passé antérieur**	
me trouvai	nous trouvâmes	me fus trouvé(e)	nous fûmes trouvé(e)s
te trouvas	vous trouvâtes	te fus trouvé(e)	vous fûtes trouvé(e)(s)
se trouva	se trouvèrent	se fut trouvé(e)	se furent trouvé(e)s
4 futur		**11 futur antérieur**	
me trouverai	nous trouverons	me serai trouvé(e)	nous serons trouvé(e)s
te trouveras	vous trouverez	te seras trouvé(e)	vous serez trouvé(e)(s)
se trouvera	se trouveront	se sera trouvé(e)	se seront trouvé(e)s
5 conditionnel		**12 conditionnel passé**	
me trouverais	nous trouverions	me serais trouvé(e)	nous serions trouvé(e)s
te trouverais	vous trouveriez	te serais trouvé(e)	vous seriez trouvé(e)(s)
se trouverait	se trouveraient	se serait trouvé(e)	se seraient trouvé(e)s
6 présent du subjonctif		**13 passé du subjonctif**	
me trouve	nous trouvions	me sois trouvé(e)	nous soyons trouvé(e)s
te trouves	vous trouviez	te sois trouvé(e)	vous soyez trouvé(e)(s)
se trouve	se trouvent	se soit trouvé(e)	se soient trouvé(e)s
7 imparfait du subjonctif		**14 plus-que-parfait du subjonctif**	
me trouvasse	nous trouvassions	me fusse trouvé(e)	nous fussions trouvé(e)s
te trouvasses	vous trouvassiez	te fusses trouvé(e)	vous fussiez trouvé(e)(s)
se trouvât	se trouvassent	se fût trouvé(e)	se fussent trouvé(e)s

Impératif
trouve-toi; ne te trouve pas
trouvons-nous; ne nous trouvons pas
trouvez-vous; ne vous trouvez pas

Où se trouve le bureau de poste? Where is the post office located?
Trouve-toi dans ce café à huit heures ce soir. Be in this café at 8 o'clock tonight.
Vous avez été malade; allez-vous mieux maintenant? —Oui, je me trouve mieux, merci! You have been sick; are you feeling better now? —Yes, I'm feeling better, thank you!

See also **trouver.**

290

to unite, to join

The Seven Simple Tenses		The Seven Compound Tenses	
Singular	Plural	Singular	Plural
1 présent de l'indicatif		**8 passé composé**	
unis	unissons	ai uni	avons uni
unis	unissez	as uni	avez uni
unit	unissent	a uni	ont uni
2 imparfait de l'indicatif		**9 plus-que-parfait de l'indicatif**	
unissais	unissions	avais uni	avions uni
unissais	unissiez	avais uni	aviez uni
unissait	unissaient	avait uni	avaient uni
3 passé simple		**10 passé antérieur**	
unis	unîmes	eus uni	eûmes uni
unis	unîtes	eus uni	eûtes uni
unit	unirent	eut uni	eurent uni
4 futur		**11 futur antérieur**	
unirai	unirons	aurai uni	aurons uni
uniras	unirez	auras uni	aurez uni
unira	uniront	aura uni	auront uni
5 conditionnel		**12 conditionnel passé**	
unirais	unirions	aurais uni	aurions uni
unirais	uniriez	aurais uni	auriez uni
unirait	uniraient	aurait uni	auraient uni
6 présent du subjonctif		**13 passé du subjonctif**	
unisse	unissions	aie uni	ayons uni
unisses	unissiez	aies uni	ayez uni
unisse	unissent	ait uni	aient uni
7 imparfait du subjonctif		**14 plus-que-parfait du subjonctif**	
unisse	unissions	eusse uni	eussions uni
unisses	unissiez	eusses uni	eussiez uni
unît	unissent	eût uni	eussent uni
		Impératif	
		unis	
		unissons	
		unissez	

s'**unir**   to join together, to marry
réunir   to reunite;   se **réunir**   to meet together
les **États-Unis**   the United States
les **Nations-Unies**   the United Nations
une **union**   union, alliance

unir en mariage   to join in marriage
Elle unit l'intelligence au courage.
She combines intelligence with courage.

vaincre	Part. pr. **vainquant**	Part. passé **vaincu**

to vanquish, to conquer

The Seven Simple Tenses		The Seven Compound Tenses	
Singular	Plural	Singular	Plural
1 présent de l'indicatif		8 passé composé	
vaincs	vainquons	ai vaincu	avons vaincu
vaincs	vainquez	as vaincu	avez vaincu
vainc	vainquent	a vaincu	ont vaincu
2 imparfait de l'indicatif		9 plus-que-parfait de l'indicatif	
vainquais	vainquions	avais vaincu	avions vaincu
vainquais	vainquiez	avais vaincu	aviez vaincu
vainquait	vainquaient	avait vaincu	avaient vaincu
3 passé simple		10 passé antérieur	
vainquis	vainquîmes	eus vaincu	eûmes vaincu
vainquis	vainquîtes	eus vaincu	eûtes vaincu
vainquit	vainquirent	eut vaincu	eurent vaincu
4 futur		11 futur antérieur	
vaincrai	vaincrons	aurai vaincu	aurons vaincu
vaincras	vaincrez	auras vaincu	aurez vaincu
vaincra	vaincront	aura vaincu	auront vaincu
5 conditionnel		12 conditionnel passé	
vaincrais	vaincrions	aurais vaincu	aurions vaincu
vaincrais	vaincriez	aurais vaincu	auriez vaincu
vaincrait	vaincraient	aurait vaincu	auraient vaincu
6 présent du subjonctif		13 passé du subjonctif	
vainque	vainquions	aie vaincu	ayons vaincu
vainques	vainquiez	aies vaincu	ayez vaincu
vainque	vainquent	ait vaincu	aient vaincu
7 imparfait du subjonctif		14 plus-que-parfait du subjonctif	
vainquisse	vainquissions	eusse vaincu	eussions vaincu
vainquisses	vainquissiez	eusses vaincu	eussiez vaincu
vainquît	vainquissent	eût vaincu	eussent vaincu

	Impératif
	vaincs
	vainquons
	vainquez

convaincre qqn de qqch to convince, to persuade someone of something
vainqueur victor, victorious; conqueror, conquering
convaincant, convaincante convincing
les vaincus the defeated, the vanquished
s'avouer vaincu to admit defeat
Nous vaincrons. We shall conquer; we shall overcome.

to be worth, to be as good as, to deserve, to merit, to be equal to

The Seven Simple Tenses		The Seven Compound Tenses	
Singular	Plural	Singular	Plural
1 présent de l'indicatif		8 passé composé	
vaux	valons	ai valu	avons valu
vaux	valez	as valu	avez valu
vaut	valent	a valu	ont valu
2 imparfait de l'indicatif		9 plus-que-parfait de l'indicatif	
valais	valions	avais valu	avions valu
valais	valiez	avais valu	aviez valu
valait	valaient	avait valu	avaient valu
3 passé simple		10 passé antérieur	
valus	valûmes	eus valu	eûmes valu
valus	valûtes	eus valu	eûtes valu
valut	valurent	eut valu	eurent valu
4 futur		11 futur antérieur	
vaudrai	vaudrons	aurai valu	aurons valu
vaudras	vaudrez	auras valu	aurez valu
vaudra	vaudront	aura valu	auront valu
5 conditionnel		12 conditionnel passé	
vaudrais	vaudrions	aurais valu	aurions valu
vaudrais	vaudriez	aurais valu	auriez valu
vaudrait	vaudraient	aurait valu	auraient valu
6 présent du subjonctif		13 passé du subjonctif	
vaille	valions	aie valu	ayons valu
vailles	valiez	aies valu	ayez valu
vaille	vaillent	ait valu	aient valu
7 imparfait du subjonctif		14 plus-que-parfait du subjonctif	
valusse	valussions	eusse valu	eussions valu
valusses	valussiez	eusses valu	eussiez valu
valût	valussent	eût valu	eussent valu
		Impératif	
		vaux	
		valons	
		valez	

---

la valeur value
valeureusement valorously
valeureux, valeureuse valorous
la validation validation
valide valid
Mieux vaut tard que jamais. Better late than never.

Cela vaut la peine.
It's worth the trouble.
faire valoir to make the most of, to invest one's money

vendre

Part. pr. **vendant**   Part. passé **vendu**

to sell

The Seven Simple Tenses		The Seven Compound Tenses	
Singular	Plural	Singular	Plural
1 présent de l'indicatif		8 passé composé	
vends	vendons	ai vendu	avons vendu
vends	vendez	as vendu	avez vendu
vend	vendent	a vendu	ont vendu
2 imparfait de l'indicatif		9 plus-que-parfait de l'indicatif	
vendais	vendions	avais vendu	avions vendu
vendais	vendiez	avais vendu	aviez vendu
vendait	vendaient	avait vendu	avaient vendu
3 passé simple		10 passé antérieur	
vendis	vendîmes	eus vendu	eûmes vendu
vendis	vendîtes	eus vendu	eûtes vendu
vendit	vendirent	eut vendu	eurent vendu
4 futur		11 futur antérieur	
vendrai	vendrons	aurai vendu	aurons vendu
vendras	vendrez	auras vendu	aurez vendu
vendra	vendront	aura vendu	auront vendu
5 conditionnel		12 conditionnel passé	
vendrais	vendrions	aurais vendu	aurions vendu
vendrais	vendriez	aurais vendu	auriez vendu
vendrait	vendraient	aurait vendu	auraient vendu
6 présent du subjonctif		13 passé du subjonctif	
vende	vendions	aie vendu	ayons vendu
vendes	vendiez	aies vendu	ayez vendu
vende	vendent	ait vendu	aient vendu
7 imparfait du subjonctif		14 plus-que-parfait du subjonctif	
vendisse	vendissions	eusse vendu	eussions vendu
vendisses	vendissiez	eusses vendu	eussiez vendu
vendît	vendissent	eût vendu	eussent vendu
		Impératif	
		vends	
		vendons	
		vendez	

---

un vendeur, une vendeuse   salesperson
une vente   a sale
maison à vendre   house for sale
revendre   to resell
en vente   on sale
une salle des ventes   sales room

vendre à bon marché   to sell at
   a reasonably low price (a good buy)
une vente aux enchères   auction sale
vendre au rabais   to sell at a discount
On vend des livres ici.   Books are
   sold here.

294

Part. pr. **venant**   Part. passé **venu(e)(s)**   **venir**

to come

The Seven Simple Tenses		The Seven Compound Tenses	
Singular	Plural	Singular	Plural
1 présent de l'indicatif		**8 passé composé**	
viens	venons	suis venu(e)	sommes venu(e)s
viens	venez	es venu(e)	êtes venu(e)(s)
vient	viennent	est venu(e)	sont venu(e)s
2 imparfait de l'indicatif		**9 plus-que-parfait de l'indicatif**	
venais	venions	étais venu(e)	étions venu(e)s
venais	veniez	étais venu(e)	étiez venu(e)(s)
venait	venaient	était venu(e)	étaient venu(e)s
3 passé simple		**10 passé antérieur**	
vins	vînmes	fus venu(e)	fûmes venu(e)s
vins	vîntes	fus venu(e)	fûtes venu(e)(s)
vint	vinrent	fut venu(e)	furent venu(e)s
4 futur		**11 futur antérieur**	
viendrai	viendrons	serai venu(e)	serons venu(e)s
viendras	viendrez	seras venu(e)	serez venu(e)(s)
viendra	viendront	sera venu(e)	seront venu(e)s
5 conditionnel		**12 conditionnel passé**	
viendrais	viendrions	serais venu(e)	serions venu(e)s
viendrais	viendriez	serais venu(e)	seriez venu(e)(s)
viendrait	viendraient	serait venu(e)	seraient venu(e)s
6 présent du subjonctif		**13 passé du subjonctif**	
vienne	venions	sois venu(e)	soyons venu(e)s
viennes	veniez	sois venu(e)	soyez venu(e)(s)
vienne	viennent	soit venu(e)	soient venu(e)s
7 imparfait du subjonctif		**14 plus-que-parfait du subjonctif**	
vinsse	vinssions	fusse venu(e)	fussions venu(e)s
vinsses	vinssiez	fusses venu(e)	fussiez venu(e)(s)
vînt	vinssent	fût venu(e)	fussent venu(e)s
		Impératif	
		viens	
		venons	
		venez	

venir de faire qqch to have just done something
Je viens de manger. I have just eaten.
venir à + inf. to happen to; **Si je viens à devenir riche . . .** If I happen to become rich . . .

faire venir to send for
venir chercher to call for, to come to get
D'où vient cela? Where does that come from?

295

visiter	Part. pr. **visitant**	Part. passé **visité**

to visit

The Seven Simple Tenses		The Seven Compound Tenses	
Singular	Plural	Singular	Plural
1 présent de l'indicatif		8 passé composé	
visite	visitons	ai visité	avons visité
visites	visitez	as visité	avez visité
visite	visitent	a visité	ont visité
2 imparfait de l'indicatif		9 plus-que-parfait de l'indicatif	
visitais	visitions	avais visité	avions visité
visitais	visitiez	avais visité	aviez visité
visitait	visitaient	avait visité	avaient visité
3 passé simple		10 passé antérieur	
visitai	visitâmes	eus visité	eûmes visité
visitas	visitâtes	eus visité	eûtes visité
visita	visitèrent	eut visité	eurent visité
4 futur		11 futur antérieur	
visiterai	visiterons	aurai visité	aurons visité
visiteras	visiterez	auras visité	aurez visité
visitera	visiteront	aura visité	auront visité
5 conditionnel		12 conditionnel passé	
visiterais	visiterions	aurais visité	aurions visité
visiterais	visiteriez	aurais visité	auriez visité
visiterait	visiteraient	aurait visité	auraient visité
6 présent du subjonctif		13 passé du subjonctif	
visite	visitions	aie visité	ayons visité
visites	visitiez	aies visité	ayez visité
visite	visitent	ait visité	aient visité
7 imparfait du subjonctif		14 plus-que-parfait du subjonctif	
visitasse	visitassions	eusse visité	eussions visité
visitasses	visitassiez	eusses visité	eussiez visité
visitât	visitassent	eût visité	eussent visité
		Impératif	
		visite	
		visitons	
		visitez	

---

rendre visite à qqn to visit someone, to pay a call
un visiteur, une visiteuse visitor, caller
une visite de douane customs inspection
une visite à domicile a house call
passer à la visite médicale to have a physical exam

rendre une visite à qqn to return a visit
les heures de visite visiting hours
une visitation visitation

The Seven Simple Tenses		The Seven Compound Tenses	
Singular	Plural	Singular	Plural
1 présent de l'indicatif		8 passé composé	
vis	**vivons**	**ai vécu**	**avons vécu**
vis	**vivez**	**as vécu**	**avez vécu**
vit	**vivent**	**a vécu**	**ont vécu**
2 imparfait de l'indicatif		9 plus-que-parfait de l'indicatif	
vivais	**vivions**	**avais vécu**	**avions vécu**
vivais	**viviez**	**avais vécu**	**aviez vécu**
vivait	**vivaient**	**avait vécu**	**avaient vécu**
3 passé simple		10 passé antérieur	
vécus	**vécûmes**	**eus vécu**	**eûmes vécu**
vécus	**vécûtes**	**eus vécu**	**eûtes vécu**
vécut	**vécurent**	**eut vécu**	**eurent vécu**
4 futur		11 futur antérieur	
vivrai	**vivrons**	**aurai vécu**	**aurons vécu**
vivras	**vivrez**	**auras vécu**	**aurez vécu**
vivra	**vivront**	**aura vécu**	**auront vécu**
5 conditionnel		12 conditionnel passé	
vivrais	**vivrions**	**aurais vécu**	**aurions vécu**
vivrais	**vivriez**	**aurais vécu**	**auriez vécu**
vivrait	**vivraient**	**aurait vécu**	**auraient vécu**
6 présent du subjonctif		13 passé du subjonctif	
vive	**vivions**	**aie vécu**	**ayons vécu**
vives	**viviez**	**aies vécu**	**ayez vécu**
vive	**vivent**	**ait vécu**	**aient vécu**
7 imparfait du subjonctif		14 plus-que-parfait du subjonctif	
vécusse	**vécussions**	**eusse vécu**	**eussions vécu**
vécusses	**vécussiez**	**eusses vécu**	**eussiez vécu**
vécût	**vécussent**	**eût vécu**	**eussent vécu**

Impératif
vis
vivons
vivez

---

revivre   to relive, to revive
survivre à   to survive
Vive la France!   Long live France!
avoir de quoi vivre   to have enough
   to live on
vivre de   to subsist on
la joie de vivre   the joy of living

savoir-vivre   to be well-mannered
Vivent les Etats-Unis!   Long live the
   United States!
le vivre et le couvert   room and board
la vie   life; **j'aime la vie.**   I love life.
C'est la vie!   That's life!

voir	Part. pr. **voyant**	Part. passé **vu**

to see

The Seven Simple Tenses	The Seven Compound Tenses

Singular	Plural	Singular	Plural
1 présent de l'indicatif		8 passé composé	
vois	voyons	ai vu	avons vu
vois	voyez	as vu	avez vu
voit	voient	a vu	ont vu
2 imparfait de l'indicatif		9 plus-que-parfait de l'indicatif	
voyais	voyions	avais vu	avions vu
voyais	voyiez	avais vu	aviez vu
voyait	voyaient	avait vu	avaient vu
3 passé simple		10 passé antérieur	
vis	vîmes	eus vu	eûmes vu
vis	vîtes	eus vu	eûtes vu
vit	virent	eut vu	eurent vu
4 futur		11 futur antérieur	
verrai	verrons	aurai vu	aurons vu
verras	verrez	auras vu	aurez vu
verra	verront	aura vu	auront vu
5 conditionnel		12 conditionnel passé	
verrais	verrions	aurais vu	aurions vu
verrais	verriez	aurais vu	auriez vu
verrait	verraient	aurait vu	auraient vu
6 présent du subjonctif		13 passé du subjonctif	
voie	voyions	aie vu	ayons vu
voies	voyiez	aies vu	ayez vu
voie	voient	ait vu	aient vu
7 imparfait du subjonctif		14 plus-que-parfait du subjonctif	
visse	vissions	eusse vu	eussions vu
visses	vissiez	eusses vu	eussiez vu
vît	vissent	eût vu	eussent vu

Impératif
vois
voyons
voyez

---

revoir to see again
faire voir to show
voir la vie en rose to see the bright side of life
Voyez vous-même! See for yourself!

entrevoir to catch a glimpse, to glimpse
C'est à voir. It remains to be seen.
Cela se voit. That's obvious.
Voyons! See here now!

to fly, to steal

The Seven Simple Tenses		The Seven Compound Tenses	
Singular	Plural	Singular	Plural
1 présent de l'indicatif		8 passé composé	
vole	volons	ai volé	avons volé
voles	volez	as volé	avez volé
vole	volent	a volé	ont volé
2 imparfait de l'indicatif		9 plus-que-parfait de l'indicatif	
volais	volions	avais volé	avions volé
volais	voliez	avais volé	aviez volé
volait	volaient	avait volé	avaient volé
3 passé simple		10 passé antérieur	
volai	volâmes	eus volé	eûmes volé
volas	volâtes	eus volé	eûtes volé
vola	volèrent	eut volé	eurent volé
4 futur		11 futur antérieur	
volerai	volerons	aurai volé	aurons volé
voleras	volerez	auras volé	aurez volé
volera	voleront	aura volé	auront volé
5 conditionnel		12 conditionnel passé	
volerais	volerions	aurais volé	aurions volé
volerais	voleriez	aurais volé	auriez volé
volerait	voleraient	aurait volé	auraient volé
6 présent du subjonctif		13 passé du subjonctif	
vole	volions	aie volé	ayons volé
voles	voliez	aies volé	ayez volé
vole	volent	ait volé	aient volé
7 imparfait du subjonctif		14 plus-que-parfait du subjonctif	
volasse	volassions	eusse volé	eussions volé
volasses	volassiez	eusses volé	eussiez volé
volât	volassent	eût volé	eussent volé

Impératif
vole
volons
volez

---

un vol flight, theft
le voleur thief
à vol d'oiseau as the crow flies
vol de nuit night flying (airplane), night flight
New York à vol d'oiseau
  bird's eye view of New York

survoler to fly over
le volant steering wheel
se mettre au volant to take the (steering) wheel

vouloir　　　　Part. pr. **voulant**　　　　Part. passé **voulu**

to want

The Seven Simple Tenses		The Seven Compound Tenses	
Singular	Plural	Singular	Plural
1　présent de l'indicatif		8　passé composé	
veux	voulons	ai voulu	avons voulu
veux	voulez	as voulu	avez voulu
veut	veulent	a voulu	ont voulu
2　imparfait de l'indicatif		9　plus-que-parfait de l'indicatif	
voulais	voulions	avais voulu	avions voulu
voulais	vouliez	avais voulu	aviez voulu
voulait	voulaient	avait voulu	avaient voulu
3　passé simple		10　passé antérieur	
voulus	voulûmes	eus voulu	eûmes voulu
voulus	voulûtes	eus voulu	eûtes voulu
voulut	voulurent	eut voulu	eurent voulu
4　futur		11　futur antérieur	
voudrai	voudrons	aurai voulu	aurons voulu
voudras	voudrez	auras voulu	aurez voulu
voudra	voudront	aura voulu	auront voulu
5　conditionnel		12　conditionnel passé	
voudrais	voudrions	aurais voulu	aurions voulu
voudrais	voudriez	aurais voulu	auriez voulu
voudrait	voudraient	aurait voulu	auraient voulu
6　présent du subjonctif		13　passé du subjonctif	
veuille	voulions	aie voulu	ayons voulu
veuilles	vouliez	aies voulu	ayez voulu
veuille	veuillent	ait voulu	aient voulu
7　imparfait du subjonctif		14　plus-que-parfait du subjonctif	
voulusse	voulussions	eusse voulu	eussions voulu
voulusses	voulussiez	eusses voulu	eussiez voulu
voulût	voulussent	eût voulu	eussent voulu
		Impératif	
		veuille	
		veuillons	
		veuillez	

---

un voeu　a wish
meilleurs voeux　best wishes
Vouloir c'est pouvoir.　Where there's a will there's a way.
vouloir dire　to mean; **Qu'est-ce que cela veut dire?**　What does that mean?
vouloir bien faire qqch　to be willing to do something
sans le vouloir　without meaning to, unintentionally
en temps voulu　in due time
en vouloir à qqn　to bear a grudge against someone
Que voulez-vous dire par là?　What do you mean by that remark?

to travel

The Seven Simple Tenses		The Seven Compound Tenses	
Singular	Plural	Singular	Plural
1 présent de l'indicatif		8 passé composé	
voyage	voyageons	ai voyagé	avons voyagé
voyages	voyagez	as voyagé	avez voyagé
voyage	voyagent	a voyagé	ont voyagé
2 imparfait de l'indicatif		9 plus-que-parfait de l'indicatif	
voyageais	voyagions	avais voyagé	avions voyagé
voyageais	voyagiez	avais voyagé	aviez voyagé
voyageait	voyageaient	avait voyagé	avaient voyagé
3 passé simple		10 passé antérieur	
voyageai	voyageâmes	eus voyagé	eûmes voyagé
voyageas	voyageâtes	eus voyagé	eûtes voyagé
voyagea	voyagèrent	eut voyagé	eurent voyagé
4 futur		11 futur antérieur	
voyagerai	voyagerons	aurai voyagé	aurons voyagé
voyageras	voyagerez	auras voyagé	aurez voyagé
voyagera	voyageront	aura voyagé	auront voyagé
5 conditionnel		12 conditionnel passé	
voyagerais	voyagerions	aurais voyagé	aurions voyagé
voyagerais	voyageriez	aurais voyagé	auriez voyagé
voyagerait	voyageraient	aurait voyagé	auraient voyagé
6 présent du subjonctif		13 passé du subjonctif	
voyage	voyagions	aie voyagé	ayons voyagé
voyages	voyagiez	aies voyagé	ayez voyagé
voyage	voyagent	ait voyagé	aient voyagé
7 imparfait du subjonctif		14 plus-que-parfait du subjonctif	
voyageasse	voyageassions	eusse voyagé	eussions voyagé
voyageasses	voyageassiez	eusses voyagé	eussiez voyagé
voyageât	voyageassent	eût voyagé	eussent voyagé
		Impératif	
		voyage	
		voyageons	
		voyagez	

---

un voyage   a trip
faire un voyage   to take a trip
un voyageur, une voyageuse   traveler
une agence de voyage   travel agency
Bon voyage!   Have a good trip!
Bon voyage et bon retour!   Have a good trip and a safe return!
J'aime le roman *Voyage au centre de la terre* **de Jules Verne.**
   I like the novel *Journey to the Center of the Earth* by Jules Verne.

Index of English-French Verbs

The purpose of this index is to give you instantly the French verb for the English verb you have in mind to use. This saves you time if you do not have at your fingertips a standard English-French word dictionary.

If the French verb you want is reflexive (*e.g.,* **s'appeler** or **se lever**), you will find it alphabetically among the verbs under the first letter of the verb and not under the reflexive pronoun *s'* or *se.*

When you find the French verb you need through the English verb, look up its verb forms in this book, where all the verbs are listed alphabetically at the top of each page. If it is not listed among the 301 verbs in this book, consult the list of over 1,000 French verbs conjugated like model verbs among the 301 that begins on p. 312. If it is not listed there, consult my more comprehensive book, *501 French verbs fully conjugated in all the tenses,* 4th edition, with new features.

A

able, be **pouvoir,** 217
accept **accepter,** 1
accompany **accompagner,** 2
acquainted with, be **connaître,** 61
act (in a play) **jouer,** 155
add **ajouter,** 11
admire **admirer,** 6
admit **admettre,** 5
adore **adorer,** 7
advance **avancer,** 30
afraid, be **craindre,** 71
aid **aider,** 9
allow **laisser,** 156; **permettre,** 208
amaze **étonner,** 118
amuse **amuser,** 15; **égayer,** 100
amuse oneself **s'amuser,** 16
angry, become **se fâcher,** 124
annoy **ennuyer,** 107
answer **répondre,** 245
apologize **s'excuser,** 121
appear **paraître,** 193
arrange **arranger,** 21
arrest **arrêter,** 22
arrive **arriver,** 24
ascend **monter,** 173

ask (for) **demander,** 81
assist **aider,** 9
assist (at) **assister,** 26
assure oneself **s'assurer,** 27
astonish **étonner,** 118
attend **assister,** 26

B

babble **bavarder,** 36
be **être,** 119
be a matter of **s'agir,** 8
be a question of **s'agir,** 8
be able **pouvoir,** 217
be acquainted with **connaître,** 61
be afraid **craindre,** 71
be as good as **valoir,** 293
be born **naître,** 179
be busy **s'occuper,** 188
be enough **suffire,** 277
be like **ressembler,** 249
be located **se trouver,** 290
be named **s'appeler,** 18
be necessary **falloir,** 127
be present (at) **assister,** 26
be quiet **se taire,** 279

be silent **se taire,** 279
be situated **se trouver,** 290
be sufficient **suffire,** 277
be the matter **s'agir,** 8
be worth **valoir,** 293
beat **battre,** 34
become **devenir,** 90
become angry **se fâcher,** 124
begin **commencer,** 57;
   se mettre, 172
believe **croire,** 73
beware **se méfier,** 168
bite **mordre,** 175
blow **souffler,** 271
bore **ennuyer,** 107
born, be **naître,** 179
borrow **emprunter,** 105
break **casser,** 45; **se casser,** 46;
   rompre, 257
bring **amener,** 14; **apporter,** 19
bring down **descendre,** 86
bring up (take up) **monter,** 173
brush **brosser,** 40
brush oneself **se brosser,** 41
build **bâtir,** 33; **construire,** 62
burden **charger,** 52
burn **brûler,** 42
burst **rompre,** 257
busy, be **s'occuper,** 188
buy **acheter,** 4

C

call **appeler,** 17
call again **rappeler,** 231
call back **rappeler,** 231
call oneself **s'appeler,** 18
can **pouvoir,** 217
carry **porter,** 215
carry away **enlever,** 106
cast **jeter,** 153
catch **attraper,** 29
cause **causer,** 47
cease **cesser,** 49

change **changer,** 50
charge **charger,** 52
chase **chasser,** 53
chat **bavarder,** 36; **causer,** 47
chatter **bavarder,** 36
cheer up **égayer,** 100
chide **gronder,** 142
choose **choisir,** 55
clean **nettoyer,** 181
close **fermer,** 128
come **venir,** 295
come back **revenir,** 254
come in **entrer,** 110
command **commander,** 56
commence **commencer,** 57
commit sin **pécher,** 201
complain **se plaindre,** 211
complete **finir,** 130
conduct **conduire,** 60
conquer **vaincre,** 292
construct **construire,** 62;
   bâtir, 33
continue **continuer,** 64
cook **cuire,** 75
correct **corriger,** 65
cost **coûter,** 69
count **compter,** 59
cover **couvrir,** 70
cross **traverser,** 288
cry **pleurer,** 213
cry out **crier,** 72
cure **guérir,** 143
cut **couper,** 67

D

damage **gâter,** 138
dance **danser,** 76
defend **défendre,** 79
demand **exiger,** 122
depart **partir,** 196
derange **déranger,** 85
descend **descendre,** 86
describe **décrire,** 78

deserve **valoir,** 293
desire **désirer,** 87
destroy **détruire,** 89
detest **détester,** 88
die **mourir,** 176; **périr,** 207
dine **dîner,** 92
dirty **salir,** 259
discover **découvrir,** 77
dislike **détester,** 88
display **montrer,** 174
distrust **se méfier,** 168
disturb **déranger,** 85
do **faire,** 126
doubt **douter,** 96
dream **songer,** 268
dress oneself **s'habiller,** 144
drink **boire,** 39
drive (a car) **conduire,** 60
drive out **chasser,** 53
dwell (in) **habiter,** 145

E

earn **gagner,** 136
eat **manger,** 165
embrace **embrasser,** 101
employ **employer,** 104
end **finir,** 130; **terminer,** 282
enjoy oneself **s'amuser,** 16
enliven **égayer,** 100
enough, be **suffire,** 277
enter **entrer,** 110
entertain **amuser,** 15; **égayer,** 100
excuse oneself **s'excuser,** 121
exhibit **montrer,** 174
explain **expliquer,** 123
extinguish **éteindre,** 116

F

fail **faillir,** 125
fall **tomber,** 283
fear **craindre,** 71

feed **nourrir,** 182
feel **sentir,** 265
fight **se battre,** 35
fill **remplir,** 240
find **trouver,** 289
finish **finir,** 130; **terminer,** 282
fish **pêcher,** 202
flee **fuir,** 134
fly **fuir,** 134; **voler,** 299
follow **suivre,** 278
forbid **défendre,** 79; **interdire,** 149
force **forcer,** 131
forget **oublier,** 191
forgive **pardonner,** 194
freeze **geler,** 139
frighten **effrayer,** 99
fry **frire,** 133

G

gain **gagner,** 136
gather **cueillir,** 74
get **obtenir,** 186; **recevoir,** 233
get angry **se fâcher,** 124
get dressed **s'habiller,** 144
get up **se lever,** 161
give **donner,** 94
give back **remettre,** 238; **rendre,** 242
go **aller,** 12
go away **s'en aller,** 13
go back **retourner,** 251
go down **descendre,** 86
go forward **avancer,** 30
go in **entrer,** 110
go out **sortir,** 270
go to bed **se coucher,** 66
go up **monter,** 173
gossip **bavarder,** 36
grasp **saisir,** 258
greet **accueillir,** 3
grow (up, grow taller) **grandir,** 141

stay **rester,** 250; **demeurer,** 82
steal **voler,** 299
stink **puer,** 227
stop (oneself) **s'arrêter,** 23
stop (someone or something)
  arrêter, 22
stretch (oneself) **s'étendre,** 117
stretch out (oneself) **s'étendre,** 117
strike (beat) **battre,** 34
strike (hit) **battre,** 34
study **étudier,** 120
stun **étonner,** 118
submit **soumettre,** 274
succeed **réussir,** 252
suffer **souffrir,** 272
suffice **suffire,** 277
sufficient, be **suffire,** 277
sweep **balayer,** 32
swim **nager,** 178

Index of Common Irregular French Verb Forms Identified by Infinitive

The purpose of this index is to help you identify those verb forms that cannot be readily identified because they are irregular in some way. For example, if you come across the verb form *fut* (which is very common) in your French readings, this index will tell you that *fut* is a form of **être.** Then you look up **être** in this book and you will find that verb form on the page where all the forms of **être** are given.

Verb forms whose first three or four letters are the same as the infinitive have not been included because they can easily be identified by referring to the alphabetical listing of the 301 verbs in this book.

A

a **avoir**
ai **avoir**
aie **avoir**
aient **avoir**
aies **avoir**
aille **aller**
ait **avoir**
as **avoir**
aurai, *etc.* **avoir**
avaient **avoir**
avais **avoir**
avait **avoir**
avez **avoir**
aviez **avoir**
avions **avoir**
avons **avoir**
ayant **avoir**
ayons, *etc.* **avoir**

B

bu **boire**
bûmes **boire**
burent **boire**
bus **boire**
bussent **boire**
but **boire**

bûtes **boire**
buvant **boire**

C

crois **croire**
croit **croire**
croyais, *etc.* **croire**
cru **croire**
crûmes **croire**
crurent **crolre**
crus **croire**

D

dîmes **dire**
disais, *etc.* **dire**
disse, *etc.* **dire**
dit, dît **dire**
dois **devoir**
doive, *etc.* **devoir**
dors **dormir**
dû, due **devoir**
dûmes **devoir**
dus, dussent **devoir**
dut, dût **devoir**

E

es **être**
est **être**
étais, *etc.* **être**
été **être**
êtes **être**
étiez **être**
eu **avoir**
eûmes **avoir**
eurent **avoir**
eus **avoir**
eusse, *etc.* **avoir**
eut, eût **avoir**
eûtes **avoir**

F

faille **faillir, falloir**
fais, *etc.* **faire**
fasse, *etc.* **faire**
faudra **faillir, falloir**
faudrait **faillir, falloir**
faut **faillir, falloir**
faux **faillir**
ferai, *etc.* **faire**
fîmes **faire**

firent **faire**
fis, *etc.* **faire**
font **faire**
fûmes **être**
furent **être**
fus, *etc.* **être**
fut, fût **être**
fuyais, *etc.* **fuir**

I

ira, irai, iras, *etc.*
  aller

L

lis, *etc.* **lire**
lu **lire**
lus, *etc.* **lire**

M

meure, *etc.* **mourir**
meus, *etc.*
  mouvoir
mîmes **mettre**
mirent **mettre**
mis **mettre**
misses, *etc.* **mettre**
mit **mettre**
mort **mourir**
mû, mue **mouvoir**
mussent **mouvoir**
mut **mouvoir**

N

naquîmes, *etc.*
  naître
né **naître**

O

omis **omettre**
ont **avoir**

P

pars **partir**
paru **paraître**
peignis, *etc.*
  peindre
peuvent **pouvoir**
peux, *etc.* **pouvoir**
plu **plaire,**
  pleuvoir
plurent **plaire**
plut, plût **plaire,**
  pleuvoir
plûtes **plaire**
pourrai, *etc.*
  pouvoir
prîmes **prendre**
prirent **prendre**
pris **prendre**
prisse, *etc.* **prendre**
pu **pouvoir**
puis **pouvoir**
puisse, *etc.* **pouvoir**
pûmes, *etc.* **pouvoir**
purent **pouvoir**
pus **pouvoir**
pusse **pouvoir**
put, pût **pouvoir**

R

reçois, *etc.* **recevoir**
reçûmes, *etc.*
  recevoir
reviens, *etc.* **revenir**
revins, *etc.* **revenir**
riiez **rire**
ris, *etc.* **rire**

S

sache, *etc.* **savoir**
sais, *etc.* **savoir**
saurai, *etc.* **savoir**
serai, *etc.* **être**
sers, *etc.* **servir**
sois, *etc.* **être**
sommes **être**
sont **être**
sors, *etc.* **sortir**
soyez **être**
soyons **être**
su **savoir**
suis **être, suivre**
suit **suivre**
sûmes **savoir**
surent **savoir**
susse, *etc.* **savoir**
sut, sût **savoir**

T

tiendrai, *etc.* **tenir**
tienne, *etc.* **tenir**
tînmes **tenir**
tins, *etc.* **tenir**
tu **taire**
tûmes **taire**
turent **taire**
tus **taire**
tusse, *etc.* **taire**
tut, tût **taire**

V

va **aller**
vaille **valoir**
vais **aller**
vas **aller**
vaudrai, *etc.* **valoir**
vaux, *etc.* **valoir**
vécu **vivre**

vécûmes, *etc.*
   vivre
verrai, *etc.* **voir**
veuille, *etc.*
   vouloir
veulent **vouloir**
veux, *etc.* **vouloir**
viendrai, *etc.*
   venir

vienne, *etc.*
   venir
viens, *etc.* **venir**
vîmes **voir**
vînmes **venir**
vinrent **venir**
vins, *etc.* **venir**
virent **voir**
vis **vivre, voir**

visse, *etc.* **voir**
vit **vivre, voir**
vît **voir**
vîtes **voir**
vont **aller**
voudrai, *etc.*
   vouloir
voyais, *etc.* **voir**
vu **voir**

Over 1,000 French Verbs Conjugated Like Model Verbs Among the 301

The number after each verb is the page number in this book where a model verb is shown fully conjugated. At times there are two page references; for example, **abréger** is conjugated like **céder** on p. 48 because **é** changes to **è** and like **manger** on p. 165 because **abréger** and **manger** are both **-ger** type verbs.

If the French verb you want is reflexive (*e.g.*, **s'appeler** or **se lever**), you will find it listed alphabetically under the first letter of the verb and not under the reflexive pronoun *s'* or *se*.

317

AT A GLANCE Series

Barron's new series gives travelers instant access to the most common idiomatic expressions used during a trip—the kind one needs to know instantly, like "Where can I find a taxi?" and "How much does this cost?"

Organized by situation (arrival, customs, hotel, health, etc.) and containing additional information about pronunciation, grammar, shopping plus special facts about the country, these convenient, pocket-size reference books will be the tourist's most helpful guides.

Special features include a bilingual dictionary section with over 2000 key words, maps of each country and major cities, and helpful phonetic spellings throughout.

Each book paperback, 256 pp., 3 ¾" x 6"

ARABIC AT A GLANCE, Wise (0-7641-1248-1) $8.95, Can. $12.50
CHINESE AT A GLANCE, Seligman & Chen (0-7641-1250-1) $8.95, Can. $12.50
FRENCH AT A GLANCE, 3rd, Stein & Wald (0-7641-1254-6) $6.95, Can. $9.95
GERMAN AT A GLANCE, 3rd, Strutz (0-7641-1255-5) $6.95, Can. $9.95
ITALIAN AT A GLANCE, 3rd, Costantino (0-7641-1256-2) $6.95, Can. $9.95
JAPANESE AT A GLANCE, 3rd, Akiyama (0-7641-0320-2) $8.95, Can. $11.95
KOREAN AT A GLANCE, Holt (0-8120-3998-X) $8.95, Can. $11.95
RUSSIAN AT A GLANCE, Beyer (0-7641-1251-1) $8.95, Can. $12.50
SPANISH AT A GLANCE, 3rd, Wald (0-7641-1257-0) $6.95, Can. $9.95

Barron's Educational Series, Inc.
250 Wireless Blvd., Hauppauge, NY 11788
Call toll-free: 1-800-645-3476
In Canada: Georgetown Book Warehouse, 34 Armstrong Ave.
Georgetown, Ont. L7G 4R9, Call toll-free: 1-800-247-7160
Visit our website at: www.barronseduc.com

Books may be purchased at your bookstore, or by mail from Barron's. Enclose check or money order for total amount plus sales tax where applicable and 18% for postage and handling (minimum charge $5.95). Prices subject to change without notice.
Can. $ = Canadian dollars

3 Foreign Language Series From Barron's!

The **VERB SERIES** offers more than 300 of the most frequently used verbs. The **GRAMMAR SERIES** provides complete coverage of the elements of grammar. The **VOCABULARY SERIES** offers more than 3500 words and phrases with their foreign language translations. Each book: paperback.

FRENCH GRAMMAR
ISBN: 0-7641-1351-8
$5.95, Can. $8.50

GERMAN GRAMMAR
ISBN: 0-8120-4296-4
$6.95, Can. $8.95

ITALIAN GRAMMAR
ISBN: 0-7641-2060-3
$6.95, Can. $9.95

JAPANESE GRAMMAR
ISBN: 0-7641-2061-1
$6.95, Can. $9.95

RUSSIAN GRAMMAR
ISBN: 0-8120-4902-0
$6.95, Can. $8.95

SPANISH GRAMMAR
ISBN: 0-7641-1615-0
$5.95, Can. $8.50

FRENCH VERBS
ISBN: 0-7641-1356-9
$5.95, Can. $8.50

GERMAN VERBS
ISBN: 0-8120-4310-3
$7.95 Can. $11.50

ITALIAN VERBS
ISBN: 0-7641-2063-8
$5.95, Can. $8.50

SPANISH VERBS
ISBN: 0-7641-1357-7
$5.95, Can. $8.50

FRENCH VOCABULARY
ISBN: 0-7641-1999-0
$6.95, Can. $9.95

GERMAN VOCABULARY
ISBN: 0-8120-4497-5
$6.95, Can. $8.95

ITALIAN VOCABULARY
ISBN: 0-7641-2190-1
$6.95, Can. $9.95

JAPANESE VOCABULARY
ISBN: 0-8120-4743-5
$6.95, Can. $8.95

RUSSIAN VOCABULARY
ISBN: 0-8120-1554-1
$6.95, Can. $8.95

SPANISH VOCABULARY
ISBN: 0-7641-1985-3
$6.95, Can. $9.95

Barron's Educational Series, Inc.
250 Wireless Blvd., Hauppauge, NY 11788 • Call toll-free: 1-800-645-3476
In Canada: Georgetown Book Warehouse
34 Armstrong Ave., Georgetown, Ontario L7G 4R9 • Call toll-free: 1-800-247-7160
www.barronseduc.com

Can. $ = Canadian dollars

Books may be purchased at your bookstore or by mail from Barron's. Enclose check or money order for total amount plus sales tax where applicable and 18% for postage and handling (minimum charge $5.95 U.S. and Canada). Prices subject to change without notice. New York residents, please add sales tax to total after postage and handling. (#26) R 1/03